3RD EDITION

ANTIQUE GOLF COLLECTIBLES

A PRICE AND REFERENCE GUIDE

Chuck Furjanic

©2004
by Chuck Furjanic

Published by

krause publications
An F+W Publications Company

700 East State Street • Iola, WI 54990-0001
715-445-2214 • 888-457-2873
www.krause.com

Our toll-free number to place an order or obtain a free catalog is 800-258-0929.

Library of Congress Catalog Number: 99-66998
ISBN: 0-87349-672-8

Designed by Kay Sanders
Edited by Dennis Thornton

Printed in USA

Table Of Contents

Dedication

To Maria, my loving wife and editor of this book.

Acknowledgments

I would like to express my sincere gratitude to the many people who helped put this book together. Without them this presentation would have never become a reality: Wayne Aaron, Hank Alperin, Archie Baird, Paul Biocini, Bob Burkett, Jim Cooper, Lee Christ, Mike Daniels, Art DiProspero, Mark Emerson, Jim Espinola, Keith Foster, Pete Georgiady, Roger Gilchrist, Bob Gowland, David Griffiths, Gary Hilgers, Roger Hill, Johnny Henry, Tom and Karen Kuhl, Bob Kuntz, George Lewis, Ralph Livingston, Chuck McMullin, Dick Moore, Norm Moreau, Joseph Murdoch, Gordon Page, Don Paris, Will Roberto, Tim Smartt, Jerry Sprung, and Bob Zajac. Dan Alexander provided the impetus and a multitude of photographs for this reference.

A special thank you to Teresa Ferrieri-Bisigato, for her enthusiasm and research assistance, and Maria C. Furjanic, for without her editorial skills this work would not have been possible.

Introduction

What started centuries ago, when men hit feather balls with wooden clubs on the rolling hills of Scotland, has evolved into a professional game where athletes routinely pound 300-yard drives on immaculately groomed courses using high-tech golf balls and titanium drivers in front of a worldwide television audience.

It's now the Tiger Woods era. The young golfer has matured from a precocious 3-year-old hitting golf balls on the Mike Douglas TV show into a global sports personality who has joined the biggest legends in sports—Babe Ruth, Muhammad Ali, Michael Jordan. Greatest golfer ever. Single-handedly transforming a sport from a leisurely pastime to a major spectator sport rivaling baseball and basketball for TV ratings. Those opinions are becoming the consensus of golfers, writers, and even sports historians. If Tiger enters a tournament and doesn't win, it's considered an upset. If he doesn't win in three or four tournaments, writers call it a "slump." And he may have another 30 to 40 years more of record-smashing performances ahead of him.

For collectors of golf equipment and memorabilia, that means the time is now to stock up on everything Tiger Woods touches or endorses. That's why we included a big, new chapter on Woods in a book called Antique Golf Collectibles. Autographed Woods materials are already fetching huge prices, and there's every possibility that a vast assortment of Woods collectibles will be treasured by collectors for generations.

Even if he never won another tournament, Woods' legend would be established. No one else in the history of the game has won the "Tiger Slam," when Woods won all four of golf's major tournaments consecutively. Still in his 20s, Woods is on the path to shattering Jack Nicklaus' record of 18 major championships.

Spectators line the golf course dozens deep to watch Tiger whack a drive or coax in a long putt, whether he's at Augusta or in Thailand.

Golf courses are being constructed everywhere and high-tech equipment is flying off the shelves. Nike has suddenly become a major force in golf equipment and attire, ever since Tiger started his affiliation with the company.

Not since the days of Bobby Jones, the legend who inspired a golf boom in the Roaring Twenties, has a golfer so transformed the sport.

Golf's boom in the late 1990s and early 21st Century also has inspired a new wave of golf collecting fervor. Fairway "woods" once really were made of hickory and gutta-percha was the modern golf ball of choice in a bygone era. That makes those items prized collectibles today, even though brassies, niblicks, and cleeks have been replaced in golfers' bags by metal woods, sand wedges, and long-handled putters.

So enjoy your journey through the world of golf collectibles, from the 19th Century and before, through Tiger's time.

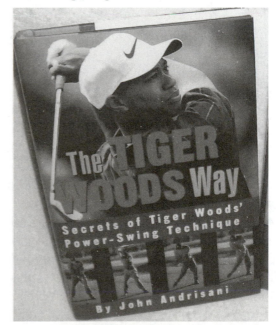

Books about Tiger Woods are among a growing number of collector's items featuring the young golf star. Woods' popularity has fueled a new wave of collectors' interest in the centuries-old sport.

Preface

For the past 16 years, I have heard thousands of collectors, club professionals, antique dealers, and curious people with collectibles ask the same questions: "What is this worth?" and "Is there a reference book giving current pricing for all golf collectibles?"

This book is designed to answer both these questions, and more.

Collecting old golf memorabilia, clubs, books, and balls is not a new fad. Classified advertisements for "Feather Balls," old "Gutta Percha Balls," and wooden head clubs made by "Hugh Philp" were published in the British publication, Golf Illustrated, circa 1900. Harry B. Woods assembled a fine collection and, in 1911, published Golfing Curios and the Like.

In 1987, my thirst for information concerning collectible golf equipment was at its peak. The references available were Stirk and Henderson's Golf in the Making, The Encyclopedia of Golf Collectibles by the Olmans, the Golf Collectors Society's Bulletin, a few dealers publishing catalogues, and auction catalogues from several British auction houses.

Determined to acquire and share up-to-date information, I began publishing a retail catalogue in 1989. In 1991, interesting articles by expert collectors and dealers were also included, helping the catalogues become both informative and a retail sales vehicle. The catalogues include a wide variety of golf collectibles, such as wood shaft clubs, balls, books, tees, memorabilia, and ephemera, all offered for sale. There is also a listing of events, gatherings, and meetings involving golf collectors and collectibles, articles that will bring you back to the nostalgic times, and offerings of hard-to-find grips, tacks, and whipping for care and repair of old hickories. I am presently the only dealer publishing a monthly catalogue for the golf collectibles hobby, and have published nearly 160 as of this writing.

In 1993, I began conducting mail auctions that provided two essential services to the collector: A way to sell duplicates from their collections and a way to add collectibles at "their price." Chuck Furjanic, Inc. now holds four auctions each year: Spring and Fall live sales, and Winter and Summer absentee sales. If a collector cannot attend the auction "in person," where lots may be viewed prior to sale, a profusely illustrated catalogue allows them to bid confidently by mail.

When Dan Alexander, former president of Books Americana, suggested I write a price and reference guide on golf collectibles, the intent was clearly set in producing a truly comprehensive work encompassing the entire spectrum of golf collectibles. To accomplish this, I called for input from a number of knowledgeable, well-respected dealers and collectors who are experts in their field. Throughout the years, I have been privileged to know the finest, and several of them assisted in presenting accurate, up-to-date information and pricing of collectibles. Their perspective and knowledge are a refreshing and valued addition to this price and reference guide.

It was also the goal of my publisher, the contributors, and mine, to provide as many photographs as possible to make these listings and prices come alive for the collector. Anyone using this guide will find the photographs incredibly helpful in bringing you back to the times and the history of the game, as well as providing visual references to the collectibles.

Thus, this guide is the result of such an effort; I am very confident it will be of great help to the numerous collectors asking that familiar question, "How much is this item worth?"

Golfingly,
Chuck Furjanic
Irving, Texas, 2003

Chapter 1

Collecting Tiger Woods

By Mark Allen Baker and Bob Zajec

Eldrick "Tiger" Woods has not only transformed the PGA tour by setting new levels of accomplishment, but has introduced collectors to a new "mind set," a new way of collecting. No longer can collectors simply walk into the area collectibles store and find everything there is to collect on a sports legend. Certainly the basics are there: trading cards, posters, autographs, etc. But gone are the days of Elvis and The Beatles, where licensing covered everything from ashtrays to key chains.

"The days of controlled collecting are upon us," one golf collector said. "Research is now the key to building a comprehensive collection." The collector brings up an excellent point: no longer can glancing through a price guide provide you with the definitive answers to collecting. While it can certainly assist you in your efforts, some subjects just take work. Tiger is one of them.

A Tiger Woods T-shirt colorfully sums up the dynamic persona of the PGA superstar. $5-$10

A Wild Horse limited edition cachet from 2000 commemorates Tiger Woods' entry into the select group of five golfers who have won all four major golf tournaments. $75

Although I watched the Mike Douglas TV show when Tiger appeared, I didn't really start collecting him until his early amateur days. Similar to other collectors, I quickly realized that I have to change my approach to be successful with my subject. This meant dissecting every event and determining its collecting ramifications. Unlike tracking Derek Jeter trading card releases, this project I knew was going to take some effort.

From advertisements, programs, tickets, press kits, and brochures, to videotapes, cereal boxes, and golf balls, a Tiger Woods collector quickly becomes a detective. Since there is no definitive guide about the golfer, nor is golf one of the most understood areas of collecting, a collector is challenged to piece together what is often not obvious. And patience is a virtue, because Tiger Woods material collected now and saved might appreciate in value considerably later in Tiger's career, which promises to be long and likely historic.

In building this cursory overview, this is exactly what I hope to provide to the collector: a foundation for new collectibles and even forgotten older items. Through the interaction of you and other collectors, we can use this information as a springboard, and maybe someday a dedicated book.

Speaking of books, as a contributor to what I think is one of the best books ever written about the sport, I would like to take this time to thank both the author and publisher for allowing me to contribute such a small piece to a greater project.

Bob Zajac also contributed a large number of photos, as well as pricing, to this modern, although important, field of Tiger Woods collectibles. Zajac has been involved in the sports collectibles business since 1978 and has specialized in golfing collectibles and memorabilia since 1990. His store is in Cape Cod, Mass., and he will send a catalog to anyone upon request. He is a member of the USGA and the Golf Collectors' Society and is also an avid golfer. Zajac can be reached at: (508) 760-8100 or e-mail: zgolfcards@capecod.net.

The Tiger Mind Set

With future NBA and PGA stars being plucked from the high school ranks, gone are the traditional days of collecting. It seemed we always had the time to recognize a phenom years before his or her emergence. Such is no longer the case. Instead of "kicking it up a notch," we are going to have to " kick it down a notch" into university and even high school collectibles.

We live in a society that demands perfection at a very impatient price. With profit as its only motive, commercialism has no age, ethnic, religious, or political affiliation. To become a millionaire overnight is beyond the comprehension of most, yet still an occasional option for those in professional sports.

New stars are created overnight and lured by lucrative endorsement agreements. These commitments are geared toward profit and not necessarily longevity. Fortunately, such has not been the case with Tiger Woods.

Much has been expressed about Woods and by him. His motives are understood and convictions legitimized by his actions. While this has been an exception with most athletes, it hasn't been with Woods. His beliefs have been forged through his parents and in a manner we may never see for a lifetime. Not only are we witnessing history on the golf course, but off it as well. There is a unique bond around all those in "Team Tiger." They are members of a group determined to preserve his integrity, focus on his mission, and meet the demands of the public. They are preserving the mantra, "Tiger Gives Back, Where Others Haven't."

Collecting Tiger Woods means understanding the subject first, the memorabilia second. If you know Tiger, you understand why he won't be showing up on the face of a drink cup at your local convenience store. The package has to fit the model.

As a child prodigy, memorabilia was created far sooner than most. Early photographs, videotapes, and tournament information are now treasures, but who would have thought? Perhaps since he is still young enough, many of these items may still be out there waiting to be uncovered by a diligent collector.

Since there are no Tiger Wood collector stores, there is no easy method to collecting. Finding treasures for your collection will depend on awareness, creativity, and knowledge: both of him, the sport, and financial resources. Endorsements, such as Nike, Buick, Upper Deck, and Titleist, will be the key to your success. Many programs, campaigns, and even event collectibles are generated by them and have a future in your collection.

There have been many books written about Tiger Woods, with even more in the works, but none have tried to build a foundation for collecting his memorabilia. We know why now, and have a new understanding about our subject. This section is not intended to be comprehensive but a new beginning into an enjoyable hobby. If you want to collect golf memorabilia you have chosen the best subject, Tiger Woods.

A Look Back

As a collector, you must understand your subject first. Doing so will guide and strengthen your purchases. It will enable you to seek and find associated items that are often unknown to the novice collector. From Western High School yearbooks to Fred Haskin dinner award programs, you will understand how they relate to Tiger and if they are worthy and in some cases even authentic pieces of memorabilia.

In the collectibles section we listed Tiger's participation as an amateur in professional events. So let's look further back.

Before we have even explored his professional career, we quickly realize that there is a wealth of memorabilia in the form of videotapes, programs, tickets, posters, photographs, magazines, and even yearbooks waiting to be found and added to our collection.

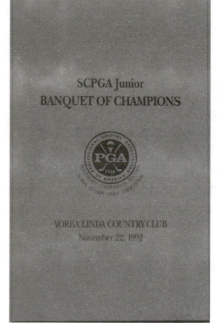

An example of Tiger Woods collectibles from his early days is a SCPGA Junior Banquet of Champions program from the Yorba Linda Country Club, Nov. 22, 1992. It is valued at $350 today.

Some Early Achievements

1996 NCAA Champion at Stanford University; All-American - First Team; Jack Nicklaus Award winner - Collegiate Golfer of the Year.

1994-1995: PAC-10 Player of the Year; The Masters - first major tournament, only amateur to qualify, silver medal winner; Walker Cup - member U.S. Team.

1993: Dial Award - Top High School Athlete in Country.

1991: Titleist-Golfweek National Amateur of the Year; U.S. Junior Amateur Championship - winner, youngest player ever.

1990: Insurance Youth Golf Classic National - winner, youngest ever; PGA National Junior Championship – second; appeared in *Sports Illustrated* "Faces in the Crowd" on Sept. 24, 1990, at the age of 14.

At age 6, Tiger played a two-hole exhibition with Sam Snead.

At age 5, Tiger appeared on the TV show, *That's Incredible.*

At age 3, he won a pitch, putt, and drive competition.

At age 2, he appeared as a guest on *The Mike Douglas Show.* The clip also appeared on the *CBS Network News.*

TIGER WOODS COLLECTIBLES

Advertisements

"There are still golf courses in the United States that I cannot play because of the color of my skin. I'm told I'm not ready for you. Are you ready for me?" and "I am Tiger Woods" are just two advertising campaigns by Nike that feature Tiger Woods. The first created significant controversy and ended up being pulled by Nike much sooner than the company anticipated. The latter, its replacement, was a success. Not only is Tiger-related advertising effective and even controversial, it is also highly sought by collectors.

Collector intrigue with advertising begins with the creative element. You've seen the commercial with Tiger bouncing a golf ball on a club between his legs, then hitting it like a Sammy Sosa shot to left field. It then evolves into "I have to have it!" I have to have copies of all videotapes, press releases, photographs, ad campaigns, sound bites, etc.

People laugh at me when I tell them that I have magazines from the 1930s where the

An ad in USA TODAY in 2000 for American Express card saluted Tiger Woods as Sportsman of the Year. $20-$30

A quarter-page ad in USA TODAY from 1997 promotes TV coverage of the PGA championship. $5-$10

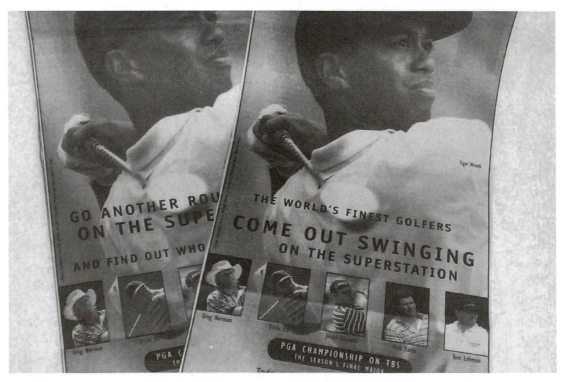

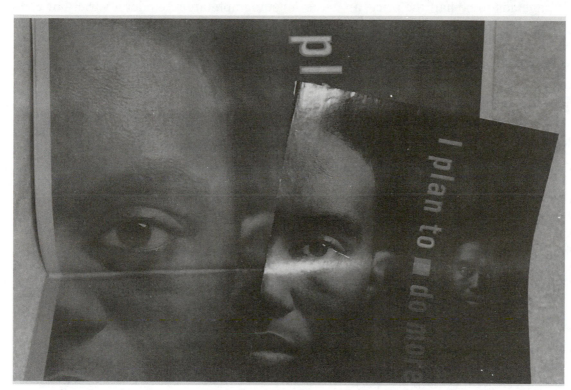

A full-page 1997 ad for American Express featuring Tiger says: "I plan to do more." $20-$30

advertisements are worth more than a hundred times the initial cost. Remember when people bought packs of baseball cards for the gum? The same is going to be true in the future for advertising especially when it relates to an individual such as Tiger Woods.

"There are still golf courses in the United States that I cannot play because of the color of my skin. I'm told I'm not ready for you. Are you ready for me?" this Nike campaign, as controversial as it was, generated collector interest. The "Hello World" campaign first ran as a three-page ad in the *Wall Street Journal*, followed by television spots that same week. Costing nearly $275,000, it caught the interest of many, but for the wrong reasons. Controversy is collected, just try finding one today.

Tiger's lucrative Nike and Titleist contracts have allowed him to be more selective in evaluating other endorsement opportunities. Naturally a player like Tiger Woods could have all the endorsements he could handle, but selection is the key. Image and over-exposure are paramount concerns of both Tiger and his agency IMG (International Management Group).

Advertising in all forms is collectible, but what Tiger collectors seek most are large, colorful, and powerful images that represent an event or key endorsement. For example, the American Express advertisement associated with the campaign "If you're going to take on the world you'd better be prepared," this full page ad that ran in many periodicals also appeared in *USA TODAY* on Nov. 19, 1997, was very impressive. Newspaper advertisements such as this are what Tiger collectors dream about. Large, full-color, perfect imagery, representing a key campaign and running in a daily source, makes a sound investment.

Pricing *

Full page ad.... Color (13 1/4" x 22"),
         example listed above $20-$30
(figure half price for magazine ads)

Full page ad....Black & white (13 1/4"
         x 22"), example *USA TODAY*,
         American Express ad,
         12/4/2000 Tiger in front
         of a credit card........... $15-$20

* Controversial ad campaigns, short-run campaigns or event driven can double a price.

Figure half page ads to be half the price, a quarter page, a quarter price, etc. Prominent newspapers will command more than monthly magazine ads. Networks such as TBS, ABC, and NBC promote their tournaments with very collectible ads using Tiger's image. The greater the significance of the tournament, the more valuable the ad.

Autographs

Tiger Woods has probably signed more autographs in the last 15 years than anyone on earth. Yet, there is a mystique about him and the autograph hobby in general. Collecting autographs, while a great hobby, always has that apprehension associated with it - especially with sports autographs. Because of the autographed sports boom at the end of the last century, many collectors are fearful (and they should be), always wondering if the signature is real.

Since Tiger was five years old he has been signing autographs. Because he couldn't write script, however, he printed his name in block letters. (Good luck trying to authenticate these examples in the future.) As a child prodigy, he has been targeted throughout his entire life

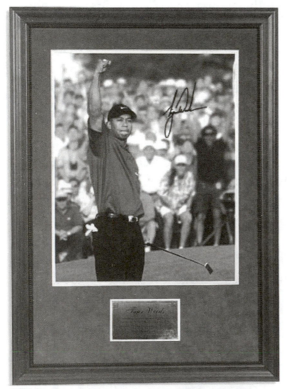

Upper Deck Authenticated photo display. **$1000**

as an autograph target. Under a variety of conditions, terms, and concerns, he has almost always complied.

Over the years, Tiger has willingly signed everything from golf bags to hand bags. Authentic autographed programs, tickets, hats, shirts, and golf balls had routinely found their way into collections. It wasn't until he turned pro that influences in his life decided to create a "fear factor" surrounding his signature. Yes, there have indeed been unscrupulous individuals who have offered questionable signatures for sale. But most have been prosecuted or acquitted for their actions.

Fact: Tiger Woods signed thousands of autographs before turning pro was even an option. Fact: Tiger Woods still signs autographs. Fact: Tiger Woods will probably be signing autographs for the rest of his life. In recent years, many organizations associated with Tiger have tried and failed to intimidate the autograph collectors. Simply put, they don't want you to get an autograph for free, if there is such a thing! When an agency tells you your autograph is fake, simply tell it, "I won't forget."

Access to Tiger is limited. He lives in the exclusive, gated, and guarded Isleworth community in Orlando, Fla. Since I have been collecting autographs for nearly 40 years, and just happen to live near Tiger's home, let me give you some advice. Tiger is a gentleman, in every sense of the word. He, his family, and friends should be treated with dignity and respect at all times. Tiger is only a public figure during public events. In your quest for his signature, never approach him if he is eating, with his family, or in his home town. He is smart enough to realize when a person would like an autograph and will comply when he feels like doing so.

During tournaments he has extensive security, uniformed and plain clothed, watching his every move and any move by the gallery. He does take time to sign autographs in public and under the proper conditions, which means not during a tournament, as he sees fit. During his many clinics, which he conducts annually, he will sign for attendees, often Titleist visors or Nike propaganda. If you send autograph requests to Tiger via IMG, his agency, you will receive a machine-generated signature.

His signature does vary considerably, especially from his amateur days, and often due to circumstance. I have seen fake signatures look real and vice versa. Patience, perseverance, knowledge, and dealing with reputable dealers can usually guarantee an authentic signature.

As one might imagine, autographed Tiger Woods memorabilia is abundant and varied in form. The price guide is based upon thousands of sales. His signature in some forms is very dynamic and should be monitored as such through available resources.

Pricing is subject to scarcity and desirability. Items authenticated as being prior to his turning professional are relatively scarce. Many experts in the field question the authenticity of half or more of all Tiger Woods autographed items. The Upper Deck Authenticated items are one sure way of guaranteeing authenticity; the other is obtaining items and autographs "in person."

Autograph Price Guide

Form	Price Range
Golf Ball pre-1997	**$1,000-$1,500**
Golf Ball 1998-2003	**$450-$700**
Photograph pre-1997	**$1,000-$2,000**
Photograph 1998-2003	**$500-$1,000**
Trading Card pre-1997	**$400-$700**
Trading Card 1998-2003	**$250-$450**
Visor or Glove pre-1997	**$500-$800**
Visor or Glove 1998-2003	**$350-$550**
Signed Book	**$250-$400**
Signed Flags from Majors:	
......Masters 1997	**$2,500**
......Masters 2001-2002	**$1,200**
......British Open	**$750**
......U.S. Open	**$750**
......PGA	**$750**
Index cards	**$30-$50**
Document	**$125-$150**
Posters	**$150**
Scorecard	**$200**
Program/Magazine/Gallery Guide	**$45-$50**
Baseball	**$100-$125**
Wheaties Box	**$45-$60**

A flag from the 2002 U.S. Open at Bethpage Black was autographed by Woods, who won. **$8,600**

Banners & Billboards

This is an area bigger than life for any Tiger collector, but believe it or not, they are purchased. Overseas billboards, some printed and others hand-painted, have been made available to collectors. The issues facing such a form are obvious: space, cost, shipping. There is no sense spending much time on this form of collecting.

Of greatest interest are tournament, advertising, or associated event-related pieces. This might include a Tiger Woods Foundation banner or a Nike advertising campaign billboard. Images including Tiger's image, be it printed or painted, bring a greater price. Because advertising campaigns, such as Nike's "I am Tiger Woods," come and go so quickly, concentrate on the most successful. Memorabilia associated with failed releases or campaigns will probably not appreciate significantly over time.

A good early example of a great Tiger billboard was the Asian Honda Classic sign that appears in many background photographs from the tournament.

Books

Collecting books on Tiger can be a significant challenge. From finding first editions, limited quantity (low-press runs) releases, to acquiring smaller-size books and even books for children, titles can often be elusive. Since the shelf life of a title varies due to its success, bestsellers and books by well-known publishers are the easiest to find and should be a great place to begin your collection.

Like many other forms of collectibles, condition is everything. Superb first edition hard covers, with dust jackets, are the preferred approach to sports book collecting. Often forgotten by the novice is that the condition of the dust jacket is a key part of the book's value. Try to collect the finest hardcover books that fit your budget.

Speaking of damage, softcover issues can often be found with bent corners or chipped (missing ink) covers. This is why many collectors opt for the latest paperbacks concerning Tiger, before others have handled the book.

The popularity of Tiger Woods led to a whirlwind of book releases, especially in 1997. Many of the books were over-produced and ended up on the bargain shelves. Other titles that had moderate success were updated and re-released with a new chapter or even a new cover. Some successful titles however had subsequent audiotapes/compact disks - another area of Tiger collecting.

Remember, the release of a book can often include many collectibles in the form of advertisements (periodicals), sound bites (audio releases), press releases, press kits, photographs, displays, buttons, posters, standees (life-size cardboard images of a person or book cover), and much more.

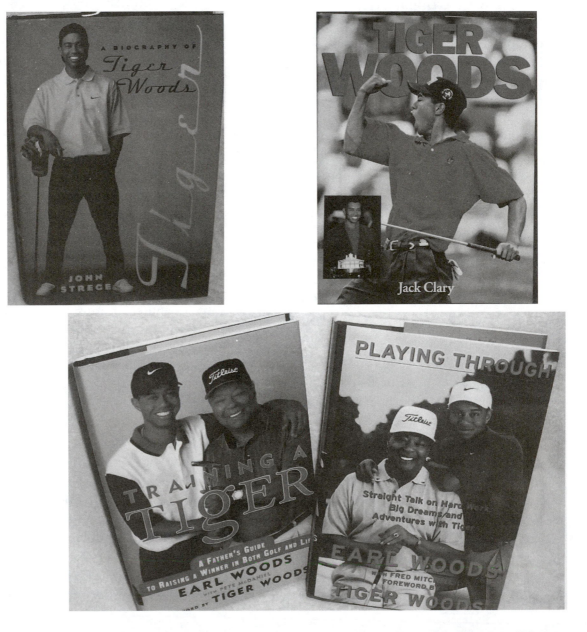

Books on Tiger Woods.
$15-$25 each

Selected books on, about, or including Tiger Woods
 ** = significant price variations ..*** = a must for your collection

Title/Author	Notes	Price
Training a Tiger	by Earl Woods, with Pete McDaniel	$18
	Foreword by Tiger Woods, Harper Collins, 1997, 190 pgs.	
Playing Through	by Earl Woods, with Fred Mitchell	$24
	Foreword by Tiger Woods, Harper Collins, 1998, 270 pgs.	
The Ultimate Encyclopedia of Golf	1995-97, Carlton Books Limited, 256 pgs.,	$15 **
	Tiger on the cover, Good overall resource,	
	large format, great photos	
A Biography of Tiger Woods	by John Strege Broadway Books, 1997, 238 pgs.,	$25 ***
	nice design, strong content	
Tiger Woods, The Making of a Champion	by Tim Rosaforte St. Martins Press, 1997, t	$22 ***
	240 pgs., good content	
Tiger Woods	by Jack Clary Smithmark Publishers, 1997,	$15
	64 pgs., large format	
18 Holes with Tiger	Beckett, 144 pgs., great photos, limited text	$25 **
Stalking the Tiger	by Vartan Kupelian Sleeping Bear Press,	$22 ***
	1997, 196 pgs., good content	
Tiger Woods, The Grandest Slam	Triumph Books, 2001, 112 pgs.	$15 **

Buttons/Pins/Badges

"Tigermania," similar to "Beatlemania," creates a significant amount of desire for fans to show their support of their hero. Buttons and pins, most of which are not licensed, have entered the market. They range in price from $3 to $10 in most cases.

The only legitimate, or so it seems, buttons and badges that have entered the market are those associated with an advertising campaign or an event. These can range from $5 to $15 each (doesn't include event badges). To be safe in your collecting, I would stick to these. Typically, no licensing means no value.

Clothing and Accessories

You don't believe Tiger can push a product? Each day during the U.S. Amateur at Pumpkin Ridge, Tiger wore a black cap with a U.S. Amateur logo, with the bill bent upward. Once television viewers took notice, phone orders began streaming into the clubhouse, depleting the existing stock before the tournament even finished.

At the advent of Woods' professional career, Nike wanted to make an impressive debut with its new marketing messiah. So they shipped dozens of shirts and pants to Tiger in multi-pocketed Nike bags. While Tiger was more impressed with the bags, he did manage to show up at Brown Deer Park Golf Course in Milwaukee for the pro-am, attired in Nike swooshes from head to toe, 11 in fact.

Nike provides Tiger's tournament wardrobe. It is predetermined to assure customers that they can purchase identical items at the club's pro shop or vending stands. Serious wardrobe collectors, who can quickly spend hundreds of dollars, should concentrate on purchasing a full wardrobe replication, especially the attire worn at a Major, such as The Masters. This includes purchasing the items in the proper sizes.

Pricing on all clothing items, including Nike, varies but here are some average prices: hats from $10 to $25; polo shirt, $30 to $40; sweaters/vests, $35 to $45; shorts, $30 to $40; sunglasses, $40 to $70; shoes, $50 to $150. Naturally, styles, colors, and sizes vary.

Other than gloves and hats, tournament-worn Tiger attire has not yet found its way into the market. But it is only a matter of time.

Provenance, size, color, style, and tagging will then become paramount concerns.

Just a few collectors' notes:

* According to Tiger's mom, Tida, Tiger wears red in final rounds because it's his lucky color.

* Tiger's green jacket that he won at the Masters was a 42-long.

* Tiger has a 28-inch waist (1997), a 35-inch sleeve length, and wears size 9 1/2-medium shoes.

Tiger Woods' affiliation with Nike has benefited his bank account, and Nike's golf apparel and equipment sales. $30-$40 for shirt

A colorful Tiger Woods T-shirt features photos from his early days in golf. $10-$15

* Tiger wears solid-black golf shoes, because two-tone shoes distract him from putting.

Currency and Commemoratives

Yes, it's hard to believe that Tiger has appeared on currency, but he has, sort of. A variety of fake bills bearing Tiger's image have been used as promotional pieces. While they are neat, the thrill wears off fast. However you might want to pick up a few cheap versions for your collection.

The most controversial issue in this form was a sterling-silver medal produced by the Franklin Mint in commemoration of Tiger Woods' Masters win, and removed from the market after Woods sued over the unauthorized use of his likeness. The legal battle raged, and Tiger prevailed. The coins were marketed at a price of $37.50 each.

Dishes and Glassware

Some of these items have found their way into the market, however most are unlicensed.

Promotional mugs are common and average about $15.

Fan Club Related Items

Real Tiger Woods fans belong to "Club Tiger," the Official Tiger Woods Fan Club. In addition to online interaction with Tiger and other fans, a member can play trivia, listen to audio clips, design your own golf course, and enter contests.

When you enter you will receive a limited edition Nike T-shirt, Titleist collectible golf ball, American Express Golf Wall Map, Topps glossy photo, member certificate, bag tag and membership ID card, and a special All-Star Cafe gift. Also, as a part of your membership you are entitled to an All-Star Cafe VIP card (Tiger is part owner of the All-Star Cafe chain, along with Shaquille O'Neal, Ken Griffey Jr., and Andre Agassi).

The shirt is identical to the Nike "I am Tiger Woods" T-shirt but is missing the "Nike Apparel" cardboard tag. Silkscreened on the

An official golf ball and shirt are part of the Club Tiger membership package.

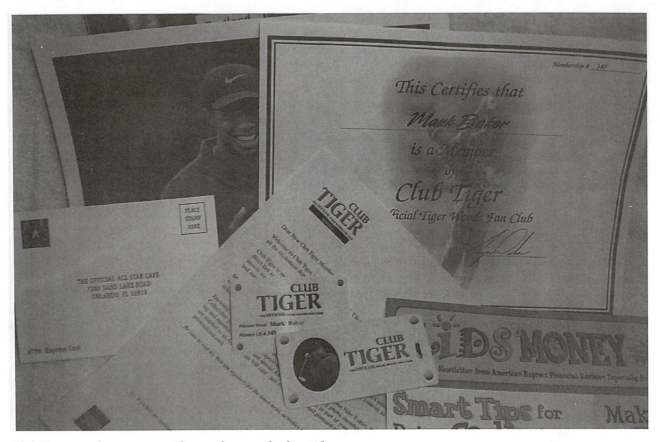

Club Tiger members get a certificate, photo, and other gifts.

left sleeve (or side of golf ball) is "CLUB TIGER" (red ink with a black drop shadow and partial outline), "THE OFFICIAL TIGER WOODS FAN CLUB" (the word "OFFICIAL" is in red ink, all other text in black).

To join, visit http://www.clubtiger.com or call (888) 43-TIGER. I wanted to get Member ID No. 1 when I joined but didn't make it, so I am happy with No. 349 (1/98).

Surprisingly few individual items in the club package have surfaced in the collectors market. They are certainly valuable.

Golf Equipment

Since golf equipment and a professional player's game are dynamic, so is the relationship between the two. A player may change his equipment due to changes in his game, the type of course he is playing, and even due to the conditions of the round. Naturally, new equipment developments always draw curiosi-

ty with professional players, as do new endorsement contracts.

There is a symbiotic relationship between professional golfers and equipment manufacturers. While it is tempting for any professional to sign a lucrative deal with a manufacturer, the thought of changing equipment and how it's going to affect his game, or even his life, is always paramount. For those who develop new equipment, there is no better affirmation of a product than a key player of the PGA using their latest development.

For a player such as Tiger Woods, there is no equipment manufacturer on the face of the earth that wouldn't want to find its product in his arsenal. Since 1997 was his breakout year, let's look at his equipment. Titleist, a major endorser, supplied him with a custom black and white leather golf staff bag with his name embroidered in gold beneath the front pocket. The name Titleist appeared prominently on the bag and in great contrast to the surrounding areas. Now, he could discard the lightweight Ping carry bag he used during the U.S. Amateur. He also used a black and white Titleist umbrella and cover, along with a Titleist head cover for his Titleist PT metal 3-wood. His driver, with a headcover made by his mother (stitched with Thai words that translate to "Love from Mom") covered a Cobra steel driver. Cobra was a company that Titleist's parent company American Brands had purchased.

For his irons, he chose Mizuno three through nine, a Cobra 1-iron, and a variety of Cleveland wedges. Putters, perhaps the most sacred among all the tools of a professional golfer, can vary considerably. Here Tiger has chosen a Titleist Scotty Cameron model. It is appropriate to state again that professional golfers often have hundreds of golf clubs available to them. The deal he signed with Titleist meant he would eventually have to switch over to its golf clubs once the company made a set that struck Tiger just right.

Golf balls vary significantly and often, including changes in compression, outer design, and inside construction. Suffice it to say that Tiger was using the top-of-the-line

Titleist golf ball (Titleist Tour Balata) when he won the 1997 Masters. During that year, Titleist offered six families of golf balls. Visit your local pro shop for pricing information and modifications.

Speaking of golf balls, Titleist provided Woods with 2000 Tour Balata golf balls, 100 compression, to practice with. After practicing with them on the range, they are collected and placed on his front porch. Since the range is so close, he just uses his golf cart to drive from his house.

Tiger has made changes since his first Augusta win, including clubs, balls, and gloves. He currently opts for Nike balls and interchanges equipment as needed.

Authenticating tournament-used equipment can be a very difficult procedure and, since virtually none of Tiger's equipment has turned up for sale, collectors should only be aware that it can be done. Golf clubs are often custom made and as such include certain measurements unique to that individual. It's a procedure similar to what major league baseball players do with their bats. Golfers define elements of the equipment to better serve their particular game. These measurements involve shaft length, grip size, swing weights, and

---

Equipment Price Listed - Selected items (not used by Woods)

KIWI putter cover for Tiger's Cameron 983 putter $15
Nike golf towels..$15-$20
Titleist 975 JVS Tiger Woods Headcover (Japan) $35
One dozen Nike/Buick promotional golf balls..$25
Tiger Woods Foundation /Coca Cola bag..$25
1997 Tiger Woods Masters golf ball marker $55
Nike golf Tiger Woods Windshear II umbrella..$30
Tiger Woods Titleist Headcovers $70
Tiger Woods Nike Junior stand bag..$60
Scotty Cameron/Tiger Woods Newport putter ....**Price varies**
Tiger Woods Buick Staff Golf Bag..$675
Nike Forged Irons complete Tiger Woods set..$725
Titleist 681T stamped irons, 2-PW, Tiger Woods $700
1996 Box of 6 Commemorative U. S. Amateur Pumpkin Ridge Titleist Balls with the "U.S. Amateur, 1996, Pumpkin Ridge" logo. Limited to 1,000 with certificate of authenticity, copy #, insert about Pumpkin Ridge Golf Club in a presentation box. $295

many other measurements important to the manufacturer and eventually to the collector.

The Nike Commemorative Series tins are perhaps my favorite Tiger collectible. The die-cast stamped commemorative tins include a dozen balls, segmented by specific round in four full-color custom boxes. Inside each box are three Nike balls (include logo and number) stamped on one side with "TIGER" (black ink) and the other side with specific commemorative, such as "2000 129th Open Champion" (blue ink).

2000 Nike tin of 12 balls commemorating Tiger's winning of the 4 major tournaments. Each sleeve has the score of respective days. and the balls are imprinted with the tournament and "TIGER."

2000 U. S. Open	**$25**
2000 British Open	**$25**
2000 PGA	**$25**
2001 Masters	**$35**

Jewelry/Watches/Crystal

With Rolex (Tudor) as a sponsor, Tiger can guarantee himself an outstanding collection of watches. For example the Tiger Woods Automatic Chronograph can cost about $1,700. If you can't afford the watches, try the many forms of advertising that Tiger appears in on behalf of Tudor.

Jewelry is available, including Tiger chains, etc., but most is not licensed. There is talk of creating a Buddha replica (a family heirloom) piece in honor of the one Tiger wears around his neck.

There is a Tiger Woods Waterford crystal piece that has entered the market, however I am unaware if it is licensed or is a custom piece. It typically brings about $100.

Miscellaneous Items

This not only a difficult area to track for collectors, but also for researchers. Endorsement agreements and those around "Team Tiger," his coach, and agency, while they work fine together as a team, often forget that fans and collectors are monitoring their success. New agreements mean new collectibles. Some items will be licensed, others counterfeited. The hobby would be far better off if we could understand Tiger's endorsements and how it will affect collectors. This would save us money and allow Tiger to receive the money he deserves. Our only options now are to trust the seller and hope we have made a good purchasing decision.

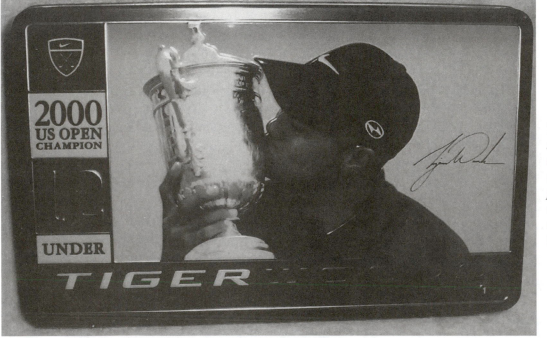

Tiger Woods smacks the winning U.S. Open trophy in the photo on a Nike commemorative tin from 2000. $25

Inside the Nike commemorative U.S. Open tin from 2000 are four sleeves of golf balls with photos from the tournament. $25

A photo from the 2000 British Open decorates a Nike collectors tin. $25

A 1996 U.S. Amateur commemorative golf ball box from Pumpkin Ridge was limited to 1,000 boxes. Tiger Woods won that title. $295

Items listed below may or may not be licensed.

Upper Deck Tiger Woods Christmas Card **$20-$25** *(licensed)*

September 1995 New England Golfer with cover photo and caption "Tiger Woods U.S. Amateur Victory at Newport CC" ...$25

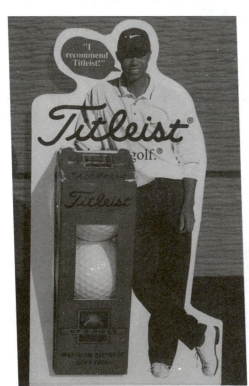

Titleist stand-alone plastic item with picture of Tiger leaning on the space for a sleeve of Titleist balls while saying "I recommend Titleist." 9"x 4" $85

Titleist plastic display with double-sided photos of major players. Full color photos measure 6 1/2" x 4". Stand measures 9 1/2" x 5" and has space for a sleeve of balls. ... $65

1997 Masters Spectator Guide. $45

2000 Tiger Woods Foundation sponsored "Start Something" ad and application form. $15

Tiger Woods - Hot Wheels Golf Cart	**$10**
Tiger Woods mouse pad	**$10**
Tiger Woods street sign	**$12**
Tiger Woods light switch cover	**$10**
Tiger Woods phone cards	Numerous
brands at different values	
Tiger Woods wall clock (8")	**$10**
Tiger Woods flip-book	**$10**
Tiger Woods playing cards	**$5**
"I am Tiger Woods" promotional ball markers	**$10**
"I am Tiger Woods" wooden golf tees	**$10**
Tiger Woods assorted bag tags	**$10-$20**
Tiger Woods money clips	**$40-$150**
Tiger Woods postage stamps - sheet of 9	**$10** .
(various countries)	
Tiger Woods philatelic releases (various)	**$30- $45**
Tiger Woods leader board name plate	**$25-$50**
(event dependent)	
Tiger Woods high school yearbook	**$150-$200 (Sr.)**, **$250-$300 (soph.)**

Tiger Woods pencils (various)	**$5**
T-shirts (various)	**$10-$25**
Periscope - "Eye of the Tiger," and others	**$15**
1992 SCPGA Junior Banquet of Champions, Yorba Linda CC, Nov. 22, 1992.	**$350**
1995 U. S. Amateur Championship Program	**$35**
1996 U. S. Amateur Championship Program	**$25**
2001 Masters Spectator Guide	**$25**
2002 Masters Spectator Guide	**$15**
2000 NBC pin from the 2000 U. S. Open at Pebble Beach	**$95**

Not listed above is any memorabilia from Tiger's transportation: a Citation X jet. In the Fall of 1997, he spent $1.95 million for a one-eighth interest in the corporate jet. This includes a monthly fee just under $10,000 and a seat fee of $1,840 for each hour the plane is occupied. It's just a matter of time before some flight-used trinkets enter the market.

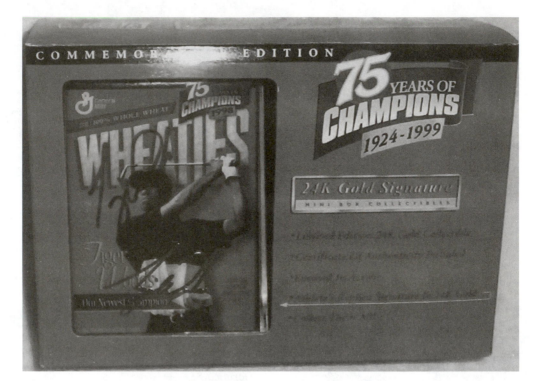

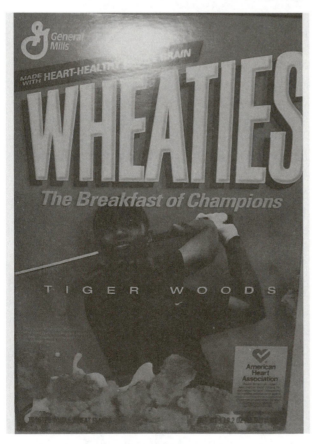

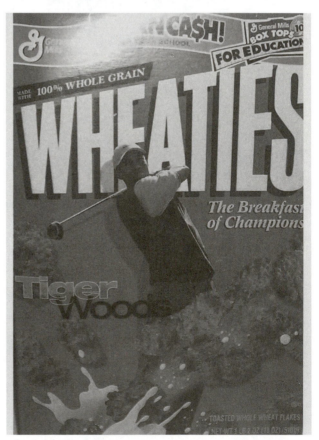

Cereal Boxes

1998 Wheaties, 5 different boxes **$12**
1999 Wheaties **$10**

1999 mini Wheaties box w/24k gold facsimile signature. Commemorative Edition encased in acrylic. Limited edition **$25**
2000 Wheaties **$10**

1997 Tiger Wins Masters No. 117-12 **$20**

COMMEMORATIVE CACHETS

1997 Masters Winnner - Z Silk Cachets	**$75**
1997 Masters Winner - Wild Horse Cachets	**$95**
1999 Ryder Cup "The Tiger" - Wild Horse	**$75**
2000 U. S. Open "Tiger on the Loose" - Wild Horse Cachets	**$75**
2000 "The Grand Slam of Golf" with Nicklaus, Hogan, Sarazen, and Player. Wild Horse Cachets	**$75**
2000 "Tiger Woods Wins PGA Playoff" - unknown	**$10**
2000 "Tiger Woods Sportsman of the Year" - unknown	**$10**
2001 "Tiger Woods Wins the Bay Hill Invitational"	**$10**
2001 "Tiger Woods Wins the Masters" - unknown	**$10**

COMMEMORATIVE CARDS and BOXES

1997 Grand Slam Ventures Titleist Give-Away set with purchase of one dozen Titleist balls.   **$395**

1997 Grand Slam Ventures box. **$295**

2001 Tiger Reigns Supreme, Grolier No. 136-14 **$10**

2001 Legends Magazine full page Masters Champion card w/complete scorecard on reverse. **$15**

1998 Grand Slam Ventures box	**$275**
2001 Masters Champion, limited to 100,000	**$15**
2001 Tigers Career Grand Slam, limited to 5,000	**$29**
Postcards of Legends Magazine Tiger covers.	**$5 each**
2001 Buick Advertising card	**$10**

Grolier collectible cards

1998 Ryder Cup, No. 121-8	**$10**
1999 Mark O'Meara, No. 126-15	**$10**

Newspapers

The newspaper vending boxes in Edicott, N.Y., during Tiger's appearance at the B.C. Open touted "There's a TIGER in town!" Yes, Tiger Woods sells newspapers and plenty of them. Speaking of plenty, there are an incredible amount of newspapers that have featured Tiger on the front page of the paper, front page of a section in advertisements, and even on newspaper vending boxes.

2001 Buick advertising postcard for Buick Bengal 2+2 concept car. **$17.50**

Newspapers? You mean people actually collect these things? Guess what? I have sold newspapers for hundreds of dollars, some not even that old. Significant events, such as Tiger's appearances in the four majors, sell newspapers and are very attractive to collectors. Not all are valuable yet, but wait a few years, just wait.

Prominent newspapers, with bold headlines, sell best. Minor markets, although marketable, will never reach the value of the major papers. *USA TODAY, The New York Times*, and the region of the country where a Tiger tournament victory has taken place will show the greatest appreciation. Value range: **$5-$50.**

Newspapers are also collected for their advertising. Full-page advertisements, such as some that have appeared with Tiger for American Express or Nike, sell best. Naturally a large colorful advertisement in a prominent daily adds value to the newspaper.

Newspapers are highly acidic and prone to many environmental characteristics of deterioration. They should be stored under the proper environmental conditions using archival materials only. Advertisements should also be placed with acid-free backing boards and in archival bagging before storing properly.

April 14, 1997 - The Atlanta Constitution	**$10**
April 9, 2001 - New York Post	**$5**
April 15, 2002 - The Augusta Chronicle	**$5**

Periodicals

What Tiger does for television ratings, a huge increase in ratings during his appearances, he also does for magazines. A Tiger Woods cover means increased circulation. This has grown to such an extent that I own magazines with him on the cover, yet he's not in the issue.

Collectors in this area prefer major magazine issues with Tiger featured predominantly on the cover, especially those that refer to a major event such as a win at "The Masters" or an annual award such as *Sports Illustrated* "Sportsman of the Year." Novelty issues, such as those that contain posters, trading cards, booklets, postcards, etc., are also very popular.

Since condition is a factor in value, always store periodicals carefully in archival materials and conditions. Most choose acid-free bags and backing boards for each issue. All periodicals should be in original state, with no items removed or added. Some collectors will purchase more than one novelty issue in order to remove a poster for display or the trading cards to be graded.

Selected below are a diverse group of periodicals, from *Ebony* and *American Legacy*, to *Penthouse, Sports Illustrated*, and *Golf Digest*, Tiger Woods is big news to everyone. During the end of 1996, the Tiger periodical boom began, appearing on covers of *Golf World* five times, *Golf Digest* once, *Golf* once, *Newsweek* once and *Sports Illustrated* twice. Since 1997, he seems to be living in a goldfish bowl, with everything he says or does documented. So routine is his picture on the cover of a magazine that nearly any trip to a newsstand should add a new addition to your collection.

Selected Periodicals

Sports Illustrated, Sept. 24, 1990, "Faces in the Crowd," his first of many appearances inside the magazine.   **$75**

Sports Illustrated, Appearances inside the magazine prior to his first cover: Prices vary dramatically with inside articles. Range   **$5-$20**
March 9, 1992, Aug. 9, 1993, Sept. 5, 1994, Oct. 17, 1994, March 27, 1995, April 17, 1995, July 17, 1995, Sept. 4, 1995, April 8, 1996, June 10, 1996, June 24, 1996, Sept. 9, 1996, Sept. 23, 1996, Sept. 30, 1996, Oct. 14, 1996. The price ranges for these issues vary   **($10-$20)**

Sports Illustrated, Oct. 28, 1996, "Tiger!" His Disney win landed him on the SI cover, a must collectible! Inside includes Titleist ad with Tiger. Considered his rookie cover! **$60**
Sports Illustrated, Dec. 23, 1996, "Sportsman of the Year," a must for collectors! Includes an American Brands ad inside with Tiger. **$40**
SI For Kids, 1996. Includes Tiger Card. **$200-$300**

   Legends Sports Memorabilia, Vol. 9 No. 4, 1997, Tiger on Cover. A controversial and highly sought issue due to a nine-card insert panel (included were three Ted Williams cards, three Tiger Woods cards, two Ernie Banks cards and one Rod Carew card) and a three-card postcard insert of cover art including Ted Williams, Tiger and Greg Maddux. This issue sparked controversy over what trading card is actually his rookie card. See Trading Card section. Prices vary significantly.
Golf World International, Vol. 38 No. 6. "Tiger Talks." **$15**
Fortune, May 12, 1997. Tiger on cover, great shot. **$25**
Links, The Best of Golf, April, 1997. "Tiger Takes Aim at Augusta," weak article. **$10**

Golf Monthly, June 1997. "Tiger Walks Alone," great cover shot. **$12**

People, June 16, 1997. Tiger & Earl Woods on cover, popular. **$17**

Golf Digest, June 1997. Black & white photograph on the front. "How he became a Tiger" by Earl Woods. Includes Titleist small booklet with Tiger inside; also Pocket Tips insert booklet. Tiger appears in two Titleist ads along with him using a King Cobra driver in an American Brands ads. A must collectors issue. **$20**

GQ, April 1997, Tiger on Cover. "The Coming of Tiger Woods, Sports Next Messiah" by Charles P. Pierce. One of the most controversial articles ever written about Tiger Woods. It created an uproar with all associated with the sport. **$20**

Sports Illustrated, April 21, 1997. "The New Master." Included a pull-out panorama at the beginning of the article. **$10**

Sports Illustrated For Kids, August 1997. "I am Tiger Woods" ad campaign spread inside along with a "Big Shot" poster of Tiger. **$10**

Golf Magazine June 1997. "Tigermania," great cover. **$5**

Golf Digest, October 1997. "The Spirit of Tiger Woods." Finding Col. Phong, Earl Woods on cover, a fantastic issue and a must for all Tiger collectors **$15**

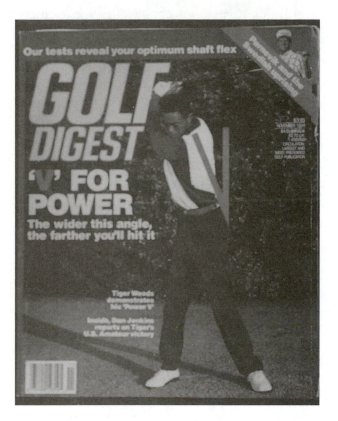

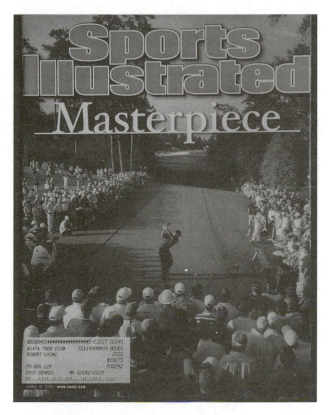

Payne Stewart's Guide to Golf, Premier Issue. Includes a Tiger profile inside, a scarce issue for obvious reasons. **$15**

Golf Digest, August 1997. "Tiger signs to write articles exclusively for *Golf Digest* this month."

"Tiger Tips" now becomes a collectible column. Issue includes a Tudor watch ad featuring Tiger also a Fortune Brands ad. Tiger is also featured on the inside "Pocket Tips" book, a small tear out section. **$10**

Black Enterprise, September 1997. "Tiger Woods & The Business of Golf." Tiger and Earl Woods on the cover. Issue includes Nike "I won't forget" two-page spread. **$6**

Golf World International, Vol. 39 No. 4. Great black and white photo on the cover, Masters Edition, Special double foldout of Tiger's swing, a must for collectors! **$14**

Golf Digest, January 1998. Double foldout of Tiger's swing, two-page Titleist spread with Tiger, "Pocket Tips" removable booklet with Tiger on cover, a great edition! **$10**

Golf Week's Pro Golf 1998. Great statistic book, include two-page Titleist ad. **$6**

Sports Illustrated, June 26, 2000. "Any Questions?" nice cover. **$10**

Sports Illustrated, Dec. 18, 2000. "Sportsman of the year," great issue. **$15**

Time, Aug. 14, 2000. "Tiger's Tale," nice article. **$10**

Sports Illustrated, Aug. 28, 2000. "Guts and Glory," wins third major of the year (PGA). **$10**

Sports Illustrated For Kids, January 2001. Great Tiger cover, plus huge Tiger poster, nine-card multiple sport trading card insert, four Tiger Woods Athlete of the Year trading cards, a must for all collectors! **$22**

People Weekly, Dec. 25, 2000. "The 25 Most Intriguing People 2000," Tiger on front. **$5**

Golf Digest, January 2001. "How He Did It," features Tiger with all his trophies, Tiger poster pull-out, Tiger "Pocket Tips" insert, a must for any collector! **$10**

Sports Illustrated, April 16, 2001. "Masterpiece," great cover, outstanding issue. **$6**

Golf World, January 2001. "The Tiger Effect," great issue, a must for collectors. **$9**

TV Guide. June 9-15, 2001. Four Collector covers commemorating Tiger Woods' major titles. "Tiger's Slam Dance." **$30**
Eye on the Tiger, "The Tiger Woods Quarterly." Gold Collectors Series Sports Guide Magazine, Vol. 1, No.1, a must for collectors! **$8.50**
Eye on the Tiger, "The Tiger Woods Quarterly." Gold Collectors Series Sports Guide Magazine, Vol. 1, No.2, a must for collectors! **$8**
Tiger Woods Tribute, Grand Slam Champion 2000. Gold Collectors Series Sports Guide Magazine. **$5.50**

Posters, Postcards, Prints

As one might anticipate, there are many Tiger Woods posters available. Most posters fall in the $10 to $20 range. Collectors should try to concentrate on those associated with advertising campaigns, many of which have limited distribution and a short shelf life. Nike and Buick related posters have been extremely popular with collectors. For example, the Tiger Woods six foot Nike "Hope" poster sealed can bring as much as $25 and the Nike "Intensity" about $20.

Similar to posters, postcards are widely available in the hobby. Mass marketed issues being worth far less than those with limited distribution, such as Buick promos. Endorsement related postcards average about a dollar each, while mass marketed about half that. Keep in mind that postcards can also appear as inserts in magazine and bring a far greater value.

Photography is an art form and marketed as such, at least most of the time. Tiger has been a photography subject for years, with prints now appearing in the market on a daily basis. Similar to other forms of artwork, prices vary significantly. The quality of the photograph, photographer, event, and distribution will all play a major role in determining value. Like artwork, quality is not cheap. A good example of this is the *Golf Digest* January 2001 cover shot. It is a beautiful and relevant photograph showing Tiger with all his major trophies. Sales from prints of the photo benefited the Tiger Woods Foundation Inc. Framed and matted prints were available exclusively from Famous Photography Inc. for $199, $299, and $349, not including shipping and handling.

Topps released its first set of authorized sports photographs in 1997. The facts around this release were:

* Six professional, 8" x 10" photographs
* All photos selected by Tiger Woods
* Official Tiger Woods Poster was also available
* Superb shots from the '97 Masters, and more
* Each photo included a "Topps Genuine Issue" holographic stamp
* All photos were sealed in an archival quality envelope
* The issue was exclusively distributed by The Topps Company

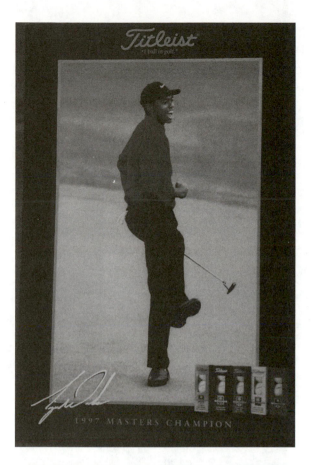

Since the release seemed to meet with a mediocre response from the hobby, little interest has been seen in the market.

There have also been a number of framed (21" x 17") prints entering the market from Pro Tour. They typically bring about **$40 to $50.** 1997 Masters Champion by Titleist. One of the Major Championship Winners series. Full color. 18" x 12". **$75**
Angelo Marino, limited edition of 900, full color, 9" x 12", signed by the artist. **$95**
"Tiger's Triple" Series of three original pencil sketches of Tiger after his three U. S. Amateur wins. Signed by the artist Michael Astrachan and limited to 950 pieces. 22" x 10". **$195**
"A Tribute to Tiger Woods," lithograph poster limited edition by Julio Cardozo Henriques. Black and white and signed by the artist. **$150**
"A Championship Season" full color litho by Robert Tannenbaum of the cover of Legends Sports Memorabilia magazine #112. Limited to 2001 issues. Signed and numbered by the artist. 16" x 20" **$295**

Standees and Displays

This area could prove worthwhile for collectors over the long haul. At least that has been the case in other areas of collecting. Standees (life-size cardboard cutouts) and merchandise displays are often overlooked by collectors or simply forgotten.

Some standees have entered the market, many being custom made. One prominent one, although I don't know the manufacturer, is a picture celebrating his victory at The Masters. It also includes a facsimile signature, which leads me to believe it's authentic (licensed). Standees can vary significantly in price from $30 to $100.

Displays are common to many forms of collecting such as books, golf balls, cereal boxes, etc. The problem is that they are often reused, disassembled or destroyed. Most are cardboard. While I have seen some in stores, very few are offered in the open market. Complete displays, depending on subject matter and appearance, can bring $50 to $100. There are always some areas of collecting that you will have to monitor and this is one of those areas.

Tour Programs/Passes/Related items

Anyone who has attended a PGA event knows just how exciting it can be. From the time you purchase your ticket, you are deluged with vendors marketing their products. Many hand out "freebies" such as golf balls or cushions. By the time you get to the first tee, many visitors have a handful of memorabilia in one hand and their program in the other. Speaking of programs, most are free and include a pairing sheet for that round. Programs come in all shapes and sizes, as do pairing sheets that are either inserted or included in the magazine.

Tickets also vary by tournament, from detachable stubs to a single-round printed form. Most tickets include a string that is used to attach it to the attendee; tickets must be displayed at all times. There are many types of tickets, such as sponsor, event staff, V.I.P., etc. The greater the distribution of a certain type of ticket, badge or identification, the less value it will have.

Final-round memorabilia and key-round articles command more money. Complete tournament packages (program, pairing sheets, and tickets) also bring greater value.

Programs

1996 Greater Milwaukee Open, first Pro Tour tournament as a professional **$50**

1996 Las Vegas Invitational, first professional win **$75**

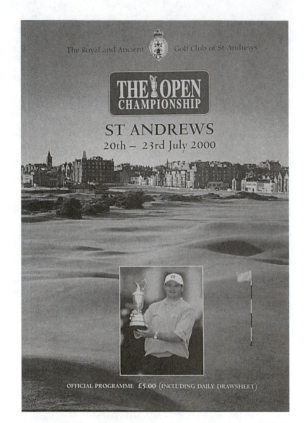

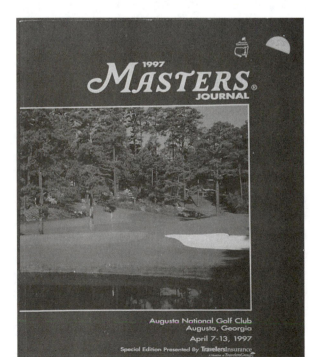

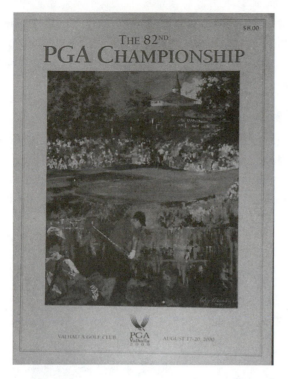

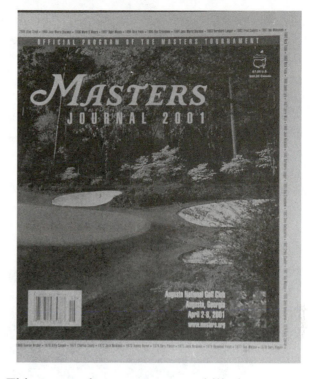

1997 Masters	**$45**
2000 U. S. Open	**$25**
2000 British Open	**$45**
2000 PGA	**$45**
2001 Masters	**$35**
All other programs	**$10-$25**

Tiger Tour Event Tickets

Amateur Career Record in Professional Events (1992-96)

Tournament: ticket(s) **$45 to $50, $75** with program

Masters/Majors: ticket(s) **$100, $175** with program

Professional Career Record

Tiger Woods' professional career began at the Greater Milwaukee Open in August 1996. Tiger was allowed to play in the TPC (Tour Players Championship) at the end of the year because his total winnings moved him into the top 30 money winners for that year. He won twice, at the Las Vegas Invitational and at Disney World.

Keep in mind as a collector that both tournament attendance and corporate involvement increases by 25 percent when Tiger attends.

This means that more memorabilia is produced at these tournaments.

1996

First win (Las Vegas Invitational): ticket(s) **$125, $200** with program

Second win (Walt Disney/Oldsmobile): ticket(s) **$100, $165** with program

First tournament (Greater Milwaukee Open): ticket(s) **$125, $170** with program

Prior to first win: ticket(s) **$55, $110** with program

All other 1996: ticket(s) **$40, $80** with program

1997

First place tournament: ticket(s) **$40, $65** with program

Major(s): ticket(s) **$50, $100** with program

Masters: ticket/badge(s) **$200, $300** with program

All other 1997: ticket(s) **$30, $50** with program

Following the "Tigermania" boom of 1997, more and more tournament items were being produced at events he planned on attending. While this has always been the case, even as an amateur, his victory at The Masters solidified his position of being the "meal ticket" on the PGA Tour.

Tiger Tour Victories 1998-2003
First place tournament: ticket(s) **$40, $50** with program
Major(s): ticket(s) **$50, $100** with program
Masters: ticket/badge(s) **$100, $200** with program
All other 1998-2003: ticket(s) **$30, $50** with program

Tiger Woods was the 2002 Money Leader with five wins at only 18 events. To get into the top 10 list of money leaders, some players had to play more than 30 events.

Original Scorecards

November 15-19, 2000, Alpine Golf & Sports Club, European PGA Tournament held in Germany. Tiger Woods scorecards from all 4 rounds. (below and next page)   **$10,000**

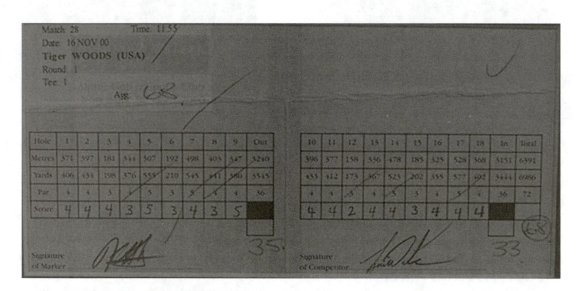

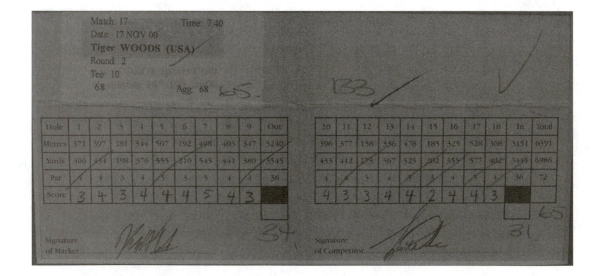

Match: 27 Time: 11.40
Date: 18 NOV 00
Tiger WOODS (USA)
Round: 3
Tee: 1
68 65 Agg: 133 65.

198.

Hole	1	2	3	4	5	6	7	8	9	Out
Metres	371	397	181	344	507	192	498	403	347	3240
Yards	406	434	198	576	555	210	545	441	380	3545
Par	4	4	3	4	5	3	5	4	4	36
Score	4	4	3	4	4	3	3	4	4	33

Hole	10	11	12	13	14	15	16	17	18	In	Total
Metres	396	377	158	336	478	185	325	528	368	3151	6391
Yards	433	412	173	367	523	202	355	577	402	3444	6986
Par	4	4	3	4	5	3	4	5	4	36	72
Score	4	4	3	3	4	2	4	4	4	32	65

Signature of Marker
Signature of Competitor

Match: 27 Time: 11.35
Date: 19 NOV 00
Tiger WOODS (USA)
Round: 4
Tee: 1
68 65 65 Agg: 198 65. 263

Hole	1	2	3	4	5	6	7	8	9	Out
Metres	371	397	181	344	507	192	498	403	347	3240
Yards	406	434	198	376	555	210	545	441	380	3545
Par	4	4	3	4	5	3	5	4	4	36
Score	4	4	3	4		4	3	4	4	3	33

Hole	10	11	12	13	14	15	16	17	18	In	Total
Metres	396	377	158	336	478	185	325	528	368	3151	6391
Yards	433	412	173	367	523	202	355	577	402	3444	6986
Par	4	4	3	4	5	3	4	5	4	36	72
Score	3	4	3	4	4	3	3	4	4	32	65

Signature of Marker
Signature of Competitor

Scorecards (Not official USGA or PGA)

Masters 1997	**$800**
Masters 2001-2002	**$500**
British Open	**$250**
US Open	**$250**
PGA	**$250**
Other PGA or Charity Event Score Cards	**$200**

Toys, Costumes, Games, etc.

Interest in this area surrounds video game releases: new, used, and counterfeit. Naturally Nintendo Gamecube, Playstation 2, Gameboy, and others are constantly being sold in the market. Price range: $25 to $50. There are also a variety of hand-held video games that I don't believe are licensed, but are being sold. Sharper Image markets The Tiger Woods Ultimate Golf Game, but I am unsure if it is licensed or not. Prices for the unit run about $15.

Yes, there are Tiger Woods Halloween costumes and the mask ranges from $10 to $15. Also figurines do enter the market: for example the Art of Sports figurine with trophy that sells at about $100.

Where would we be without a Tiger Woods Bobble Head? Both Nike and Upper Deck have provided a fun line. Most average $10 to $15 per figure in original state, unopened.

This is an area filled with unlicensed and counterfeit products. Always exercise caution. If you are a real Tiger collector, don't waste your time with fakes and forgeries.

Trading Cards

Although this is a popular area of collecting, it is also very confusing. Primarily fueled by the enormous television exposure of the 1997-98 Grand Slams Ventures Masters Collection, collectors became confused by manufacturer claims to "Rookie Card" rights. Many collectors realized that the December 1996 magazine *Sports Illustrated For Kids* included a Tiger Woods card. Not to mention a trip to your local card store during this period could yield a handful or more of unauthorized Woods trading cards. Will the real Tiger Woods please step to the tee?

In 1997, Tiger Woods agreed to just one licensed card and it appears in Grand Slam Venture's 1997 "Champions of the Masters Collection." Unlicensed cards, that did not come from a set and were inserted into a magazine, are not considered by hobby professionals to be true rookie cards. They recognize Tiger Woods' 2001 Upper Deck #1 and 2001 SP Authentic #45 as his only rookie cards.

Tiger Woods trading card pricing is not an exact science. It is not consistent, far too subjective and dynamic. When you find cards being sold at 10 times more or 10 times less than listed in a price guide, something is wrong. Therefore, collectors should research their purchases, use a grading service that is consistent and accurate, and find a price guide that seems to reflect what you are experiencing in the hobby.

Remember whatever price you are quoted could change dramatically with another major win by Tiger.

With Upper Deck's appearance in the market, everything has changed since 2001. Simply stated: it has revolutionized the golf trading card market. The company has brought legitimacy and fun back into Tiger card collecting.

Tiger Woods Selected Card Checklist (Mint)

1997-98 Grand Slam Ventures Masters Collection	$40
1997-98 Grand Slam Ventures Masters Gold Foil	$200
2001 Upper Deck Golf #1	$20
2001 Upper Deck Golf Player's Ink TW	$750
2001 Upper Deck Golf Tour Threads (red)	$750
2001 Upper Deck Golf Tour Threads (white)	$400
2001 SP Authentic #45 (autograph-500)	$1,150
2001 SP Authentic TW (autograph)	$525
2001 SP Authentic Tour Swatch	$240
2002 SP Authentic #1	$4
2002 SP Authentic Course Classics TW	$175
2002 SP Authentic Sign of the Times (autograph)	$250
2002 Upper Deck Golf America's Best	$200
2002 Upper Deck Golf Fairway Fabrics	$240
2002 Upper Deck Golf Fairway Fabrics (autograph)	$1,250
2002 Upper Deck Golf Combo Shirt	$375
2002 Upper Deck Golf Authentic Golf Glove	$200
2002 SP Game-Used Scorecard Signatures	$250
2002 SP Game-Used Course of a Champion Tiger Woods Auto	$250
2002 SP Game-Used Front 9 Fabric	$70
2002 SP Game-Used Front 9 Fabric (autograph-100)	$400
2003 Upper Deck Golf	$3

Legends Sports Memorabilia

Hobby Edition #78 - Tiger Woods cover, includes three Tiger Woods cards plus one Tiger Woods postcard along with Ted Williams cards and postcards. **$295**

Vol. 13, No. 1, Hobby Ed. #112 - Tiger Woods cover. Includes nine gold foil-edged cards of Tiger and an eight-page article w/many photos. **$27.50**

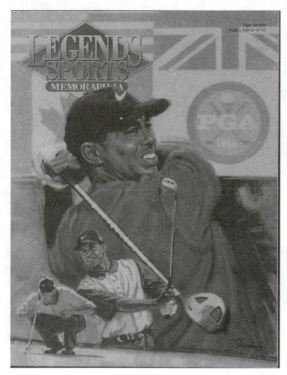

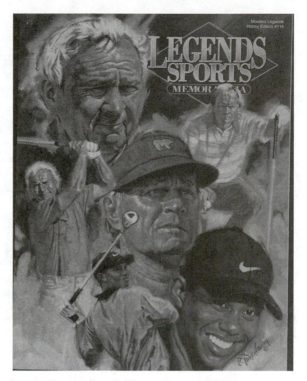

Vol. 13, No. 3, Hobby Ed. #114 – Daytona cover w/Dale Earnhardt, Jeff Gordon, and Dale Jarrett. Includes a Tiger Woods card and the first in a series of Grand Slam winners with a Gene Sarazen card. **$27.50**

Vol. 13, No. 4, Hobby Ed. #115 – New York Yankees cover. Has Tiger Woods and Gary Player Grand Slam winner cards. **$15**

Vol. 13, No. 5, Hobby Ed. #116 – Masters Legends cover w/Nicklaus, Palmer & Woods. Has eight Masters Champions cards and one Jack Nicklaus Grand Slam winner card. **$20**

Tiger Woods Special Collector's Edition pays tribute to Tiger Woods victory at the 2001 Masters. 32 pages devoted to Tiger and two special gold-foiled inserts. One features nine images of Tiger Woods at the Masters. The second is a full page gold foiled image of Tiger wearing the green jacket. **$25**

Videotape/DVD related

Collecting Tiger Woods videos, which include all of his televised golf tournaments, can be a costly and challenging undertaking. From appearances at halftime during a *Monday Night Football* telecast to ABC's *World News Tonight* and news show *Nightline*, Tiger seems to pop up everywhere. Even Tiger's former caddie, Mike "Fluff" Cowan, starred in his own ESPN commercial.

Most collectors start with acquiring copies of Tiger's major tour victories and work their way back to his amateur days. It is conceivable to acquire a complete videotape set of his appearances on the professional tour, as many networks have archive departments, but it will take time and money.

Collecting network appearances of Tiger will be much harder. Finding copies of shows such as *The Mike Douglas Show, CBS Network News, That's Incredible, The Today Show, Good Morning America,* and *Oprah*, where Tiger appeared, can be tricky. This will take some research on your part, along with a constant monitoring of the networks.

Of the videotapes available, here are my favorites. The first is "Tiger's Triple!" It's the phenomenal story of Tiger Woods' unprecedented three straight U.S. Amateur Championships. This 60 minute tape, produced for the United States Golf Association, chronicles Tiger's victories at TPC at Sawgrass in 1994, Newport in 1995, and at Pumpkin Ridge in 1996. Produced and written by Bruce J. Smith, this is a must addition to any Tiger collection. It costs about $18.

Three popular Tiger Woods videos include, from left, Tiger Woods, Son, Hero & Champion; Highlights of the 1997 Masters, and Tiger's Triple!
$15 each

Another favorite is "Highlights of the 1997 Masters Tournament," presented by IBM and available through Monarch Home Video (Cat. #36269). Narrated by Chris Schenkel, this 52 minute tape takes you back to Tiger's third Masters and documents his win as the youngest champion in history at the age of 21. This production costs about $10 on videotape.

The last is "Tiger Woods, Son, Hero & Champion." This 58-minute tape, produced by CBS video (#4098), takes collectors back to Tiger's tour debut. It includes his hole-in-one in Milwaukee and history-making Masters win. Some never-before-released footage is also included. This tape averages about $15.

There are many more video images of Tiger, but this will give you a start. No doubt many more memories are to come, so keep some blank videotapes on hand.

Tiger Woods at a Glance

Name: Eldrick Woods

Nickname: "Tiger," named after Earl's friend Nguyen Phong

Date of birth: Dec. 30, 1975, in Long Beach, California

Early years: Grew up in Cypress, Calif., southeast of Los Angeles.

Parents: Earl and Kultida Punsawad Woods, married in 1969.

Relations: Tiger has two half brothers and one half sister from his father's previous marriage.

Childhood idol: Greg Norman

Ethnicity: African-American, Chinese, Native American, Thai, and Caucasian.

Religion: Buddhism

High school: Western High School in Anaheim   **Coach:** Don Crosby

College: Stanford University

Coach: Wally Goodwin

College major: Economics

Favorite meal: McDonalds Big Mac and fries

Coach: Butch Harmon, son of 1948 Masters champion Claude Harmon

Agent: Hughes Norton, IMG, 1 Erie View Plaza, Cleveland, OH 44114

Sports psychologist: Jay Brunza

Chapter 2

Playing With Hickories

By C. W. McMullin, Jr.

Chuck McMullin has been collecting and playing with antique clubs for nearly 20 years. He won the Scottish Hickory Championship and has placed in the top five in numerous World Hickory Championships. He and I are great friends and as a result I asked him to write an article on play with hickories. Many thanks, as his profusely illustrated dissertation is far more than I anticipated!

Historic Clubs – Pre 1880

Playing sets as we know them today weren't introduced into the game of golf until about the turn of the century. Early photographs suggest that a player in the mid 1800s would choose from local craftsmen a variety of clubs that suited his or her game. The caddy then carried them under the arm during the game. The playing clubs available in the mid 1800s were mostly wooden-headed clubs such as the Robert Forgan shown.

A "set" of playing clubs would have looked similar to the group of clubs shown.

A player would assemble a mixture of this type of club, depending upon his ability and desire to have "all the shots." Play clubs or driving-type clubs had extremely long and thin shafts, quite flexible at times, plus long, narrow, and shallow heads, often with a slightly "hooked" face. Spoons, or fairway-type clubs, were available in several lengths and lofts for a variety of approach shots. One could assemble six or eight or more varieties of long,

Robert Forgan made this wooden-headed club in the mid 1800s.

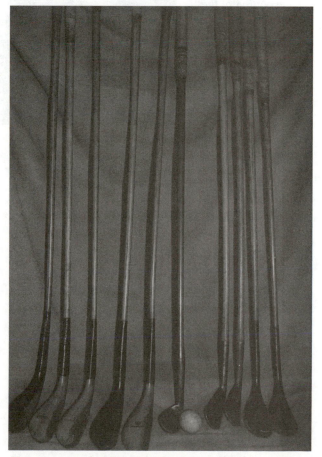

Here is a set of 1800s playing clubs.

Another view shows a close-up of a set of wooden playing clubs.

The evolution of the golf ball included the feather ball, hard rubber ball, and, eventually, multiple-piece rubber balls. A representative ball from each generation is depicted here.

short, and baffing spoons. Putters were not just one type either. They could be of an approaching putter style with a little more loft for longer range shots, or they could be the more normal short-range putters.

In the mid 1800s, the player only had two basic choices of iron clubs available: a lofted iron, which was mostly used from sand and dirt lies, and the track iron, a small rounded-head iron for extricating oneself from cart tracks, footprints, and other nasty lies. Although the gutta percha (rubber) ball was introduced in 1848, the feather ball was widely in use well into the 1860s, and probably into the 1870s by some diehard users. Assembling a playing set today with these his-

toric clubs is cost prohibitive and not practical for use. These clubs are truly collectibles.

Over the years, the ball evolved from a feather-stuffed leather-covered ball to a hard rubber ball and eventually to multiple-piece rubber balls.

Transitional Clubs – 1880-1910

By the 1880s, the feather ball was virtually extinct. Golfers were using the more versatile rubber ball, the gutty. It was more reliable and flew farther than the feather ball. But it was a harder consistency and therefore was more abusive to the wooden-headed clubs. The delicate nature and elegant style of the play club was forced to give way to a more practical and

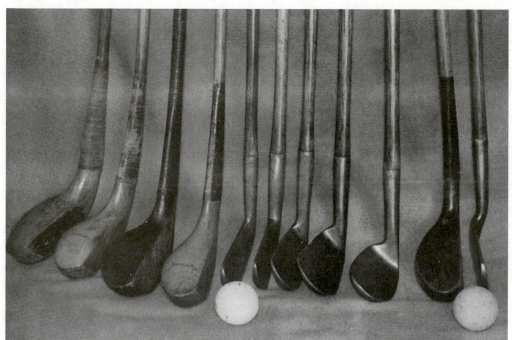

This early "playing set" made by the famous Wm. Park Jr. is displayed with line cut and bramble guttie balls. It features woods, irons, and both a wooden and iron putter.

Transitional clubs, used when the gutta-percha ball replaced the featherie, were made from the 1880s through 1910s and featured tougher club heads for the harder balls.

sturdier club head. This not only changed the look and versatility of the wooden headed clubs forever, but it was the beginning of the infiltration of iron headed clubs as a regular part of the playing sets. This type of look in the wooden-headed clubs became known as the "transitional" style, as it was in between the early "historic" club design and what we now affectionately refer to as the "modern" hickory club design (1920s and '30s).

Golfers began to see that a golf shot with a gutty ball could be controlled somewhat better with an iron head than with a wooden head. Finesse was being discovered as an integral part of the game. For distance, one still used wooden headed clubs, though a smaller number of choices were available and they were still scare or splice neck in construction. The making of iron-headed clubs became a vocation for many craftsmen, as opposed to just a select few iron makers a couple of decades earlier. New types of shot making were created with new types of club names. "Cleeks," "irons," "lofters," and "niblicks" were adopted by golfers everywhere to enhance the art of shot making.

A "playing set" assembled from one maker began to surface in the 1880s and 1890s.

A set of Park's clubs is carried in the Osmond club carrier that was available about the turn of the century.

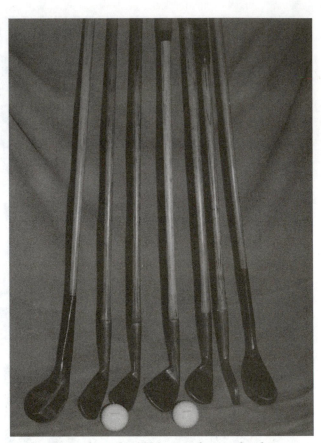

A playing set from the 1890s was designed to hit a hard rubber ball with a variety of "mesh" patterns for spin and maneuverability. The author uses this playing set at Oakhurst Links, White Sulphur Springs, W. Va.

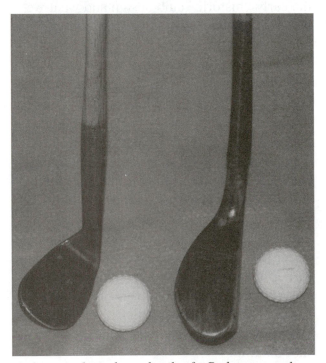

A close-up photo shows details of a Park putter and a smooth-face niblick.

Typical of this idea would be a group of clubs from the famous Wm. Park Jr., two time Open Champion in his own right and son of four-time Open Champion "Old Willa" Park of Musselburg.

One could choose from a number of lofted wooden clubs and as well as a larger variety of iron clubs. Both wooden and iron putter choices are shown here.

By the 1890s, and certainly by the turn of the century, one could avail oneself of a club carrier such as the Osmond carrier shown.

As we moved into the 1890s, the ball was still a hard rubber ball, but with a variety of "mesh" patterns, raised surfaces on the ball for spin and maneuverability. Typical of this era is the playing set shown here that I use at Oakhurst Links, White Sulphur Springs, W. Va.

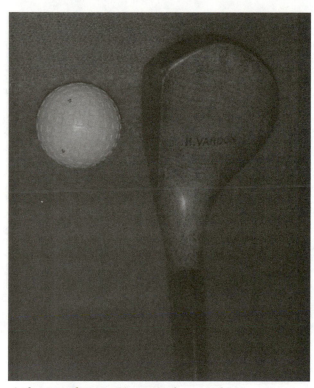

A close-up shows a Harry Vardon wood

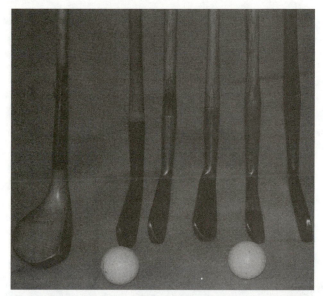

These Harry Vardon clubs are typical of the last of the era of splice neck woods and smooth-face irons. (Above and below)

It consists of driving clubs, one of which is a Wm. Park spoon c. 1890s. The irons are all smooth faced and there are two putter choices, either wooden or iron headed.

They offer a variety of shot making ability with lofts ranging from 24 degrees in a cleek, 30 degrees in an "iron," 42 degrees in a lofter, to 51 degrees in a niblick. The putter varieties are a Wm. Park 1880s style transitional wooden head design and a 1890s brass blade putter.

Assembling a playing set of clubs from this era can be a bit expensive, but sturdy splice neck woods and smooth-faced irons are out there to be found. The good news is that one only needs a few clubs to have an effective set. At this writing, the National Hickory Championship at Oakhurst is the only tournament using these clubs.

Transitional clubs after the turn of the century were forced to progress with the innovative evolution of the ball. Gradually they transformed from the splice neck variety with shorter, more round-shaped heads such as the Harry Vardon driver shown here to a socket head design where the shaft screwed into the head.

A close-up shows a typical hickory wood from the 1920s.

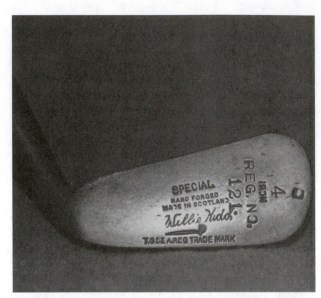

By the 1920s, irons were beginning to be made with much smaller degrees of difference in loft so as to provide a club for nearly every distance encountered.

These Vardon clubs are typical of the last of the era of splice neck woods and zsmooth-face irons. The wood may have been made by Vardon and the irons were made for Vardon by Tom Stewart.

From this time forward, the heads continued to take on a more round shape, were shorter in length, and had much deeper faces. The old straight and somewhat "hooked" faces gave way to a slight convex or bulged face. They were referred to as "bulger" faced woods. Shot makers of the day were designing irons first with dots punched on the face and then lines scored across the face. The markings on the ball and now the markings on the clubs would forever change the level of play from the shot makers. Names for the irons were creative and numbers were introduced on some of them. Assembling a set of clubs from this era is currently done only for collection purposes.

Modern Hickory Clubs

By 1920, nearly every wooden club maker was producing bulger-faced, socket headed drivers, brassies, and spoons. Most of the iron makers were making larger six- to 10-club sets, mostly with lined scored faces. Also, irons were beginning to be made with much smaller degrees of difference in loft so as to provide a club for nearly every distance encountered. Consistency of construction was more prevalent in this era so the clubs lasted longer. They were being produced for a far larger group of golfers worldwide so the cost was more affordable to the public.

Since metal shafts didn't permanently invade club making until 1935, we have about a 15-year period from which to assemble a set of good playables. The vast majority of clubs available today at collectors gatherings are from this era. By this time, there were millions of golfers playing with millions of clubs and many thousands have survived. Good playables are available and not expensive at this time, although the interest in tournament play with hickory clubs has increased sharply in recent years.

Featured here is a matched set of irons made in St. Andrews, Scotland, by Tom Stewart for Willie Kidd of Interlochen Golf

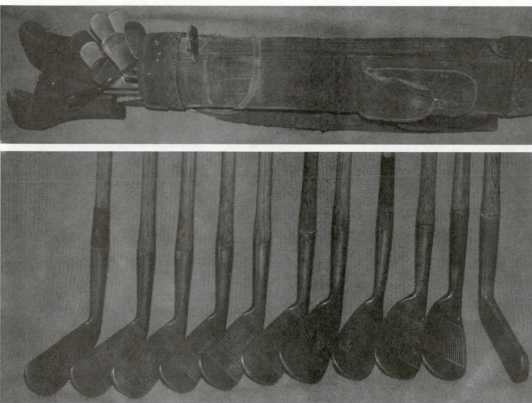

A set of hickory playables is ready for play in an antique golf bag.

A "modern set" of hickory clubs includes bulger faced, socket headed drivers, brassies, and spoons, as well as irons and a putter.

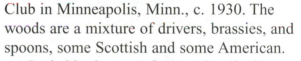

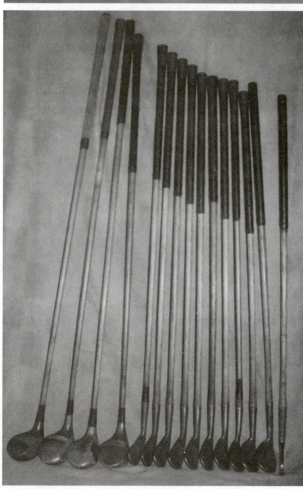

Club in Minneapolis, Minn., c. 1930. The woods are a mixture of drivers, brassies, and spoons, some Scottish and some American.

Probably the most frequently asked question of me when I'm out playing with my hickory clubs is, "Aren't you afraid you will break them?" My response is always that players of every era swing hard or soft, fast or slow, and with care or with abandon. Nothing is new today. Well-made clubs always seem to survive longer than players.

If you haven't hit a hickory club, you are missing one of life's most rewarding pleasures. Playing world famous courses with hickory clubs is an experience of a lifetime.

Featured here is a matched set of irons made in St. Andrews, Scotland, by Tom Stewart for Willie Kidd of Interlochen Golf Club in Minneapolis, Minn., c. 1930.

Collecting Wood Shaft Patent Golf Clubs

By Gordon Page

I always enjoy talking with collectors about patent golf clubs. Over the years, I have frequently been asked how can collectors make their golf club collection more unique or focused, rather than loading the collection with just any wood shaft golf club. Many of us can say, "been there, done that." The answer to the question of what type of club to concentrate on is not an easy one, as a collection can focus on woods, irons, putters, maker, country of manufacture, and age. However most veteran collectors will point in the same direction.

Patent Golf Clubs

Each patented club seems to have a story to tell, usually quite unique, and it stands out in any collection. In some instances, they are the forerunners of today's high tech clubs. If we look at the Carruthers bore-through hosel, there is very little change in the design of the 1925 models and the 2003 designs. Also, consider the Park wry neck putter design, patented in the late 1800s. That same style of bent neck hosel is currently being made by several manufacturers.

Yet difference is a patent club's middle name, for example, the bullet shaped Streamliner of the 1920s, the Gibson Snail putter, or the Giant niblick. Examples of patent clubs can be found at price levels from moderate to high end and, thus, can be admired and purchased by the beginning collector on a budget to the veteran collector eyeing the highly treasured ones.

Let's reflect a moment on history and its relationship to many of the patent clubs. Several events in history collided around the 1890s through the early part of the 1900s that brought forward the proliferation of unusual, patent clubs. The Industrial Revolution brought manufacturing techniques to the golf industry that were not available prior to that time. Hand forging, with its limited volume, started to be replaced by mass production and the ability to work with various metals in new and sometimes very unique designs. Instead of hundreds or thousands of clubs being produced, the industry was producing millions, yes, millions of clubs. The interest in golf was exploding. While the game was played previously by a few golfers on a few courses, golf courses were being built at a rapid pace for the multitude of eager novices. As companies looked for an advantage to sell their clubs and profit from this groundswell of interest, designers conceived hundreds of patentable club shapes, sizes, and forms. The golfer picked up the game with a fervor and many looked for the magic crutch to assist them in getting from tee to green in as few strokes as possible. This total mix resulted in "fertile" ground for patent club design and production.

The next section describes why certain clubs were invented and is categorized by availability/price. I have concentrated on the period from the 1890s to the 1930s, when patent clubs proliferated the golfing field. An overly simplistic statement of availability suggests that the less the patent appealed to the golfer at that time and the less it improved his game, the fewer clubs were made. Thus, the least desirable clubs of that era are the most desirable to today's collector.

This first list gives some examples of moderately priced, more available clubs, generally under $500 to $600, followed by a list of higher priced, high end clubs.

Fancy Faces

The "DINT"

Moderately Priced Woods

Face inserts (Fancy Faces) were used on some models to protect the hitting surface. Many styles resulted from using inserts of gutta percha, brass, steel, aluminum, ivory, etc. Look for Spalding Kro-Flite series and Wilson's Walker Cup series. Even thin metal was used, such as the DINT. This club had a single face plate that covered both sole and face of the club. This was reported in golf advertisements as offering increased strength.

Head materials were developed in an attempt to make the heads impervious to the elements. Included were Forgan's Forganite and Kroydon's Kroydonite with their synthetic or compressed wood materials, as well as aluminum heads by Standard Golf Co. of Sunderland, England. Their options of materials were limited, primarily in materials selection and manufacturing methods.

Structural designs were fairly standard at the turn of the century. All club heads were basically "copy cats." Shape was universal for the most part. However, one club that went its own way was the MacGregor Streamliner.

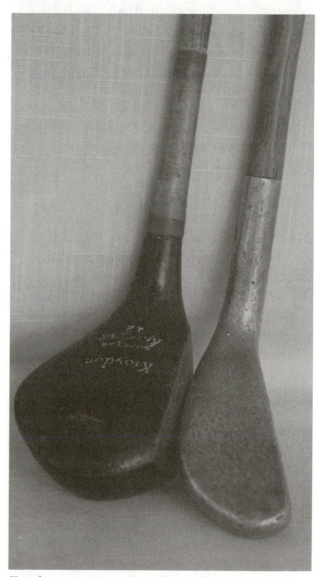

Kroydonite compressed wood and aluminum head

MacGregor Streamliner

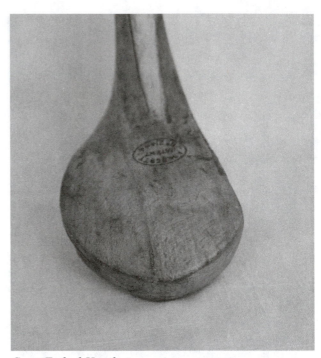

Scott Forked Hosel.

This head is bullet shaped and was an attempt at using aerodynamics to affect club head speed. It has an early chrome over steel shaft. This is one steel shaft you can collect, as it was used in the wood shaft era as well. If you didn't hit the small sweet spot on this head, you probably missed the ball completely.

Neck designs were developed to strengthen the shaft/neck joint. Scott's Forked Hosel allowed the grain on head and hosel to be oriented in one direction, thus strengthening the joint.

Moderately Priced Irons

Sweet spot weighting was patented in a multitude of designs, all aimed at concentrating weight at the sweet spot. Included were: mussel backs, diamond backs, flange backs, and heel/toe weighting.

Hosel designs were also developed to add weight to the club head by removing it from the hosel. Two popular designs are the Maxwell holes made in the hosel and the slotted holes seen on MacGregor clubs. Another of the many designs was the Carruthers hosel featuring a short hosel with bore-through shaft, as seen on some Spalding clubs. It is interesting to note that modern club designs still use such designs as flanges, Carruthers hosels, but moved in the opposite direction from sweet spot weighting to cavity back enlargement of the sweet spot. Modern manu-

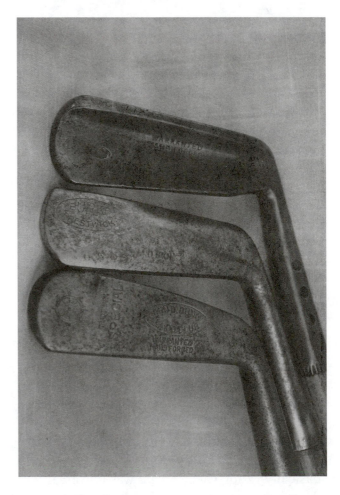

Sweet spot weighting

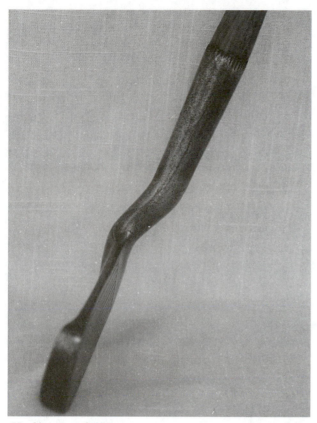

Heel/toe weighting

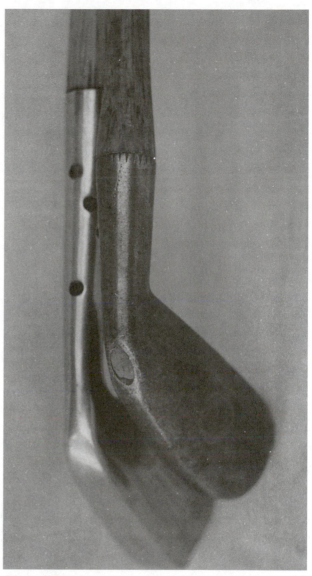

Maxwell hosel

Carruthers hosel

facturing techniques allowed for working with many unique designs.

Deep Groove Clubs were developed to help the golfer put "spin" on the ball in order to stop quickly on the green. MacGregor made slots and corrugated-style deep groove clubs, Spalding made waterfall designs, Kroydon and Burke designed waffle and brick faces. Many of these designs were declared illegal by the Royal and Ancient, and the USGA in the 1920s.

Flanged Niblicks were designed as players recognized their lack of a good wedge to negotiate the ball out of soft sand. The most popular of these, from a collecting standpoint, is the Walter Hagen concave sand wedge with its large flange and concave face. Scotland's answer to this concept was the "Skoogee" with concave face and large flange by Winton of Montrose. These clubs were subsequently declared illegal due to the propensity of striking the ball during the follow through (two strokes).

Deep Groove Clubs

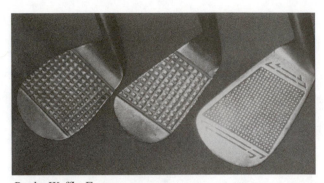

Burke Waffle Face

Hagen Sand Wedge

Mac and Mac Co., Large Dimple

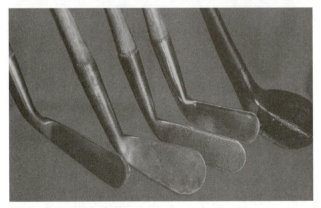

W. Park Bent Neck Putter

Skoogee Sand Wedge

Flangeback and GEM style

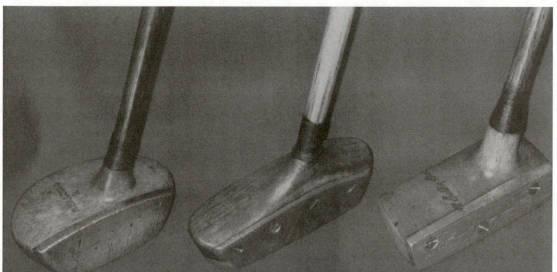

Wood mallets

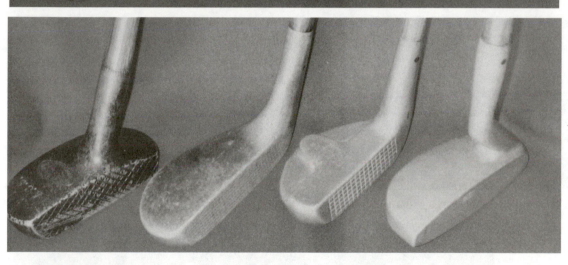

Aluminum mallets

Materials for heads, other than iron, were tried over the length of the wood shaft era, from the late 1800s through the 1930s. It would be several decades before titanium would go from the periodic table to the golf club designer's table. Materials tried included: stainless, chrome coating, brass, monel metal, Perma Frost by Spalding (don't ask), Duralite by MacGregor, and many permutations and combinations.

Moderately Priced Putters

Putter designers must have been tuned in to the golfer's "yips" on the green, as there were a prodigious number of design concepts being offered in this time span. Hosel/Neck designs were developed that gave the golfer a better view of the blade striking area by bending the hosel "out of the way." The Willie Park patented bent neck putter was one of the first in this traditional bent neck style that has survived through the present. The Patented Park putter is shown on the right side of a group of early patented Park clubs.

Weighting of the head for balance and feel includes: heavy flange back by Cochrane and GEM style by Gibson Wood mallet models by Spalding, MacGregor, and others, and aluminum mallet models by Spalding, Standard Golf Co. Also, hollow backs.

Some of the more unusual putters include: hollow backs by Gibson and Spalding, Sayers "Benny" putter with a ribbed sole, MacGregor's aluminum mallet putter with lead face inserts, steel blade putter with lead face insert by Noirit. Another dramatic putter is the Bussey Patent putter, incorporating a

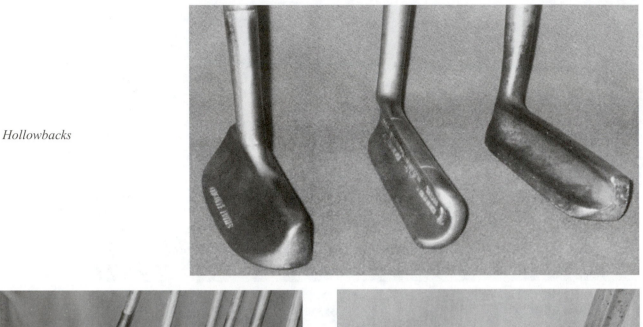

Hollowbacks

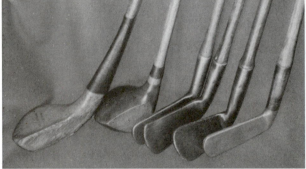

Bussey Brass Putter

Lead face inserts

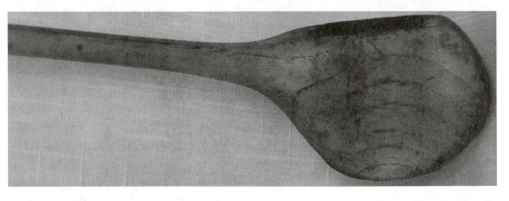

One-piece woods

brass head attached to an iron hosel. In the picture it is shown with its sister clubs: Brass putter, lofter, mashie, driving cleek, brassie, and semi long nose driver.

For those collectors who have come to the point they would like to expand their collection to some of the rarer patent clubs, the following very unusual, highly visual examples would be a good start.

High End Woods

Neck designs to strengthen the head/shaft interface included Slazenger, with a reverse thread screw-in shaft design that is rarely found in good condition, suggesting the concept didn't live up to advertised expectations. The reverse threading resulted in tightening of the joint each time the club hit the ball. The one-piece woods by BGI, Spalding and others offered another technique for a stronger joint.

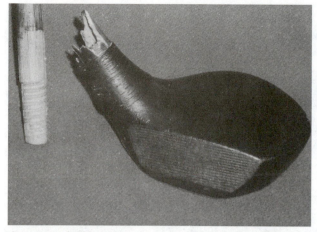

Screw-in shaft

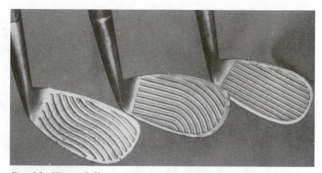

Double Waterfall

Cran wood face and Spring Face insert

Giant Size Head

Duplex aluminum clubs

Structural designs would include clubs like the Brewster Simplex, shaped like an elongated triangle. As with the Streamliner clubs, mentioned in the first list, this design considered aerodynamics of a center-shafted wood for head speed and accuracy. The aluminum duplex heads by St. Golf were designed for both a left- and right-handed swing with the same club.

High End Irons

Deep Groove Clubs to impart spin on the ball went to the ultimate with Spalding's double waterfall. The reverse S shape of the face grooves would impart not only a spin, but also a cut shot with spin, or so they say.

Face Inserts to absorb the shock of the club head hitting the ball and/or to impart more distance include the Spalding Cran wood insert and the Spalding Spring Face steel insert.

Club Head Size was exaggerated with the Giant niblick by Winton and others in order to give the golfer an advantage in the sand. It was never very popular, as it was found to be a rather clumsy club. It only dug you deeper in the trap while flinging buckets of sand out of the trap.

Adjustable Irons were designed with the intent of lightening the load for the golfer with a club that had multiple lofts. You can picture the following foursome's consternation as the golfer pulled his adjusting wrench from his hip pocket and "fiddled" with the adjusting mechanism and then "refiddled" after changing his mind. Among the many designs available, look for the very collectible Urquhart Club, the Master Club, and the Goodrich Club.

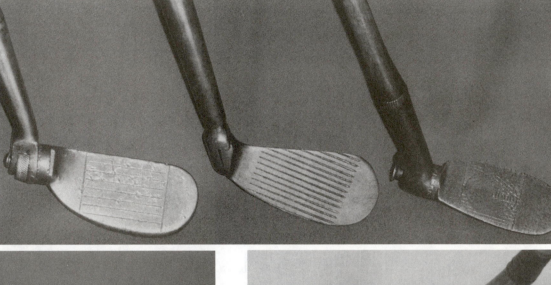

Adjustable irons

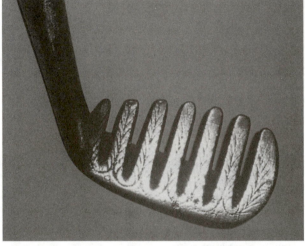

Rake Iron

Grand piano

Forked hosel

Unusual Design prize has to go to the Brown rake iron series. These clubs, with face perforations or teeth like slots in the face, were intended to extract the ball from water, sand, and heavy rough. They are a highly sought after, rare, and unusual club.

High End Putters

Unusual Designs can pretty well cover the range of very collectible and scarce high-end putters. Look for the "grand piano" shaped, large wooden mallet putter by Gassiat of France. I guess if you are having trouble putting, big may be better.

The aluminum forked hosel mallet by Otto Hackbarth is an unusual bifurcated design to get center balance advantages.

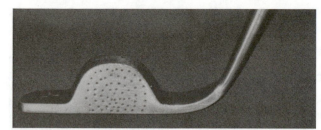

JONKO putter

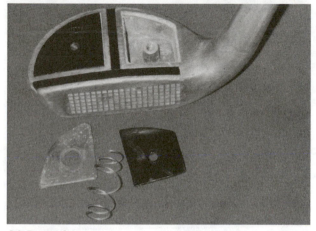

McDougal

Adjustable putters

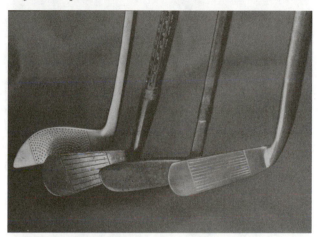

Early steel shafts

Limbershaft

How's this for unusual? The JONKO by Gibson Co. putter with large hump centered on top of the blade takes the form of a snail.

Adjustable putters allowed for left- and right-handed play, lie and/or loft. Again you can imagine the "grinding of teeth" by the following foursome as he adjusts and re-adjusts his club. These highly collectible and scarce putters include the block rectangular shaped Sprague, the Boye putter, and the Baltimore putter with its unique triangular head shape. Also, an aluminum adjustable-weight mallet putter called the McDougal has an elaborate system of springs and lead weight inserts for adjustable weighting. Try that while your partners are waiting for you to putt.

While golf heads were being significantly changed in this time frame, grips, shafts, training aids, golf carriers, etc., were also looking at possible change. A few examples are shown:

Shafts

Limbershaft, from Tarpon Springs, Fla., as loose as a buggy whip.

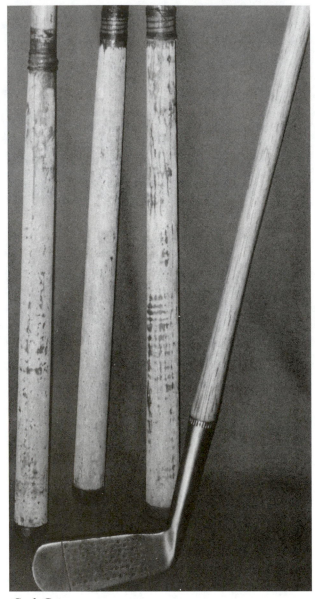

Cork Grip

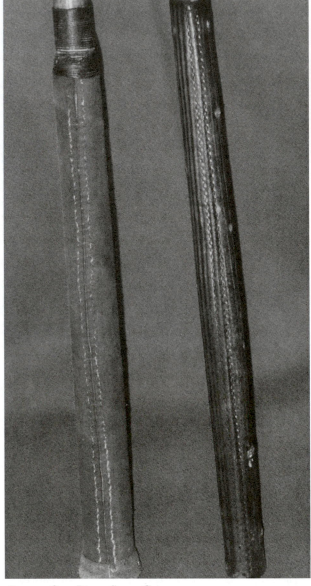

Bussey One-Piece Sewn Grip

Olympic Square shaft tubing for strength.

Lard Whistler with a steel perforated shaft for weight reduction.

Shivas Oval Steel Shaft for strength.

All three of these steel shaft clubs are highly collectible as forerunners to our current shafts.

The Limbershaft is most unique for its flexibility.

Grips included cork, leather, wood, underlisting, fabric, etc. Unusual is the Bussey one-piece leather sewn grip. Cork grips were used on a series of irons by Hillerich and Bradsby.

Training Aids

Training aids were developed, including a mechanical swing analyzer, a measuring club for shaft length, and a Golfex, 28" practice club, which could be swung indoors. "Watch the lamp, honey."

Golf Club Carriers

Golf club carriers had progressed a long way from the 1800s, when the caddie hand carried all the clubs needed. Several mechanical tripod style carriers were patented as well as unusual wicker styles.

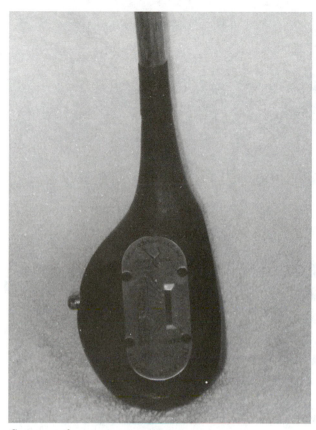

Swing analyzer

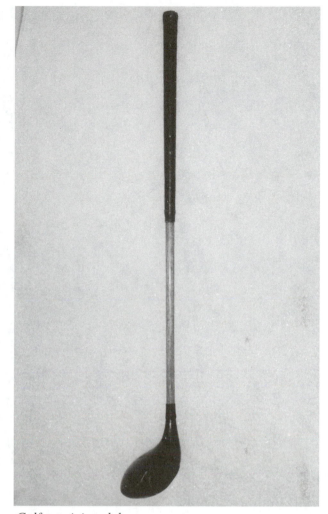

Golfex training club

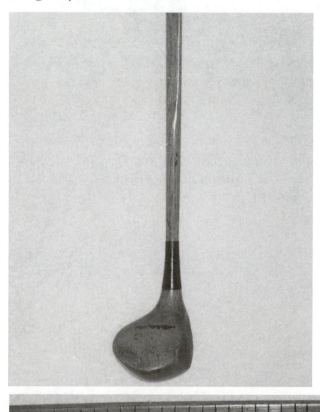

Spalding measuring club

Hopefully this information on patent clubs will help those of you looking for the unusual and visually dramatic clubs for a collection focus. What will the future bring for patent collecting? Certainly they are going to rise in value and dwindle in availability. More collectors are choosing to focus in the patent club area and thus competition will be high as these clubs come to the open market. Your best opportunities for acquiring these type clubs will be auctions, Golf Collector shows, networking with other collectors and dealers. Because some dealers see many more clubs than the average collector, they will maintain a

140 Tripod carrier

Wicker carrier

"wish list" for their customers. Don't forget the Internet. This is a whole new arena and more and more collectors are using this venue to buy/sell clubs, and trade information. Whatever we focus on for a collection, it's the thrill of the hunt, and most of all the thrill of "bragging" rights with our fellow collectors!

Gordon Page is a long time friend collector and dealer in golf antiques. Gordon can be contacted by e-mail gpage@innet.com or telephone (813) 780-8841.

Chapter 3

The Heritage of Golf

By Archie Baird

Aberlady, Scotland

Archie Baird is an avid golf collector and historian as well as a good golfer and past Captain of Gullane. He is a member and a director of both the British and American Golf Collectors Societies, and founder and curator of the Golf Museum next to the pro-shop at Gullane Links, Gullane, Scotland. He is one of the most knowledgeable and respected authorities on clubs, balls, books, and golf memorabilia in the hobby.

Early Golf 1300-1700 AD

We begin with the Dutch derivation and, by means of paintings, prints and photographs, show the variety of conditions and costumes in which the game was played. It was played in church yards, on the streets and roads, on the fields and harvest, and on the ice in winter.

Who brought it to Scotland? It may have been soldiers or sailors. There were many Scottish mercenary soldiers in Holland and dozens of marriages with Dutch girls are recorded. Scotland's main export was wool and, if the wind were unfavorable, Scottish sailors would be forced to stay in Holland for days or weeks. The Van der Velde painting of 1668 shows two kilted players with clubs.

The flowerings of Dutch landscape paintings coincided with the popularity of the game and, in most outdoor scenes, at least one fig-

Early golf artwork shows scenes of 17th century "Kolf" played on the ice in Holland, above and at right.

This painting depicts early 19th century golf in Scotland. Pre-1900 golf art is a popular collectible.

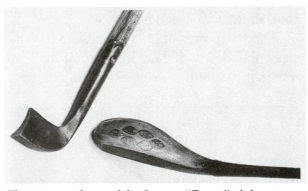

These are replicas of the famous "Troon" clubs.

A W. & J. Gourlay feather ball, size 26, is rare, especially in mint condition.

ure carries a club. The game disappeared about 1700 and was succeeded by an indoor variation.

The spread to Scotland from Holland looks likely when the early Scottish links are marked on a map. They are all near east coast ports: e.g. Dunbar, North Berwick, Aberlady, Musselburgh, Leith, Elie, St. Andrews, and so on up the coast to Dornoch. The earliest inland golf was at Bruntsfield Links, just south of Edinburgh Castle.

In all these places, there were rolling linksæland where rabbits and grass vied for existence. Smooth areas nibbled short and marked by rabbit "scrapes" (the 1st hole?) alternated with rough grass. The "greens" were connected by sheep paths of varying widths. Rabbits and sheep were therefore the first golf course architects!

The Feathery Ball Era

Up until 1850, the feather ball was used. It was a leather-stitched case stuffed with enough boiled feathers to fill a top hat. It was a skilled and arduous job to make a feather ball and a man could only complete two or three in a day. This made them as expensive as a club and controlled, to some extent, the popularity of golf.

Because the "feathery" was easily damaged by iron clubs, irons were only used in sand or in a rut. The player carried nearly all wooden clubs and there was a great variation in loft and length. The first club makers were bow makers who fashioned beautiful delicate woods and carpenters who made heavier, clumsier clubs. There were no "sets" of clubs, as the player chose or ordered them to his preference, and no two clubs made before 1890 were the exactly the same. The heads were long, narrow, and shallow with a concave or "hooked" face. They were made of beech, apple, pear, or thorn. The shafts were ash or hazel until about 1830 when hickory was found to make much better shafts.

The wood heads were attached to the shaft by a long diagonal splice or "scare." These are known as "scared head" clubs. They had lead poured into the back and a strip or horn was fitted into the leading edge of the sole. Very early clubs had no grips and the shafts were thick enough to grip. Sheepskin was used as a grip from about 1800. Leather became popular much later, about 1880. Early irons were made by blacksmiths and were heavy and cumbersome. They were only used "in extremis" for fear of damaging the leather cover of the feather ball. The hosel was thick and the shaft fitted into the socket, which was "knurled" to help grip the wood shaft. The cruder the "nicks," the earlier is the iron. During the "feather" era, there were two main irons: the sand iron with a large concave face and the rut iron with a very small head to play out of the tracks formed as carts brought back sand from the beach.

The courses at this time were as nature made them. There was very little green keeping and they played the ball as it lay. Rules were simple and about 14 in number. Stroke play was very rare; match play was almost always the game. Societies were few, only 17 being formed by 1850. Dress was a personal choice except that most societies made the wearing of red jackets compulsory so that golfers could be seen easily on the busy links. Colored facings and lapels were often described, and silver or brass buttons with club insignia and motto were increasingly popular.

Costumes

The story of golf clothing is more varied than the clubs and the balls.

Styles of male and female golfers of the 1890s tended toward what we would consider formal attire.

MISS BEATRIX HOYT,
WOMAN CHAMPION GOLFER '97-'98.

MRS. CHARLES S. BROWN.
CHAMPION WOMAN GOLFER, 1896.

Styles of male and female golfers of the 1890s tended toward what we would consider formal attire.

A print by F.T. Richards depicts an Elizabethan woman's golf costume.

A print by F.T. Richards depicts an Elizabethan man's golf costume.

In the "feathery" era, red coats with swallow tails and even the occasional top hat were seen. A man's everyday suit was considered correct and the ladies wore the long-skirted gowns that were fashionable at the time. An unbuttoned jacket was rare before 1920.

Waterproof clothing and spike shoes are fairly recent innovations. There is surely a wonderful book to be written on golfing costume.

Personalities

Being essentially a solo game, golf has had its share of personalities. The Parks and the Morrises; the Triumvirate; Braid, Taylor and Vardon; Harold Hilton and John Ball, Hoylake's tremendous pair; the prince of them all Bobby Jones; Joyce Weathered and Babe Zaharias; Hagen and Hogan; Player and Palmer; Nicklaus and Watson are only a few. Any golfer could add a hundred names because no two people ever played the game the same way.

What Gutta-Percha Did for Golf

Just before 1850, probably in Musselburgh, the first gutta-percha balls were produced by immersing the gum-like substance in hot water and hand rolling until round. They were cheap and tough, and a man could make dozens in a day. But they would not fly properly when they were smooth. At first they were hand ham-mered to produce a rough surface, then they were made in molds with a wide variety of patterns. Bramble, dimple squares, and circles are only a few. They were never painted successfully and survivors are all dark brown. Like the featheries, they were made in varying weights and sizes. Their moderate price and resilience allowed golf to grow quickly. The Scots had kept the game alive for 400 years but now it expanded rapidly.

Golf Clubs and Societies

Year	1850	...1870....	1890	1910
No. of Clubs and				
Societies ....17........34........			387	4,135

This expansion was aided by the spread of the railways but the "gutta" and its composition successor, the "guttie," made it possible.

They also changed the shape and the choice of clubs. The long-nose woods that swept the "featherie" along could not stand up to the "gutta-percha." Leather faces and vulcanite insets, brass soles and broader heads all appeared. Irons became more popular and blacksmiths who made clubs became "cleek-makers," refining the sand iron and the rut-iron into niblicks, mashies, and cleeks. They even made iron putters!

Greenskeeping became a necessary and canny craft. The skills became more special-

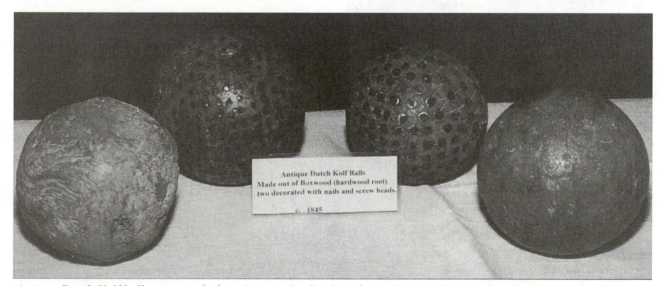

Antique Dutch Kolf balls were made from Boxwood, a hardwood root. Two are decorated with nails and screw heads.

ized and numerous, and the local club makers or professionals had seldom the time or the inclination to "keep the green."

Rubber Core

At the turn of the century from the U.S. came the "Haskell" ball. This was made by winding hundreds of feet of elastic onto a central core, then coating it with gutta-percha. These balls flew farther and a bad shot could still go a long way. The rubber core ball traveled so far, golf courses had to be changed to contain it.

On the negative side, the cover was easily cut on these new balls and many improvements were tried over the next 75 years. Recently, some solid one-piece balls have gained in popularity with manufacturers, who are always trying to improve them further.

During the gutta and rubber core domination, club face design became important. Lines or dots on the face enabled backspin to be applied to the ball. When the grooves became too deep, the R & A ruled them illegal. Hickory shafts finally gave way to steel in the 1920s, partly due to steel's superiority, but mostly because the hickory forests were depleted.

A Guide to Values

"How much is this Calamity Jane putter worth?"
"What condition is this book, The Curious History of the Golf Ball*?"*
"How much is this sterling silver trophy worth in this condition?"
"How would you rate that Vardon Flyer ball on a 1 to 10 scale?"

Condition affects value, and experience is the collector's best ally in understanding how it affects the value of golf collectibles. Many collectors purchase only the best quality items; though their collection may be small, it is of high quality. Other collectors acquire items simply because they are available regardless of condition. The ultimate common thread is receiving value for dollar spent, no matter what golf collectible you buy. There is an old cliche worth mentioning here: "Quality remains long after the price has been forgotten." Quality and value go hand in hand.

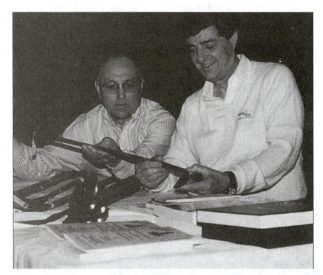

Chuck Furjanic, right, and noted golf collectibles author Peter Georgiady discuss a rare club at the Midwest Golf Collectors Show and Sale in Chicago.

Here are examples of smooth, hand-hammered, and line cut gutta-percha balls from the 1850s (left), 1870s, and 1890s

How to Receive the Best Value For Dollar Spent

Set collecting goals. If your goal is to collect everything related to golf, or only long-nose putters made by Robert Forgan during September 1886, stick with your goal. Acquire what you like and achieve your collecting goals rather than purchasing golf collectibles touted as a good buy.

Acquire collectibles in the best condition you can afford, even if it means buying a G-2 condition scarcity or rarity that fills a void in your collection. Most of all, be happy with the items you acquire. Sort out the items that do not conform to your collecting goals and find collectors or dealers who will take them in trade towards items that will enhance your collection.

Learn as much as possible about the golf collectibles you have set goals to acquire. Building a good reference library to go with your golf collectibles will be an invaluable asset.

Once you have set your goals and have armed yourself with knowledge, you can begin locating dealers and collectors who will respect your collecting aspirations and help you fulfill them. If purchasing from a dealer, buy only from those who offer return privileges regardless of reason. If you buy at auction, inspect lots or have someone you trust inspect and bid on your behalf. You can bid confidently by mail if the auction company will allow you to return lots you are not happy with.

What Determines the Value of a Golf Collectible?

Value is based on condition, rarity, availability, competition, and desirability.

Rarity is based on the availability of a golf collectible factored by its condition and desirability.

For example, a McEwan Play Club from 1880 is moderately scarce, but frequently available in the marketplace in grades ranging from G-5 to G-8. In near mint condition (G-9), it is decidedly rare and highly desirable.

Common mesh pattern golf balls—circa 1930 from Worthington, Dunlop or Spalding—in above average condition (G-7) sell for about $75. An identical ball, but with a cover cut, or teeth marks from the family pet, will bring only $10 or $15. "Faroid" or "Park Royal" are balls so rare and seldom offered that even damaged examples are highly sought after and bring premium prices.

Availability of a golf collectible has a great effect on the price, especially at public auctions. Let's imagine a nice example of John Kerr's *The Golf Book of East Lothian,* limited edition, signed and numbered, is offered at auction. We know the book is not rare because there were 250 copies printed in 1896. But this is the only example to be offered publicly for nearly a year and three book collectors attending the sale are interested in bidding on the book. In this case, availability and competition will determine the ultimate value.

In another example, two Royal Doulton punch bowls in similar condition were offered by two different companies at their July auctions held during British Open week. Only two serious pottery buyers were in attendance, and each was able to acquire one at a reasonable price. Availability, in this scenario, has had an adverse affect on value, even though the punch bowls are quite rare.

Let's use our imagination again. We are back in 1980 and a famous collection is being auctioned. A circa 1865 rut iron by Carrick is touted as the finest example available to collectors. At the time, only four or five collectors worldwide have enough sophistication and knowledge to believe the cataloguer; only one attends the auction and the club brings a modest $200.

Ten years from now, let's say the same club is offered when literally thousands of collectors are actively seeking clubs and several hundred have the knowledge, sophistication, and resources to take the cataloguer seriously. Several hop a flight, inspect the club, and try to determine who in attendance will be competition for acquiring it. Dealers carefully inspect the club, try to "feel the mood" of those present, and contact anxious clients to determine if a high "four-figure" or low "five figure" bid is appropriate.

If you think the last paragraph is pure folly, think again! Let's look at what actually took place at an auction during 1996. A Willie Dunn "Stars & Stripes" ball in mint condition was estimated at the $6,000 level. Three bidders were actively bidding at $18,000 and the final hammer price was $26,000 plus a 10 percent buyer's fee for a total of $28,600! And

to top that off, the collector who purchased the ball was offered a handsome profit (which he graciously refused) within a short time after the auction.

What does this mean to the antique golf collector? Since the mid-1980s, thousands of new collectors have entered the hobby. In addition, tens of thousands have expressed curiosity in golf antiques. The highly visible collectibles such as long-nose woods, feather balls, art, pottery and any other collectibles will be the center of attention, and quality will become the determining factor of value.

A Grade Scale for Golf Collectibles

Any golf collectible that has deviated from its initial manufactured mint new condition must be evaluated by how much change it exhibits. A grade scale (G-) on a basis of 1 to 10 has been formulated to evaluate the golf collectibles in this reference.

G-10 - Absolutely mint new as it left the factory. Showing no signs of wear, circulation, play or any deviation from "as made."

G-9 - The ultimate collectible, but not mint new. Exhibits "as made" originality with virtually no imperfections.

G-8 - An outstanding example, with minor imperfections and minimal wear.

G-7 - A desirable collectible in an above average state of preservation. A nice example exhibiting all the characteristics of originality, but with evident imperfections and visible wear.

G -6- A slightly better than average collectible. Should look original with evident imperfections and wear. Still very desirable to the collector who cannot locate a better example because of rarity or financial reasons.

G-5 - An "average" example showing moderate to heavy wear. An affordable collectible with moderate desirability.

G-4 - A below average collectible, with moderate to major problems. Unless the collectible is very scarce or rare, the advanced collector will not be interested in an item of this grade.

G-3- Collectibles with obvious major problems such as broken parts, and or replacement parts that are not matching. Unless the collectible is very scarce or rare, the advanced collector will not be interested in an item of this grade.

G-2 - A collectible that borders on being a non-collectible. Only the scarce or rare items will have any collectible interest.

G-1 - A non-collectible item.

Chapter 4

Golf Clubs

Introduction to Collecting Wood Shaft Clubs

The Earliest Clubs

Feather ball-era clubs were usually made by carpenters, bow makers, barrel makers, wheelwrights, and other craftsmen who had woodworking backgrounds. The irons were forged by the local armor maker or blacksmith.

The woods were very long and narrow, almost half-pear-shaped, with a head usually measuring between 5 and 6 inches in length. The face was shallow and slightly hooked to promote control of the feather ball. The neck was delicate and curved usually producing a flat lie. The shaft was long and whippy, about 44 to 47 inches, which permitted the ball to be "swept" from the turf. The head and shaft were joined together by a "scare" or "splice," usually 5 to 7 inches in length. The shaft and neck were glued together and a heavy linen twine was wrapped over the splice to help reinforce and strengthen. The linen twine was treated with "pitch" to act as adhesive and preservative for the splice. The grip was formed by an underlisting of wool wrappings tacked to the end of the shaft and covered by goat, lamb, sheep, or deer skin.

Woods, putters, and irons with wooden shafts are sought after by collectors of antique golf clubs.

A Scotsman, whose name was MacIver,
Put weights on his opponent's driver.
The guy took a whack
And threw out his back.
Would you call the old Scot a conniver?
By Edwin De Bell

Handsome Sean had a lie nice and grassy.
So he "let it all oot" with a brassie.
He was filled with delight.
The ball ended its flight.
At the feet of a charmin' young lassie.
By Edwin De Bell

A "play club" was used from the teeing ground; a "brassie" was used to strike long, low shots from the fairway. The "long spoon" and "mid-spoons" were used to hit moderately long-lofted shots and the "short spoon" (sometimes also called a baffie) was used to hit short-lofted shots around the green or over trouble. Next time you play golf, look at the variety of woods in the bags: Ginties with runner soles, No. 5, 7, 9 and 11 woods—even some I've not heard of. The feather ball era was not much different, as many players had variations made of a long spoon or baffie to suit a particular playing style or a specific type of terrain where most of their golf was played.

The iron-head clubs generally consisted of three, although all golfers did not carry all three. The "rut" iron had a small, rounded head with the face concave or cupped. The hosel was generally 5 to 6 inches long and very thick, as this club was a "trouble" club. It was used to extricate the ball from cart ruts, hoof prints or bad lies in the gorse and heather. The club was designed to propel the ball for only a few yards from impending disaster to a more playable lie. According to the player's preference, there were tiny heads (2 to 2 1/4 inches wide) and larger heads (2 1/2 to 2 3/4 inches wide) with anything in between. The concavity of the face also varies from being nearly straight to "ice cream scoop" proportions, and some were made with twisted hosels. During this era, the blacksmith didn't make clubs until he had an order. The clubs were, therefore, made to the golfer's specifications. In many cases, the golfer brought the club back to the blacksmith, having him re-heat and re-hammer the head to produce just the right loft or concavity to suit his game.

The "bunker" or "sand" iron was a large-head, concave-faced, heavy gauge metal iron with the similar use of our modern sand wedge. Most courses were laid out over links land between the sea and arable land, and most of the terrain was sandy. The head was rounded and generally 3 to 4 inches wide with a thick hosel usually about 5 inches long. The stoutness of shaft and hosel, combined with the heavy weight of the head, afforded the golfer to take a forceful slash at the ball, propelling it, with moderate distance, back into play, or onto the green.

The "cleek" was an iron with very little loft and a long face that could measure 4 to 5 inches in length. Usually the heel and toe were nearly the same depth, giving the head a "rectangular" appearance. The hosel was generally very long, as much as 6 inches, and the shaft was held in place with heavy nicking hammered down into the shaft. Many old re-shafted irons had the nicking sawed off to remove the shaft. When I see an older-style club without nicking, this indicates to me that the shaft is a replacement and the original heavy sawtoothed hosel nicking was sawed away when removing the original shaft. The hosel pin replaced nicking as a head and shaft fastener. The cleek was primarily used for hitting long, low shots from bad lies instead of using a long spoon or brassie, which were more susceptible to damage when not swung with a sweeping motion. The cleek was also used to hit low shots into a strong wind or to hit running approach shots to the green.

Many players carried two putters, sometimes three. The "driving" putter had a large thick head with a rather deep face and a large heavy back weight. This was used to approach the hole from a long distance over a relative flat area. The approaching cleek or putter was a slightly lofted iron with a shaft shorter than a cleek, but longer than a putter. This was

---

Wooden-shafted clubs in this section will be valued on a scale of 10 grades as outlined in Chapter 3. Current prices will be provided in conditions G-5, G-7, and G-9. The criteria for these conditions are as follows:

G-9 - The ultimate collectible, but not *mint new*. Exhibits "as made" originality with virtually no imperfections. The head, shaft, and grip must be original. The head, whether wood or metal, must be "as made." Shaft will be straight and have original finish. Grip must be an original or a replacement done "in-period" in order to appear as the original when inspected by the most fastidious experts. Whipping may be replacement, but must be the correct size and color for the club's period.

G-7 - A desirable collectible in an above average state of preservation. A nice example exhibiting all the characteristics of originality, but with evident imperfections and visible wear. Imperfections may include an "in period" grip, signs of moderate play or a weak "maker's mark." A very desirable collectible. Clubs prior to 1890 will show more use and the woods may have slight grain separations or a leather face insert nicely done "in period." This club must be esthetically appealing. For the collector who wants the best, but finds it difficult to locate a better example.

G-5 - An "average" example showing moderate to heavy wear. An affordable collectible with moderate desirability. May exhibit a slight warping of the shaft or a tattered original looking grip. If there are any markings on pre-1900 clubs, they should be readable enough to properly identify the maker. An acceptable example for the person not seeking perfection, or on a limited budget. A well done in-period cracked shaft repair can actually add "character" and desirability.

There was an old duffer from Troon
Who played by the light of the moon.
He putted for par,
The ball went too far.
He'd mistakenly hit with a spoon!
By Edwin De Bell

Illustrated by Sharri Lou Casey

used to run the ball to the hole when the terrain prohibited the use of the driving putter. The "holing out" putter was either a delicately made wood-head putter or an iron head putter with minimal loft used for more control and accuracy when in close proximity to the hole.

A heavy white linen thread or cord was used at both ends of the grip. It was coated with pitch and many weathered whippings appear more brown than black. This same thick thread or cord was used for covering the splice joint of shaft and head on the woods and putters. A thick coating of tar or pitch was used to cover the splice whipping for added protection from moisture and handling.

Clubs from the 1890s Through the Early Teens

During the boom period beginning with the 1890s, many innovations in club making took place. There were many patents filed on clubs with aluminum heads, adjustable heads, laminated heads, laminated shafts, one-piece woods, screw-socket woods, bifurcated hosels, steel sockets, one-piece grips, various back weightings, socket wood joint, cushioned iron face, wooden face irons, rake irons, waterfall irons, concave face irons—the list goes on and on.

Club makers went from hand forging to drop forging to conserve time and increase production. The cleek maker who hand forged only hundreds of clubs a month was replaced by factories (or he built his own) producing thousands of clubs a week. With the advent of the rubber-cored "Haskell" ball, golf went into another gear and companies such as Spalding, MacGregor, Stewart, Anderson, Nicoll, Forgan, and Gibson produced millions of clubs yearly.

Clubs from the Teens Through the 1930s

During the roaring 1920s and early 1930s, new American companies such as Burke, Hillerich & Bradsby, Wilson, Kroydon, Draper-Maynard, and Scottish companies Cochrane's Ltd., Hendry & Bishop as well as the aforementioned Forgan, Nicoll, etc., produced more than 100 million wood-shaft clubs of various quality. Millions upon millions of low quality clubs were made by Burke, Wright & Ditson, and others to be marketed at department, hardware, and sporting good stores.

With the advent of legalization of steel-shaft clubs for the 1926 season in America, and 1930 in Great Britain, Spalding, MacGregor, Walter Hagen, Hillerich & Bradsby, Forgan, Sayers, Nicoll, Gibson, and other mainstream makers began to market sets of high quality hickory-shaft clubs. The Gibson "Stella" series was a great playable

How Much Are These Clubs Worth?

Every day, someone calls our offices saying "I can't find this club in your book."

It is our intention to list collectible clubs in this reference. Listing all the clubs that were made would require volumes. The following will help you understand why most clubs you encounter may not be in this book.

Chuck Furjanic, Peter Georgiady, and Bub Duffner, *Golfiana Magazine,* (1987-1994) have collaborated to bring you the following information:

Auction houses and club dealers usually sell the finest-grade museum-quality scarcities or rarities. Reports of these prices realized cause the uninformed to overestimate the value of grandpa's clubs. Metal-shafted clubs with coated or painted shafts made to look like "cane" or "wood" have no collectible value to the woodshaft collector.

Collectors and dealers feel fewer than 5 percent of all wood-shafted clubs have interest or value beyond decorative or playable worth. In effect, this means about 24 out of every 25 clubs you have, or encounter at flea markets or garage sales, are common.

One must realize during the period 1920-1935, millions of low-grade clubs were made and sold through department, hardware, and sporting goods stores. Spalding, MacGregor, Burke, Kroydon, Hillerich & Bradsby, Wilson, Wright & Ditson, and scores of others made clubs with line, dot, hyphen, and other face markings.

About 99 percent of these are common and have no value beyond decorative, conversational or playable items.

---

iron, as well as MacGregor's "Duralite," Burke's "Long Burke," and Spalding's "Kro-Flite" series, just to name a few.

You can identify common clubs by:

- No manufacturer's name, or names like: Biltmore, Hollywood, Thistle, Bonnie, Metropolitan, Columbia, Ace, Majestic, etc.
- Metal caps at the end of the grip.
- Yardage ranges stamped on the back (145-155 yds.).
- Chromed, chromium, or stainless steel heads.
- Numbered irons from sets, or "matched set" irons.
- Irons with dots, hyphens, lines or other face scoring.

Clubs that have not been "cleaned, or refinished" that look all original and slightly used, are worth more than clubs that show use, have some rust or are not of "high quality." Clubs that have been restored, cleaned, have warped or cracked shafts and/or hosels, heavy rusting, pitting, bad or missing grips, bring substantially less.

Retail prices for common clubs in outstanding, museum or playable condition:

Irons.	$45-$75
Putters	$50-$90
Woods	$85-$135

Here's how to identify scarce or rare clubs:

- Irons with no face markings, or unusual face markings.
- Irons or putters with unusual head shapes. Wood head putters.
- Woods with a thick, curved, oval neck covered with 4 or 5 inches of string whipping.
- Smooth face irons with the following names: Anderson, Army & Navy, Ayres, Carrick, Forgan, Gray, Morris, Park, and White. Certain Spalding, MacGregor, Condie, Nicoll, Stewart, Gibson, and Wright & Ditson with smooth faces.
- Clubs are valuable because collectors want them. Common clubs are not in demand by collectors.

Golf Clubs: The Most Collectible Makers and Prices

Prices are for grades G-5, G-7, and G9.

LINE FACE IRONS
$35	$45	$75

Circa 1920s made by Burke Mfg.

ABERCROMBIE & FITCH
NEW YORK CITY

Abercrombie & Fitch sold golf equipment and wood shaft clubs from the 1910s through the 1930s. Most of the clubs were made by Burke, Newark, Ohio, and were stamped with the "A & F" Monogram.

MONEL METAL BLADE PUTTER
$40	$50	$75

Circa 1925 offset blade with Abercrombie & Fitch monogram

STAINLESS STEEL BLADE PUTTER
$40	$50	$75

Circa 1920s made by Burke Mfg.

SOCKET PLAIN FACE WOODS
$70	$90	$135

Circa 1920s Usually with a two-tone Persimmon head.

AITKEN, ALEX
GULLANE, SCOTLAND
Aitken was the professional at Royal Portrush from 1892-1895 and at Gullane Links from 1905-1917.

ACCURATE PUTTER
$60	$85	$140

Circa 1910. Offset blade. Stamped "Alex Aitken, Maker, Gullane."

RUSTLESS PUTTER
$60	$85	$150

Circa 1915. Offset blade. Stamped "Alex Aitken, Maker, Gullane."

SOCKET WOODS
$70	$100	$175

Circa 1910-1915. Driver, brassie, or spoon marked "A. Aitken."

SPLICED NECK WOODS
$220	$325	$850

Circa 1890-1895. Transitional bulger beech head play club marked "Aitken."

JOHN ALLAN
WESTWARD HO!
Allan was the professional at Royal North Devon (Westward Ho!) from 1867-1886 and at Prestwick, St. Nicholas from 1886-1895. He made long nose and transitional putters and woods. He was a well respected clubmaker.

LONG NOSE PUTTER
$1,200	$2,200	$4,800

Circa 1880-1890. Beech head driving putter stamped "J. Allan."

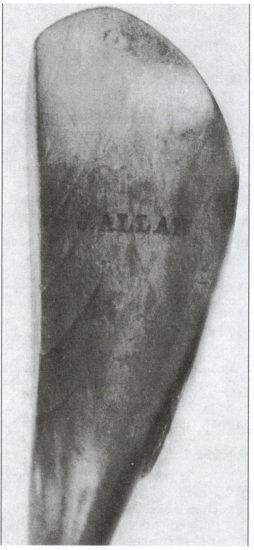

TRANSITIONAL WOODS

$350   **$700**   **$1,850**

Circa 1885-1895. Beech head play club or brassie marked "J. Allan."

LONG NOSE WOODS

$1,500   **$2,800**   **$6,500**

Circa 1880-1890. Beech head play club marked "J. Allan."

AMPCO MGFR CO.
MILWAUKEE, WI

Ampco began forging clubs about 1926 and by the early 1930s was out of business. It made irons and putters from an alloy resembling bronze or brass. When cleaned or polished, they have a golden appearance.

AMPCO IRONS

$50   **$75**   **$125**

Circa 1926-1930. Line scored. All irons.

LION & GLOBE IRONS

$150   **$250**   **$500**

Circa 1895-1905. Smooth-face iron, mashie, or mashie-niblick. Large "Lion and Globe" mark.

AMPCO PUTTER

$50   **$75**   **$125**

Circa 1926-1930. Line scored face.

AMPCO ALUMINUM WOODS

$220   **$350**   **$600**

Circa 1926-1930. Driver, brassie, or spoon. "Ampco, Milwaukee, Wis." on crown with a brass face insert.

ANDERSON, ANDERSON & ANDERSON

Anderson, Anderson & Anderson clubs were made by Anderson of Anstruther and bear the large "Lion and Globe" mark.

LONG BLADE PUTTER

$150   **$275**   **$600**

Circa 1895-1905. "Lion and Globe" maker's mark. Smooth-face blade.

PUTTING CLEEK

$150   **$250**   **$500**

Circa 1900. "Lion and Globe" mark.

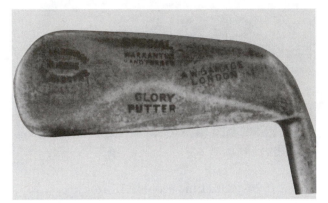

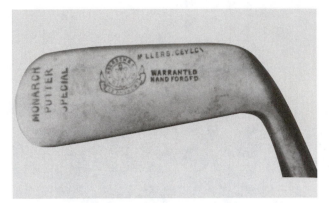

GLORY PUTTER		
$60	$100	$175

Circa 1915. "Diamond" back design.

MONARCH PUTTER		
$40	$60	$100

Circa 1920s. "D. Anderson & Sons" in a circle mark.

BRASS BLADE PUTTER		
$190	$350	$650

Circa 1900. Steel face inlay. "Lion and Globe" mark.

ANDERSON & BLYTHE
ST. ANDREWS, SCOTLAND

The firm of Anderson & Blythe began operations shortly before 1910 and was dissolved prior to 1915. It made wooden-head putters, but iron-head clubs with its stampings were forged by other makers, principally Tom Stewart.

WEYMESS PATENT IRON		
$100	$140	$250

Circa 1910. Dot-faced iron. Two level back marked "R E Weymess Patent No 16070."

LONG NOSE PERSIMMON PUTTER		
$250	$400	$700

Circa 1908-1914 stamped "Anderson & Blythe."

SOCKET WOODS		
$70	$125	$225

Circa 1910. Driver brassie or spoon marked "Anderson & Blythe Special."

WOODEN-HEAD CLEEK		
$100	$150	$250

Circa 1910. Small persimmon head. Lofted wooden cleek.

ANDERSON, D & SONS
ST. ANDREWS, SCOTLAND

Club and golf ball production began in St. Andrews about 1893 with David and his five sons. They exported many clubs to the United States. They were instrumental in the revival of Ash shafts during the mid 1890s.

LONG-NOSE PUTTERS		
$700	$1,150	$2,250

Circa 1893-1900. Spliced neck, beech head stamped "D Anderson."

BRASS-HEAD PUTTERS		
$60	$90	$150

Circa 1910. Dot Ball face.

LINE SCORED PUTTER		
$45	$70	$100

Circa 1920s. "Double Circle and Ribbon" mark.

EXCELSIOR PUTTER		
$50	$75	$135

Circa 1910. "Diamond-Dot" face scoring.

SPECIAL ACCURATE PUTTER		
$40	$60	$100

Circa 1920s. "Calamity Jane" style offset blade.

BENT NECK PUTTER		
$60	$100	$175

Circa 1900-1910. "Criss-cross" with "diamond-dot" face scoring.

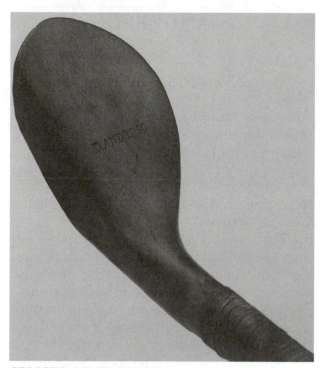

MAXWELL HOSEL IRONS
$60   **$90**   **$150**
Circa Teens. Flanged back with Maxwell holes drilled into hosel.

SPLICED NECK WOODS
$150   **$250**   **$550**
Circa 1900. Beech head driver, brassie, or spoon marked "D. Anderson, St Andrews." May have a leather-face insert.

D. ANDERSON IRONS
$50   **$80**   **$150**
Circa 1900. Cleek, iron and lofting iron. Smooth face.

MONARCH IRONS
$35   **$50**   **$90**
Circa 1920s. All irons.

GLORY IRONS
$40   **$70**   **$135**
Circa 1915. "Diamond" back design. Dot punched face.

MAXWELL HOSEL IRONS
$50   **$75**   **$150**
Circa 1910-1915. Flanged back with Maxwell drilled holes in hosel.

SAMMY IRON
$60   **$100**   **$175**
Circa 1910-1915. Rounded sole. "Diamond" back.

GLORY JIGGER OR CLEEK
$60   **$100**   **$150**
Circa 1915. "Diamond" back design. Dot punched face.

ANTI-SHANK IRONS
$120   **$220**   **$350**
Circa 1920s. Stainless steel "Smith's Mashie."

SPLICED NECK WOODS
$150   **$225**   **$450**
Circa 1910. Driver, brassie, or spoon. "D. Anderson & Sons, St Andrews, Special" in Gothic lettering.

SOCKET WOODS
$60   **$100**   **$175**
Circa 1915. Driver, brassie, or spoon with "D Anderson & Sons, St Andrews" on the head.

ANDERSON OF ANSTRUTHER, SCOTLAND

By Pete Georgiady

Most collectors have seen the circular mark containing the name "Anderson-Anstruther" at one time or another but few realize the history behind the firm. That mark was used by a father and son whose club production spanned 75 years. Their business was located in the Fife coastal town of Anstruther (pronounced "Anster"), located about 25 miles from St. Andrews.

The firm's founder, James Anderson, was born in 1845 and became a blacksmith and ferrier. He was undoubtedly approached to make a club head or two at some point and did such a fine job that more such work was sent his way. This is conjecture but it makes for a sound hypothesis since at that time, the early 1860s, Anstruther had no golf links and Anderson himself was never known to have played golf.

There is no acknowledged year when he made his first club heads but several sources suggest either 1862 or 1865, in a decade when John Gray and the Carricks would have been his chief competition. Anderson quickly prospered and, by 1880, he had moved primarily into golf club heads and was probably not shoeing horses any longer.

He eventually became a master smith. Among the alumni of those once apprenticed to him was Robert Condie, who started his own golf club forge in St. Andrews and achieved considerable fame in later years.

In 1892, Anderson patented his first club, a roll face putting cleek that he named the Kurtos model—Kurtos meaning curved in ancient Greek. Since he ran the premier cleek-making business of his day, many other makers and patentees sought him out to produce their iron heads. He forged Carruthers' (drilled hosel), Forester's (concentric), and George Lowe's (anti-shank) patent club heads as well as many others for F.H. Ayers, Willie Park Jr., and Robert Anderson.

Some people credit James Anderson with the invention of the diamond-back shaped iron club head. Whether or not this is true, he produced some magnificent old irons with that design in the late 1880s and early 1890s.

James Anderson died early in life in 1895 and was succeeded in the business by his son Alexander. Alex did a fine job of transitioning the company from his father's moderately-sized shop to a large-volume production company making heads in the hundreds of thousands yearly.

Anderson used several cleek marks over the years. James' first mark appeared in about 1875 and was used up to his death in 1895. It is the classic Anderson-Anstruther name in a circle measuring only 1/2 inch diameter, usually stamped in the center of the back of the club head. Alex then switched to a similar mark with a double circle that he used for about 15 years before reverting to the original design his father used, only in a slightly larger 5/8 inch circle.

It was Alex who began to use the "arrow" cleek mark for which the firm is now so famous. Also around this time, 1905, Anderson devised a numbering system for club heads to increase sales through catalogs. A two- or three-digit model number can be found stamped on most of their heads. Many Anderson heads were exported to North America and one of the largest sellers of Anderson headed clubs was The Golf Shop, Chicago, a MacGregor retail outlet. Alex Anderson produced a registered design bent neck putting cleek (#277771) similar to that of Willie Park Jr. around 1900. He also produced a wide variety of iron heads in many styles including concave faced irons, "Hold-em" model deep groove irons, as well as a healthy variety of putter types.

To today's golf collectors, the Andersons are the quintessential cleek making firm. James Anderson was known even in the 1890s as the original hand-forged cleek maker. His iron club heads were viewed as examples of the finest craftsmanship as golf entered its first modern era. Later, in Alex's generation, the company continued to produce a quality product while keeping up with modern production methods and new designs until their demise before World War II.

BRASS MALLET PUTTER
$150   **$275**   **$600**

Circa 1915. Brass head with a steel face plate. Double circle mark.

BRASS-HEAD PUTTERS
$110   **$140**   **$275**

Circa 1890. Straight blade putter with small "Circle" mark.

SMOOTH-FACE PUTTER
$100   **$140**   **$250**

Circa 1895-1900. Rounded back with small "Circle" mark.

DEEP-FACE PUTTER
$50   **$70**   **$150**

Circa 1905. Smooth face with small "Circle" mark.

BRASS BLADE PUTTER
$75   **$120**   **$250**

Circa 1900. Smooth-face blade. Small circle mark. Large "P" stamped at the toe.

DIAMOND BACK PUTTER
$40   **$70**   **$150**

Circa 1910. Smooth face. Bent neck hosel. Small circle mark.

RIDGE BACK PUTTER
$150   **$250**   **$475**

Circa 1915-1920. "Ridge" runs along the center of the back. Dot punched face. "Arrow" mark at toe.

TRIUMPH PUTTER
$190   **$300**   **$600**

Circa 1920. Pyramid top line of blade. "Diamond-dot" face scoring.

JAMES ANDERSON IRONS
$350   **$650**   **$1,800**

Circa 1870-1880. Cleek. Small "Circle" mark. Five inch hosel.

JAMES ANDERSON IRONS
$220   **$350**   **$750**

Circa 1880-1890. Lofted general purpose iron with small "Circle" mark.

SMALL HEAD NIBLICK
$220   **$450**   **$1,150**

Circa 1895-1900. Smooth-face rut niblick. Small "Circle" mark.

SHORT BLADE CLEEK
$60   **$90**   **$225**

Circa 1900. Small "Circle" mark.

FOR ARMY & NAVY STORES
$85   **$125**   **$250**

Circa 1900. Cleek, iron, or lofting iron marked "A N C S L" with small "Circle" mark.

VARDON SIGNATURE IRONS
$50   **$90**   **$175**

Circa 1905-1910. All irons. Arrow mark at toe.

VARDON SMALL HEAD NIBLICK
$190   **$350**   **$900**

Circa 1905-1910. Small smooth-face niblick. "Arrow" mark at toe.

MAGIC MASHIE
$80   **$120**   **$225**
Circa 1920-1925. A raised ridge bisects back from heel to toe. Lined face. Large double circle mark.

SMOOTH-FACE CLEEK
$40   **$75**   **$135**
Circa 1910-1915. Large double circle mark.

DEEP-FACE MASHIE
$45   **$75**   **$140**
Circa 1910. Smooth face. Large double circle mark.

OVAL-HEAD NIBLICK
$50   **$90**   **$150**
Circa 1915-1920. Line or dot face. Arrow and large double circle marks.

MUSSEL BACK IRONS
$50   **$85**   **$145**
Circa 1920s. Cleek, iron, mashie, or mashie-niblick. Arrow and large double circle marks.

CRISS-CROSS FACE IRON
$50   **$80**   **$150**
Circa 1905-1910. "Arrow" mark at toe.

CONCAVE FACE IRONS
$80   **$130**   **$225**
Circa 1915. Mashie-niblick 30. Dot punched face. "Arrow" at toe.

DIAMOND BACK IRONS
$40   **$65**   **$120**
Circa 1920. Driving iron, mid-iron, mashie, jigger, mashie-niblick, or niblick. Large double circle mark.

Illustrated by Sharri Lou Casey

MacAfee, whose swing was oblique,
Said an ace he would get with his cleek.
So he took quite a cut
And fell down on his butt.
Holes in one nevermore will he seek.
By Edwin De Bell

PYRAMID BACK IRONS
$40   **$65**   **$120**
Circa 1920s. All irons. Arrow and large double circle mark.

BALL FACE LOFTING IRON
$50   **$90**   **$175**
Circa 1905-1910. Deep face. Small circle mark.

"A 5" SAMMY IRON
$120   **$175**   **$350**
Circa 1920. Ridge bisects the back from heel to toe. Box-dot scoring.

RUSTLESS NIBLICK
$40   **$60**   **$100**
Circa 1925-1930. Dot face. Large single circle mark.

STEEL BLADE PUTTER
$50 $80 $150
Circa 1905-1910. Large double circle mark.

GENERAL PURPOSE IRON
$100 $225 $475
Circa 1890-1895. Long, moderately-lofted smooth face. "Anderson & Sons, Princess St., Edinburgh" markings.

THROUGH HOSEL PATENT WOODS
$80 $140 $250
Circa 1900. Driver, brassie or spoon marked "Anderson & Sons, Edinburgh, Patent."

THROUGH HOSEL PATENT WOODS
$120 $250 $475
Semi-long nose, circa 1891-1900. Play Club, brassie, or spoon marked "Anderson & Sons, Edinburgh, Patent."

ALUMINUM WOODS
$240 $400 $750
Circa1900-1910. Various lofts. Head marked "Anderson, Edinburgh."

ARMY & NAVY COOPERATIVE STORES, LTD.

Began selling clubs about 1885 and began manufacturing and assembling clubs during the early 1890s. The mark they used was "A & N C S L" and usually included "London" on the pre-1900 wood head putters and semi-long nose woods.

LONG-NOSE PUTTER
$500 $1,000 $2,200
Circa 1890-1900. Beech head spliced neck marked "Army & Navy C S L, London."

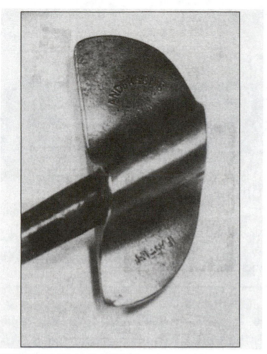

CRESCENT HEAD IRON
$900 $1,500 $2,750
Center shafted crescent shaped head.

SMITH ANTI-SHANK IRONS
$120 $175 $350
Circa 1920-1925. All irons.

JAMES ANDERSON RUT IRON
$650 $1,200 $3,000
Circa 1885. Tiny rounded head. Small "Circle" mark.

ANDERSON, ROBERT
EDINBURGH, SCOTLAND, PRINCESS STREET
Began making clubs during the early 1890s. Patented the first through-hosel shafted woods.

BRASS-HEAD PUTTERS
$75 $150 $275
Circa 1890-1900. Smooth-face blade marked "R Anderson & Sons, Princess St, Edinburgh."

CONCENTRIC-BACK CLEEK
$60 $140 $250
Circa 1900. Shallow smooth-face cleek.

SMOOTH-FACE IRONS
$75 $150 $275
Circa 1895-1905. Cleek, iron, or lofter. Marked "R Anderson & Sons, Edinburgh."

SMOOTH-FACE IRONS
$125   **$175**   **$325**

Circa 1890-1900. Iron or lofting iron. "A & N C S L" on head.

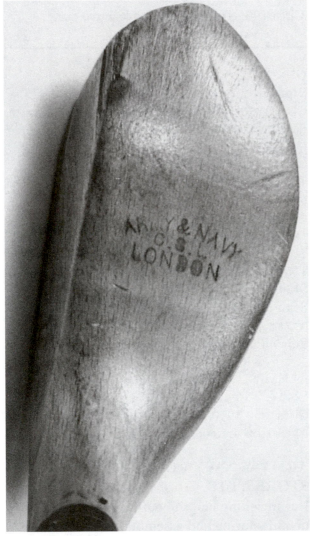

LONG-NOSE WOODS
$900   **$1,750**   **$3,750**

Circa 1890. Play club or brassie. Beech head marked "Army & Navy C S L, London."

DEEP-FACE MASHIE
$75   **$140**   **$250**

Circa 1900-1905. Stamped "Hold Fast" and "A & N C S."

SHORT-BLADE CLEEK
$175   **$325**   **$600**

Circa 1893-1897. Stamped "W & G Ashford, Mild Steel" with "Cat" mark. Many have a one-piece leather grip.

SPLICED-NECK WOODS
$190   **$300**   **$600**

Circa1900-1910. Driver, brassie, or spoon. "Army & Navy A N C S L, London."

ASHFORD, W & G
BIRMINGHAM, ENGLAND

Made clubs during the mid-1890s. They used a "Fox" head as a maker's identification mark. Many clubs had the patented one-piece sewn grip.

SMOOTH-FACE IRONS
$175   **$275**   **$600**

Circa 1893-1897. General purpose iron or lofting iron. Marked "W & G Ashford, Mild Steel" with "Cat" mark. Many have a one-piece leather grip.

DRIVING IRON
$200   **$350**   **$600**

Circa 1893-1897. Driving iron marked "W & G Ashford, Mild Steel" with "Cat" mark. Many have a one-piece leather grip.

AUCHTERLONIE, D & W
ST. ANDREWS, SCOTLAND

David and Willie Auchterlonie formed their company during the late 1890s. Their mark was simply "D & W Auchterlonie, St Andrews."

STAINLESS STEEL PUTTER
$50   **$70**   **$110**

Circa 1930-1935. Offset flanged back blade putter. Marked "D & W Auchterlonie, St Andrews".

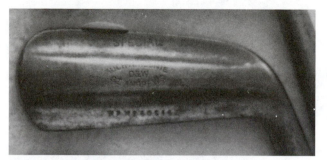

RIDGE-BACK PUTTER
$150   **$250**   **$450**
Circa 1905-1910. Patent No. 405445. Fancy "Chain Link" face scoring.

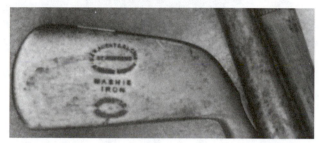

ALL SMOOTH-FACE IRONS
$50   **$80**   **$140**
Circa 1905-1910. Stamped "D & W Auchterlonie, N B, St Andrews."

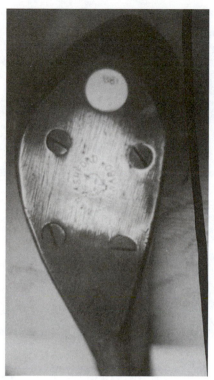

SPLICED-NECK WOODS
$350   **$750**   **$1,500**
Circa 1893-1897. Pear-shaped heads with "Cat" and "W G Ashford" markings. Many have a one-piece leather grip.

D & W BRAND PUTTER
$75   **$125**   **$225**
Circa 1910-1915. Patent No. 726896. Two-level back. Dot face.

SOCKET WOODS
$75   **$110**   **$175**
Circa 1915-20. Driver, brassie or spoon. Marked "Auchtie" in script below "D & W Auchterlonie, St Andrews."

SPLICED NECK PUTTERS
$250   **$550**   **$950**
Circa 1910-1915. Long nose style persimmon head. Marked "Auchterlonie Special."

AUCHTERLONIE, TOM
ST. ANDREWS, SCOTLAND
He began his business in St. Andrews at the turn of the century and continued until the 1980s. His mark was "T Auchterlonie" in block lettering.

ELLICE PUTTER
$45   **$65**   **$100**
Circa 1925-1930. Bent-neck line-scored blade.

WOOD HEAD SOCKET PUTTER
$175   **$325**   **$500**
Circa 1910-15. Marked "T Auchterlonie."

HOLING-OUT PUTTER
$175   **$325**   **$550**
Circa 1920. Wide sole and beveled heel and toe.

"AUCHTERLONIE" IRONS
$35   **$55**   **$90**
Circa 1925. All irons. "Auchterlonie" in large script.

DELUXE SOCKET WOODS
$75   **$100**   **$175**
Circa 1920s. Driver, brassie, or spoon. Stamped "T Auchterlonie, St Andrews, Deluxe."

SPLICED-NECK PUTTERS

$220	$425	$900

Circa 1910. Long-nose style putter. Marked "T. Auchterlonie."

HAND MADE SOCKET WOODS

$75	$100	$175

Circa 1920s. Driver, brassie, or spoon. Stamped "Auchterlonie Special, Hand Made."

GOLD MEDAL SOCKET WOODS

$75	$100	$175

Circa 1920s. Driver, brassie, or spoon. Stamped "Auchterlonie Gold Medal."

AYRES, F H

LONDON, ENGLAND

F.H. Ayres began as a sporting goods house at the beginning of the 19th century. About 1885, it purchased clubs from different manufacturers, and stamped them with their "F H Ayres, London" block letters mark. It also began making its own clubs and used the same mark until about 1900, when it began to use the "Maltese Cross" mark. The business ended during the dark days of the Great Depression. Many of the original shafts were marked "F H Ayres & Co."

FLANGED BACK PUTTER

$50	$80	$150

Circa 1915-1920. Offset blade stamped with the "Maltese Cross" mark.

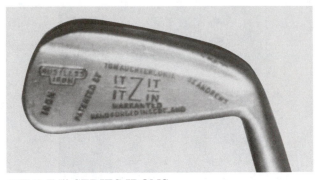

"IT-Z-IN" SERIES IRONS

$60	$90	$160

Circa 1920s. All irons. Marked "Patented by Tom Auchterlonie."

LONG NOSE PUTTERS

$600	$1,350	$2,250

Circa 1885-1895. Long-nose putter. Beech head.

GEM PUTTER

$50	$80	$150

Circa 1915. "Maltese Cross" mark and "Putter" at toe.

STRAIGHT BLADE PUTTER

$70	$100	$190

Circa 1890. Smooth face with "P" at toe. Steel head.

FACET PUTTER

$60	$90	$160

Circa 1915-1920. "The Facet" in a "Triangle Sweet Spot" on a dot faced straight blade. "Maltese Cross" mark at toe.

STRAIGHT BRASS BLADE PUTTER

$80	$125	$250

Circa 1890. Brass head. Smooth face with "P" at toe.

WINKWORTH SCOTT PUTTER

$190	$350	$575

Oval hosel and oval shaft putter similar to the "Winkworth Scott" Patent. "Rainbow" face.

O'Casey, a golf games indulger,
Was known as a secrets divulger.
When his foe hit a shot
Which was right down the slot
He confided the club was a bulger.
By Edwin De Bell

LONG NOSE PUTTERS
$450　　　　**$800**　　　　**$1,650**
Circa 1890-1900. Transitional shorter rounded-head putter. Beech head.

BOBBIE IRON
$45　　　　**$65**　　　　**$110**
Circa 1915. Rounded sole. "Maltese Cross" mark.

VARDON SERIES IRONS
$60　　　　**$90**　　　　**$150**
Circa 1920s. All irons. "Maltese Cross" mark at toe.

ROUND FACE NIBLICK
$60　　　　**$90**　　　　**$175**
Circa 1910-1915. "Maltese Cross" mark. Dot-punched face.

THE CERT IRONS
$140　　　　**$190**　　　　**$350**
Circa 1920s. "Maltese Cross." Sole extends below the heel and toe.

SMOOTH FACE IRONS
$90　　　　**$190**　　　　**$450**
Circa 1885-1895. Large block letters.

DRIVING IRON
$80　　　　**$135**　　　　**$300**
Circa 1890-1900. "D" marked at toe. "F H Ayres, London" mark.

ANTI-SHANK IRONS
$120　　　　**$190**　　　　**$350**
Circa 1915-1925. All Smith Patent irons.

ANTI-SHANK IRONS
$120　　　　**$190**　　　　**$350**
Circa 1900-1910. All Fairlie Patent irons with smooth face.

SMALL-HEAD NIBLICK
$150　　　　**$300**　　　　**$650**
Circa 1900-1905. "Maltese Cross" mark.

RUT IRON
$375　　　　**$750**　　　　**$1,750**
Circa 1885-1895. "Maltese Cross" mark.

SOCKET WOODS
$75　　　　**$100**　　　　**$175**
Circa 1915-1925. Driver, brassie, or spoon. "F H Ayres" mark.

Illustrated by Sharri Lou Casey

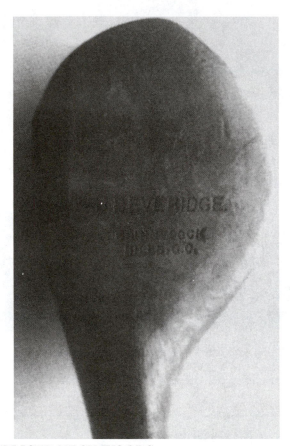

SPLICED NECK WOODS

$275   **$500**   **$900**

Circa 1890s with transitional pear-shaped heads, many stamped Shinnecock Hills.

SOCKET WOODS

$80   **$125**   **$200**

Circa 1915-1925. Wood cleek or Bull Dog trouble wood.

SPLICED-NECK WOODS

$160   **$275**   **$550**

Circa 1895-1910. Traditional head shape. Driver, brassie, or spoon. "F H Ayers" stamping.

LONG-NOSE WOODS

$500   **$800**   **$1,750**

Circa 1895-1900. Transitional semi-long nose driver, brassie, or spoon. "F H Ayers" stamping.

LONG NOSE WOODS

$900   **$1,500**   **$2,750**

Circa 1885-1895. Play club, brassie, or spoon. "F H Ayres" on beech head.

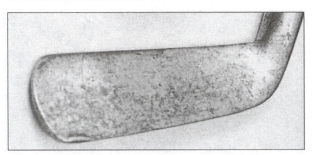

PAR-A-LEL IRONS

$90   **$125**   **$190**

Circa late 1920s with interesting face pattern of semi-circular lines.

SMOOTH-FACE CLEEK

$1,500   **$3,500**   **$9,500**

Circa 1840-1860. Five-inch-long hosel with crude heavy nicking.

BEVERIDGE, JAMES

SHINNECOCK HILLS

Beveridge began making clubs in Scotland about 1880. He immigrated to America in the early 1890s and was the professional at Shinnecock Hills until his death in 1899. His clubs are highly collectible, as he was an important early American clubmaker.

SMOOTH-FACE CLEEK

$140   **$225**   **$400**

Circa 1890s stamped Southhampton, NY.

BILLINGS AND SPENCER

HARTFORD, CT.

Began making iron-head clubs in the late 1920s. They only produced wood shaft clubs for a few years.

BLACKSMITH MADE

Clubs made by makers of armor, wheelwrights, metal workers, etc. and blacksmiths. Usually made prior to the 1870s and have crudely-forged heads and heavy hosel nickings.

HOLING-OUT PUTTER

| $1,500 | $4,000 | $9,000 |

Circa 1840-1860. Very thick long hosel with crude heavy nicking.

BUNKER OR SAND IRON

| $2,000 | $5,500 | $12,500 |

Circa 1840-1860. Very thick long hosel with crude heavy nicking. Usually with a concave face.

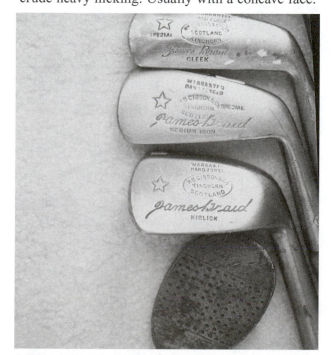

DOT FACE IRONS

| $60 | $75 | $120 |

Usually having Wm Gibson's "Star" stamp.

RUT IRON

| $1,500 | $4,500 | $10,000 |

Circa 1840-1860. Small cupped face. Long thick hosel with heavy nicking.

ORION FLANGED BACK PUTTER

| $120 | $160 | $275 |

"James Braid, Orion" in script. Heavy flange with flat side to hosel.

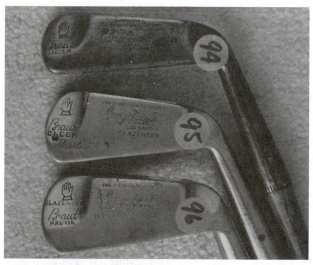

MUSSEL BACK IRONS

| $70 | $90 | $140 |

Made by Nicoll.

BRAID, JAMES

WALTON HEATH, ENGLAND

Maker of very few clubs. Most of the iron-head clubs bearing his name were made by Wm. Gibson, Kinghorn and George Nicoll, Leven. As a five-time British open champion, his clubs were very popular.

ALUMINUM-HEAD WOODS

| $325 | $650 | $1,350 |

Circa 1894-1900. "Braddell Patent 4624." Leather face insert.

BRADDELL
BELFAST, IRELAND

BRASS BLADE PUTTER

| $90 | $160 | $300 |

Circa 1895-1900. Stamped "Braddell, Belfast."

SMOOTH FACE CLEEK

| $60 | $100 | $250 |

Circa 1900 Stamped "Braddell Patent."

ALUMINUM-HEAD WOODS

| $450 | $700 | $1,350 |

Circa 1900-1910. Model C or G. Stamped "Braddell Patent." "Carruthers" shafting and a leather face insert.

BRAND, CHARLES
CARNOUSTIE, SCOTLAND

Charles Brand was from Carnoustie and began making clubs about 1890. He used "C. Brand, Carnoustie" in block letters, inside a double oval and also used a "Lion" mark. He produced clubs until his death in 1922.

IRON-HEAD BLADE PUTTER

| $50 | $80 | $150 |

Circa 1910-1915. Stamped "C Brand, Carnoustie." Hatched face scoring.

BRASS-HEAD PUTTERS

| $80 | $125 | $225 |

Circa 1900-1910. Stamped "C Brand, Carnoustie." Smooth face.

Illustrated by Sharri Lou Casey

O'Keefe, once a star of the gridiron,
Was a scrub when it came to the mid-iron.
So he stashed it away,
And to this very day,
That club is but known as a hid iron.
By Edwin De Bell

WOOD-HEAD SOCKET PUTTER

| $190 | $350 | $700 |

Circa 1900-1910. Stamped "C Brand."

SPLICED-NECK PUTTER

| $450 | $900 | $1,800 |

Circa 1895. Stamped "C. Brand" on beech head.

LINE-SCORED IRONS

| $40 | $60 | $100 |

Circa 1920s. All irons. Stamped "C Brand, Carnoustie" in a double circle.

SMOOTH-FACE IRONS

| $75 | $125 | $250 |

Circa 1895-1905. Cleek, iron, and lofter. Stamped "C Brand, Carnoustie."

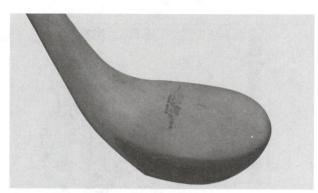

PUTTING CLEEK

$50   **$90**   **$200**

Circa 1900. #110 on shaft. "Diamond W" mark on the hosel.

SPLICED-NECK PUTTER

$375   **$750**   **$1,500**

Circa 1899-1901. "Arrow-BGI-Arrow" mark. Dogwood head. #96 on heel

BRIDGEPORT GUN & IMPLEMENT CO.
Bridgeport, Connecticut

Bridgeport Gun Implement Co. produced clubs, balls, and bags from 1896 to 1904 in its Bridgeport, Conn., plant. Most pre-1899 clubs sold by BGI were imported or made by Spalding before the J H Williams Co., Brooklyn, N.Y., became its major supplier. Many aluminum-head putters and fairway woods were imported from Standard Golf Company, Sunderland, England, and were stamped "B G I, CO" on the sole. Some Anderson of Anstruther clubs can also be found with the block letter "B G I CO." stamp. About the turn of the century, BGI began numbering its clubs and placed those numbers on the shaft just below the grip and on the heel of the wood head clubs.

Its clubs were of high quality and very popular in their day, competing favorably with MacGregor and Spalding. Today many collectors focus on BGI clubs, as they represent a good portion of early American golf history.

Other brand names BGI used were Fairfield, Edinboro, Aberdeen, and Dunn Selected. The Fairfield and Aberdeen marked clubs are priced slightly less than the other BGI marked clubs.

In 1904, the company was sold to the Bridgeport Athletic Mfg. Co. and the "BAM" trade mark, 1904-1907, replaced the familiar BGI oval marks.

Don Paris, who is currently writing a book on BGI, has contributed photos, information, and pricing.

Jim Cooper has written the definitive work on Spalding, which is profusely illustrated and contains sections on BGI and Wright & Ditson as well. Every BGI collector should have this reference in his library. It is available from the author, or Jim Cooper. There are also BGI Retail Catalogue reprints from 1900, 1903, and 1904 available from the author of this book.

FAIRFIELD PUTTER

$50   **$90**   **$200**

Circa 1900. "Fairfield" in script. "220" on the shaft.

DEEP FACE BLADE PUTTER

$70   **$125**   **$275**

Circa 1900. Smooth face. "BGI" oval mark. "Diamond W" mark on the hosel.

BRASS-HEAD PUTTERS

$60   **$130**   **$275**

Circa 1900. Two-way blade. "BGI" oval mark.

PARK-STYLE PUTTERS

$90   **$175**   **$425**

Circa 1900. Goose Neck, severely offset blade. "BGI Arrow" mark.

SCHENECTADY-TYPE PUTTER

$150   **$350**   **$600**

Circa 1903-1904. "BGI Co" on the sole.

·B.G.I·
Socket Golf Clubs

Made with Persimmon Heads of the
Finest Quality, Thoroughly Seasoned

One Piece Drivers

add 20 yards to your drive

All B. G. I. GOLF GOODS described in Complete Catalogue
including Book of Instruction to Beginners,
Free upon application

Golf Clubs supplied with Professionals
for short or long engagements.
Golf Courses Laid Out at moderate cost.

The Bridgeport Gun Implement Co.
313-315 BROADWAY, NEW YORK

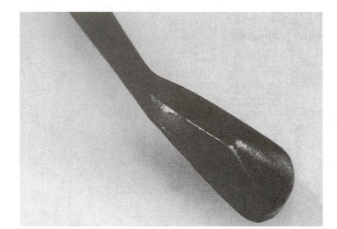

CENTRA-JECT MASHEY
$50   **$100**   **$225**
Circa 1899-1904. Weight concentrated in center of back. #105 on shaft.

SMOOTH FACE IRONS
$40   **$85**   **$150**
Circa 1900. All irons. "BGI" oval mark.

FAIRFIELD IRONS
$40   **$75**   **$150**
Circa 1900. All irons.

CARRUTHER'S MODEL CLEEK
$65   **$125**   **$275**
Circa 1900. #103 on shaft. Carruther's through hosel shafting.

SPLICED NECK WOODS
$150   **$300**   **$600**
Circa 1900. "Arrow-B G I-Arrow." All woods.

SOCKET WOODS
$80   **$160**   **$350**
Circa 1900-1905. "Arrow-B G I-Arrow" mark. All woods.

FAIRFIELD WOODS
$75   **$125**   **$275**
Circa 1900. "Fairfield" in script. All woods. Socket heads.

FORKED SPLICE WOODS
$350   **$650**   **$1,200**
Circa 1900. All woods.

ONE-PIECE WOOD
$1,000   **$1,500**   **$3,500**
Circa 1898-1902. Driver or brassie one-piece hickory head and shaft. Has a leather face insert.

BRITISH GOLF CLUB COMPANY
LONDON, ENGLAND
Began making iron head clubs shortly after the turn of the century.

OFF SET BLADE STEEL PUTTER
$50   **$70**   **$110**
Straight Line Stamp.

SMOOTH FACE CLEEK
$65   **$85**   **$145**
Straight Line Stamp.

BRODIE & SONS, ROBERT
ANSTRUTHER, FIFE, SCOTLAND
Like Tom Stewart, Brodie made steel club heads to be sold on a wholesale basis to assemblers. Tom Morris' shop was one of their biggest customers. The "Tom Morris" Signature clubs were made by Brodie in the 1920s. Brodie began making heads in the late 1890s. A "Triangle" with "B S & A" inside was stamped on the heads.

IRONS WITH TOM MORRIS STAMP
$75   **$100**   **$160**
Lined face with Triangle stamp.

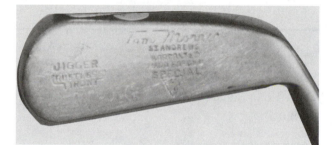

JIGGER WITH MORRIS STAMP
$100   **$125**   **$200**
Rustless head with Triangle stamp.

ZENITH IRONS
$40   **$50**   **$85**
Dot punched face, Triangle stamp.

STAINLESS STEEL IRONS
$35.   **$45**   **$75**
Triangle stamp.

BUHRKE CO., R H
CHICAGO, IL
Began making clubs in the early 1920s. R.H. Buhrke made many different clubs, mostly department or sporting goods quality clubs. The most sought after series is the "Classic" with a brass "plug" in the face. They used a "Key" mark and used trade names of "Medalist," "Burr-Key-Bilt," "Classic," "Finalist," and others.

ANDY ROBERTSON IRONS
$30   **$40**   **$80**
Circa late 1920s. All irons. Line scored face. Chromed head.

MORRIS STAMPED BLADE PUTTER
$90   **$120**   **$180**
Lined or dot punched face, Triangle stamp.

STRAIGHT LINE PUTTER
$75   **$95**   **$140**
Two level back, Triangle stamp.

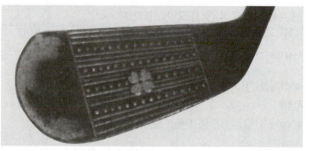

STYLIST SERIES IRONS
$30   **$40**   **$80**
Circa 1925-1930. All irons. Line scored blade, "Flower" at the sweet spot. Chromed head.

ANDY ROBERTSON PUTTER
$30   **$45**   **$90**
Circa late 1920s. Line scored face. Chromed head.

CLASSIC SERIES PUTTER
$50   **$90**   **$150**
Circa 1920s. Brass plug face insert in sweet spot.

MAJESTIC SERIES IRONS
$30   **$40**   **$80**
Circa 1920s. All irons. Line scored face.

PRETTY FACE WOODS
$70   **$110**   **$190**
Circa 1925. "Burr-Key-Bilt Regal." Driver, brassie, or spoon.

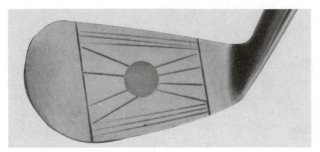

CLASSIC SERIES IRONS
$50   **$70**   **$115**
Circa 1920s. All irons. Brass plug face insert in sweet spot.

PRETTY FACE WOODS
$90   **$175**   **$300**
Circa 1925. Half-moon aluminum face insert. Driver, brassie, or spoon.

MAJESTIC SERIES PUTTER
$30   **$45**   **$90**
Circa 1920s. Line scored face.

STYLIST SERIES PUTTER
$30   **$45**   **$90**
Circa 1925-1930. Line scored blade. Chromed head.

BURKE MFG. CO.
NEWARK, OH
Burke began forging irons about 1910. It made millions upon millions of low and medium quality clubs that were sold in dry good and department stores throughout the Midwest. It used many marks including a "Hand with Scales," "Bee," "Daisy," "Thistle," "Crown," and others. Its top-of-the-line clubs were the "Grand Prize" series.

MONARCH PUTTER
$30   **$40**   **$90**
Circa 1920. Flanged back hyphen scored blade with a large "Crown" mark.

PICCADILLY PUTTER
$65   **$120**   **$200**
Circa 1920s. Large flange with a "Swastika" type mark.

BURR-KEY-BILT IRONS
$30   **$40**   **$125**
Circa 1920s. All irons. "Burr-Key-Bilt" mark with "Key."

STERLING PUTTER
$30   **$40**   **$90**
Circa 1920. Square punch marked face. Crown and Lion marks.

PRESTWICK PUTTER
$30   **$40**   **$90**
Circa 1920. Line scored blade putter.

ST. ANDREWS SPECIAL PUTTERS
$30   **$40**   **$90**
Circa 1915-1920. Dot punched face. "Crown" mark.

GRAND PRIZE PUTTERS
$30   **$40**   **$90**
Circa 1920s. Hyphen scored face.

BEE AND FLOWER MARK PUTTERS
$30   **$40**   **$90**
Circa 1920s. Various assemblers.

COLUMBIA SPECIAL PUTTERS
$30   **$40**   **$90**
Circa 1915-1925. "Rampant Lion" and "Crown" markings.

GLENCOE PUTTERS
$65   **$90**   **$190**
Circa 1920s. Flanged back putter with alternating "Line and Dot Punched" face scoring.

GRAND PRIZE PUTTERS
$30   **$40**   **$90**
Circa 1920s. Offset hosel blade.

*A fine golfer whose name was
O'Crofter
Tried a shot from the sand with a
lofter.
But the ball came straight out,
Hit the greenskeeper's snout.
How he wished that the shot had
been softer!
By Edwin De Bell*

Illustrated by Sharri Lou Casey

COLUMBIA SPECIAL IRONS
$30	$40	$75

Circa 1915-1925. All irons. "Rampant Lion" and "Crown" markings.

X 69 PUTTER
$80	$120	$225

Circa 1920s. Flanged back, wide sole.

GIRAFFE-NECK PUTTER
$90	$150	$250

Circa 1920s. Six-inch-long pencil-thin hosel.

ALUMINUM-HEAD PUTTER
$80	$100	$175

Circa 1920s. Mills-type aluminum-head mallet.

X 78 BENT-NECK PUTTER
$80	$120	$200

Circa 1920s. Park-style, severely bent neck, smooth-face putter.

CRESCENT-HEAD PUTTER
$90	$140	$250

Circa late 1910s. Crescent head, broad sole, and pointed toe.

END GRAIN PUTTER
$275	$400	$800

Circa 1920. Rectangular wood head.

DIAMOND BACK IRONS
$40	$55	$90

Circa 1910-1915. "Rampant Lion" mark at the toe.

PRESTWICK IRONS
$30	$40	$75

Circa 1920. All irons.

ST. ANDREWS SPECIAL IRONS
$30	$40	$75

Circa 1915-1920. Dot punched face. "Crown" mark at the toe.

GLENCOE IRONS
$30	$40	$75

Circa 1920s. All irons.

COMMANDER IRONS
$30	$40	$75

Circa late 1920s. All irons. Grip has aluminum end cap.

BURKE STAINLESS IRONS
$30	$40	$75

Circa 1925-1930. All irons.

GRAND PRIZE IRONS
$30	$40	$75

Circa 1920s. All irons.

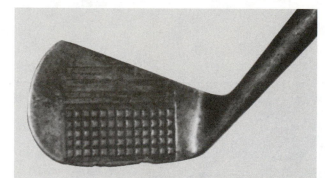

ROTARY ILLEGAL IRONS

$250   **$400**   **$750**

Circa 1920. All clubs. Half waffle pattern, half slot deep groove. Monel metal.

LONG BURKE IRONS

$30   **$40**   **$75**

Circa 1925-1930. All irons. "Shield" mark.

BALL WITH WINGS SOCKET WOOD

$80   **$100**   **$190**

Circa 1920s. Driver, brassie, or spoon.

MONEL METAL IRONS

$35   **$50**   **$95**

Circa 1920-1930. All clubs.

DEEP GROOVE IRONS

$80   **$120**   **$200**

Circa 1915-1922. Corrugated deep grooves. All irons.

DEEP GROOVE IRONS

$85   **$125**   **$225**

Circa 1915-1922. All clubs. Monel metal heads.

DEEP GROOVE IRONS

$90   **$140**   **$250**

Circa 1915-1922. Slot deep grooves. All irons.

GRAND PRIZE IRONS

$80   **$120**   **$175**

Circa 1915. Foulis-type concave head.

BRASS HEAD NIBLICK

$120   **$175**   **$300**

Circa 1925. Large hyphen scored brass head.

HARRY VARDON SIGNATURE IRONS

$30   **$40**   **$90**

Circa 1925-1930. All irons.

CHAMPION WOODS

$65   **$90**   **$150**

Circa 1920s. Driver, brassie, or spoon.

GRAND PRIZE WOODS

$65   **$90**   **$150**

Circa 1915-1925. Driver, brassie, or spoon.

TED RAY SIGNATURE IRONS

$30   **$40**   **$90**

Circa 1925-1930. All irons.

GLENCOE WOODS

$65   **$90**   **$150**

Circa 1920s. Driver, brassie, or spoon.

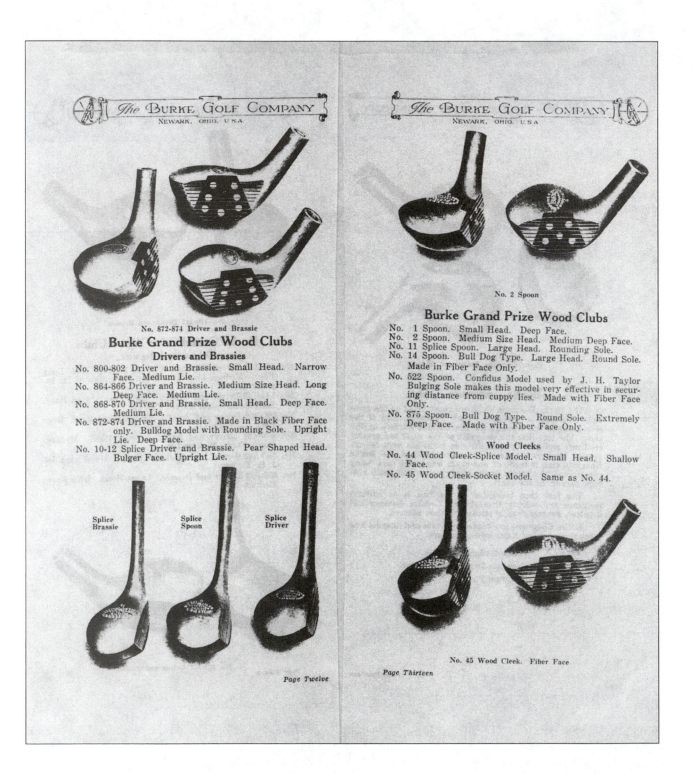

The Burke Golf Company
NEWARK, OHIO, U.S.A

No. 872-874 Driver and Brassie

Burke Grand Prize Wood Clubs

Drivers and Brassies

No. 800-802 Driver and Brassie. Small Head. Narrow Face. Medium Lie.

No. 864-866 Driver and Brassie. Medium Size Head. Long Deep Face. Medium Lie.

No. 868-870 Driver and Brassie. Small Head. Deep Face. Medium Lie.

No. 872-874 Driver and Brassie. Made in Black Fiber Face only. Bulldog Model with Rounding Sole. Upright Lie. Deep Face.

No. 10-12 Splice Driver and Brassie. Pear Shaped Head. Bulger Face. Upright Lie.

Splice Brassie   Splice Spoon   Splice Driver

Page Twelve

The Burke Golf Company
NEWARK, OHIO, U.S.A

No. 2 Spoon

Burke Grand Prize Wood Clubs

No. 1 Spoon. Small Head. Deep Face.
No. 2 Spoon. Medium Size Head. Medium Deep Face.
No. 11 Splice Spoon. Large Head. Rounding Sole.
No. 14 Spoon. Bull Dog Type. Large Head. Round Sole. Made in Fiber Face Only.
No. 522 Spoon. Confidus Model used by J. H. Taylor Bulging Sole makes this model very effective in securing distance from cuppy lies. Made with Fiber Face Only.
No. 875 Spoon. Bull Dog Type. Round Sole. Extremely Deep Face. Made with Fiber Face Only.

Wood Cleeks

No. 44 Wood Cleek-Splice Model. Small Head. Shallow Face.
No. 45 Wood Cleek-Socket Model. Same as No. 44.

No. 45 Wood Cleek. Fiber Face

Page Thirteen

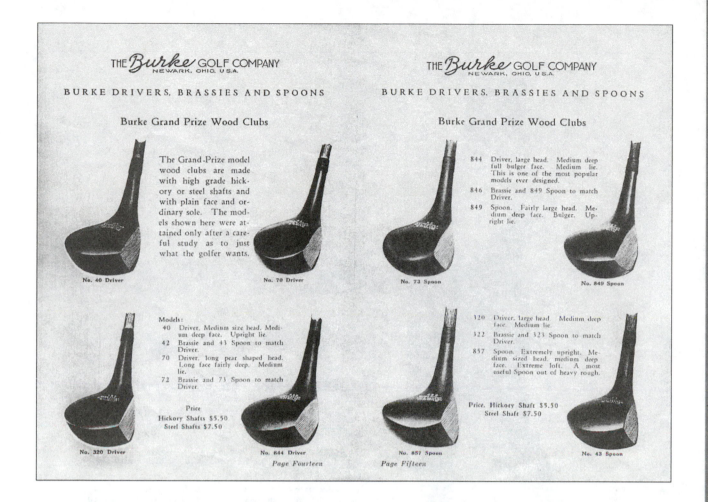

THE *Burke* GOLF COMPANY
NEWARK, OHIO, U.S.A.

BURKE DRIVERS, BRASSIES AND SPOONS

Burke Grand Prize Wood Clubs

The Grand-Prize model wood clubs are made with high grade hickory or steel shafts and with plain face and ordinary sole. The models shown here were attained only after a careful study as to just what the golfer wants.

No. 40 Driver

No. 70 Driver

Models:
40 Driver. Medium size head. Medium deep face. Upright lie.
42 Brassie and 43 Spoon to match Driver.
70 Driver. long pear shaped head. Long face fairly deep. Medium lie.
72 Brassie and 73 Spoon to match Driver.

Price
Hickory Shafts $5.50
Steel Shafts $7.50

No. 320 Driver

No. 844 Driver

Page Fourteen

THE *Burke* GOLF COMPANY
NEWARK, OHIO, U.S.A.

BURKE DRIVERS, BRASSIES AND SPOONS

Burke Grand Prize Wood Clubs

844 Driver, large head. Medium deep full bulger face. Medium lie. This is one of the most popular models ever designed.
846 Brassie and 849 Spoon to match Driver.
849 Spoon. Fairly large head. Medium deep face. Bulger. Upright lie.

No. 73 Spoon

No. 849 Spoon

320 Driver, large head. Medium deep face. Medium lie.
322 Brassie and 323 Spoon to match Driver.
857 Spoon. Extremely upright. Medium sized head. medium deep face. Extreme loft. A most useful Spoon out of heavy rough.

Price. Hickory Shaft $5.50
Steel Shaft $7.50

No. 857 Spoon

No. 43 Spoon

Page Fifteen

COLUMBIA SPECIAL WOODS
$65 **$90** **$150**
Circa 1915-1925. Driver, brassie, or spoon.

VARIOUS WOODS
$65 **$90** **$150**
Circa 1925-1928. Driver, brassie, or spoon. "Golfrite," De Luxe," "Plus-Four," Autograph series," "Sportsman," and "Skippers."

PRESTWICK WOODS
$65 **$90** **$150**
Circa 1920s. Driver, brassie, or spoon.

JUVENILE CLUBS
$30 **$40** **$70**
Circa 1920s. All irons and putter. Smooth faces.

JUVENILE CLUBS
$60 **$80** **$140**
Circa 1920s. All woods.

HAGEN SERIES IRONS
$30 **$40** **$85**
Circa 1925. All clubs.

BUSSEY & CO.
LONDON, ENGLAND

George Bussey began making clubs in London during the late 1880s and made a two-piece club called the "Patented Steel Socket." He also patented a one-piece grip that was sewn up the back. He used a monogram "GGB" mark with an arrow through it and "Thistle." On many clubs, the name of the club, (mashie, iron, etc.) was stamped on the shaft.

STEEL SOCKET PATENT CLEEK
$190 **$275** **$550**
Circa 1890-1900. Smooth face cleek. "Thistle" below "Bussey & Co., London."

Hagen's Own Clubs—for You!

WALTER HAGEN—the Incomparable Sir Walter—has granted Burke (and only Burke) the right to copy his bag of clubs.

So here are shown the leading Burke-Hagen models—*actual duplicates* of his record-breaking clubs, each autographed *Walter Hagen*.

If Walter uses them, they MUST be unrivalled in design, in material, in finish. Have you ever wondered how a set of these *proven* clubs will help your score?

Quit wondering—and find out!

In Monel metal or in steel at Pros and Sporting Goods Stores

Hagen Driver: Socket model. Deep face with metal insert. Easy to learn.

Hagen Brassie: Made exactly as the Driver but with a little more loft.

Hagen Driving Iron: A confidence-building club for the long one-shotters.

Hagen Mashie Iron: His pet club. You will use it more than any other in a round.

Hagen Mashie: Well lofted. Medium in size and weight. Practical in every way.

Hagen Mashie Niblick: Heavy head but a small blade. An excellent trouble-escape.

Hagen Putter: Slightly goose-neck. His selection from 100 models.

GRAND PRIZE

BURKE

CLUBS · BAGS · BALLS

A COPY of the new Burke Catalog, picturing and describing the full line, sent on request.

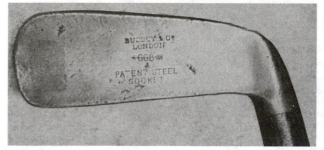

STEEL SOCKET BRASS PUTTER

$200   **$400**   **$900**

Circa 1890-1900. Brass blade, steel socket. "Bussey & Co, London" and "Thistle" marks. Many have a one-piece leather grip.

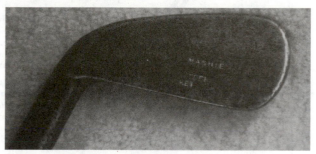

STEEL SOCKET PATENT PUTTER

$150   **$250**   **$450**

Circa 1890-1900. "Bussey & Co, London" and "Thistle" marks.

STEEL SOCKET PATENT IRONS

$150   **$250**   **$500**

Circa 1890-1900. Smooth iron or mashie. "Thistle" below "Bussey & Co., London."

BUTCHART-NICHOLS

GLENBROOK, CT

They were famous for shafts made of alternating strips of bamboo and hickory. They used a "Bird" mark and the letters "BTN."

BAMBOO-SHAFT PUTTER

$45   **$55**   **$100**

Circa 1920s. Dot punched face.

BAMBOO-SHAFT IRONS

$40   **$50**   **$90**

Circa 1920s. All irons. Dot punched face.

BUTCHART BILT WOODS

$80   **$120**   **$220**

Circa 1920s. Driver, brassie or spoon. Many have steel face inserts. Laminated bamboo shaft.

CAMPBELL, WILLIE

SCOTLAND, and BOSTON, MA

Willie Campbell began his club-making career in Scotland and immigrated to the U.S. and became a professional at The Country Club, Boston, 1894. He died at an early age in 1901. His clubs are highly sought after by collectors of early American clubs.

BRASS BLADE PUTTER

$85   **$110**   **$200**

Straight blade with "Willie Campbell, Franklin Park" stamp.

SMOOTH FACE IRONS

$75   **$95**   **$175**

Diamond stamp.

SOCKET WOODS

$85   **$110**   **$185**

SPLICED NECK WOODS

$150   **$220**   **$375**

LONGER "LIFE"—BETTER TIMING PERFECT BALANCE

Golfers everywhere will be pleased to learn of the association of two great golf experts, now organized into a company producing new and superior model golf clubs in 3 Woods and 12 Irons.

Butchart-Nicholls clubs are a distinct advance in the art of clubmaking. They are the final achievement of two skilled clubmakers. Made of laminated bamboo and hickory by a new patented process, the shafts of B-T-N clubs maintain enduring straightness. Possessing all the advantages of first-grade hickory shafts, they retain longer "life" and in addition are uniform, durable and more dependable. Players of every class are finding the perfectly balanced B-T-N clubs an aid to greater distance on every shot.

Facilities for manufacture of B-T-N clubs at the up-to-date Glenbrook, Conn., factory include only the newest and most modern equipment. Every improved device for excellence and precision in clubmaking has been installed.

**MADE IN
3 WOODS
12 IRONS**

BTN

**EVERY SHAFT
GUARANTEED**

Now golfers, professionals and sporting goods dealers should acquaint themselves with the superior qualities of the Butchart-Nicholls clubs. Exponents of the game have long awaited golf clubs which measure up to Butchart-Nicholls quality—a superiority that is carefully built into each club shaft and each club head by expert craftsmen.

Write, wire or telephone us today for additional information. Our representative will gladly call and display these models and quote you prices.

PLAY BETTER GOLF WITH B-T-N CLUBS

BUTCHART-NICHOLLS COMPANY, INC.
Glenbrook, Connecticut · · · Telephone: Stamford 6785

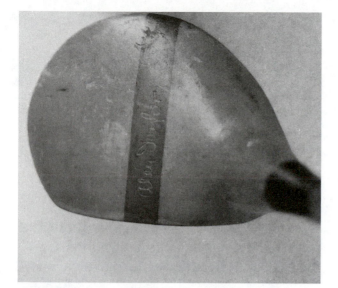

ALUMINUM MALLET PUTTER
$175   **$275**   **$475**
Circa 1915 with a raised sight line.

CANN & TAYLOR
LONDON, ENGLAND

A London-area firm, it used "Cann & Taylor, Winchester" in block letters 1894-1897, a "J H Taylor" signature and an odd looking "Flywheel" mark into the 1930s.

TWISTED HOSEL PUTTER
$80   **$125**   **$275**
Circa 1905-1915. "Cann & Taylor" with "J H Taylor" signature marks.

DOT FACE BLADE PUTTER
$40   **$50**   **$100**
Circa 1910-1915. "Cann & Taylor" with "J H Taylor" signature marks.

GEM PUTTER
$70   **$90**   **$150**
Circa 1910-1920. Flywheel mark. Rounded back. Dot punched face.

SMOOTH FACE PUTTER
$75   **$110**   **$225**
Circa 1900. "Cann & Taylor, Winchester and...... Richmond" stampings.

CYNOSURE SERIES IRONS
$40   **$50**   **$85**
Circa 1925. All irons. "Flyweel" mark.

AUTOGRAPH MODEL IRONS
$40   **$50**   **$95**
Circa 1915. All irons. Bordered hyphen face.

CONVEX FACE NIBLICK
$50   **$60**   **$100**
Circa 1920.

SMOOTH FACE AUTOGRAPH IRONS
$60   **$80**   **$150**
Circa 1900-1910. Cleek, iron, mashie, and lofting iron.

RADIAL SOLE DRIVING MASHIE
$60   **$100**   **$150**
Circa 1915. "Flywheel" mark.

DRIVING MASHIE
$60   **$100**   **$150**
Circa 1920. "Flywheel" mark.

RUT NIBLICKS
$110   **$180**   **$350**
Circa 1900-1905. Stamped "Cann & Taylor Niblick."

CYNOSURE SERIES WOODS
$80   **$110**   **$190**
Circa 1920s. Driver, brassie, or spoon.

SPLICED NECK WOODS
$110   **$200**   **$350**
Circa 1910-1915. Driver, brassie, or spoon.

SPLICED NECK WOODS
$220   **$375**   **$750**
Circa 1891-1897. Transitional beech head. Leather face insert. Bulger driver or brassie.

CROSS MARKED CLEEK

| $400 | $750 | $1,500 |

Circa 1870-1880. Stamped only "Carrick." "Cross" mark.

CARRICK, F & A

MUSSELBURGH

The Carrick brothers, who were initially blacksmiths, began forging iron heads about 1860 through the early 1900s. They used two marks: "F & A Carrick, Musselburgh" and simply "Carrick" in block letters. All their clubs carried a "Cross" cleek mark. They are quite scarce and highly collectible.

STEEL-BLADE PUTTER

| $300 | $550 | $1,200 |

Circa 1890-1895. Smooth face blade putter. "Cross" mark.

EARLY STEEL-BLADE PUTTER

| $400 | $650 | $1,500 |

Circa 1870-1885. Smooth face straight blade. "Cross" mark.

GENERAL PURPOSE IRON

| $400 | $650 | $1,350 |

Circa 1870-1880. "F & A Carrick, Musselburgh" above the "Cross" mark.

CROSS MARKED CLEEK

| $400 | $700 | $1,400 |

Circa 1870-1880. Stamped "F & A Carrick, Musselburgh."

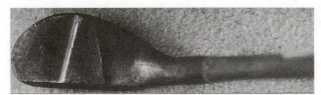

ALUMINUM HEAD MALLET

| $90 | $150 | $250 |

Circa 1910. "Cassiday 'V'" on the sole.

CASSIDAY, J L

Aldburgh, England

Cassiday began making clubs shortly after the turn of the century. He is known for his patented "V" sight line aluminum putters.

PERSIMMON HEAD PUTTER

| $140 | $250 | $450 |

Circa 1910. "Cassiday, Aldburgh" on the socket, semi-long nose head.

CLARK, J & D

MUSSELBURGH, SCOTLAND

The Clark brothers apprenticed under Willie Park and many of their clubs were made by Park or in his style. In the short period of time during the late 1890s and early 1900s, they used two marks: "J & D Clark, Musselburgh" in a circle similar to Park's mark, and the same in very tiny letters.

LONG NOSE BEECH HEAD PUTTER

| $750 | $1,500 | $2,750 |

Circa 1890-95 most likely made by Willie Park.

SMOOTH FACE BLADE PUTTER

| $80 | $120 | $225 |

Circa 1895-1905. Stamped "J & D Clark Musselburgh".

BRASS BLADE PUTTER

| $100 | $160 | $300 |

Circa 1895-1905. Stamped "J & D Clark Musselburgh".

MARKED FACE IRONS

| $50 | $80 | $150 |

Circa 1910-1920. All irons. Stamped "J & D Clark Musselburgh".

STAINLESS IRONS

$40	$50	$95

Circa 1925-1930. All stainless irons. "Bow-line" mark.

SMOOTH FACE IRONS

$75	$110	$200

Circa 1895-1905. Cleek, iron, and lofting iron. Stamped "J & D Clark Musselburgh."

SPLICED NECK BRASSIE

$250	$450	$900

Circa 1895. Transitional pear shaped head stamped "J & D Clark Musselburgh."

COCHRANE'S LT'D

EDINBURGH, SCOTLAND

This Edinburgh-based firm used several marks including the "Knight" in armor holding a sword, and a "Bowline Knot". They also used "J P Cochrane's, Lt'd, Edinburgh" in script. The company made clubs well into the late 1930s.

PUTTING CLEEK

$40	$60	$110

Circa 1910-1915. "Knight" mark. Hyphen scored straight blade putter.

MUSSEL BACK PUTTER

$45	$60	$125

Circa 1920. "Knight" mark.

WALTER HAGEN PUTTER

$45	$60	$120

Circa 1925-1930. Stainless steel putter. "Bowline" mark.

PUTTING CLEEK

$45	$60	$120

Circa 1920. Dot faced blade. "Bowline Knot" mark.

"NIGGER" PUTTER

$140	$225	$425

Circa 1920. Seven inch long hosel. Dot faced blade. "Bowline Knot" mark.

FLANGED BACK PUTTER

$50	$60	$120

Circa 1920-1925. "Knight" mark.

BENT NECK PUTTER

$50	$60	$120

Circa 1915. Stamped "Bent Neck Putter." "Knight" mark.

HOLEM PUTTER

$65	$90	$175

Circa 1915. "Mussel" back. "Knight" mark.

CHALLENGER RUSTLESS PUTTER

$80	$130	$250

Circa 1920s. "Knight" mark. Park-style severely bent neck hosel.

"X X X" FLANGED PUTTER

$80	$130	$225

Circa 1920. Flat hosel and shaft.

U O T PUTTER

$450	$750	$1,150

Circa 1920. "Knight" mark. "Spur" at toe.

CRUICKSHANK SIGNATURE IRONS

$40	$50	$90

Circa 1925-1930. "Bowline Knot" mark.

CARDINAL SERIES IRONS

$40	$50	$80

Circa 1920s. 1 through 9 irons. Dot punched face.

HAGEN SERIES IRONS

$40	$50	$80

Circa 1930. All irons marked rustless. "Bowline Knot" mark.

OFFSET BLADE PUTTER

| $45 | $55 | $90 |

Circa 1915. Knight mark. Dot punched face.

LIGHT MASHIE

| $50 | $70 | $120 |

Circa 1920-1925. "Knight" mark. Line-scored face.

MAXWELL HOSEL IRONS

| $50 | $70 | $140 |

Circa 1910-1920. All flanged back irons. Maxwell holes drilled in hosel.

CARDINAL SERIES IRONS

| $75 | $90 | $175 |

Circa 1920s. Dreadnought niblick.

DEEP GROOVE IRONS

| $120 | $175 | $275 |

Circa 1915-1922. "DEDLI" pitcher with five slot grooves.

GIANT NIBLICK

| $900 | $1,300 | $1,900 |

Circa 1925-1930. "Mammouth Niblick." "Stainless" "Fort Mason, Picadilly, London" "Bowline Knot" mark.

CARDINAL GIANT NIBLICK

| $900 | $1,350 | $2,000 |

Circa 1920s. Bowline Knot mark.

PRETTY FACE WOODS

| $80 | $120 | $190 |

Circa 1910-1920. Driver, brassie, or spoon. "Triangular" black face insert.

KIRKWOOD SERIES WOODS

| $80 | $120 | $190 |

Circa 1925-1930. Driver, brassie, or spoon. "Genuine Joe Kirkwood Model."

PUTTING CLEEK

| $60 | $80 | $150 |

Circa 1900-1910. Smooth face blade. "Flower" mark.

HAGEN SERIES WOODS

| $80 | $120 | $190 |

Circa 1925-1930. Driver, brassie, or spoon. "Genuine Walter Hagen Model."

SEMI-SOCKET PATENT.

| $120 | $190 | $300 |

Circa 1910.

SPLICED NECK WOODS

| $120 | $200 | $350 |

Circa 1900-1910. Driver, brassie, or spoon. Persimmon head.

CONDIE, ROBERT

ST. ANDREWS, SCOTLAND

Robert Condie began as a cleek maker during the early 1880s in St. Andrews. His mark was "R. Condie, St Andrews" surrounding a "Flower" mark. More than 10 different sizes and shapes of Condie's "Flower" have been catalogued. During the 1890s, he briefly used single and double "Fern" marks. Clubs with the "Fern" marks are very scarce and are highly sought after by collectors.

EXCELSIOR PUTTER

| $50 | $70 | $120 |

Circa 1920. Dot faced blade. "R Condie, St Andrews" surrounding his "Flower" mark.

CALAMITY JANE TYPE

| $50 | $70 | $125 |

Circa 1910. Offset blade. "Flower" mark.

BRASS-HEAD PUTTERS

| $70 | $100 | $180 |

Circa 1900-1910. Smooth face blade. "Flower" mark.

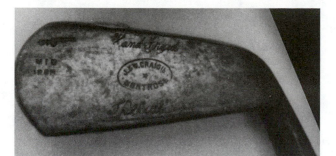

SINGLE FERN IRONS		
$200	$325	$600

Circa 1890-1895. Iron or lofter.

LINE-SCORED JIGGER		
$40	$60	$100

Circa 1920. "Flower" mark.

ROUND-HEAD NIBLICK		
$40	$60	$95

Circa 1915-1920. "Flower" mark. Dot punched face.

OVAL-HEAD NIBLICK		
$40	$60	$95

Circa 1915-1920. "Flower" mark. Dot punched face and offset hosel.

SMOOTH-FACE IRONS		
$50	$70	$120

Circa 1900-1910. Iron or lofter. "Flower" mark.

SMOOTH-FACE CLEEK		
$50	$70	$120

Circa 1900-1910. "Flower" mark.

EARLY CONDIE IRONS		
$80	$130	$250

Circa 1890-1900. Smooth face iron or lofter. "Flower" mark. Shafted and stamped by D McEwan, Ben Sayers, R Simpson, and others.

SWILCAN PITCHER		
$75	$110	$175

Circa 1920. "Flower" mark. Wide sole, beveled heel and toe. Dot punched face.

SMOOTH FACE NIBLICK		
$75	$110	$190

Circa 1900-1910. "Flower" mark.

DOT PUNCHED FACE IRONS		
$45	$55	$90

Circa 1915-1920. All irons. "Rifle" mark.

EARLY CONDIE CLEEKS		
$80	$130	$250

Circa 1890-1900. "Flower" mark surrounded D McEwan, Ben Sayers, R Simpson, and others.

CONCAVE FACE LOFTER		
$110	$160	$275

Circa 1895. "Flower" mark.

ANTI-SHANK IRONS		
$120	$190	$325

Circa 1900-1910. Fairlie Patent smooth face iron, lofter or niblick. "Flower" mark.

SINGLE FERN CLEEK		
$250	$350	$600

Circa 1890-1895.

DOUBLE FERN IRONS		
$250	$375	$600

Circa 1890-1895. Iron or lofter.

DOUBLE FERN CLEEK		
$275	$400	$650

Circa 1890-1895.

CRAIGIE, J & W
MONTROSE, SCOTLAND

The Craigie brothers began forging clubs during the mid-1890s and continued through the 1920s. Their mark was "J & W Craigie, Montrose" in block letters and they used a "Rifle" cleek mark.

OFFSET BLADE PUTTER		
$40	$60	$100

Circa 1915-1920. "Rifle" mark.

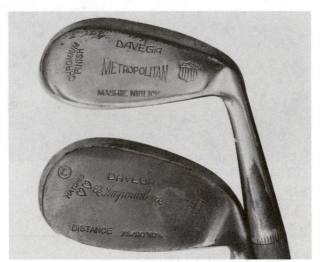

IRON OR STAINLESS STEEL IRONS
$30   **$40**   **$65**
"Davega," "Wicklow," or "Metropolitan" stamps.

BUNNY PUTTER
$100   **$135**   **$200**
Mallet style with brass plug in face.

SPLICED NECK PUTTER
$450   **$800**   **$1,750**
Circa 1895. Transitional shaped beech head.
"Craigie" in block letters.

RUT NIBLICK
$160   **$250**   **$450**
Circa 1900-1905. Smooth face. "Rifle" mark.

DAVEGA
NEW YORK CITY SPORTING GOODS STORE

BLADE PUTTER
$40   **$50**   **$75**
"Davega," "Wicklow," or "Tommy Armour"
stamps.

ILLEGAL DEEP GROOVE IRONS
$90   **$125**   **$190**
Corrugated face.

SILVER DINT WOODS
$175   **$275**   **$475**
Circa 1915. Wooden baffie. Patented one-piece
silver face and sole plate. "Pat. No. 22777/13."

RANGEFINDER IRONS
$40   **$55**   **$85**
Circa 1925-1930. All rustless irons. Dot-punched
face.

SOCKET WOOD
$65   **$85**   **$125**
"Davega," "Wicklow" or "Metropolitan" stamps.

DINT PATENT GOLF CO., LTD
Made wood clubs with "Dint" in script on the
sole plate. The one-piece face and sole plate
were made of silver.

SILVER DINT WOODS
$160   **$250**   **$450**
Circa 1915. Driver, brassie, or spoon. Patented one
piece Silver face and sole plate. "Pat No.
22777/13."

DONALDSON, J
GLASGOW, SCOTLAND
James Donaldson made clubs from the early
1920s through the early 1930s. He used a
"Rangefinder" circular mark.

IONIC IRONS
$45   **$60**   **$100**
Circa 1915-1920. All line scored irons.

LUCKY DOG SOCKET WOODS
$80   **$120**   **$190**
Circa 1925-1930. Driver, brassie, or spoon.

SMOOTH FACE IRONS
$80   **$120**   **$200**
Circa 1905-1910. All irons. Large "Crown and Ribbon" mark.

THE SKELPIE IRONS
$45   **$60**   **$110**
Circa 1925-1930. All rustless irons. Dot punched face.

RANGEFINDER WOODS
$80   **$120**   **$190**
Circa 1925-1930. Driver, brassie, or spoon. Two-tone heads.

DRAPER & MAYNARD
PLYMOUTH, NH
Made inexpensive clubs during the 1920s and 1930s. Babe Ruth was one of the spokesmen for Draper & Maynard baseball and golf goods.

IDEAL PUTTER
$40   **$55**   **$90**
Circa 1925-1930.

IDEAL IRONS
$35   **$45**   **$80**
Circa 1925-1930.

LUCKY DOG BRAND IRONS
$35   **$45**   **$80**
Circa 1925-1930.

DUNN, JOHN D
BOURNEMOUTH, ENGLAND
Began making clubs in the early 1890s. He patented the "One-Piece" wood while in Bournemouth, England, circa 1894. He later moved to New York.

BRITISH MAKE IRONS
$60   **$80**   **$150**
Circa 1900. All smooth face irons.

ONE-PIECE WOOD
$1,000   **$1,600**   **$3,300**
Circa 1895. "John D Dunn, Bournemouth" on shaft.

PARK-STYLE PUTTER
$100   **$150**   **$300**
Circa 1900-1910. "Dunn Selected" mark. Severe bent neck.

DUNN IRONS ARDSLEY NEW YORK
$150   **$250**   **$450**
Circa 1895. All smooth face irons with tiny "Eagle" mark.

CROWN MARKED WOODS
$80   **$120**   **$190**
Circa 1905-1910. All socket woods.

DUNN, SEYMOUR
LAKE PLACID, NY
Made clubs in America circa 1910-1920. Used a large "Crown and Ribbon" mark.

DOT FACE IRONS
$70   **$100**   **$200**
Circa 1915. Large "Crown and Ribbon" mark.

ANTI-SHANK IRONS
$140   **$250**   **$500**
Circa 1910. Fairlie style. Smooth face mashie-niblick or niblick. Large "Crown and Ribbon" mark.

SOCKET WOODS
$80   **$130**   **$225**
Circa 1910. Driver, brassie, or spoon. Large "Crown and Ribbon" mark.

DUNN, WILLIE
NEW YORK
Willie Dunn began forging clubs in the late 1880s at Westward Ho! In 1895, he began a club-making business in New York. His clubs

SMOOTH-FACE IRONS
$100   **$150**   **$275**
Circa 1897-1903. All irons stamped "Willie Dunn, New York" in large block letters.

---

were marked "Ardsley C. C., New York." During the period from 1897 to 1900, he worked as club designer for B.G.I., MacGregor, and Spalding. After 1900 his clubs were marked "Dunn Selected" or "Willie Dunn, New York" in block letters.

OFFSET BLADE PUTTER
$60   **$100**   **$150**
Circa 1910. "Rampant Lion" mark.

BALL-FACE BLADE PUTTER
$60   **$100**   **$160**
Circa 1910. "Rampant Lion" mark.

SMOOTH-FACE BLADE PUTTER
$70   **$100**   **$200**
Circa 1900-1905. Stamped "Willie Dunn, New York."

DUNN SELECTED IRONS
$70   **$120**   **$195**
Circa 1900-1905. All smooth face irons.

APPROACHING CLEEK
$100   **$150**   **$275**
Circa 1897-1903. "Willie Dunn, New York" in block letters.

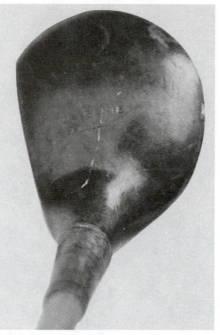

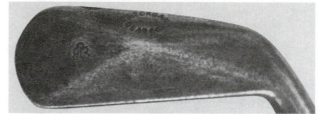

BRASS BLADE PUTTER

$120 $190 $325

Circa 1900. Pear Tree mark. "Andrew Forgan, Glasgow" stampings.

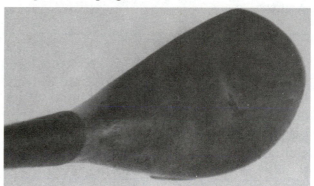

SOCKED HEAD WOODS

$80 $100 $160

Circa 1905-1920s.

DUNN SELECTED WOODS

$100 $175 $325

Circa 1900-1905. Socket-head driver, brassie, or spoon.

SPLICED-NECK WOODS

$160 $300 $600

Circa 1900-1905. Spliced-head driver, brassie, or spoon.

DUNN SELECTED WOODS

$160 $300 $600

Circa 1900-1905. Spliced-neck driver, brassie, or spoon.

FERNIE, WILLIE

TROON, SCOTLAND

Willie Fernie began making clubs around 1880 and was a professional at Troon from 1887 to 1923. His clubs were popular because he was a great player. He won the British Open in 1883 and was runner-up four times.

SMOOTH FACE CLEEK

$100 $125 $200

Circa 1885-90 "W Fernie" oval stamp.

SPLICED NECK WOODS

$175 $325 $650

Circa 1895-1900. Driver, brassie, or spoon. "Tree" mark.

SMOOTH FACE BLADE PUTTER

$90 $120 $180

Circa 1885-90 "W Fernie" oval stamp.

IRON HEAD CLUBS

$50 $65 $100

Dot or line face with Oval stamp circa 1910-1920s.

TRANSITIONAL SPLICED NECK WOOD

$250 $325 $650

Circa 1880-90.

FORGAN, ANDREW

GLASGOW, SCOTLAND

Brother of Robert Forgan. He made clubs during the mid-1890s. He used the marks "A Forgan, Glasgow" in block letters and a "Pear" tree with "Regd" beneath.

STEEL BLADE PUTTER

$100 $150 $250

Circa 1895-1900. Pear Tree mark. "Andrew Forgan, Glasgow" stampings.

PLUME MARK BRASS PUTTERS
$80	$160	$325

Circa 1895. Smooth face brass blade with a short, straight, thick hosel. "R Forgan & Sons, St Andrews" mark.

FORGAN, ROBERT
ST. ANDREWS, SCOTLAND

Robert Forgan was one of the foremost and prolific clubmakers of his time. His shop was adjacent to the 18th green of the Old Course in St. Andrews, Scotland.

Robert apprenticed under Hugh Philp (Philp died in 1856). During that time, his reputation had grown to capture the attention of the Prince of Wales, who commissioned him to make his clubs. This explains why the firm used the Prince of Wales "Plume" mark as its trademark from the 1880s onward. When the Prince became King Edward in 1901, the firm adopted the "Crown" mark and used it until about 1910 and subsequently during the late 1920s. When the firm of James Spence was acquired in 1926, its "Flag in the Hole" maker's mark was also used. Each club had "R Forgan & Son, St Andrews" stamped into the head as well as the "mark" (woods sometimes did not bear the "trade mark"). Pre-1910 clubs and post-1910 premium quality clubs usually had "R Forgan & Sons, St Andrews Selected" stamped into the shaft just below the grip.

Today the St. Andrews Woolen Mills occupies the building, which still has "R. Forgan & Son" spelled out on the sidewalk in front of the main entrance as a reminder of its glorious clubmaking past.

EARLY STEEL PUTTERS
$190	$350	$600

Circa 1880-1890. "R Forgan and Sons, St Andrews" marking. Face nearly two inches vertical.

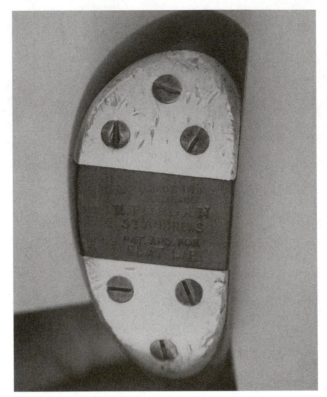

MAXMO PUTTER
$160	$250	$500

Circa 1920. Persimmon head mallet. Metal sole plates at heel and toe. Wood portion of sole marked "R Forgan, St Andrews."

CROWN MARKED PUTTERS
$60	$100	$200

Circa 1901-1908. Smooth face. Heavy gauge steel.

CROWN MARKED PUTTERS
$60	$100	$150

Circa 1901-1908. #100 dot faced, centra-ject back weighted.

CROWN MARKED BRASS PUTTERS
$65	$100	$200

Circa 1901-1908. Brass blade with "R Forgan & Sons, St Andrews" mark.

SCOTIA SERIES PUTTER
$35	$50	$100

Circa 1920. Line scored blade.

GEM PUTTER
$55	$85	$150

Circa 1926-1930. Wide rounded back broad sole. "Forgan" in large block letters on back.

TOLLEY PUTTER
$190   **$300**   **$600**
Circa 1925-30. Heel shafted socket putter made of "Forganite," a plastic-type material.

DIAMOND BACK IRONS
$45   **$60**   **$110**
Circa 1920s.

GIRAFFE NECK PUTTER
$120   **$180**   **$300**
Circa 1920. "Flag" mark. Slender five-inch-long hosel.

PUTTERS EXPORTED TO INDIA
$100   **$160**   **$275**
Circa 1901-1908. Brass blade putter. "Crown" mark. "Wager & Co., Bombay" stamping.

LONG-NOSE PUTTERS
$1,250   **$2,400**   **$6,000**
Circa 1856-1870. Beech head. "R Forgan" large block letters mark. Long head. Large lead back weight.

SPLICED NECK PUTTERS
$190   **$450**   **$900**
Circa 1910-1920. "R Forgan" in block letters on long narrow head.

GOLD MEDAL SERIES IRONS
$40   **$55**   **$100**
Circa 1920s. All irons with line scored face.

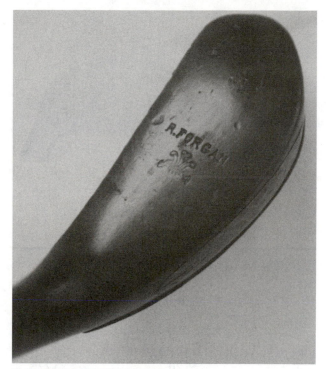

LONG-NOSE PUTTERS
$900   **$1,500**   **$3,500**
Circa 1870-1890. "R Forgan" and "Plume" mark. Medium-size head. Medium weight.

PLUME MARKED IRONS
$80   **$150**   **$375**
Circa 1890-1900. Lofting iron marked "R Forgan & Sons, St Andrews."

PLUME MARKED IRONS
$80   **$150**   **$375**
Circa 1890-1895. Long blade cleek marked "R Forgan & Son, St Andrews."

PLUME MARKED IRONS
$175   **$350**   **$750**
Circa 1880-1890. Large head lofting iron marked "R Forgan & Sons, St Andrews".

PLUME MARKED IRONS
$700   **$1,350**   **$3,250**
Circa 1880-1890. Rut iron with a small cupped head. "R Forgan & Sons, St Andrews" marks.

CROWN MARKED IRONS
$60   **$90**   **$150**
Circa 1901-1908. Jigger marked "R Forgan & Sons."

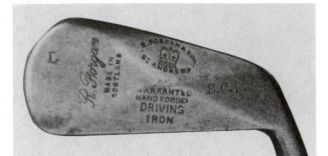

CROWN MARKED IRONS
$50   **$70**   **$150**
Circa 1901-1908. Cleek or driving iron with a smooth face.

CROWN MARKED IRONS
$60   **$90**   **$150**
Circa 1901-1908. Diamond back and dot punched "BALL" face.

CROWN MARKED IRONS
$80   **$120**   **$225**
Circa 1901-1908. Driving mashie with a smooth face marked "R Forgan & Sons, St Andrews."

CROWN MARKED IRONS
$220   **$375**   **$750**
Circa 1901-1908. Niblick with a rounded head and smooth face. "R Forgan & Sons, St Andrews" markings.

CELTIC SERIES IRONS
$40   **$50**   **$100**
Circa 1920s. All irons with dot punched face.

SELECTED SERIES IRONS
$40   **$50**   **$100**
Circa 1920s. All irons with line scored face.

BIG BALL SERIES IRONS
$40   **$50**   **$100**
Circa 1930. All irons marked "Made especially for the big ball."

ROYAL SERIES IRONS
$40   **$50**   **$100**
Circa 1930. All irons line scored face.

SCOTIA SERIES IRONS
$40   **$50**   **$100**
Circa 1920s. All irons with dot punched face.

FLAG-IN-HOLE SERIES IRONS
$40   **$50**   **$100**
Circa 1926-1930. All irons with dot or lined face.

METEOR RUSTLESS IRONS
$50   **$65**   **$100**
C-1930 line scored face.

SMITH ANTI-SHANK IRONS
$100   **$160**   **$275**
Circa 1915-1920. Dot face. Cleek, mid-iron, mashie, mashie-niblick and niblick.

ANTI-SHANK IRONS
$120   **$175**   **$300**
Circa 1900-1915. "Fairlie's Patent" cleek, mid-iron, mashie, mashie-niblick and niblick.

JUVENILE CLUBS
$50   **$70**   **$110**
Circa 1926-30. Smooth face. "Flag-in-Hole" mark.

LONG NOSE WOODS
$1500   **$3500**   **$9,000**
Circa 1860-1880. Long nose without "Plume" mark.

PLUME MARKED WOODS
$375   **$950**   **$2,000**
Circa 1885-1895. Play club, brassie, spoon. Beech transitional pear-shaped head.

CROWN MARKED WOODS
$80   **$120**   **$250**
Circa 1901-1908. Driver, brassie, or spoon. "R Forgan, St Andrews" above "Crown" mark.

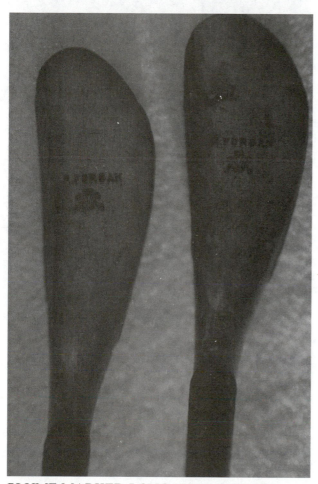

PLUME MARKED WOODS

$300	$600	$1,500

Circa 1890-1900. Spliced-neck bulger face play club, brassie and spoon.

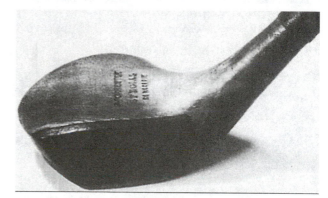

SPLICED NECK WOODS

$140	$225	$375

Circa 1900-1910. Driver, brassie, or spoon. Stamped "George Forrester, Elie, Earlsferry."

PLUME MARKED LONG NOSE WOODS

$1,100	$2,400	$7,500

Circa 1870-1890. Play club, brassie, spoon. Beech transitional pear-shaped head.

GOLD MEDAL SERIES WOODS

$80	$100	$190

Circa 1920s. Driver, brassie, or spoon marked "Forgan, St Andrews Gold Medal" on persimmon head.

SCOTIA SERIES WOODS

$80	$100	$190

Circa 1920. Driver, brassie, or spoon. "R Forgan & Son, St Andrews" mark.

FORGANITE WOODS

$90	$160	$290

Circa 1910-1915. Driver, brassie, and spoon. "Forganite" in an elongated "Diamond." Forganite is a plastic-type material. No sole plate.

DREADNOUGHT WOODS

$100	$175	$300

Circa 1920. Large head driver, brassie, or spoon. "RForgan" in block letters. Black triangular face insert.

ANGLE-SHAFT WOOD

$150	$275	$500

Circa 1905-1910. "Crown" mark, "Angle-Shaft Patent No. 10194" and "R Forgan" markings. The shaft is oval shaped and "Angled" for strength.

FORRESTER, G

EARLSFERRY, ELIE, SCOTLAND

George Forrester began making clubs in the late 1880s and continued through 1930. His mark was "Geo. Forrester, Elie, Earlsferry" in block letters.

SMOOTH FACE IRONS
$90   **$115**   **$175**
Circa 1890-1900. Nicoll stamp.

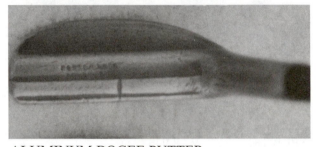

ALUMINUM BOGEE PUTTER
$190   **$300**   **$550**
Circa 1920. "Registered No. 696416." Wide soled
sloped back aluminum-head putter. Square hosel.

BRASS HEAD PUTTERS
$70   **$100**   **$175**
Circa 1895-1900. Long face blade putter. "George
Forrester, Earlsferry, Elie" circle mark.

CONCENTRIC BACK IRONS
$80   **$120**   **$225**
Circa 1900. Smooth face. Patent "No. 125240."

GENERAL PURPOSE IRON
$120   **$180**   **$350**
Circa 1890. Smooth long face. "George Forrester,
Earlsferry, Elie" circle mark.

ROUNDED FACE IRONS
$140   **$225**   **$400**
Circa 1895-1900. "Patent #53386" rounded back
cleek or iron. The face is rounded from heel to toe,
much like a "bulger" face wood.

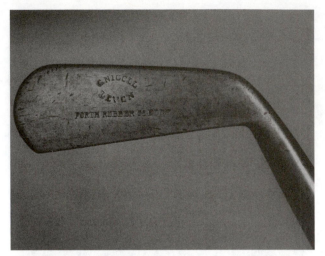

SMOOTH FACE CLEEK
$100   **$125**   **$190**
Circa 1890-1900. Nicoll Stamp.

FORTH RUBBER COMPANY
EDINBURGH, SCOTLAND
The Forth Rubber Company had several stores
in Scotland that sold Gutta Percha balls and a
full line of clubs, c-1890s through the turn of
the century. Its mark was block lettering inside
a rectangle. Many of the irons had Nicoll
stampings as well.

SMOOTH FACE PUTTER
$100   **$125**   **$200**
Name in rectangle. Circa 1900.

SPLICED NECK WOODS
$225   **$300**   **$600**
Bulger or transitional. Circa 1890-1900.

FOSTER BROTHERS
ASHBOURNE
The Foster Brothers produced clubs for only a
short time after World War I. They used a
human "Skeleton" swinging a club as their
mark. They also made clubs bearing "The
Bogee" stampings.

BOGEE IRONS
$60   **$120**   **$200**
Circa 1915-1920. All irons. Dot punched face.
Marked with a "Skeleton" swinging a club.

FOULIS, JAMES

WHEATON, IL

By Pete Georgiady

On his first day attending St. Andrews University, Charles Blair MacDonald was taken to meet the Grand Old Man of Golf, Tom Morris. The Morris shop was one of Scotland's golfing headquarters. Situated close to the 18th green, it was a place where golfers gathered and stories were told by the game's early devotees. Spending time in the company of those golfers left its mark on the student MacDonald, and he knew exactly who to call when the club he formed, the Chicago Golf Club, required a pro—a real Scottish pro. Old Tom, himself, was entrusted to nominate a suitable candidate for the Chicago Golf position. Thus Tom went to his foreman, James Foulis Sr., the father of five sons, each of whom played a highly respectable game, and encouraged him to send his best son to America where golf missionaries were required.

But James Foulis Jr. was not the first choice for the position. Brother Robert was already a professional at the Ranfurly Golf Club, Bridge o' Weir, and the most experienced, but he turned down the opportunity. Instead of moving to Chicago, he chose to honor his one-year contract and suggested that Jim take the job offer instead. Jim was, after all, the better golfer and he arrived in Wheaton, Ill., in March 1895, ready to assume his responsibilities.

Strictly speaking, young Jim Foulis was not a golf professional in 1895. Foulis' occupation was a clubmaker in the Robert Forgan works, at the time the world's largest clubmaking firm. The rules defining golf professionalism allowed him to compete as an amateur. A member of the famed St. Andrews Golf Club, he was a skilled competitor and at age 22 won the club's 1893 medal competition. Although not highly competitive, his family had been in the golfing world for many years. James'

great-grandfather, a shepherd, had also mown the grass on the St. Andrews links during the time of George III. His father was employed in the Morris club works for more than 30 years.

With golf courses being created all across America, the need for more professionals and greenskeepers was quickly growing. Once in Chicago, Jim sent for younger brother David to be his assistant. Soon after that, Foulis wired home again and instructed Robert to join him immediately, "expenses paid!" Once Bob arrived, he was quickly put to work overseeing the final phases of construction at the Lake Forest Golf Club (the name would shortly be changed to Onwentsia), finishing the work Jim had begun that spring. He was appointed Lake Forest's first pro and stayed for another five years.

Jim played in the first U.S. Open at Newport in 1895, winning $50 for finishing third behind Horace Rawlins and Willie Dunn. The following year the Open was played at Shinnecock Hills and the train from Illinois carried two challengers from the American West, Jim Foulis and C. B. MacDonald.

The '96 Open would be remembered for two important non-golf events outside of the tournament. The threatened boycott of professional contestants opposed to the entry of two local Shinnecock caddies, John Shippen and Oscar Bunn, fell apart two days before the championship. The other mix up occurred when Willie Park Jr., the odds-on favorite to clean the field, arrived a day after the tournament had ended, having missed his original steamship to New York.

In the early days of the U.S. Open, only two 18-hole rounds were played, both on the same day. Jim Foulis shot a 78 in the morning round, leaving him in a six-way tie for the lead among the 33 contestants. In the afternoon, he deftly stroked a 74 to outdistance defending champ Horace Rawlins by three, setting an 18-hole record that was not broken until the advent of the rubber-wound ball. It is interesting to note that James Foulis Jr. stood only 5 feet 5 inches tall, but had a barrel chest, stout arms and legs, and enormous hands, which gave him excellent club control.

One of the trademarks Jim Foulis applied to the game was the invention of the special Foulis patent mashie-niblick. The American game differed from Scottish golf in large part because of course design and native vegetation. Thick long grass around greens prohibited the traditional Scottish approach shot we now refer to as the "bump and run." A lofted shot, hopefully stopping dead, was required and to this end Foulis perfected a new club. It had a deeply concaved face with a blade rounded on top and was very flat at the sole. It assumed the name of the "Foulis club" and every manufacturer on both sides of the Atlantic copied it after its introduction in 1904. Earlier, he had invented a club called the Octagon Niblick with its modified diamond-back design.

America was good to the Foulis family. In 1899, with three sons enjoying successes in American golf, James Sr. brought the remainder of the family—wife, daughter and two sons—to Chicago to live permanently. Robert subsequently moved to Minneapolis and, afterward, St. Louis, initially to Glen Echo, then became the first pro at Bellerive. David worked with Jim at Chicago Golf (clubs marked "J & D Foulis") and was made the club's professional after Jim moved to Calumet C.C. on Chicago's far south side in 1905. Later Jim received the appointment to the pro's post at Olympia Fields. The fourth brother, John Foulis, worked at Chicago Golf as a ball maker until his untimely death in 1907. The youngest brother, Simpson, remained an amateur throughout his career.

The life and career of James Foulis are interwoven with the very heart of early American golf history. He was the second national champion and had a close relationship with C.C. MacDonald, a founding father of the USGA, Chicago Golf and National Links clubs. He served as the first professional at America's first full 18-hole course and the first golf pro west of the Alleghenies. Foulis was an expert clubmaker and inventor, and with his brothers, he had a hand in laying out more than 20 courses in the Chicago and St. Louis areas.

PATENTED MASHIE-NIBLICK
$140   **$250**   **$450**
Circa 1905. Concave smooth face.

SMOOTH-FACE IRONS
$140   **$200**   **$325**
Circa 1900. Iron or lofter. "J & D Foulis, Selected" mark.

SMOOTH FACE CLEEK
$145   **$200**   **$400**
Circa 1900. "J & D Foulis, Selected" mark.

SOCKET WOODS
$120   **$250**   **$450**
Circa 1905. Driver, brassie, or spoon.

SPLICED NECK WOODS
$250   **$450**   **$1,000**
Circa 1905. Driver, brassie, or spoon.

GASSIAT, JEAN
BIARRITZ, FRANCE
He made the famous "Grand Piano"-style head putter circa 1910 that today is called simply "The Gassiat." He used his name in script as his mark.

PIANO-SHAPED WOOD PUTTER
$375　　　　**$650**　　　　**$1,100**
Circa 1910. "Jean L Gassiat" and "Regd. No. 627732" on the broad wood head.

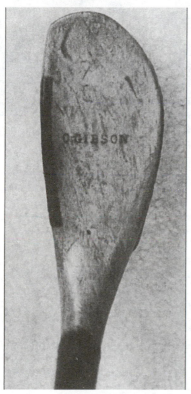

TRANSITIONAL BULGER DRIVER
$600　　　　**$1,200**　　　　**$2,500**
Circa 1885-1895. Beech head stamped "C. Gibson."

GIBSON, CHARLES
WESTWARD HO!
Charles Gibson began making clubs about 1890 and used the mark "Charles Gibson, Westward Ho!" in block lettering on his earliest clubs. About 1910, he adopted a "Rampant Stallion" mark and later the "Phoenix" bird mark.

RUSTLESS PUTTER
$100　　　　**$160**　　　　**$275**

OFFSET BLADE PUTTER
$60　　　　**$90**　　　　**$150**
Circa 1915-1920. "Rampant Stallion" mark.

Circa 1925-1930. Long blade with "G-in-Star" mark. Corrugated sole.

RUT NIBLICK
$160　　　　**$300**　　　　**$600**
Circa 1895-1900. Stamped "C Gibson, Westward Ho!"

SOCKET WOODS
$80　　　　**$120**　　　　**$190**
Circa 1910-1915. Driver, brassie, or spoon. "C Gibson, Westward Ho!" mark.

SOCKET-HEAD PUTTER
$190　　　　**$300**　　　　**$450**
Circa 1915-1920. Persimmon mallet. Stamped "C Gibson Special."

PHOENIX MARKED IRONS
$40　　　　**$60**　　　　**$100**
Circa 1925. All irons. Line-scored face. "Phoenix" bird mark.

EXCELLAR IRONS
$40　　　　**$60**　　　　**$100**
Circa 1920. All irons. "Phoenix" bird mark.

MAXWELL HOSEL IRONS
$50　　　　**$70**　　　　**$125**
Circa 1915-1920. All irons. Flanged back. "Rampant Stallion" mark.

GENERAL PURPOSE IRON
$90　　　　**$175**　　　　**$325**
Circa 1890. "C. Gibson" mark.

SOCKET WOODS
$80　　　　**$120**　　　　**$200**
Circa 1900-1920. "C. Gibson" in block letters.

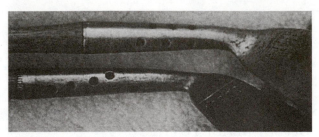

STAR MAXWELL SERIES PUTTER

| $50 | $70 | $145 |

Circa 1915. Flanged back with Maxwell holes drilled in hosel.

"G" IN CIRCLE MARKED PUTTER

| $40 | $55 | $90 |

Circa 1930. Stainless blade. "Star" inside circle.

GIBSON, WILLIAM
KINGHORN, SCOTLAND

One of the most prolific clubmakers during the wood-shaft era, Gibson began forging iron-head clubs in the mid-1890s in Edinburgh. Before the turn of the century, he relocated in Kinghorn on the northern shore of the Firth of Fourth. His maker's mark was a "Star," which varied in size and style during the nearly 50 years it was used.

He produced the first "flanged" back irons and the "Maxwell" drilled hosel irons in large quantities for a variety of clients who assembled clubs. He forged many patent clubs including the heel and toe weighted "Smith's Patent" anti-shank irons. Collecting only Gibson forged clubs would be a formidable task.

KINGHORN SERIES PUTTERS

| $55 | $90 | $150 |

Circa 1910. Emoried smooth face straight blade.

BRAID SERIES PUTTERS

| $50 | $75 | $150 |

Circa 1915. Putting cleek.

VARSITY PUTTER

| $110 | $190 | $350 |

Circa 1910. Crook in hosel. Bulge weight at toe.

DOMINIE PUTTER

| $120 | $150 | $225 |

Center shafted aluminum head with "G" in "Star" mark.

STAR MAXWELL SERIES PUTTER

| $40 | $60 | $100 |

Circa 1915. Blade putter, regular hosel.

SAVILLE SERIES PUTTER

| $40 | $55 | $90 |

Circa 1930. Stainless steel blade putter.

FIFE GOLF CO. SERIES PUTTERS

| $50 | $70 | $125 |

Circa 1930. Flanged back offset blade putter with "Maxwell" holes drilled in the hosel.

ESKIT RUSTLESS PUTTER

| $40 | $55 | $90 |

Circa 1930-1935. Offset blade, dot face. "G inside a Star" mark.

ORION PUTTER

| $100 | $190 | $425 |

Circa 1910-1920. Flanged back with flat hosel and shaft.

GEM PUTTER

| $70 | $100 | $175 |

Circa 1920-1925. Stainless steel head.

DOT FACE GIBSON IRONS
$40   **$50**   **$85**
Circa 1915-1920. 1 through 9 irons.

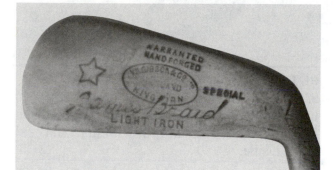

BRAID SERIES IRONS
$45   **$65**   **$120**
Circa 1915. James Braid signature full or light irons.

BROWN-VARDON PUTTER
$100   **$175**   **$325**
Circa 1910-1915. Crescent shaped steel head. Oval hosel and shaft.

BRAID SERIES IRONS
$45   **$60**   **$100**
Circa 1915. James Braid signature mid-iron, mashie, mashie-niblick, or niblick.

BRAID SERIES IRONS
$100   **$175**   **$250**
Circa 1915. "James Braid Autographed Dreadnought" niblick.

GENII MODEL IRONS
$40   **$50**   **$100**
Circa 1915-1920. Marked face irons with offset hosel.

GENII MODEL IRONS
$50   **$60**   **$125**
Circa 1910. Smooth face irons with offset hosel.

AKROS MODEL IRONS
$40   **$55**   **$100**
Circa 1915. All irons. Geo. Duncan signature.

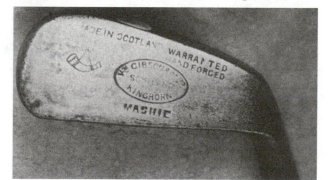

POWDER HORN SERIES
$40   **$55**   **$100**
Circa 1925-1930. Stainless steel heads. 1 through 9 irons.

STAR MAXWELL IRONS
$40   **$50**   **$85**
Circa 1915. Regular hosel.

STAR MAXWELL IRONS
$50   **$65**   **$125**
Circa 1915. Maxwell holes drilled in hosel.

FIFE GOLF CO. SERIES IRONS
$40   **$50**   **$85**
Circa 1925. Stainless steel head. All irons.

SAVILLE SERIES IRONS
$40   **$50**   **$85**
Circa 1930. Stainless steel 1 through 9 irons.

STELLA SERIES IRONS
$40   **$50**   **$85**
Circa 1925-1930. 1 through 9 irons.

KINGHORN SERIES IRONS
$40   **$50**   **$85**
Circa 1930. "Star-in-Circle." All irons.

Examples of both the Fairlie's and Smith's anti-shank irons. Various face scoring.

SUPERIOR SERIES IRONS
$40	$50	$85

Circa 1925-1930. Stainless steel heads. 1 through 9 irons.

SUPERIOR SERIES IRONS
$115	$200	$325

Circa 1925-1930. Anti-shank irons.

PIXIE SAMMY
$60	$80	$125

Circa 1920. Line scored face.

BAXPIN SERIES
$100	$170	$235

Circa 1914-1922. Corrugated deep groove irons.

BAXPIN SERIES
$100	$180	$250

Circa 1914-1922. Slot deep groove irons.

JERKO DEEP GROOVE IRONS
$120	$200	$300

Circa 1920. Mashie, mashie-niblick, or niblick.

ANTI-SHANK IRONS
$120	$190	$275

Circa 1910. Fairlie style anti-shank irons. Various face scoring.

SKOOGEE SAND IRON
$240	$375	$650

Circa late 1920s. Wide flat sole and deeply concave face.

RUT NIBLICK
$350	$500	$950

Circa 1895. Small rounded head. "Wm Gibson & Co, Kinghorn" in an oval with his "Star" mark inside.

GIANT NIBLICK
$1,000	$1,400	$2,000

Circa 1925. Big Ben Model.

GIBSON KINGHORN WOODS
$80	$100	$175

Circa 1920s. Driver, brassie, or spoon.

GOURLAY, JAMES
CARNOUSTIE, SCOTLAND

James Gourlay began forging clubs during the mid-1890s and continued into the Great Depression. He had a number of marks including an "Anchor," a "Crescent and Star," a "Crescent" and small circle, and a "Horseshoe"-type mark.

DIAMOND BACK IRONS
$40	$60	$100

Circa 1905-1915. All irons "Crescent and Star" mark.

MUSSEL BACK PUTTER
$50	$60	$110

Circa 1910-1915. Smooth face. "Crescent and Star" mark.

DIAMOND BACK PUTTER
$50	$70	$125

Circa 1905-1915. Smooth face. "Crescent and Star" mark.

OFFSET BLADE PUTTER
$40   **$50**   **$90**
Circa 1915-1920. "Crescent and Star" mark. Dot punched face.

PARK STYLE PUTTER
$80   **$120**   **$190**
Circa 1910. Severely bent neck. "Crescent and Star" mark.

BRASS HEAD MALLET PUTTERS
$180   **$325**   **$475**
Circa 1915. Brass head, steel face insert. "Crescent and Star" mark.

SWAN NECK PUTTER
$350   **$600**   **$900**
Circa 1905-1910. P.A. Vaile Patent of 1905.

SMOOTH FACE IRONS
$50   **$70**   **$125**
Circa 1900-1910. Iron or lofter. "Crescent and Star" mark.

MAXWELL HOSEL IRONS
$50   **$70**   **$110**
Circa 1910-1915. All irons. Smooth face, flanged back. "Crescent and Star" mark.

SMOOTH FACE CLEEK
$50   **$70**   **$135**
Circa 1900-1910. "Crescent and Star" mark.

SAMMY IRON
$60   **$80**   **$135**
Circa 1915. Dot face. Rounded sole. "Crescent and Star" mark.

JUMBO NIBLICK
$80   **$150**   **$250**
Circa 1925. Dot punched face. Head size is 3 3/4 x 2 3/4 inches.

SMOOTH FACE CLEEK
$750   **$1,400**   **$3,500**
Circa 1860-1880. Long blade, 5 inch hosel. Stamped "Jn Gray."

ANTI-SHANK IRONS
$120   **$200**   **$300**
Circa 1905-1910. All irons. Fairlie's Patent. "Crescent and Star" mark.

RUT NIBLICK
$125   **$250**   **$500**
Circa 1900-1910. Smooth face. "Crescent and Star" mark.

PERFECT BALANCE IRONS
$300   **$600**   **$1,000**
Circa 1910. All irons. "Lump" back weighting. "Patent No. 21307" and "R Simpson, Carnoustie" at toe. "Crescent and Star" mark.

GRAY, JOHN
PRESTWICK, SCOTLAND
John Gray started as a blacksmith in Prestwick and began forging iron heads from about 1850 to the 1880s. He used at least two stampings to identify his clubs. "J. Gray," "Jn. Gray," and I've seen several simply marked "Gray." His clubs are very scarce and highly prized by collectors.

GENERAL PURPOSE IRON
$700   **$1,200**   **$2,800**
Circa 1870-1885. Hooked face iron. Stamped "Jn Gray."

DISHED FACE LOFTER
$750   **$1,350**   **$2,950**
Circa 1860-1875. Stamped "Gray."

RUT IRON

$1,500	$3,500	$8,000

Circa 1860-1880. Small cupped head. 5 inch hosel. Stamped "Jn Gray."

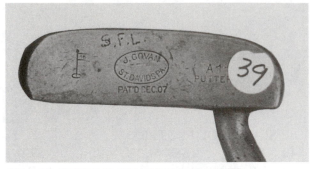

BRASS CENTER SHAFTED PUTTER

$250	$350	$600

"J Govan, St Davids, PA" stamp and "Pat'd Dec, '07."

GOVAN, JAMES
PINE VALLEY, NEW JERSEY

James Govan was the first professional at the famous Pine Valley course. He made very few clubs himself, and sold many made by Spalding stamped with his Oval mark.

SPALDING PUTTER

$85	$110	$175

Circa 1910-1915.

SPALDING IRONS

$75	$100	$150

Circa 1910-1915.

GREAT LAKES GOLF COMPANY
MILWAUKEE, WISCONSIN

This company produced clubs during the late 1920s and 1930s. Most notable were clubs endorsed by famous pros Tommy Armour and Bobby Cruickshank. Most carried their "GL" monogram either on the face or on the back.

TOMMY ARMOUR PUTTER

$45	$55	$85

"GL" Monogram on lined face. "Tommy Armour Open Champion," C-1928-30.

CRUICKSHANK AUTOGRAPH PUTTER

$45	$55	$85

Chromium plated head.

CRUICKSHANK AUTOGRAPH IRONS

$35	$45	$75

Chromium plated head –1930.

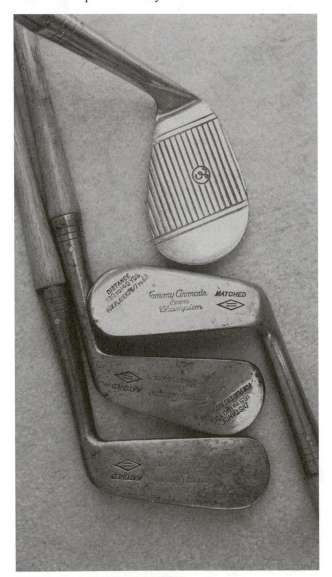

TOMMY ARMOUR IRONS

$40	$50	$80

"GL" Monogram on lined face. "Tommy Armour Open Champion," C-1928-30.

HACKBARTH PUTTER
$325   **$650**   **$1,000**
Patented 1901. Bifurcated hosel.

MONARCH PUTTER OR IRONS
$30   **$40**   **$65**
"Monarch" in large block letters.

KILTIE PUTTER OR IRONS
$30   **$40**   **$65**
Chromium plated head circa 1930

HACKBARTH, OTTO
CINCINNATI, OHIO
Circa 1920. Famous for manufacturing the bifurcated hosel putter commonly known as "The Hackbarth."

SPLICED NECK CLEEK
$135   **$190**   **$375**
Circa 1920. Wooden cleek marked "Otto Hackbarth."

HALLEY, JAMES B., & CO.
LONDON, ENGLAND
Halley & Co. began selling golf clubs about 1900, but did not make its own brands until much later. It had several marks: The "Pyramid" most often found on brass putters, a "Shell," "Circled 'H,'" and a "Crossed Swords" mark.

SPECIAL PUTTER
$40   **$60**   **$100**
Circa 1920. Offset hosel. "Crossed Swords" mark.

RUSTLESS PUTTER
$50   **$65**   **$120**
Circa 1925. Monel metal head. "Pyramid" mark.

BRASS-HEAD PUTTERS
$50   **$65**   **$120**
Circa 1920s. "Pyramid" mark. Line scored blade.

LINE SCORED IRONS
$40   **$55**   **$85**
Circa 1925-1930. All irons. "Crossed Swords" mark.

CONCENTRIC BACK IRONS
$40   **$55**   **$90**
Circa 1915. All irons. Dot punched face.

CIRCLE "H" MARKED IRONS
$40   **$55**   **$90**
Circa 1920. All irons. "Diamond-dot" scoring.

MAXWELL HOSEL IRONS
$50   **$70**   **$120**
Circa 1915. All irons. Circle "H" mark. Flanged back. Holes drilled in hosel.

DREADNOUGHT NIBLICK
$60   **$100**   **$190**
Circa 1915-1920. Hyphen scored face. "Pyramid" mark.

PRETTY FACE WOODS
$90   **$135**   **$200**
Circa 1920s. Ivorine pegs in circular configuration.

PER WIT PUTTER

$400   **$750**   **$1,200**

Circa 1920. "Patent No 247116." Hollowed out back and rounded face. The head gives the appearance of a pipe sawed lengthwise. "Bishop's Hat" mark.

THE VIPER PUTTER

$50   **$70**   **$120**

Circa 1920s. Long blade. "Bishop's Hat" mark.

JUVENILE CLUBS

$30   **$40**   **$65**

Circa 1920. Putter, iron, mashie or niblick. "Crossed Swords" mark.

JUVENILE CLUBS

$75   **$100**   **$150**

Circa 1920. Juvenile wood. "Crossed Swords" mark.

HENDRY & BISHOP, LT'D

EDINBURGH, SCOTLAND

Hendry & Bishop began producing clubs about 1910 and used the "Bishop's Hat" mark. It also made the "Cardinal" brand by which many of its clubs can be identified.

WRY-NECK PUTTER

$40   **$60**   **$100**

Circa 1920s. Chromed head. "Bishop's Hat" mark.

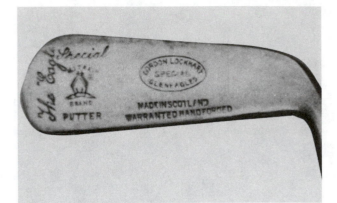

THE EAGLE PUTTER

$45   **$60**   **$100**

Circa 1920s. "Bishop's Hat" mark.

THE SNIPER PUTTER

$120   **$190**   **$300**

Circa 1920s. "Pencil" thin seven inch hosel. "Bishop's Hat" mark.

CARDINAL SERIES IRONS

$40   **$55**   **$90**

Circa 1925. All irons. Dot punched face.

DEEP FACE MASHIE

$40   **$55**   **$100**

Circa 1915. Dot punched face. "Bishop's Hat" mark.

LARGE-HEAD SPADE MASHIE

$40   **$60**   **$110**

Circa 1915. Dot punched face. "Bishop's Hat" mark.

CONCENTRIC BACK IRONS

$50   **$70**   **$110**

Circa 1915. All irons. "Mitre Brand" mark.

DREADNOUGHT NIBLICK

$60   **$120**   **$200**

Circa 1920. Large head, dot punched face. "Bishop's Hat" mark.

PITCH-EM IRON

$60   **$110**   **$150**

Circa 1915. Dot punched face. "Bishop's Hat" mark.

LOFTING IRON
$100	$160	$275

Circa 1895. Smooth face lofting iron. Marked "Hiatt's Mild Steel".

SMOOTH-FACE CLEEK
$120	$200	$325

Circa 1895. Long face. Stamped "Hiatt's Mild Steel."

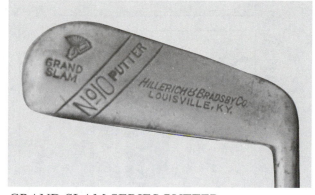

GRAND SLAM SERIES PUTTER
$30	$40	$80

Circa 1920s. "Hand Holding Playing Cards" mark.

BRASS HEAD PUTTERS
$100	$175	$275

Circa 1895. Smooth face blade. "Hiatt" stamped on back.

GENERAL PURPOSE IRON
$100	$175	$300

Circa 1895. Stamped "Hiatt's Mild Steel."

RUT NIBLICK
$400	$600	$1,200

Circa 1895. Small smooth faced head. Marked "Hiatt's Mild Steel."

CARDINAL DREADNOUGHT NIBLICK
$80	$170	$250

Circa 1925. Head measures 3 1/2 x 2 5/8 inches. "Bishop's Hat" mark.

DEEP GROOVE IRONS
$90	$175	$275

Circa 1915-1922. All "Stopum" corrugated face irons.

HIATT & CO.
BIRMINGHAM, ENGLAND
Made irons during the mid-1890s. They had at least two marks, one "Hiatt's Mild Steel" in an oval configuration with very tiny lettering, the other with slightly larger lettering. Their irons are very scarce and desirable.

STEEL-HEAD PUTTERS
$80	$150	$225

Circa 1895. Smooth face blade. "Hiatt" stamped on back.

HILLERICH & BRADSBY
LOUISVILLE, KY
Began manufacturing clubs during the mid-1910s. Its early "Invincible" series irons were smooth faced. In 1918, it patented a "Kork" grip for clubs. The "Deck of Cards," "Par-X-L," and "Lo-Skore" markings were the most common on commercial quality clubs during the 1920s.

LO-SKORE SERIES PUTTER
$30	$40	$80

Circa 1920s. Chrome plated head.

INVINCIBLE SERIES PUTTER
$30	$40	$80

Circa 1925-1930. "Chromium" blade.
PHOTO H&B 5

N-9 APPROACHING PUTTER
$40	$50	$90

Circa 1920s. Lofted line scored face.

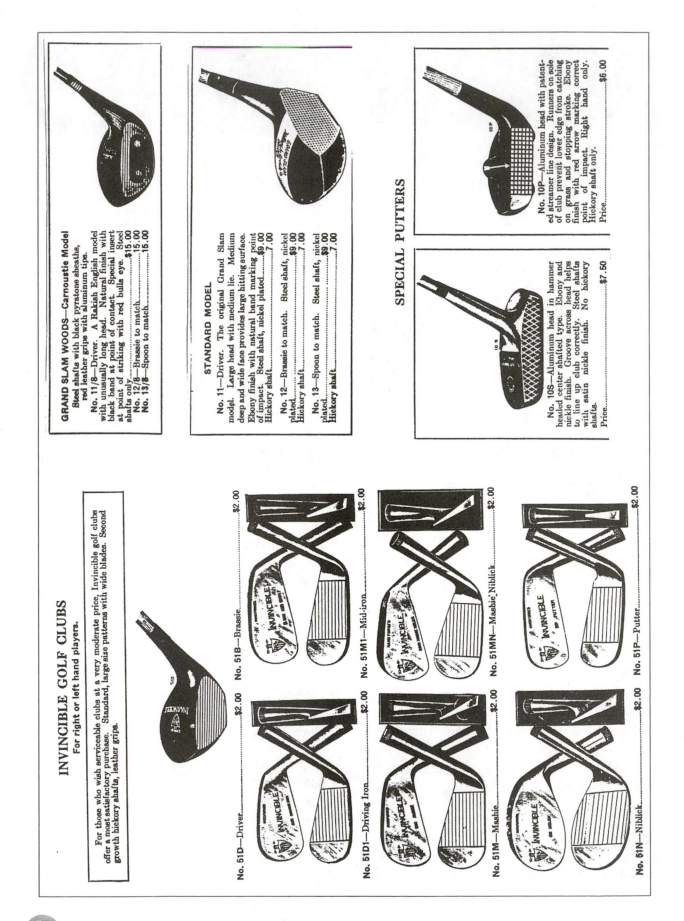

GRAND SLAM WOODS—Carnoustie Model Steel shafts with black pyratone sheaths, red leather grips with aluminum tips.

No. 11/8—Driver. A Rakish English model with unusually long head. Natural finish with black band at point of contact. Special insert at point of striking with red bulls eye. Steel shafts only $15.00
No. 12/8—Brassie to match. 15.00
No. 13/8—Spoon to match. 15.00

STANDARD MODEL

No. 11—Driver. The original Grand Slam model. Large head with medium lie. Medium deep and wide face provides large hitting surface. Ebony finish with natural band marking point of impact. Steel shaft, nickel plated $9.00
Hickory shaft. 7.00
No. 12—Brassie to match. Steel shaft, nickel plated $9.00
Hickory shaft. 7.00
No. 13—Spoon to match. Steel shaft, nickel plated $9.00
Hickory shaft. 7.00

SPECIAL PUTTERS

No. 10S—Aluminum head in hammer headed center shafted type. Ebony and nickle finish. Groove across head helps to line up club correctly. Steel shafts with satin nickle finish. No hickory shafts.
Price. $7.50

No. 10P—Aluminum head with patented streamer line design. Runners on sole of club prevent lower edge from catching on grass and stopping stroke. Ebony finish with red arrow marking correct point of impact. Right hand only. Hickory shaft only.
Price. $6.00

INVINCIBLE GOLF CLUBS
For right or left hand players.

For those who wish serviceable clubs at a very moderate price, Invincible golf clubs offer a most satisfactory purchase. Standard, large size patterns with wide blades. Second growth hickory shafts, leather grips.

No. 51D—Driver. $2.00

No. 51B—Brassie. $2.00

No. 51M1—Mid-iron. $2.00

No. 51MN—Mashie Niblick. $2.00

No. 51D1—Driving Iron. $2.00

No. 51M—Mashie. $2.00

No. 51N—Niblick. $2.00

No. 51P—Putter. $2.00

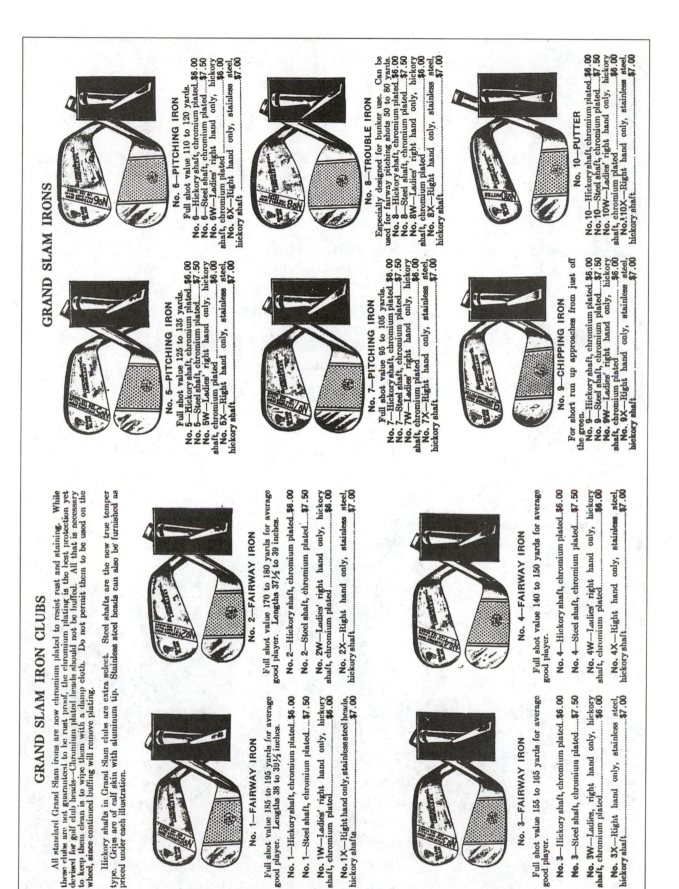

now! I can play in any Foursome

"My score ranged from 110 to 140 before I began to use Grand Slam golf clubs and it was impossible for me to arrive at any fair handicap because of this wide variance in my score. Now that I am playing balanced and graded clubs I have bettered my game materially and I can tell about what my score will be and arrange a handicap so that I am welcome in any foursome."

GRAND SLAM GOLF CLUBS

This, substantially, is the experience of many golfers who have put their game for the first time on a sound and consistent basis with the help of Grand Slams. If you have trouble getting proper distance; if you "choke" or "under-club", causing "pulling","slicing" or "topping"; if you find it hard to keep an easy, uniform swing—try playing with a set of Grand Slams, *just once.* Because the weight and balance of these clubs are scientifically accurate, they all "feel" alike; each one is graded for a certain distance, and is played the same way. The result is a standardized game, correction of your faults, improved scores, and *happier golf.*

The Grand Slam line affords a complete assortment of woods, regular and special faces, at $7.00 to $12.50, with steel and hickory shafts; six fairway irons, two trouble irons and four putters. Irons are $5.00 each; $2.00 additional with steel shaft.

Go to your dealer's and let him demonstrate these great clubs. Or write direct for our catalog "Happier Golf."

HILLERICH & BRADSBY COMPANY, *Incorporated*
468 Finzer Street,   Louisville, Kentucky.
Makers of world-standard Louisville Slugger Baseball Bats.

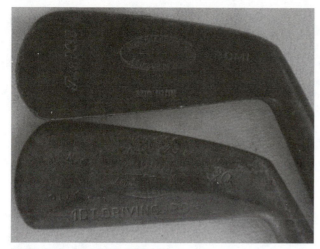

PAR-X-L SERIES IRONS
$30   **$40**   **$80**
Circa 1920s. All irons.

KERNEL SERIES IRONS
$40   **$50**   **$80**
Circa 1920s. Flanged back.

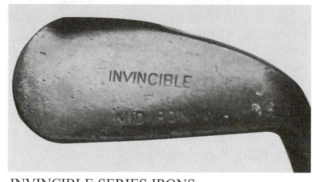

INVINCIBLE SERIES IRONS
$35   **$55**   **$100**
Circa 1915. All irons. Dot "Ball" face.

KERNEL SERIES JIGGER
$30   **$40**   **$100**

HAND MADE IRONS
$40   **$55**   **$95**
Circa 1920. "Stag-dot" face scoring. "Hand Made" and "H & B Monogram" marks.

ALUMINUM-HEAD PUTTER
$60   **$100**   **$170**
Circa 1920s. "H & B Model H 50."

SCHENECTADY PUTTER
$120   **$200**   **$350**
Circa 1920. Cork grip. "Par-X-L" mark.

GRAND SLAM SERIES IRONS
$30   **$40**   **$80**
Circa 1920s. All irons 2 through 9. "Deck of Cards" mark.

APPROACHING CLEEK
$40   **$60**   **$100**
Circa 1915-1920. "Mussel" back. "Dot-Hyphen" face scoring.

DIAMOND BACK IRONS
$40   **$60**   **$95**
Circa 1920. "Stag-dot" face scoring. "Hand Made" and "H & B Monogram" marks.

GRAND SLAM SERIES IRONS
$40   **$55**   **$95**
Circa 1920s. #1 driving iron with the "Deck of Cards" mark.

INVINCIBLE SERIES IRONS
$40   **$55**   **$95**
Circa 1915. All irons. Smooth face.

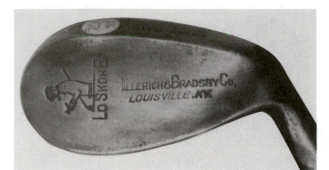

LO-SKORE SERIES IRONS

$30   40   80

Circa 1920. All irons.

CORK GRIP IRONS

$50 $70 $120

Circa 1915. All irons. Patented 1914. "Hand Made" in circle mark.

DEEP GROOVE IRONS

$80 $130 $225

Circa 1915-1922. All irons with corrugated face. Marked "Baxpin."

DEEP GROOVE IRONS

$90 $160 $250

Circa 1915-1922. All irons with slot grooves.

DEEP GROOVE IRONS

$110 $160 $250

Circa 1920. All Everbrite Monel metal slot groove.

SLOTTED HOSEL JIGGER

$120   180   275

Circa 1920s. "S-C2 Jigger." Stag-dot face scoring. "Hand Made" mark.

INVINCIBLE SERIES WOODS

$60 $90 $150

Circa 1920. Driver, brassie, or spoon.

LO-SKORE SERIES WOODS

$60 $90 $150

Circa 1920s. Driver, brassie, or spoon.

PAR-X-L SERIES WOODS

$65 $90 $150

Circa 1920s. Driver, brassie, or spoon.

NON-RUSTABLE BLADE PUTTER

$150 $200 $300

Circa 1895-1900. Smooth faced blade.

JUVENILE CLUBS

$25 $35 $65

Circa 1920. Putter, mid-iron, or mashie.

JUVENILE CLUBS

$50 $70 $120

Circa 1920. Juvenile wood.

HORTON, WAVERLY

CHICAGO, IL

Clubmaker from Chicago whose major claim to fame was the patented "Wonder Club" in 1920 with a metal-cased wooden head.

WONDER CLUB

$400 $700 $1,000

Circa 1920. Patented aluminum shell, wood face.

HUNT MFG. CO.

WESTBORO, MA

A turn-of-the-century manufacturer of rustless clubs. The clubs were a Nickel alloy and had a greenish coloring. "Hunt" in script was their mark. All Hunt-marked clubs are highly desirable to collectors.

Illustrated by Sharri Lou Casey

A hacker named Shivas MacTashy
Stepped up to the tee with his mashie.
He hit in the creek,
His ball he would seek,
But a shot out of there would be splashy.
By Edwin De Bell

Illustrated by Sharri Lou Casey

When Gwyned got hold of his sammy
His fingers began to get clammy.
Now he probably thinks
That the club is a jinx
Is that what they mean by a "Whammy?"
By Edwin De Bell

NON-RUSTABLE IRONS
$100   **$150**   **$250**
Circa 1895-1900. All irons. Smooth face.

HUNTER, CHARLES
PRESTWICK
Professional and clubmaker at Prestwick from 1868 to 1921. His clubs were marked "C. Hunter."

OFFSET BLADE PUTTER
$50   **$70**   **$110**
Circa 1915-1920. Hyphen scored face. Stamped "C & J Hunter, Prestwick."

DOT-FACE BLADE PUTTER
$50   **$70**   **$110**
Circa 1910-1915. Offset hosel. Stamped "C & J Hunter, Prestwick."

LONG-NOSE PUTTERS
$700   **$1,500**   **$2,500**
Circa 1885-1895. Transitional beech head. Marked "C Hunter."

LONG-NOSE PUTTERS
$1,000   **$2,000**   **$4,500**
Circa 1870-1880. Beech-head shallow-face putter. Stamped "C. Hunter."

HUTCHISON, JAMES H
NORTH BERWICK, SCOTLAND
Hutchison began his club making during the early 1880s in North Berwick and continued until about 1912. His clubs were well-made and popular among the better players of his era.

LONG NOSE PUTTER
$900   **$1,800**   **$3,750**
Dark stained Beech head Circa 1885-1895.

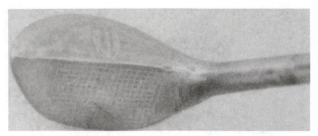

ALUMINUM-HEAD NIBLICK
$300 $550 $1,000
Circa 1915-1920. Marked "Imperial Golf Co, Sunderland, England."

PENDULUM PUTTER
$300 $500 $750
Circa 1920s. Center shafted. Hatched face scoring.

LONG NOSE WOODS
$1,500 $2,500 $5,500
Beech heads circa1885-1895.

BRASS HEAD BLADE PUTTER
$135 $175 $290
Circa1890s.

SMOOTH FACE IRONS
$120 $260 $250
Circa1890s.

SOCKET WOODS
$100 $140 $225
Circa1900-1910.

IMPERIAL GOLF
SUNDERLAND, ENGLAND
Made aluminum-head putters and fairway clubs similar to Mill's Standard Golf Co. Most of its clubs were cast during the late 1910s and early 1920s.

DOT-FACE NIBLICK
$60 $90 $150
Circa 1910. "Key" mark.

U MODEL
$90 $150 $250
Circa 1910-1920. Aluminum mallet.

RM MODEL
$130 $190 $275
Circa 1910-1920. Aluminum mallet.

THE VERDEN
$160 $225 $350
Circa 1910-1920. Rounded dome aluminum mallet.

XXX PUTTER
$160 $250 $350
Circa 1915-1920. Long Aluminum mallet. "Ivorine" sight line.

ALUMINUM-HEAD WOODS
$100 $200 $350
Circa 1915-1920. All lofts. Marked "Imperial Golf Co, Sunderland, England."

JOHNSON, FRANK A.
LONDON, ENGLAND
Used a skeleton "Key" as his mark. Made irons from about 1900 through the early 1910s.

PREMIER SPECIAL PUTTER
$55 $80 $150
Circa 1910. Line scored blade. "Key" mark.

SMOOTH-FACE IRONS
$50 $70 $135
Circa 1900-1910. All irons. "Key" mark.

ROYAL SERIES IRONS
$30   **$40**   **$80**
Circa 1920s. All irons. Widely spaced line face scoring.

BALL FACE IRONS
$40   **$65**   **$100**
Circa 1920s. All irons.

KROYDON
NEWARK, NJ

Began making clubs after World War I. The ball-face and the brick-face designs are popular collector clubs. The "Banner" series with the degree of loft on the face is also highly collectible, although not expensive.

SHALLOW-FACE PUTTER
$45   **$55**   **$90**
Circa 1920. Long blade, offset hosel. "Diamond-Dash" face scoring.

BALL FACE PUTTER
$55   **$70**   **$125**
Circa 1920s. "S-7" ball face.

ALUMINUM MALLET PUTTERS
$70   **$110**   **$160**
Circa 1920s. "Kroydon S 31 B Putter."

SCHENECTADY STYLE ALUMINUM
$80   **$150**   **$250**
Circa 1920s Model S-32-A.

SMOOTH-FACE NIBLICK
$100   **$160**   **$275**
Circa 1900-1910. Medium-size head. "Key" mark.

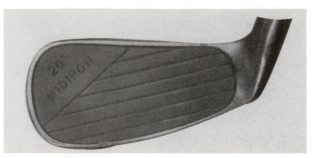

BANNER IRONS

$40   **$60**   **$90**

Circa 1920s. All irons. Name and loft of iron at toe of blade.

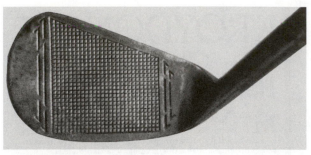

WAFFLE FACE IRON

$75   **$130**   **$190**

Circa 1920s. About 400 tiny waffles on face.

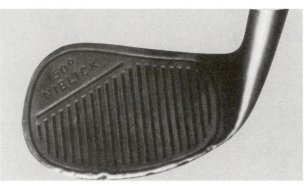

VERTICALLY SCORED NIBLICK

$200   **$300**   **$425**

Circa 1920s. "R 2, 50 Degree Niblick" with vertical deep groove face scoring.

BRICK FACE IRONS

$300   **$500**   **$725**

Circa 1920. All irons.

HEAT-TREATED IRONS

$30   **$40**   **$80**

Circa 1920s. All irons.

P SERIES IRONS

$45   **$60**   **$100**

Circa 1925-1930. All irons. Alternating "Dashes" and tiny "Diamonds" face scoring.

KROYDONITE SOCKET WOODS

$70   **$100**   **$150**

Circa 1920. Driver, brassie, or spoon.

LEE, HARRY C.
NEW YORK, NY

Sporting goods retail business that began about 1900, famous for marketing the "Schenectady" putter. Most domestic clubs were made by Burke and marked with the "Lee" stampings. It also imported clubs from more than a dozen Scottish and English makers including Jack White, Nicholl, Standard Mills, Spence, and Hendry & Bishop.

SOCKET WOODS

$70   **$100**   **$150**

Circa 1920. All woods. Many have aluminum back weights.

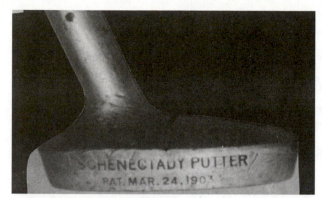

SCHENECTADY PUTTER
$150   **$275**   **$500**
Circa 1903-1915. Patent date "Mar. 24, 1903"
on back.

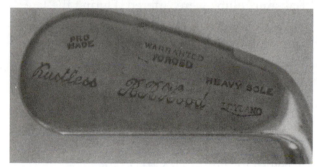

STAINLESS STEEL IRONS
$40   **$50**   **$90**
Circa 1925-1930. "Leyland" mark. Dot
punched face.

DEXTER PUTTER
$35   **$45**   **$80**
Circa 1920s. Offset blade. "Acorn" mark.

DOT-FACE BLADE PUTTER
$35   **$45**   **$80**
Circa 1915. "Acorn" mark.

LINE FACE BLADE PUTTER
$35   **$45**   **$80**
Circa 1920-1925. "Acorn" mark.

DOT FACE NIBLICK
$40   **$50**   **$90**
Circa 1915-1920. "Acorn" mark.

BALL FACE IRONS
$50   **$65**   **$120**
Circa 1910-1915. All irons. Dot ball face scoring. "Acorn" mark.

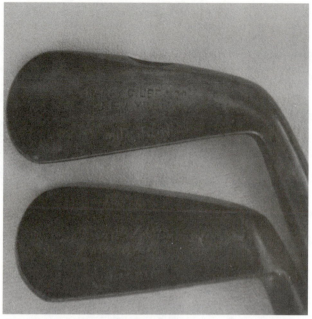

CONCENTRIC BACK IRONS
$35   **$45**   **$80**
Circa 1915. "Harry C Lee Co." mark.

HAND MADE SERIES WOODS
$70   **$100**   **$150**
Circa 1920-1925. Driver, brassie, or spoon.

LEYLAND & BIRMINGHAM RUBBER CO.
Made many "Rustless" clubs during the late
1920s.

BRASS HEAD PUTTERS
$50   **$60**   **$100**
Circa 1925-30. Stamped "L L M B" inside a
"Triangle."

MUSSEL BACK PUTTER
$45   **$55**   **$100**
Circa 1930. "Rustless Putter."

MUSSEL BACK IRONS
$40   **$50**   **$100**
Circa late 1920s. Rustless irons.

STAINLESS STEEL IRONS
$40   **$50**   **$90**
Circa 1925-1930. "Goudie Bear" mark. Dot
punched face.

CHEROKEE PUTTER

$190	$375	$600

Circa 1915. Round aluminum head marked "H Logan's, Cherokee," "T" sight line.

LOCKWOOD & BROWN

LONDON, ENGLAND

Although Lockwood & Brown did not forge its own clubs, it assembled and marked many heads with "Lockwood & Brown, London" in block letters and a monogrammed "LB" mark. It sold clubs from about 1920 through the early 1930s.

SPLICED-NECK PUTTER

$400	$650	$900

Circa 1910. Persimmon head "Gassiat" style with the back squared off. Stamped "Lockwood & Brown, Lt'd., 2 Jermyn St S."

GIANT NIBLICK

$800	$1400	$2200

Circa 1920s. Rustless giant head. Stamped "Lockwood & Brown, Lt'd., 2 Jermyn St S."

SPLICED NECK WOODS

$120	$220	$350

Circa 1910-1920. Driver, brassie, or spoon.

BULL DOG WOOD

$80	$125	$200

Circa 1910. Well lofted wood with "Triangular" black face.

LOGAN, HUGH

Logan was a club designer credited with the famous "Cherokee" aluminum-head putter and the "Genii" model series made by Wm. Gibson.

MACGREGOR

DAYTON, OH

Crawford, MacGregor and Canby began making golf clubs shortly after 1895. Initially it made wood heads until the 1900s, when it hired Willie Dunn to design clubs, including irons and putters. Its first iron-head clubs carried a mark similar to a bow tie with the monogram "W. D." Shortly after Dunn's departure, "J. MacGregor, Dayton, O" was the mark used along with a Condie-type flower mark. About 1910 "Par," "Peerless," and an economy line "Edgemont" were introduced. During the 1910s, "Superior," "Perfection," "Pilot," and "Bakspin" clubs were offered. During the late 1920s, "Duralite," "Superior," and "Nokorode" irons were the top-of-the-line clubs with "Popular," "Edgemont," and "Go-sum" being the economy brands. Other marks were "Airway-o," "Bap," "Claymore," "Paragon," "Premier," "Pro iron," "Rob Roy," "Tomahawk," "Sink-it," "Down-it," and "Worldwin."

DUNN BOW TIE MARK PUTTER

$120	$200	$375

Circa 1900. Smooth face.

DOUBLE CIRCLE MARK PUTTER

$90	$150	$250

Circa 1900. Smooth face with "J MacGregor, Dayton, O" around a "Double Circle" mark with a shamrock inside.

J MACGREGOR SERIES PUTTER

$45	$70	$140

Circa 1900-1905. Smooth face putting cleek.

EDGEMONT SERIES PUTTERS

$40	$60	$100

Circa 1910-1915. Blade putter with a "Diamond" marked face.

"O A" SERIES PUTTER

$45	$60	$120

Circa 1915. With a flanged back.

POPULAR SERIES PUTTER

$30	$40	$90

Circa 1915. "10X" with a hyphen-scored face.

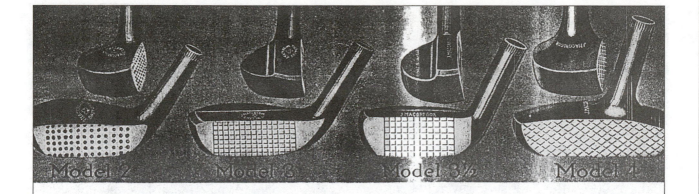

Study your putting

You know—as does every Golfer—that more games are won on the greens than anywhere else.

The man who can putt **always** has his opponent worried. Can **you** putt?

Study your putting—and your putter. Get all there is out of the club—for the club has a lot to do with it. Does your putter fit you? Does it **feel** right? Are you comfortable and natural using it? We call your attention to the

"MACGREGOR"

1919

ROB-ROY SERIES PUTTER
$30 $40 $90
Circa 1920s. Mussel back design.

GO-SUM SERIES PUTTERS
$30 $40 $90
Circa 1915-1920. Blade putter.

PILOT SERIES PUTTERS
$30 $40 $90
Circa 1915. Blade putter.

SUPERIOR SERIES PUTTERS
$30 $40 $90
Circa 1915-1920. Offset blade putter.

PERFECTION SERIES PUTTERS
$40 $50 $90
Circa 1915. Offset blade putter.

RADITE SERIES PUTTER
$40 $50 $100
Circa 1920. Offset blade.

DURALITE SERIES PUTTERS
$40 $50 $90
Circa 1928-1930. Blade putter with the line and "Pyramid" dot face.

CLIMAX-FIFE SERIES PUTTERS
$40 $50 $90
Circa 1915-1920. Dot face straight blade.

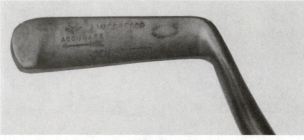

J MACGREGOR SERIES PUTTERS
$150   **$250**   **$400**
Circa 1900. Willie Park style severely bent neck smooth face blade.

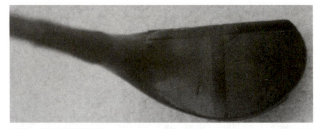

"R A" PUTTER
$190   **$350**   **$550**
Circa 1920. "Right Angle" putter. Persimmon head mallet with a black vulcanite "T-shaped sight line.

BRASS-FLANGED PUTTERS
$55   **$70**   **$140**
Circa 1915. Flanged back brass putter marked "60" or "90."

SEMI-PUTTER
$75   **$120**   **$175**
Circa 1920. Anti-shank type offset hosel.

SCHENECTADY PUTTER
$120   **$200**   **$300**
Circa 1915. With "J MacGregor" markings.

DOWN-IT 486 PUTTER
$190   **$400**   **$625**
Circa 1915-1920. Wooden-head mallet putter. Brass face plate with hatched scoring.

WORLD WIN PUTTER
$190   **$400**   **$625**
Circa 1920. Persimmon wood head, center shafted "Schenectady"-style putter. "Ivorine" sight line on head.

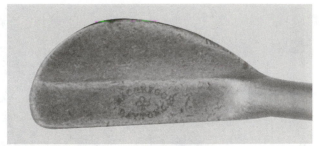

ALUMINUM-HEAD PUTTERS
$65   **$100**   **$190**
Circa 1920s. "MacGregor, Dayton, O."

IVORA PUTTER
$190   **$350**   **$550**
Circa late teens. Brass head with "Ivorine" face insert. Face marked similar to a sun with rays.

J MACGREGOR SERIES IRONS
$40   **$65**   **$110**
Circa 1900-1905. Cleek with normal shafting.

DUNN BOW TIE MARK IRONS
$120   **$200**   **$350**
Circa 1900. smooth face cleek, iron and lofter.

DUNN BOW TIE MARK IRONS
$290   **$475**   **$900**
Circa 1900. Rut niblick.

DOUBLE CIRCLE MARK IRONS
$80   **$140**   **$250**
Circa 1900. Smooth face with "J MacGregor, Dayton, O" around a "Double Circle" mark with a shamrock inside.

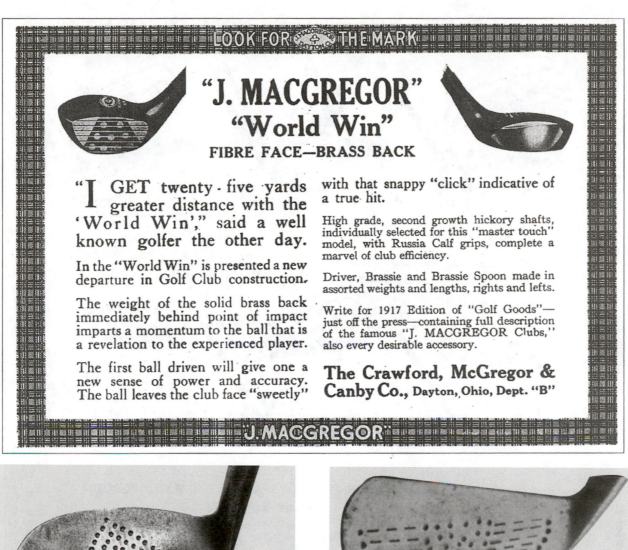

EDGEMONT SERIES IRONS
$50 $70 $140
Circa 1910-1915. "Diamond" face.

RUT NIBLICK
$250 $475 $850
Circa 1900-1905. Round concave face.

J MACGREGOR SERIES IRONS
$60 $90 $190
Circa 1900-1905. Cleek with "Carruthers" through-hosel shafting.

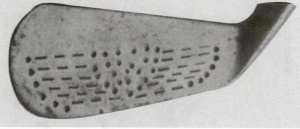

J MACGREGOR SERIES IRONS
$50 $70 $150
Circa 1900-1905. Smooth face iron or lofter.

"O A" SERIES IRONS
$45 $60 $120
Circa 1915. Flanged back.

PEERLESS SERIES IRONS
$30 $40 $80
Circa 1925-1930. Stainless steel heads.

GO-SUM SERIES IRONS
$30 $40 $80
Circa 1915-1925. Hyphen and line scored faces.

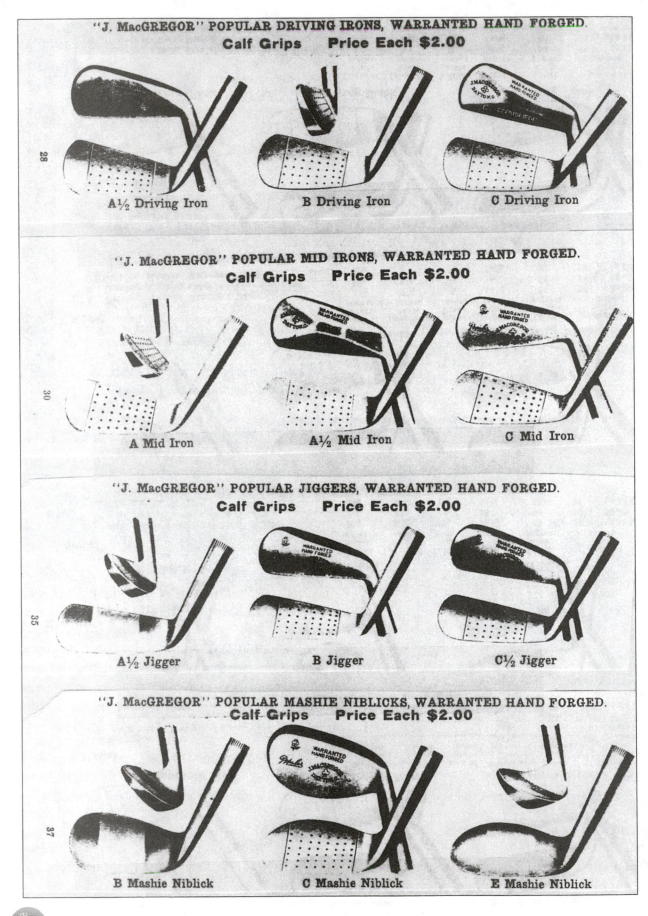

"J. MacGREGOR" POPULAR DRIVING IRONS, WARRANTED HAND FORGED.
Calf Grips   Price Each $2.00

28

A½ Driving Iron   B Driving Iron   C Driving Iron

"J. MacGREGOR" POPULAR MID IRONS, WARRANTED HAND FORGED.
Calf Grips   Price Each $2.00

30

A Mid Iron   A½ Mid Iron   C Mid Iron

"J. MacGREGOR" POPULAR JIGGERS, WARRANTED HAND FORGED.
Calf Grips   Price Each $2.00

35

A½ Jigger   B Jigger   C½ Jigger

"J. MacGREGOR" POPULAR MASHIE NIBLICKS, WARRANTED HAND FORGED.
Calf Grips   Price Each $2.00

37

B Mashie Niblick   C Mashie Niblick   E Mashie Niblick

SUPERIOR SERIES IRONS
$80	$125	$225

Circa 1918-1920. Slotted hosel patented 1918.

PILOT SERIES IRONS
$30	$40	$80

Circa 1912-1920. Various face markings.

CLIMAX-FIFE SERIES IRONS
$35	$45	$90

Circa 1915-1920. "Crown" mark. All irons.

TOMAHAWK BRAND IRONS
$80	$150	$250

Circa 1920. "Shield" marked face.

RADITE SERIES IRONS
$40	$50	$90

Circa 1920-1925. A rustless metal head with line-scored face.

RADITE SERIES IRONS
$80	$135	$250

Circa 1915-1920. Bakspin mashie, mashie-niblick, and niblick.

SUPERIOR SERIES IRONS
$30	$40	$80

Circa 1915-1920. Various face scoring.

POPULAR SERIES IRONS
$30	$40	$80

Circa 1915. Dot scored face. All irons.

POPULAR SERIES IRONS
$60	$75	$125

Circa 1915. "Popular C1/2 Sammy Jigger."

POPULAR SERIES IRONS
$45	$55	$90

Circa 1915.

POPULAR SERIES IRONS
$30	$40	$80

Circa 1915. Mussel back irons.

"G" SERIES IRONS
$60	$110	$175

Circa 1915-1920., "J. MacGregor" stamp "G" with a weighted toe bulge similar to the "Smith" patented anti-shank irons.

PERFECTION SERIES IRONS
$50	$80	$125

Circa 1915-1920. "B-4 Perfection Mashie" with wrap around "Maxwell" holes drilled in the hosel.

DURALITE SERIES IRONS
$30	$40	$80

Circa 1928-1930. Stainless steel heads with Pyramid dots over line scoring. 1 through 6 and 9 niblick.

DURALITE SERIES IRONS
$40	$65	$120

Circa 1928-1930. #7 Pitcher.

DURALITE SERIES IRONS
$100	$150	$250

Circa 1928-1930. #8 Jigger.

AIRWAY-O IRONS
$65	$90	$150

Circa 1925. Concave face, "Goal Post" scoring.

BAKSPIN SERIES IRONS

| $160 | $225 | $400 |

Circa 1915-1920. "Ribangle" face. Corrugated deep grooves with lines at an angle over deep grooves.

BAKSPIN SERIES IRONS

| $90 | $150 | $250 |

Circa 1915-1920. Slot Deep Groove.

BAKSPIN SERIES IRONS

| $150 | $250 | $375 |

Circa 1915-1920. Large dot scoring on only half the face.

PRETTY FACE WOODS

| $90 | $135 | $240 |

Circa 1920s. Small "Ivorine" inserts set around one large center insert.

SPLICED NECK WOODS

| $190 | $300 | $600 |

Circa 1898-1905. Bulger driver with "J MacGregor, Dayton, O" on the persimmon head.

"BAP" SERIES WOODS

| $80 | $100 | $185 |

Circa 1920s. Driver, brassie, or spoon. Patented 1923.

WORLD WIN SERIES WOODS

| $80 | $100 | $185 |

Circa 1920s. Driver, brassie, or spoon.

YARDSMORE SERIES WOODS

| $90 | $130 | $190 |

Circa 1925. Driver, brassie, or spoon with a black face having one large round insert and four small inserts.

Illustrated by Sharri Lou Casey

Lewellyn, a stray golf ball snitcher,
By selling them thought he'd get richer.
'Til a wild driving bloke
Soon gave him a poke
With the non-working end of his pitcher.
By Edwin De Bell

GO-SUM SERIES WOODS

| $70 | $100 | $175 |

Circa 1920s. Plain face.

DREADNOUGHT WOODS

| $90 | $110 | $200 |

Circa 1920s. Oversized heads. Driver, brassie, or spoon.

GO-SUM SERIES WOODS

| $90 | $120 | $200 |

Circa 1920s with pretty face design.

BULL DOG WOODS

| $90 | $120 | $200 |

Circa 1915-1920. Rounded sole. Marked "MacGregor, Dayton, O" and a black face insert.

AUTOGRAPH SERIES IRONS
$45   **$60**   **$95**
Lines or dot face scoring.

EDGEMONT SERIES WOODS
$80   **$125**   **$200**
Circa 1910-1915. Persimmon head driver, brassie, or spoon.

ALUMINUM-HEAD WOODS
$125   **$200**   **$400**
Circa 1915-1925. Various lofts.

SAMPSON FIBER FACE WOODS
$120   **$180**   **$325**
Circa 1915-1920. Driver or brassie.

ONE-PIECE WOOD
$1,250   **$1,850**   **$2,750**
Circa 1900. Driver or brassie one-piece hickory head and shaft. Has a leather face insert.

JUVENILE CLUBS
$30   **$40**   **$90**
Circa 1915. Edgemont putter, mid-iron, or mashie.

JUVENILE CLUBS
$60   **$90**   **$190**
Circa 1915. Edgemont driver.

MARTIN & KIRKALDY
EDINBURGH, SCOTLAND

R.B. Martin and Andrew Kirkaldy formed a partnership in 1908 and began producing clubs in Edinburgh, Scotland. The business was disbanded in the early 1920s.

O'Toole, who played golf with much vigor,
Hit all of his shots with a jigger.
Why most of those dubs
Carried all sorts of clubs
Was something he never could figer.
By Edwin De Bell

EXCELSIOR PUTTER
$75   **$90**   **$140**
Lined face with triangular back design.

ELITE SERIES IRONS
$45   **$60**   **$95**
Lines or dot face scoring.

SOCKET WOODS
$80   **$95**   **$140**
Plain face.

DREADNAUGHT DRIVER
$120   **$150**   **$250**
Kirkaldy autograph model with plain face.

SPLICED-NECK WOODS
$350   **$700**   **$1,650**
Circa 1890-1900. Play club, brassie, or spoon. Bulger face. Many have leather face inserts. Transitional head style. "McEwan" mark.

McEWAN
MUSSELBURGH, SCOTLAND
The "McEwan" name was associated with clubmaking from about 1770 through World War II. The earliest marks were simply "McEwan" and a "Thistle." Subsequent family members used either "McEwan" alone or with their first initial. Clubs made by Douglas II from about 1895 were marked "D. McEwan & Sons" and are the most obtainable in today's marketplace.

BRASS-HEAD PUTTERS
$120   **$225**   **$400**
Circa 1880-1890. "McEwan" in block letters. "Double Ringed" hosel knurling.

IRON-HEAD PUTTER
$120   **$200**   **$375**
Circa 1890-1895. Straight blade. McEwan, Musselburgh mark.

BRASS-HEAD PUTTER
$140   **$200**   **$425**
Circa 1890-1895. Straight blade. McEwan, Musselburgh mark.

LONG-NOSE PUTTERS
$700   **$1,400**   **$3,250**
Circa 1885-1895. Transitional head style. "McEwan" mark.

LONG-NOSE PUTTERS
$1,150   **$2,250**   **$4,500**
Circa 1870-1880. Long head, large lead back weight. "McEwan" mark.

LONG-NOSE WOODS
$1,150   **$2,300**   **$5,500**
Circa 1870-1880. Play club or brassie. Long head, large lead back weight. "McEwan" mark.

LONG-NOSE PUTTERS
$1,500   **$3,250**   **$7,000**
Circa Pre-1860 with Thorn head. Long head, large lead back weight. "McEwan" mark.

SOCKET WOODS
$80   **$120**   **$200**
Circa 1905-1915. Persimmon head driver, brassie, or spoon.

LONG-NOSE WOODS
$1,750   **$3,750**   **$9,250**
Circa Pre-1860 with Thorn head.   Play club or brassie. Long head, large lead back weight. "McEwan" mark.

MILLAR, CHARLES
GLASGOW, SCOTLAND
Charles Millar began forging irons about 1895. He used several types of "Thistle Brand" marks to identify his clubs. He also marked his clubs "Glasgow Golf Co." and "Thistle Golf Co."

OFFSET BLADE PUTTER
$45   **$60**   **$120**
Circa 1915. "Thistle Brand" and "The Glasgow Golf Company" marks.

SMOOTH-FACE BLADE
$50   **$70**   **$135**
Circa 1900-1910. "Thistle" mark.

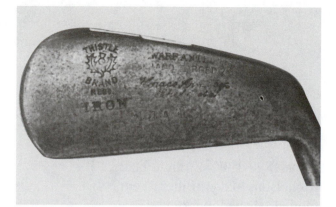

PREMIER BRAND IRONS
$40   **$55**   **$100**
Circa 1915. Dot punched face. "Thistle" mark.

PUTTING CLEEK
$50   **$70**   **$135**
Circa 1900-1910. Smooth face blade. "Thistle" mark.

PREMIER BRAND PUTTERS
$80   **$100**   **$160**
Circa 1920s. Brass blade.

APPROACHING PUTTER
$100   **$140**   **$220**
Circa 1915. Vertical line face scoring. "Thistle" mark.

RUSTLESS IRONS
$40   **$50**   **$90**
Circa 1930-1935. All irons. Dot punched face.

SMOOTH-FACE IRONS
$50   **$70**   **$125**
Circa 1900-1910. All irons. "Thistle-In-Circle" mark.

SMOOTH-FACE IRONS
$60   **$85**   **$175**
Circa 1895-1900. Cleek, iron, or lofter. "C L Millar, Glasgow" mark.

D & T SPINNER
$160   **$250**   **$400**
Circa 1915. All irons. Patent #683488. Concave face, dot scoring on bottom.

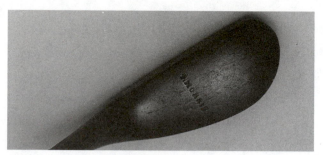

LONG-NOSE PUTTERS
$850   **$2,200**   **$4,500**
Circa 1885-1900. Beech head stamped "T Morris". Transitional head shape.

MORRIS, TOM
ST. ANDREWS, SCOTLAND
Began making clubs in the early 1850s at Prestwick. He opened a shop in St. Andrews in 1864 across the street from the 18th hole and remained there until his death in 1908. The company continued to sell clubs until the Great Depression. His marks were "T. Morris" and "T. Morris, St. Andrews, NB" in oval. After his death "Tom Morris" in script and Old Tom's portrait were used. He purchased many iron heads from Tom Stewart and Robert Condie and added his marks on them. Many of his clubs can be found with shafts marked with "T. Morris, St Andrews, N.B." The "N.B." was for North Britain.

IRON-HEAD PUTTER
$150   **$350**   **$900**
Circa 1890-1900. Smooth face usually made by Condie or Stewart.

SPLICED-NECK PUTTERS
$325   **$700**   **$1,500**
Circa 1905-1920. Long narrow head. Persimmon head.

LONG-NOSE PUTTERS
$1,200   **$3,000**   **$6,500**
Circa 1860-1880. Beech head stamped "T Morris." Long head with large lead back weight.

MORRIS MODEL IRONS
$80   **$140**   **$220**
Circa 1915. All irons. Dot punched face.

PORTRAIT IRONS

$80 **$115** **$190**

Circa 1920s. All irons. Morris' portrait stamped at toe. Most have line-scored face.

LONG-NOSE WOODS

$1,400 **$3,750** **$8,500**

Circa 1885-1900. Play club, brassie, or spoon. Beech head stamped "T Morris." Transitional head shape.

SMOOTH-FACE IRONS

$160 **$300** **$700**

Circa 1890-1905. Cleek, iron, or lofter. "T Morris, St Andrews" with Condie's "Flower" or Stewart's "Pipe" marks.

RUT IRON

$1,150 **$2,500** **$5,750**

Circa 1880. Small round head. "T Morris, St Andrews" mark.

RUT NIBLICK

$275 **$550** **$1,250**

Circa 1890-1905. Smooth face, round head. "T Morris, St Andrews" and Condie's "Flower" or Stewart's "Pipe" marks.

SMOOTH-FACE IRONS

$250 **$500** **$1,200**

Circa 1880-1890. Cleek or general purpose iron. "T Morris, St Andrews" mark.

AUTOGRAPH SERIES WOODS

$100 **$175** **$300**

Circa 1915-1925. Driver, brassie, or spoon. Two-tone head with "Tom Morris" in script.

SMOOTH-FACE BLADE PUTTER

$110 **$150** **$300**

Circa 1890-1900. Straight blade. "T Nicholson, Maker, Pittenweem" football-shaped mark.

SPLICED-NECK WOODS

$225 **$450** **$850**

Circa 1895-1910. Driver, brassie, or spoon. Persimmon head stamped "T Morris."

LONG-NOSE WOODS

$1,950 **$4,500** **$10,000**

Circa 1860-1880. Play club, brassie, or spoon. Beech or Thorn head stamped "T Morris." Long head with large lead back weight.

NICHOLSON, T.

PITTENWEEM, SCOTLAND

Tom Nicholson began forging irons in the old cleekmaker's style during the mid 1880s. Prior to winning the Gold Medal at the 1890 Edinburgh Exposition, he marked his clubs "T Nicholson, Pittenweem" in very tiny lettering. Most of these had the markings "emoried" away and are mistaken for much earlier forgings. After 1890 he used two oval marks on each club; one with "T Nicholson, Maker, Pittenweem," the other "Gold Medal Exposition, Edinburgh, 1890."

GOLD MEDAL IRONS

$75 **$110** **$250**

Circa 1890-1900. All irons.

GOLD MEDAL CLEEK

$85 **$135** **$300**

Circa 1890-1900. Smooth-face cleek.

SMOOTH-FACE IRONS

$110 **$160** **$325**

Circa 1886-1890. All irons. "T Nicholson, Maker, Pittenweem" in tiny letters.

Nicoll 'O' Leven.

By Roger Hill

Most collectors of antique golf clubs have probably come across an old club bearing the friendly upturned hand that is the cleekmark identifying a George Nicoll club. However, beyond initial identification, the collector has little to go on because much of the history of the George Nicoll Company of Leven, Fife, Scotland, remains a mystery.

Beginning in the 1920s, Nicoll clubs became popular in the U.S., with both professionals and amateurs. In this market, Nicoll sold clubs directly to professionals and golf retailers. In addition, Nicoll iron heads were shafted and sold widely by the Burke Company of Ohio as well as by the Link-Lyon Company of Nashville, Tenn. Most of these import clubs can be identified by the hand mark in the horizontal position on the back of the club, although there are exceptions. Many Nicoll clubs, mostly dating from the '20s, are available to collectors in the U.S. today. When considering a Nicoll club made before the "Golden Age," the ambitious collector should be aware of what is known about this successful club maker's history.

The story of "Nicoll 'O' Leven" begins with blacksmith and bicycle-maker George Nicoll, who began to forge iron clubs in 1881. Nicoll was a large, strong man of gentle demeanor, a "hawky" character (a local Scots word meaning very astute and careful), according to his granddaughter. The cleeks, lofters, and rut irons he made during these early years were of high quality and were the foundation for the company's excellent reputation for the next hundred years. Nicoll's famous leather-faced cleek of 1892 and the gutta percha-faced cleek that followed in 1893 are the prime and most-prized examples of this fine cleekmaker's early work. Nicoll's other patent of this period was the 1895 bent neck putter, with the hosel bent backward, toward the shaft.

Nicoll's manufacture of iron heads before 1895 has been brought into question by golf historian Aleck Watt. Citing his family's close relationship with the well-known Auchterlonie club-making family of St. Andrews and his conversations with both Laurie and Eric Auchterlonie, Watt reports that Tom Stewart made Nicoll's iron heads until 1895. Although Stewart started his own shop in 1895, he could have forged heads at Forgan's factory where he apprenticed prior to starting on his own. This idea could be supported by readily available evidence that many major cleekmakers bought and sold iron and wood heads from each other. For example, Tom Morris bought many heads from the Tom Stewart firm; many Morris clubs display both the Morris and Stewart cleekmarks.

Watt also recounts that prior to 1895, Nicoll made only wood clubs. Golf historian Pete Georgiady disputes this claim, citing his contacts with the same sources. The fact that George Nicoll was a blacksmith by trade might suggest his manufacture of iron heads rather than wood; the lack of evidence of wood clubs attributable to Nicoll prior to the mid-1920s would seem to confirm his status as a cleekmaker only.

Early Nicoll smooth-faced irons can be identified by either a circular "G. Nicoll Leven" mark or a later, oval mark of the same legend. These high quality irons, in a wide variety of shapes and weighting patterns, are expensive and scarce collectibles today. Nicoll's early "The F.G. Tait Cleek" is a prize from this clubmaker's early years.

As Nicoll 'O' Leven entered the 20th century and smooth-faced irons began to disappear in favor of face marked irons, Nicoll introduced Zenith Irons, considered to be the company's top of the line professional irons. Nicoll continued to experiment with head shapes and weighting patterns introducing the toe-weighted Able Iron, the heel-weighted Sure Iron and the rounded (concentric) back Clinker iron. In the early 20th century, Nicoll's most lasting original design was the famed Gem putter, copied by most other makers for the next 50 years.

As was the fashion in Great Britain at the time, Nicoll made anti-shank irons and putters in both the Smith's and Fairlie patterns. By 1926, Robert Nicoll, George's son, called a "proper gentleman" and "a lover of the game of golf" by a former employee, had assumed control of the company. However, George Nicoll was still actively involved and introduced Indicator irons, the first iron clubs produced as a matched set. Also at about that time, Robert Nicoll moved the company into the manufacture of socket wood clubs.

Like most cleekmakers of the late 19th century, George Nicoll chose a "cleekmark" or trademark to identify his clubs. Sometime in the late 1890s, Nicoll chose the upturned hand as his mark. Later company records refer to the upturned, palm forward hand mark, which exists in 10 or more major designs as the "hand of friendship." One also has to assume the hand mark's connection with hand forging as well.

Great debate exists among collectors as to the chronology of these hand marks. While there is little debate about the fact that Nicoll's first two early hand marks (crude outlines) date from the period of 1898 to about 1905, it seems as if there is a middle period, roughly 1905-1920, where five or six distinct variations of the hand are noted. After about 1925, only two or three new hand marks appear. It seems that nine or 10 hand marks comprise the major designs.

Collectors often claim the existence of many more hand marks. It is likely that subtle variations in the designs were caused by the constant wearing of dies (stamps) and by the remaking of stamps. It is said that two broth-ers, the Nicholsons, were responsible for stamping Nicoll iron clubs. One brother was responsible for the face, the other brother responsible for the back markings. Therefore, it is likely that many of the variations of the hand mark were created by these brothers. It is possible that changes were made when new stamps were ordered to replace worn stamps. Or perhaps the company made a conscious decision to change the mark, possibly as a marketing scheme.

Other explanations for the many variations in the hand cleekmark design have been offered. The practice of emorying clubs makes stampings difficult to distinguish from each other. There is also the possibility that the use of apprentices in the club making operation may have had an impact on the design and use of stampings and their variations. In any case, Robert Nicoll registered the hand as a trademark in 1922, but claimed continuous use back to 1898.

To complicate identification, the George Nicoll signature, found on many clubs, is of little use in determining the age of a club. At least eight variations of the signature exist, all but one only slightly different from each other. There appears to be loose correlation between the use of specific hand marks and particular signatures.

During its first 50 years, many golf professionals' names appeared on the backs of Nicoll clubs Among them were F.G. Tait, James Braid, Tommy Armour and MacDonald Smith. Because of the absence of company records, it is unclear whether a formal business relationship existed between the company and these individuals. Several Nicoll clubs were in Bobby Jones' bag during his Grand-Slam year. Many famous club professionals, such as the Bradbeers, had irons especially made by Nicoll with their names centrally positioned on the back of their clubs. As was the practice at the time, many club professionals had Nicoll make irons without a

Nicoll name stamp, leaving space for their personal stamp.

After the introduction of steel shafts in 1929, a new era began in club design and three Nicoll models that would become justly famous were introduced. The Wizard, the Pinseeker, and Pinsplitter models became instantly popular with amateurs and professionals alike. While the company ceased production at the outbreak of the Second World War, Nicoll resumed production in 1946 and continued for almost another 40 years. During the 1950s, Nicoll's association with Champion Henry Cotton became paramount. Cotton designed several successful Nicoll models while working as the company's "contract player."

Under the guidance of Robert Nicoll's son-in-law, the company prospered until the early 1980s — a one hundred year run, always under the guidance of the Nicoll family.

Modern technology, marketing, and the huge growth of American sporting goods conglomerates, as well as the growth of larger British golf companies, finally overtook the company, which closed its doors in 1983.

One further note for collectors: Nicoll continued to make putters and possibly other special clubs with wood shafts, made in the old style, until its demise in 1983. I have seen a late giant niblick with a Nicoll mark and own several Gem and White Heather putters, which can be documented as1960s purchases. Most of the putters have wrapped leather grips with a plastic end cap secured by a screw. All of these later clubs have the last Nicoll hand mark and signature mark (known as the "sickle mark") which seem to date as early as the 1930s, and were used until the company's last days, further confusing accurate club dating. Any Nicoll club with these marks must be carefully considered before purchasing.

NICOLL, GEORGE
LEVEN, SCOTLAND

A Partial Chronology of Nicoll Club Models
This list is not exhaustive; as soon as one claims to have seen all of the
models, another new variety appears.
1881-1890: Large smooth-faced irons and putters with the circular mark and no hand.
1890-1905: Oval mark until 1898, then small crude hand. Patent leather face, Patent gutta face, smaller smooth-faced irons, Patent bent neck putter, irons for the Forth Rubber Company, Tait Cleek.
1905-1919: The black, smooth leather grip becomes standard Zenith, Clinker, Excelsior, Trusty Putter, Nap, Gem putter.
Early 1920s: Stop-um, Viking, Park's Original Bent Neck putter, CrackerJack, Able, Sure, Braid, Whippett, Recorder, Indicator, Sans Souci, Precision.
Late 1920s, early 1930s: Wizard Akurazy, MacDonald Smith, Plaklub, The Gray, Bigshooter, Big Ball, Compactum Blade.

APPROACHING PUTTER

$65	$90	$150

Circa 1890-1898. Without the "Hand" mark. Smooth face straight blade.

WILLIE PARK PUTTER

$150	$250	$375

Circa 1920. Severely bent neck stamped "Willie Park's Original Bent Neck Putter."

INDICATOR SERIES PUTTER

$40	$50	$100

Circa 1925-1930. Straight blade, line scored face. "Hand" mark.

WHIPPET PUTTER

$40	$55	$110

Circa 1910s. Long narrow head, dot-punched face. "Hand" mark.

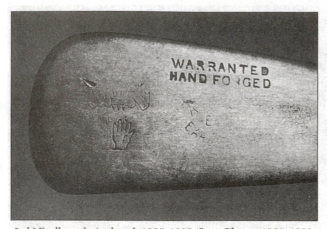

3rd Nicoll mark, 1st hand, 1898-1905. Scott Plume, 1902-1908.

5th Nicoll mark, 1910-1920.

4th Nicoll mark, 1900-1915. v.1.

6th Nicoll mark (or variation of 5th) 1910-1020.

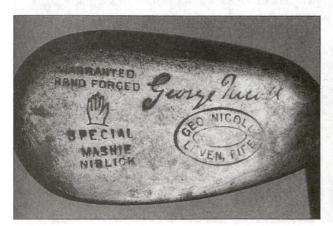

4th Nicoll mark, 1900-1915. v.2.

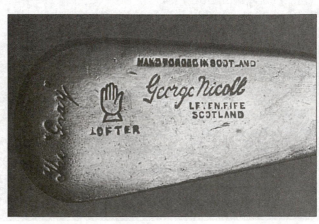

7th Nicoll mark, 1910-1920.

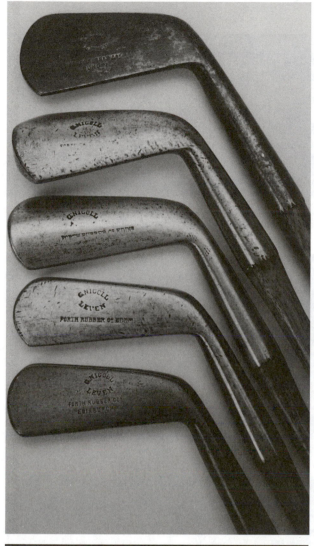

MAC SMITH SERIES IRONS
$45   **$55**   **$100**
Circa 1920s. "Duplicate of Mac Smith's" with "Hand" mark.

PRE-1898 IRONS
$90   **$125**   **$325**
Circa 1895. "G Nicoll, Leven" in block letters. Many made for "Forth Rubber Company, Dundee."

ABLE IRONS
$40   **$65**   **$145**
Circa 1910. Irons with "Geo. Nicoll, Leven Fife" mark and early "Hand" mark.

TAIT SIGNATURE IRONS
$55   **$80**   **$150**
Circa 1915, "Freddie Tait" in script.

AGLAIA PUTTER
$40   **$55**   **$110**
Circa 1920. Putting cleek. "Hand" mark.

GEM PUTTER
$45   **$80**   **$145**
Circa 1930-1935. Rustless rounded back, off-set hosel, line scored face. "Hand" mark.

PRECISION PUTTER
$50   **$90**   **$175**
Circa 1915. Flanged back and dot punched face. "Hand" mark.

NAP PUTTER
$50   **$60**   **$125**
Circa 1920. Offset hosel, line scored face. "Hand" mark.

PREMIER PUTTER
$90   **$125**   **$220**
Circa 1915. Wide sole similar to the Auchterlonie holing out putter.

PRE-1898 IRONS
$110   **$175**   **$350**
Circa 1890. Cleek with "G Nicoll, Leven Fife" mark.

ZENITH SERIES IRONS
$45   **$55**   **$100**
Circa 1925-1930. 1 through 9 irons. "Hand" mark.

PIN SPLITTER SERIES IRONS
$45   **$55**   **$100**
Circa 1925-1930. 1 through 9 irons with flanged backs.

8th Nicoll mark 1910-1920.

9th Nicoll mark, worn into the "6 finger" mark. Hand is worn down-spaces between fingers become fingers 1925-1930.

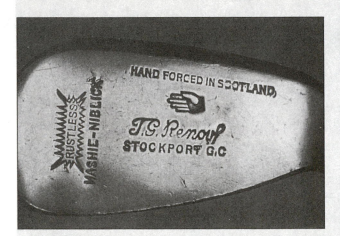

9th Nicoll mark, 1920s. v.1.

10th Nicoll mark, 1925-1930. v.1.

10th Nicoll mark, 1925-1983. v.2.

9th Nicoll mark, 1910s. v.2 or worn v.1.

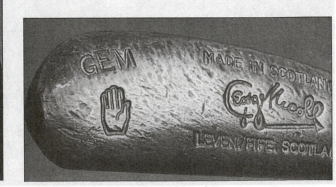

10th Nicoll mark, 1925-1983. v.3.

INDICATOR SERIES IRONS
$45   **$55**   **$100**
Circa 1925-1930. 1 through 9 irons.
Line-scored or dot face. "Hand" mark.

LEATHER-FACE IRON
$1,000   **$1,800**   **$3,450**
Patented 1892. Leather face insert. "G Nicoll,
Leven Fife" and Patent numbers.

VIKING SERIES IRONS
$45   **$55**   **$100**
Circa 1925-1930. 1 through 9 irons with large
sailing ship on back.

BRAID SIGNATURE IRONS
$55   **$80**   **$150**
Circa 1915. "James Braid" in script. Many
had flanged backs.

CRACKER JACK SERIES IRONS
$60   **$90**   **$160**
Circa 1925-1930. "Carruthers" through-hosel
shafting. 1 through 9 irons.

SMITH ANTI-SHANK IRONS
$110   **$175**   **$325**
Circa 1915-1925. Heel and toe weighted line
scored face. "Hand" mark.

CORRUGATED DEEP GROOVE IRONS
$110   **$150**   **$300**
Circa 1914-1920. "Zenith Pitcher." "Hand"
mark.

NICOLL SIGNATURE IRONS
$45   **$55**   **$110**
Circa 1915. Dot-punched faces. Driving iron
through niblick.

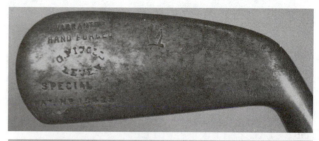

GUTTA-PERCHA FACE IRON
$1,200   **$1,900**   **$3,450**
Patented 1892. Gutta-percha face insert. "G
Nicoll, Leven Fife" and patent numbers.
About twice as rare as the leather face.

ZENITH PRECISION JIGGER
$50   **$80**   **$160**
Circa 1920s. Flanged back.

OKE, W G
FULWELL & LONDON, ENGLAND
William Oke began making clubs in the
mid-1910s and in 1923 registered the "Oak
Brand" trademark of an "Oak Tree."

LONG-HOSEL PUTTER
$125   **$200**   **$350**
Circa 1920s. Blade putter with seven-inch
pencil-thin hosel. "Oak Brand Registered"
mark.

DEEP-FACE MASHIE

$50	$70	$150

Circa 1920s. "W G Oke, Fulwell, G C" and the "Oak Brand Registered" mark.

DOT-PUNCHED IRONS

$50	$70	$135

Circa 1910. All irons.

SPECIAL PATENT PUTTER

$150	$200	$375

Circa 1900. Severely bent neck, smooth face blade.

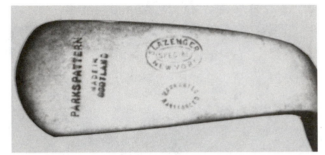

PARK'S PATTERN PUTTER

$175	$225	$350

Circa 1900. Severely bent neck, smooth face blade. Made for Slazengers.

SMOOTH-FACE BLADE PUTTER

$120	$175	$375

Circa 1890-1900. "Wm Park, Musselburgh, Maker" oval mark.

BRASS-HEAD PUTTERS

$140	$225	$450

Circa 1890-1900. Straight blade. "Wm Park, Musselburgh, Maker" oval mark.

PATENTED BENT NECK PUTTER

$200	$325	$700

Circa 1895-1900. Severely bent neck. "Wm Park, Musselburgh, Maker" oval mark.

LONG-NOSE PUTTER

$700	$1,350	$3,200

Circa 1895-1900. Transitional beech head. "Wm Park" mark.

LONG-NOSE PUTTER

$1,250	$2,500	$4,950

Circa 1885-1895. Long head, large lead weight. "Wm Park" mark.

DOT-FACE IRONS

$75	$135	$300

Circa 1910-1915. All irons. "Wm Park, Maker, Musselburgh" mark.

DIAMOND-BACK IRONS

$85	$145	$350

Circa 1910. All irons. Smooth face.

SMOOTH FACE IRONS

$135	$225	$475

Circa 1890-1900. All irons. "Wm Park, Maker, Musselburgh" mark.

PATENTED DRIVING CLEEK

$225	$400	$800

Circa 1895-1905. Smooth face compact head. "W. Park's Patent Driving Cleek" mark.

RUT NIBLICK

$300	$450	$1,250

Circa 1900-1910. Smooth face head. "Wm Park, Maker, Musselburgh" mark.

PARK, WILLIE
MUSSELBURGH, SCOTLAND

By Pete Georgiady

Undoubtedly the most versatile of all the great golfers of the 19th century was William Park Jr. Young Willie, as he was known during his lifetime, used his golfing knowledge and skills to be a champion golfer, author, course designer, real estate developer, club and ball designer and, yes, even a clubmaker, before he saw his 40th birthday.

Born in Musselburgh in 1864, his father, "Auld" Willie, had already won two Open Championships before Junior could even walk. Literally born into the golf business, Young Willie had little choice but to follow in the footsteps of his father and uncles.

His first assignment, arranged by his Uncle Mungo (himself champion in 1874), was to lay out the course and serve as professional to the golf club at Ryton, Northumberland. While there he started entering professional competitions, winning his first at age 17.

Returning to Musselburgh in 1884, he took control of his father's firm, making his first splash in the business: inventing the bulger driver in 1885 and using it in the 1885 Open. Some years later, he was challenged by Sir Henry Lamb, the prominent amateur, who also claimed to have invented the bulger in the same time frame. Through some lengthy written communications, the pair established they had both devised similar clubs concurrently without knowing that the other was involved in the endeavor. Because Willie was a clubmaker and professional continually in the public eye, he had received most of the popular acclaim for the bulger.

Over the next 10 years, Willie was the best known clubmaker in the business. His Open victories in 1887 and 1889 set the stage for the introduction of four new clubs of his invention. He received much acclaim when he brought a new lofter to market. The club was at the forefront of a new development in the game—high approaching shots—and Willie created even more attention when he received a patent for his new implement in 1889.

The Patent Lofter was followed by the Patent Driving Cleek in 1891, the Patent Compressed Driver in 1893, and the most famous club of all, the Park Patent Bent Neck Putter in 1894. His success on the links, as well as in the design, caused his business to swell and he was acknowledged to be the second-largest manufacturer of golf clubs, behind the firm of Robert Forgan. In later years, he brought out a patent groove soled brassie called the Pik-up and a patent step-faced lofter for imparting backspin.

His patent clubs are easily recognizable because they all are marked as such. He did make many other regular clubs with three types of name stamps. The vast majority of these clubs are smooth faced and it is very difficult to date them accurately since they have minimal markings and were all made in the old style, even after the firm entered the 20th century. Since Park stamped his name on the shafts of all his clubs, many are still identifiable, even if the club head markings are illegible.

The range of Park clubs available today is broad and deep. Small-headed niblicks, gun-metal-blade putters, Smith model irons, large-hosel lofters, and short-bladed mashie irons are among the more unusual clubs from his output. Some can be found in ladies' and children's models, as he was one of the first to cater to that growing segment of the market in the 1890s. Park's premium grade clubs are distinguished by his use of greenheart, purpleheart, lemonheart, or lacewood for the shafts.

Willie gradually lost interest in clubmaking and the retail business after 1910, concentrating instead in course layout. He spent a considerable amount of time in the United States and Canada, first setting up a retail outlet in New York City, and then course design offices in New York and Toronto.

He was a principal in the first modern residential-resort golf community at Huntercombe in Oxfordshire, although the lack of rail access did not encourage its success. In 1896, Willie Park's *The Game of Golf* became the first published golf instruction book written by a professional. He followed up with *The Art of Putting*, a book that discussed the skill that made him most famous. It was Willie Park who said, "The man who can putt is a match for any man." Not only was Willie a deft putter, he was the man to beat in club design, retailing, and merchandising.

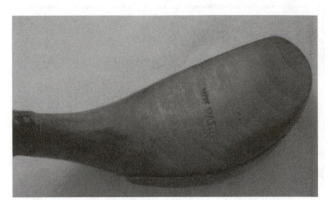

LONG-NOSE WOODS
$800   **$1,750**   **$4,250**
Circa 1895-1900. Driver, brassie, or spoon. Transitional beech head. "Wm Park" mark.

COMPRESSED-HEAD WOOD
$300   **$550**   **$1,300**
Circa 1895-1900. Spliced neck. Driver, brassie, or spoon. Spoon with "Park's Compressed Patent."

RUT IRON
$700   **$1,100**   **$2,700**
Circa 1885-1895. Small smooth face head. "Wm Park, Maker, Musselburgh" mark.

PARK PATENTED LOFTER
$300   **$500**   **$1,000**
Circa 1890-1895. Concave face.

BULL DOG WOOD
$135   **$225**   **$550**
Circa 1905-1915. Rounded sole, black triangular face insert.

SOCKET WOODS
$135   **$225**   **$525**
Circa 1905-1915. Driver, brassie, or spoon. "Wm Park" mark.

PICK-UP PATENT WOOD
$250   **$400**   **$800**
Circa 1910. Metal sole with four runners. Well lofted head.

BULGER-FACE WOODS
$400   **$650**   **$1,650**
Circa 1890-1900. Driver, brassie, or spoon. "Wm Park" mark.

TWISTED-HOSEL PUTTER
$70   **$100**   **$220**
Circa 1920. "Well-Made" horseshoe mark.

LONG-NOSED WOODS
$550   **$1,000**   **$2,500**
Circa 1885-1895. transitional head style. "A Patrick" mark.

PATRICK, ALEX

LEVEN, FIFE, SCOTLAND

The Patrick family produced clubs from the late 1840s through the 1930s. On their wooden-head clubs, the mark "A. Patrick" in block letters was used. They marked their irons and putters with "A. Patrick, Leven, Est. 1847." Shortly after the turn of the century, they stamped a "Spur" mark on the backs of their irons, and about 1920 introduced the "Well-Made" horseshoe mark.

BRASS-HEAD PUTTERS
$135   **$225**   **$400**
Circa 1890-1895. "A Patrick, Leven" mark.

LONG NOSE PUTTERS
$950   **$1,750**   **$3,750**
Circa 1885-1895. Beech head Driving putter. "A Patrick" in block letters.

HORSESHOE-MARKED IRONS
$45   **$55**   **$100**
Circa 1920s. All irons. "Well-Made" horseshoe mark.

LONG-NOSE WOODS
$1,200   **$2,250**   **$6,000**
Circa 1880-1890. Large lead back weight. "A Patrick" mark.

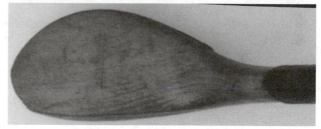

SPLICED-NECK WOODS
$250   **$500**   **$1,200**
Circa 1900. Bulger face. Driver, brassie, or spoon. "A Patrick" stamping.

CONCENTRIC-BACK IRONS
$65   **$90**   **$160**
Circa 1900-1910. Smooth face. "A Patrick, Leven" mark.

SMOOTH-FACE IRONS
$70   **$120**   **$225**
Circa 1895-1900. All irons. "A Patrick, Leven" mark.

SHALLOW-FACE CLEEK
$110   **$175**   **$375**
Circa 1890. Smooth face. "A Patrick, Leven" mark.

ACME WOODS
$90   **$120**   **$220**
Circa 1920s. Driver, brassie, or spoon.

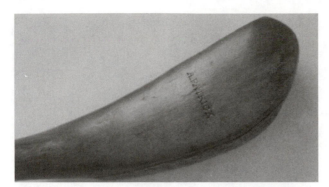

LONG -NOSE WOODS
$1,350   **$2,450**   **$6,000**
Circa 1866-1880. Long head with a large lead back weight. "A Patrick" mark. Neck is more delicate than later woods.

SMOOTH-FACE CLEEK
$300   **$450**   **$950**
Circa 1890. Smooth face. "P Paxton, Eastbourne" mark.

BULL DOG WOOD
$90   **$120**   **$220**
Circa 1910-1915. Rounded sole lofted face. Most have face inserts.

PRETTY FACE WOODS
$90   **$120**   **$220**
Circa 1920. Black face insert.

VICTORY SERIES WOODS
$100   **$150**   **$275**
Circa 1920s. Large-head driver, brassie, or spoon. "Alex Patrick, Leven, Victory" mark.

SPLICED-NECK WOODS
$150   **$225**   **$400**
Circa 1900. Driver, brassie, or spoon. "A Patrick" stamping.

SPLICED-NECK WOODS
$450   **$675**   **$1,550**
Circa 1895. Bulger face. Driver, brassie, or spoon.

LONG-NOSE WOODS
$1,100   **$1,800**   **$4,250**
Circa 1880-1890. Play club, brassie, or spoon. Long head, large lead weight. "P Paxton" stamp.

PAXTON, PETER
EASTBOURNE, ENGLAND
Paxton became an apprentice with Tom Hood at Musselburgh. He began designing and forging clubs in the early 1880s. His reputation for quality as a club and ball maker was superb. He marked his clubs "P Paxton, Eastbourne." He also used a "Crown" mark on transitional style woods.

SMOOTH-FACE LOFTER
$300   **$450**   **$900**
Circa 1890. "P Paxton, Eastbourne" mark.

LONG-NOSE WOODS
$850   **$1,500**   **$3,450**
Circa 1885-1895. Play club, brassie, or spoon. Transitional head. "P Paxton" stamp.

PHILP, HUGH
ST. ANDREWS, SCOTLAND

By Pete Georgiady

With most other golfing notables who lived prior to 1850, very little is recorded on their lives and pursuits. Hugh Philp is no exception. Much of the information existent today comes in the form of reminiscences from 40 or 50 years after his passing.

Philp was born in Cameron, Fife, in 1782, the son of a farmer. As a teen he was apprenticed to a carpenter and subsequently pursued a career as a carpenter and joiner. Philp was never known to have worked with any other clubmaker, and his bent towards that avocation apparently stemmed from his expertise as a carpenter and his love of playing golf. In time, these two skills obtained him an affiliation with the St. Andrews Society (later to be the Royal and Ancient Golf Club), for which he repaired clubs beginning in 1812. The Society had a contract with McEwan's of Edinburgh to supply clubs for its semi-annual meetings, but in 1819 they appointed Philp as their clubmaker, though they did not sever their ties with McEwan until 1827. Also beginning in 1819, Philp served the Scotscraig Golf Club in the town of that name located between St. Andrews and Dundee.

With his new patronage, Philp moved from small quarters outside the town walls to a shop along the links adjacent to the Union Parlor, a popular gathering spot for golfers. Soon afterward, he took up a position in a larger shop in the building that is today the Tom Morris shop. This shop would become a social center for golfers, congregating before and after their matches. Overhead in the shop were racks where his favored patrons could store their clubs between outings. The most remembered portion of his career was the last 11 years, when he hired James Wilson as an assistant in 1845, and Robert Forgan in 1852. Forgan was his nephew and took over the Philp business when his Uncle Hugh died in 1856.

Philp's clubmaking skills have been glorified to superior levels, though several contemporary sources say others like Peter McEwan and Alexander Munro were equally proficient. But his mere presence in the town of St. Andrews and his service to the Royal & Ancient may have decidedly aided this reputation by placing him in what little limelight could shine on such a craftsman. The gentleman and golf writer J.G. McPherson left us a romantic bit of insight, saying that "The late Hugh Philp had polished an apple tree head for a whole afternoon when modern makers would have considered it quite finished."

Late in his life, he used hickory, though he never completely adopted it in making shafts. On chance, he bought a log in the 1850s, wondering if he would ever use it all. His heads were made from apple, thorn, and beech, long and slender, some straight in the face while others were hooked.

His reputation was again enhanced when the original Mills aluminum putters were patterned after some ancient Philp models, whose beauty and utility were still greatly admired 50 years after their heyday.

Historians have also recognized the fact that forgers were prone to producing Philp clubs. As early as the 1860s, forged copies of Philp clubs were known to exist, forgeries for unwitting golfers who sought to use good clubs, not for collectors of a later age who would also covet Philp clubs. This legacy is not held by any other maker.

While he was the maker of superior grade clubs, much of the recognition he earned during his own lifetime came from his play and his association with the scions of the golf community. A player he was; like the cracks of his day, Philp was a supreme strategist, knowing at precisely which hole he should close out his opponent. He came to play infrequently, usually when he deemed the odds were in his favor. But it is also known that he would occasionally play a three ball with youthful Tom Morris and Allan Robertson.

Hugh Philp was a storyteller with a dry vein of humor. He came on in a crusty way, but in time, his inner warmth would shine through. He wore silver spectacles through which he viewed the world with glittering black eyes. In 1859, three years after he passed away, his loss was lamented, "Hugh Philp, how full of bygone pleasant memories of golf land is thy name! Thou didst make clubs for our fathers, and didst mend them for their sons."

LONG-NOSE WOODS
$4,000   **$10,000**   **$27,500**
Circa 1840-1856. "H Philp" in block letters.
Thorn head.

LONG-NOSE BAFFIE SPOON
$5,500   **$14,000**   **$33,000**
Circa 1840-1856. "H Philp" in block letters.
Thorn head.

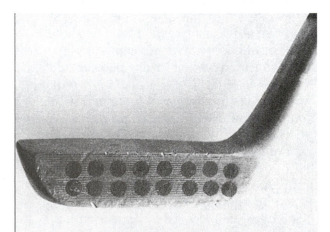

ALUMINUM HEAD PUTTER
$150   **$275**   **$500**
Circa 1910-20 with circular lead weights
across the entire face.

SEVENTY-TWO SERIES IRONS
$40   **$50**   **$75**
Wilson, Chicago with lined face.

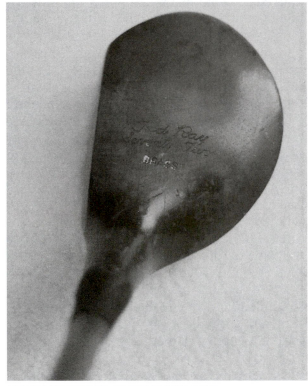

SEVENTY-TWO SERIES WOODS
$75   **$95**   **$145**
Wilson, Chicago with plain face.

LONG-NOSE PUTTERS
$1,900   **$4,500**   **$12,500**
Circa 1840-1856. "H Philp" in block letters.
Thorn head.

RANDALL, JOHN
BROMLEY, KENT, ENGLAND
Randall began making clubs shortly after
1900. He was most famous for his aluminum
head putters with lead weighting in the face.

All series: Superior Grade, Hammer Brand, Warwick, or Eagle with lined or dot scored faces.

RAY, TED (EDWARD)
OXHEY and GANTON, ENGLAND
Ted Ray was a famous English professional. He won the British Open in 1912 and finished second twice. He also won the U.S. Open in 1920 and was in the playoff for the 1913 U.S. Open won by Francis Ouimet. His clubs made in England (Scotland by Tom Morris) have the Oxhey or Ganton stamps. Wilson, Chicago, Ill., also forged the "Ted Ray Seventy-two" line during the 1920s.

GOOSE NECK BLADE PUTTER
| $60 | $75 | $110 |
With dot or lined face. Oxhey or Ganton stamps.

IRONS DOT OR LINE SCORED
| $45 | $55 | $90 |
With Oxhey or Ganton stamps.

SEVENTY-TWO SERIES PUTTER
| $45 | $55 | $85 |
Wilson, Chicago with lined face.

REACH, A J & COMPANY
PHILADELPHIA, PA
Made economy priced clubs sold through its sporting goods stores. It was owned by Spalding and carried many Spalding clubs.

KEYSTONE STAMP PUTTER
| $50. | $65 | $100 |
A J Reach & Co inside a "Keystone" stamp.

A J REACH SOCKET WOODS
| $75 | $90 | $130 |
Plain face woods.

KEYSTONE STAMP IRONS
| $40. | $55 | $90 |
A J Reach & Co inside a "Keystone" stamp.

A J REACH & CO PUTTER
| $40 | $50 | $80 |
All series: Superior Grade, Hammer Brand, Warwick, or Eagle with lined or dot scored faces.

A J REACH & CO IRONS
| $35 | $45 | $75 |

A J REACH DEEP GROOVE
| $90 | $120 | $175 |
Corrugated illegal deep groove face scoring.

KEYSTONE SOCKET WOODS
| $80. | $95 | $140 |
A J Reach & Co inside a "Keystone" stamp.

A J REACH PRETTY FACE WOODS
| $95 | $115 | $160 |
Some with six piece laminated Bamboo shafts.

ALUMINUM-HEAD PUTTER
$175   **$290**   **$500**
Circa 1920. Raised circular aiming circle.
"The Rodwell New Standard Putter #1981"
stamped on the head.

RODWELL, CHARLES
LONDON, ENGLAND
Charles Rodwell began selling clubs about
1905 and marked his clubs "Charles Rodwell,
Lt'd."

IRON-HEAD PUTTER
$80   **$110**   **$220**
Circa 1920. Long, shallow blade. Dot-punched
face.

FLANGED-BACK IRONS
$50   **$65**   **$110**
Circa 1915. All irons.

ANTI-SHANK IRONS
$150   **$200**   **$325**
Circa 1910-1915. All irons. Fairlie's Patent.
Diamond-dot face markings.

ROLLINS & PARKER
REDDICH, ENGLAND
Circa 1910-1930. They used an "EYE"
maker's mark. The firm was basically a whole-
saler of heads to assemblers, who stamped the
clubs with their marks. Very few "Eye"
stamped clubs carry the "Rollins & Parker"
name.

EXCELSIOR SERIES IRONS
$50   **$70**   **$140**
Circa 1915. All irons. Rounded back. "Eye"
mark.

DEEP-GROOVE IRONS
$100   **$160**   **$275**
Circa 1915-1922. All slot groove irons. "Eye"
mark.

MAXWELL HOSEL IRONS
$50   **$70**   **$140**
Circa 1920. Flanged back. "Eye" mark.

DEEP-GROOVE IRONS
$85   **$145**   **$240**
Circa 1915-1922. All corrugated groove irons.
"Eye" mark.

ANTI-SHANK IRONS
$135   **$195**   **$300**
Circa 1920s. All irons. Smith's model. "Eye"
mark.

ROSS, DONALD
BOSTON AND PINEHURST
Donald Ross was one of America's most
prominent golf course designers. Pinehurst is
among his most famous endeavors. He produced clubs from about 1900 through the
1920s. Many of the clubs stamped with his
name were made by Stewart, Spalding,
MacGregor, and Burke. The Donald Ross
Society is a group of golf enthusiasts who collect memorabilia related to the golf courses he
designed, as well as the clubs he produced.

SMOOTH FACE BLADE PUTTER
$110   **$135**   **$220**
Name in oval.

BLADE PUTTER
$90   **$120**   **$190**
Line or dot face, name in large block letters.

SMOOTH FACE IRONS

| $50 | $75 | $150 |

Circa 1907-1910 with "Rustless Sun" mark.

BENNY PUTTER

| $135 | $180 | $325 |

Circa 1930. Sole has 17 grooves. "Ben Sayers" in script.

SMOOTH FACE IRONS

| $100 | $120 | $190 |

Name in oval.

LINE OR DOT SCORED IRONS

| $90 | $115 | $175 |

Large block lettering.

SPLICED NECK WOODS

| $175 | $210 | $325 |

Name in script.

SOCKET HEAD WOODS

| $125 | $160 | $235 |

Name in block lettering.

RUSTLESS GOLF CLUB COMPANY
CHICAGO, ILLINOIS

The "RGCCO" began forging rustless metal heads about 1907 in Chicago. It used a "Sun" mark with a face spelling out "Rustless." Many of its clubs bear the PG Manufacturing "Anvil" mark.

ALUMINUM PUTTER

| $400 | $700 | $1,500 |

Circa 1920. Elongated sight line.

ALUMINUM MALLET PUTTER

| $135 | $225 | $450 |

Mills type with "Rustless Sun" mark.

CARRUTHERS HOSEL IRONS

| $75 | $120 | $225 |

Circa 1907-1910 with "Rustless Sun" mark. Carruther's through hosel shafting.

SAUNDERS, FRED
LONDON, ENGLAND

Fred Saunders first made clubs in Birmingham about 1896, then later moved to London.

SAYERS, BEN,
NORTH BERWICK, SCOTLAND

The Sayers family began their club business about 1890. They used the markings "B Sayers, N. Berwick" and about 1920 used a "Robin" cleek mark.

TARGET IRONS

| $40 | $60 | $100 |

Circa 1920s. All irons. "Target" sweet spot.

MAXWELL HOSEL IRONS

| $50 | $70 | $135 |

Circa 1915. All irons. Flanged back. "Ben Sayers" in script.

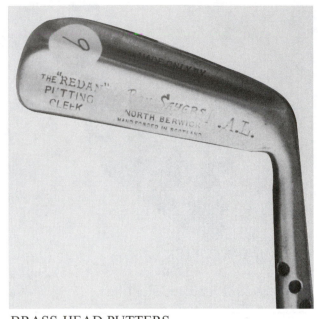

SELECTED SERIES WOODS
$90   **$120**   **$220**
Circa 1920s. All woods.

BRASS-HEAD PUTTERS
$135   **$180**   **$375**
Circa 1890-1900. Smooth face blade. "B Sayers" in block letters.

SMOOTH-FACE IRONS
$65   **$85**   **$175**
Circa 1895-1905. All irons. "Ben Sayers North Berwick" marking.

DEEP-GROOVE IRONS
$110   **$160**   **$275**
Circa 1915-1922. All irons. Corrugated face.

DEEP-GROOVE IRONS
$115   **$165**   **$300**
Circa 1915-1922. All irons. Slot face.

DREADNOUGHT WOODS
$90   **$120**   **$220**
Circa 1915-1920. Large-head driver, brassie, or spoon. "Ben Sayers Dreadnought" stamp.

SPLICED-NECK WOODS
$135   **$200**   **$375**
Circa 1900-1910. All woods.

GRUVSOL PATENT WOODS
$135   **$200**   **$375**
Circa 1920s. All woods. "Gruvsol Patent #244925." Grooves on sole plate.

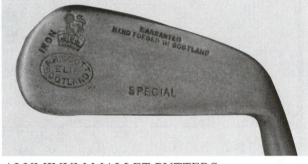

ALUMINUM MALLET PUTTERS
$110   **$160**   **$275**
Circa 1915. "Lion-on-Crown" mark.

SCOTT, A H
EARLSFERRY, ELIE, SCOTLAND
Andrew Herd Scott began forging clubs about 1894. He was clubmaker to Prince Edward and used the "Plume" mark on his clubs during his reign. About 1910, he adopted the "Lion and Crown" mark.

STRAIGHT LINE PUTTER
$90   **$150**   **$250**
Circa 1920s. Step down back design. Patent No 349407. "Lion-on-Crown" mark.

SMOOTH FACE IRONS
$65   **$90**   **$175**
Circa 1895-1905. All irons. "A. H. Scott, Elie, Earlsferry" marking.

LION-ON-CROWN IRONS
$50   **$65**   **$130**
Circa 1915. Smooth face. "A. H. Scott, Elie, Earlsferry" marking.

LION AND CROWN WOODS
$90   **$115**   **$190**
Circa 1915. All woods.

SIMPSON, ARCHIE
CARNOUSTIE, SCOTLAND
Began forging clubs during the mid-1880s. During the 1900s, his clubmaking business became prominent because of the important clientele. He marked his clubs "A Simpson, Carnoustie."

SMOOTH-FACE PUTTER
$50   **$70**   **$130**
Circa 1900. Offset blade. "A Simpson, Aberdeen" mark.

BRASS-BLADE PUTTER
$80   **$110**   **$220**
Circa 1900. "A Simpson, Aberdeen" mark.

DOT-FACE IRONS
$50   **$65**   **$120**
Circa 1915. All irons.

RUT NIBLICK
$190   **$300**   **$675**
Circa 1895-1905. Smooth face. Medium-size rounded head. "A Simpson" mark.

BULGER-FACE WOODS
$175   **$300**   **$700**
Circa 1895-1900. Driver, brassie, or spoon. "A Simpson, Aberdeen" stamp.

FORK SPLICED PATENT WOODS
$325   **$500**   **$900**
Circa 1895-1905. All woods. "A H Scott Patent No 21444." "Plume" mark.

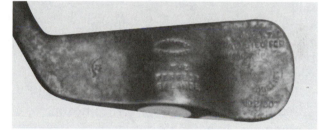

PERFECT BALANCE PUTTER
$250   **$400**   **$750**
Circa 1910. "Patent 21307." Simpson's circular mark. Bulge weight in center.

SIMPSON, R.
CARNOUSTIE, SCOTLAND
Started forging irons about 1890 with the help of his brothers, Jack and Archie. He marked his clubs simply "R. Simpson, Carnoustie." His most famous and highly collectible clubs were the ball-faced irons patented in 1903.

BRASS-HEAD PUTTERS
$90   **$125**   **$225**
Circa 1900-1910. Smooth-face blade. "R Simpson, Maker, Carnoustie" mark.

LONG-NOSE PUTTERS
$700   **$1,250**   **$2,750**
Circa 1890. Beech-head putter stamped "R Simpson."

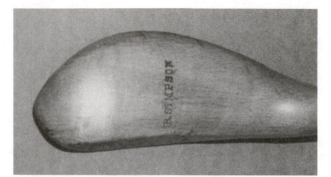

LONG-NOSE WOODS

$1,150	$2,350	$4,500

Circa 1883-1890. Play club, brassie, or spoon. "R Simpson" on a beech head. Many have leather face inserts.

LINE-SCORED IRONS

$40	$50	$95

Circa 1920s. All irons. "R Simpson, Carnoustie" with "S" and the "Anchor" mark.

SMOOTH FACE IRONS

$40	$65	$110

Circa 1900-1910. All irons. "R Simpson, Carnoustie" in a double circle.

PERFECT BALANCE IRONS

$300	$550	$1,150

Circa 1910. All irons. "Lump" back weighting. "Patent No. 21307" and "R Simpson, Carnoustie" at toe. "Crescent and Star" mark.

SIMPSON SPECIAL WOODS

$90	$120	$220

Circa 1910-1915. Driver, brassie, or spoon.

PRETTY FACE WOODS

$100	$120	$225

Circa 1910-1915. Driver, brassie, or spoon. "Ivorine" face insert.

MALINKA SERIES WOODS

$110	$150	$240

Circa 1920s. "Malinka No 367793." Driver, brassie, or spoon. "R Simpson, Carnoustie" mark.

PRETTY FACE WOODS

$100	$130	$220

Circa 1920s. "Diamond"-shaped face insert.

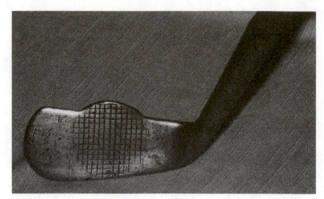

BALL FACE IRONS

$800	$1,750	$3,200

Circa early 1890s. All irons. Patent Numbers on back.

PERFECT BALANCE WOODS

$110	$175	$300

Circa 1905-1910. Driver, brassie, or spoon.

SIMPLEX WOODS

$175	$275	$600

Circa 1900-1910. Spliced neck. "Patent App. For No. 24835." "R Simpson, Carnoustie" stamp.

SEMI-LONG NOSE WOODS

$500	$800	$1,500

Circa 1890-1900. Play club, brassie, or spoon. Transitional head shape. "R Simpson" stamp.

SLAZENGER AND SONS
LONDON, ENGLAND

Slazenger's began marking and selling clubs and balls about 1890. It began by buying clubs from Tom Stewart and Robert Condie and other major makers of the time. During the wood shaft era it had outlets in London and New York and marked its clubs accordingly. The "Six-Pointed Star" was its London mark used during the late 1890s. The other mark was simply "Slazenger." It is currently making golf equipment as a subsidiary of Dunlop.

SLAZENGER, NEW YORK PUTTER

$60	$80	$155

Circa 1900-1910. Smooth face straight blade.

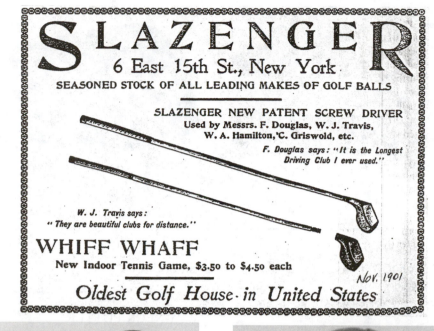

SLAZENGER NEW YORK IRONS
$50   **$70**   **$140**
Circa 1900-1910. All irons. Smooth face.

SIX POINTED STAR IRONS
$90   **$140**   **$300**
Circa 1895-1900. All irons. Smooth face.

PUTTING CLEEK
$90   **$150**   **$250**
Circa 1895-1900. Smooth face straight blade.
"Six-Pointed Star" mark.

RUT NIBLICK
$300   **$450**   **$800**
Circa 1895. Small smooth face head.
"Six-Pointed Star" mark.

THREADED SOCKET PATENT
$300   **$400**   **$750**
Circa 1901-1905. "Screw-in shaft" driver or
brassie. "Patent No.682,960 Slazenger" on the
head.

SLAZENGER SPECIAL WOODS
$90   **$120**   **$220**
Circa 1910-1915. Driver, brassie, or spoon.
"Slazenger Special, New York" stamp.

ALUMINUM-HEAD WOODS
$135   **$225**   **$400**
Circa 1910. All lofts. "Carruthers" through
hosel shafting.

TONG BRAND PUTTING CLEEK
$140 $200 $375
Circa 1910. "Tong" mark.

SPLICED-NECK WOODS
$160 $225 $450
Circa 1895-1910. Driver, brassie, or spoon.

SPALDING

DYSART, FIFE, SCOTLAND

Spalding began operations in Great Britain about 1900. Clubs from the Dysart, Fife Works carried an "Anvil" mark, "Baseball" mark stamped "Gt. Britain," "Gold Medal" series, "Tong" marked irons, and "Argyle" clubs. Jim Cooper has written the definitive work on Spalding, which is profusely illustrated. Every Spalding collector should have this reference in his library. It is available from the author, or Jim Cooper.

SMOOTH-FACE PUTTING CLEEK
$45 $65 $130
Circa 1905. "Made in Great Britain" baseball mark.

MORRISTOWN PUTTER
$70 $110 $225
Circa 1898-1902. "Made in Gr. Britain" baseball mark.

FLANGED-BACK PUTTER
$50 $70 $125
Circa 1920. "Anvil" mark.

THISTLE SERIES PUTTER
$40 $55 $100
Circa 1920-1925. Line-face blade.

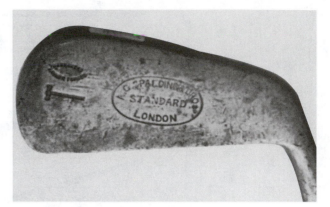

STANDARD, LONDON IRONS
$50 $80 $150
Circa 1910-1915. "Standard London" on back. Smooth face.

WRY-NECK PUTTER
$40 $55 $100
Circa 1920-1925. Line face, "Thistle" mark.

ARGYLE SERIES PUTTER
$40 $55 $100
Circa 1915-1920. Hyphen scored, offset hosel. "Thistle" marks.

GOLD MEDAL SERIES PUTTER
$40 $55 $100
Circa 1915-1920. Calamity Jane type with "Wry Neck" with "Anvil" mark.

"S R" PUTTER
$110 $175 $325
Circa 1920s. Long radial blade and 5 1/2 inch hosel. "Anvil" mark.

SCHENECTADY PUTTER
$125 $225 $500
Pre-1909. "A G Spalding, Makers" baseball trademark.

CALAMITY JANE PUTTER
$200 $375 $750
Circa 1931. "Rustless Calamity Jane" with "Spalding Kro-Flite" mark.

CENTRA-JECT MASHIE
$40 $55 $100
Circa 1910-15. "Anvil" mark.

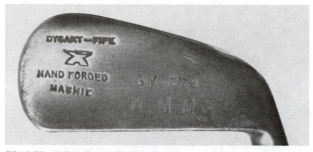

HAND-FORGED IRONS
$40	$55	$100

Circa 1915-20. "Anvil" and "Dysart-Fife" marks.

JIGGER
$40	$55	$100

Circa 1910-1915. "Hammer" mark and "Diamond-dot" face scoring.

THISTLE SERIES IRONS
$40	$55	$100

Circa 1910-1915. "Spalding" in large block letters.

GOLD MEDAL SERIES IRONS
$40	$55	$100

Circa 1910-1915. "Dysart-Fife" and "Anvil" mark.

MORRISTOWN SERIES IRONS
$65	$90	$175

Circa 1898-1902. "Made in Gr. Britain" baseball mark.

TONG BRAND IRONS
$110	$160	$325

Circa 1910-1915. "A G Spalding & Bros., Tong Brand, Scotland" marks.

FOULIS PATENT
$110	$180	$325

Circa 1905-1910. Concave, smooth face. "Hammer" mark.

LEATHER FACE SOCKET WOODS
$90	$140	$250

Circa 1900-1905. "Baseball" mark.

LARGE-HEAD BRASSIE
$65	$90	$175

Circa 1915-1920 marked "A G Spalding Bros."

CRESCENT SERIES IRONS
$40	$70	$150

Circa 1910-1915. Marked "Crescent" with the "Hammer" mark.

SPALDING MEDAL 7
$60	$100	$175

Circa 1910-1915 Driver, brassie or spoon.

IVORINE FACE WOODS
$90	$125	$225

Circa 1915-1920. Marked "A G Spalding Bros., Scotland".

BULLDOG TROUBLE WOOD
$90	$125	$225

Circa 1915. Various markings.

SPALDING, A.G. & BROTHERS
USA

Spalding began importing clubs from Scotland about 1893. They were marked with "Spalding" in block letters. During 35 years of manufacturing wooden-shafted clubs, it used a multitude of cleek marks, including the baseball trademark, Morristown, Crescent, Spalding Special, Clan, Harry Vardon, SMCO, and A. G. Spalding & Brothers model A, B, and C. From 1906 to 1918, Gold Medal in various configurations was used. In 1919, the "F" Series irons were introduced including the famous Waterfall series. During the 1920s, Spalding Medal, Spalding Forged, Dundee, and Kro-Flite were the dominant markings. In 1930, the wooden shaft Robert T. Jones, Jr. clubs were produced in very limited quantities.

Jim Cooper has written the definitive work on Spalding, which is profusely illustrated. Every Spalding collector should have this ref-

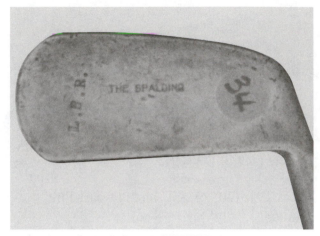

SPALDING SPECIAL SERIES PUTTER
$190   **$240**   **$375**
Circa 1894-1896. Brass blade putter.

THE SPALDING SERIES PUTTER
$135   **$200**   **$375**
Circa 1898-1902. Deep smooth face steel blade putter.

erence in his library. It is available from Jim Cooper, or the author. Spalding Retail Catalogue reprints from 1899 to 1932 are also available from the author of this book.

"SMCO" PUTTER
$250   **$375**   **$750**
Circa 1895. "Crescent Moon" mark on a straight blade putter.

CLAN SERIES PUTTER
$100   **$175**   **$350**
Circa 1895. Blade putter marked "Clan" in large block letters.

SPALDING SPECIAL SERIES PUTTER
$120   **$180**   **$275**
Circa 1894-1896. Steel blade putter.

THE SPALDING SERIES PUTTER
$90   **$125**   **$275**
Circa 1898-1902. "Park" type severe bent neck putter.

THE SPALDING SERIES PUTTER
$80   **$135**   **$275**
Circa 1898-1902. Brass blade putter with a "Diamond" back.

THE SPALDING SERIES PUTTER
$140   **$225**   **$375**
Circa 1898-1902. Deep smooth face. Brass blade putter.

MORRISTOWN SERIES PUTTER
$60   **$85**   **$165**
Circa 1898-1900. Steel head blade "Morristown" and "Baseball" marks.

MORRISTOWN SERIES PUTTER
$65   **$90**   **$190**
Circa 1902-1905. Brass putter with "Baseball" mark.

MORRISTOWN SERIES PUTTER
$70   **$110**   **$225**
Circa 1898-1902. Brass-head blade. "Morristown" mark only.

MORRISTOWN SERIES PUTTER
$70   **$100**   **$175**
Circa 1898-1902. Steel-head approaching putter with "Morristown" stamp only.

HARRY VARDON SERIES PUTTER
$110   **$160**   **$325**
Circa 1900-1903. Gooseneck putter marked "A G Spalding & Bros, Makers."

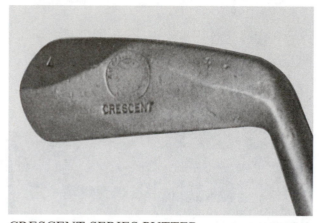

CRESCENT SERIES PUTTER

$65   **$80**   **$165**

Circa 1902-1905. Diamond back with "Baseball" mark.

CRESCENT SERIES PUTTER

$70   **$90**   **$175**

Circa 1902-1905. Brass blade with "Baseball" mark.

GOLD MEDAL SERIES PUTTER

$40   **$55**   **$100**

Circa 1906-1908 "Spalding Gold Medal 1" with dot ball face.

GOLD MEDAL SERIES PUTTER

$40   **$55**   **$100**

Circa 1906-1908. Brass blade "Spalding Gold Medal."

GOLD MEDAL SERIES PUTTER

$40   **$60**   **$110**

Circa 1912-1919. Ball face.

GOLD MEDAL SERIES PUTTER

$60   **$80**   **$160**

Circa 1912-1919. Flanged back, "Maxwell" drilled hosel.

GOLD MEDAL SERIES PUTTER

$60   **$80**   **$150**

Circa 1912-1919. Brass head.

GOLD MEDAL SERIES PUTTER

$75   **$120**   **$200**

Circa 1912-1919. Aluminum-head mallet #4.

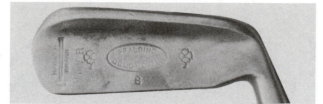

GOLD MEDAL SERIES PUTTER

$60   **$80**   **$160**

Circa 1912-1919. Flanged back, notched neck.

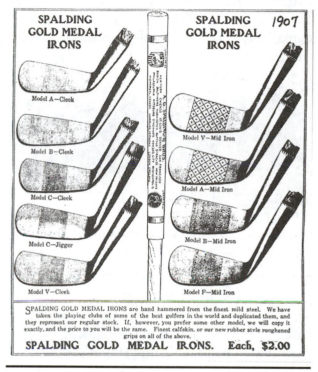

GOLD MEDAL SERIES

$40   **$60**   **$100**

Circa 1912-1919. "Gold Medal" in an oval with the "Hammer" mark at toe.

"F" SERIES PUTTER

$50   **$70**   **$130**

Patented 1-3-1922. Blade putter with three deep scoring lines.

"M" SERIES PUTTER

$40   **$55**   **$90**

Circa 1915-1922. M-11, 12, and 16 all marked "Spalding Forged."

"MEDAL" PUTTER

$40   **$55**   **$95**

Circa 1915-1920. Marked "Spalding Medal" between two "Thistle" marks.

CALAMITY JANE PUTTER

$200   **$325**   **$650**

Circa 1931. Marked "Robt. T Jones, Jr." Wood shafted.

MONEL METAL PUTTER

$70   **$135**   **$325**

Circa 1912-1913. "Ball-with-Wings" and "Baseball" marks.

KRO-FLITE SERIES PUTTER

$40   **$55**   **$90**

Circa late 1920s. Blade putter marked "Spalding Kro-Flite" with "H" on the sole.

KRO-FLITE PUTTER

$40   **$55**   **$90**

Sweet Spot "RF" putter with "Pat. Sept 13, 1927" date.

THISTLE PUTTER

$40   **$50**   **$90**

Circa 1920s. Marked "Thistle."

SEMETRIC SERIES PUTTER

$40   **$50**   **$90**

Circa mid to late 1920s. Chromed blade putter.

FLANGED-BACK PGA PUTTER

$40   **$55**   **$95**

Circa late 1920s. Marked "Pro Golfers Ass'n" with "Crossed Clubs."

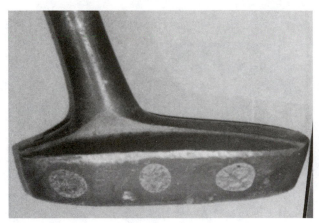

HEATHER PUTTER

$40   **$50**   **$90**

Circa 1915-1920. Marked "Spalding Heather" between two "Rose" marks.

"B V" PUTTER

$90   **$135**   **$275**

Circa 1910-1915. Crescent head shaped.

FLANGED-BACK PUTTER

$40   **$55**   **$100**

Circa 1912-1919. Marked "Spalding Gold Medal 8."

FIRE BRAND PUTTER

$50   **$65**   **$120**

One year only, 1923. "Arm & Torch" mark.

CHICOPEE PUTTER

$80   **$120**   **$225**

Circa 1920 marked "Spalding Chicopee" on the brass head. There are modern remakes with "Spalding" on the sole.

MAXWELL HOSEL PUTTER

$110   **$160**   **$250**

Ten or 12 holes in hosel. Flanged back.

ALUMINUM MALLET PUTTER

$60   **$90**   **$160**

Circa 1915-1920. "MR" on the sole. Marked "A G Spalding & Bros."

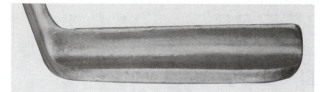

HOLLOW BACK PUTTER
$200   **$325**   **$600**
Circa late 1920s. "HB" putter with
hollowed-out back.

OLYMPIC PUTTER
$500   **$900**   **$1,800**
Circa 1914-1918. Square steel shaft. Pointed
toe on the rounded head.

ALUMINUM MALLET PUTTER
$80   **$110**   **$200**
Circa 1920. Marked "Reach" with a
"Keystone" mark.

ALUMINUM PUTTER
$70   **$90**   **$160**
Circa 1910s. "A G Spalding & Bros" and
"AHP."

ALUMINUM PUTTER
$80   **$125**   **$225**
Circa 1910s. "Gold Medal 4"

SCHENECTADY TYPE PUTTER
$110   **$160**   **$375**
Circa 1910-1920 marked "Spalding Gold
Medal H H."

SPRING FACE PUTTER
$350   **$650**   **$1,500**
Circa 1897-1915. "The Spalding," Crescent,"
and "Gold Medal" marks.

TRAVIS PUTTER
$500   **$750**   **$1,500**
Circa 1905-1910. Center-shafted persimmon
wood putter with a brass face and sole plate.

"SMCO" SERIES IRONS
$135   **$250**   **$475**
Circa 1895 Cleek, iron, and lofting iron with
the "Crescent Moon" mark.

THE SPALDING SERIES IRONS
$45   **$75**   **$150**
Circa 1898-1902. Cleek, iron, and lofting
iron.

CLAN LOFTING IRON
$125   **$190**   **$300**
Circa 1895. "Clan" in block letters on head
and shaft.

"SMCO" SERIES IRONS
$450   **$800**   **$1,550**
Circa 1895. Rut niblick with the "Crescent
Moon" mark.

CLAN SERIES IRONS
$100   **$190**   **$350**
Circa 1895. Iron and lofter marked "Clan" in
large block letters.

SPALDING SPECIAL SERIES IRONS
$80   **$135**   **$250**
Circa 1894-1896. Cleek, mid iron, lofting iron.

SPALDING SPECIAL SERIES IRONS
$300   **$600**   **$1,200**
Circa 1894-1896. Concave-face rut niblick.

Spalding discovered

that *mild steel* banishes finger fatigue

So the heads of the world's most accurately matched golf "irons" are made of this superior metal

A STEEL clubhead hits a golf ball with a terrific impact. Where does the shock of the blow go? Spalding has discovered that it depends largely upon the kind of steel used.

Brittle steel resists the blow—transmitting the shock to your fingers. A succession of such blows often causes finger fatigue—that barely perceptible tiring of the finger muscles, which, by the end of a round, can effect the accuracy of your short game.

Mild steel absorbs the shock of the blow. Your fingers are relieved of the strain—a desirable condition in all your golf, a vitally important one in tournament play.

That is why the heads of all Spalding "Irons" are made of mild steel. You notice the difference in the sweeter feel of the impact as the mild-steel clubhead hits the ball.

Mild steel makes the "Sweet Spot" sweeter still

The "Sweet Spot" is the one spot on the club face that gives greatest distance to the ball, and the sweetest feel to the shot. Every golf club has a "Sweet Spot." But it was Spalding who found that by planning the distribution of metal, it could be located in the same position on every club face. And Spalding has marked it there for you to see.

It was Spalding also who originated the idea of having golf clubs match each other. Spalding clubs are so perfectly related in balance and weight that they all *feel* exactly alike. You can time your swing the same for all of them. If you have analyzed the play of champions, you know that such uniformity is the secret of great golf. Spalding has put this uniformity into the clubs themselves.

These clubs have an exact relation of lie to lie. An exact graduation in the pitches of the blades. Even the torsion and resilience of the shafts is matched.

Your wood clubs should match too

You can buy Spalding wood clubs which are as accurately related as the Spalding irons. It is important that this relation exist, too!

Own a matched set .. Buy it complete

or *one club at a time*

YOU can now build up a perfectly related set of golf clubs, one by one if you wish. Spalding's new Kro-Flite Related Irons are sold one at a time.

There are three groups, or swinging weights, to choose from—indexed by one (.) two (..) and three (...) dots. The irons in each group are accurately related in pitch, lie, balance and feel. Buy one or two clubs of the index that suits you best. Add to them at any time by selecting additional clubs of the same index.

Each group includes a No. 1 iron (driving iron), No. 2 (mid-iron), No. 3 (mid mashie), No. 4 (mashie iron), No. 5 (mashie), and No. 6 (mashie niblick). The Kro-Flite Related Irons are $6.50 each. Kro-Flite Related Woods—Driver, Brassie and Spoon—are $12.50 each.

Spalding also offers the famous Registered Sets. These are the sets which first brought the matched club idea to golfers.

Eight perfectly matched irons comprise the Registered Kro-Flite Set, at $65. The Kro-Flite Registered Wood Set consists of twin driver and brassie, at $30. Spoon to match, made to order, is $15.

Registered Sets must be bought complete. Each set is registered by Spalding and a complete record is kept of every club. Therefore any registered club can be exactly duplicated at any time.

Ask your professional to outfit you—either one at a time with Kro-Flite Related Clubs, or all at once with a Registered Set. Spalding dealers also carry these clubs, and of course all Spalding Stores.

FREE—A GOLF CLUB BOOKLET that gives you a lot of information about clubs that you can apply to your own game. Simply request on a postal, "The First Requisite of Championship Golf" and mail to A. G. Spalding & Bros., 105 Nassau Street, New York City.

© 1927, A. G. S. & B.

Spalding
KRO-FLITE
GOLF CLUBS
Registered sets—   Related Clubs—
sold in sets only.   sold one at a time.

At the left is shown an average set of golf clubs. The dotted line connects the centers of balance. There is little relation between them. Your swing and timing for each club would be a trifle different.

At the right are six Spalding clubs. Note that they are so accurately related that a line drawn through the centers of balance parallels the tops of the shafts. The clubs all feel exactly alike. The swing and timing is the same for every one of them.

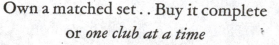

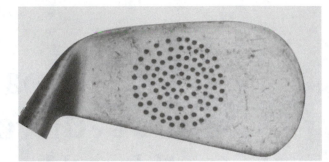

HARRY VARDON SERIES IRONS

$50 $80 $190

Circa 1900-1903. Smooth-face cleek, mid iron, and lofter marked "A G Spalding & Bros., Makers."

GOLD MEDAL SERIES IRONS

$40 $55 $100

Circa 1909-1912. Various irons with ball face designs.

THE SPALDING SERIES IRONS

$70 $135 $250

Circa 1898-1902. Cleek with "Carruthers" through-hosel shafting.

THE SPALDING SERIES IRONS

$80 $135 $275

Circa 1898-1902. Lofter with concave smooth face.

THE SPALDING SERIES IRONS

$250 $500 $1,150

Circa 1898-1902. Concave-face rut niblick.

MORRISTOWN SERIES IRONS

$45 $75 $160

Circa 1898-1900. Steel head with "Morristown" stamping. Cleek, mid iron, and lofting irons.

MORRISTOWN SERIES IRONS

$45 $70 $150

Circa 1902-1905. Steel head with "Morristown" and "Baseball" marks. Cleek, mid iron, and lofting irons.

MORRISTOWN SERIES IRONS

$200 $325 $700

Circa 1898-1900. Smooth-face niblick with "Morristown" stamping.

BASEBALL TRADEMARK IRONS

$50 $80 $150

Circa 1902-1905. "Model B" lofting iron.

HARRY VARDON SERIES IRONS

$200 $325 $600

Circa 1900-1903. Smooth-face niblick marked "A G Spalding & Bros., Makers."

MODEL SERIES A, B, C IRONS

$70 $100 $200

Circa 1899-1902. Cleek, mid iron and lofting iron with "A G Spalding & Bros., Model" in very tiny letters.

MODEL SERIES A, B, C IRONS

$250 $550 $1,000

Circa 1902-1905. Rut niblick with concave face.

CRESCENT SERIES IRONS

$45 $65 $130

Circa 1902-1905. Cleek, mid iron, lofter, and specialty clubs. Smooth face with "Baseball" mark.

GOLD MEDAL SERIES IRONS

$45 $55 $95

Circa 1912-1919. "Jigger."

GOLD MEDAL SERIES IRONS

$45 $65 $150

Circa 1906-1908. "Gold Medal" in block letters. "C" lofter with "Diamond-dot" face scoring.

GOLD MEDAL SERIES IRONS

$45 $65 $150

Circa 1906-1908. "Gold Medal 6" in block letters with a concave "Stag-dot" face.

GOLD MEDAL SERIES IRONS
$50   **$75**   **$140**
Circa 1906-1908. "Gold Medal" in block letters. Iron, lofter, and niblick.

"F" SERIES LINE GROOVES IRONS
$35   **$45**   **$90**
Patented 1-3-1922. 2 through 9 irons. "F" numbers marked on sole at toe.

*** Spalding manufactured the Robert T Jones, Jr. irons with HICKORY shafts in very limited numbers. Each set has a Registration Number that began with the letter "H" signifying "Hickory." During the 1930s through the 1950s, Spalding produced millions of sets with STEEL shafts, many coated with plastic and APPEAR TO BE WOOD.

GOLD MEDAL SERIES IRONS
$110   **$160**   **$350**
Circa 1906-08. Foulis concave mashie-niblick with "Gold Medal 3" in block letters.

CORRUGATED DEEP GROOVE IRONS
$90   **$135**   **$250**
C-54, C-67, and C-98. Mashie, mashie-niblick, and niblick.

CORRUGATED DEEP GROOVE IRONS
$90   **$135**   **$250**
"F" Series Mid-iron, mashie, mashie-niblick, and niblick.

SLOT DEEP GROOVE IRONS
$100   **$145**   **$275**
"C-91, Dedstop mashie-niblick" on the sole.

A G SPALDING & BROS. SERIES IRONS
$35   **$45**   **$90**
Circa late teens-early 1920s. Irons 1 through 9.

A G SPALDING & BROS. SERIES IRONS
$50   **$70**   **$135**
Circa late teens-early 1920s. "Bobbie iron" on a "radial" sole.

KRO-FLITE SERIES IRONS
$35   **$45**   **$90**
Circa 1925-1930. Irons 1 through 7, and 19.

KRO-FLITE SERIES IRONS
$40   **$65**   **$120**
Circa 1925-1930. Irons 8 Sky iron, 15 through 18, and 29 Sand Dabber.

R T JONES KRO-FLITE IRONS
$150   **$250**   **$375**
Irons 2 thru 8. All wood shaft irons have a REGISTRATION NUMBER PRECEDED by the letter "H." Irons that do not have the "H" prefix are metal shafted and have no real collectible value.

R T JONES KRO-FLITE IRONS
$175   **$275**   **$375**
#1 Driving iron and #9 niblick.

R T JONES KRO-FLITE IRONS
$1,950   **$3,250**   **$6,500**
Complete set 1-9 irons and Calamity Jane putter.

CUSTOM SERIES IRONS
$40   **$55**   **$110**
Exactly the same as the Kro-Flite R T Jones, but marked "Custom."

Reading from left to right: BOBBY JONES
and the Spalding Clubs he designed

HERE is Bobby Jones examining the first set of golf clubs ever made which offer his idea of what perfect golf clubs should be!

From 8 to 1, is a set of the grandest Irons that the game has ever seen. Jones, now a Spalding Director, and the Spalding experts have, by redistributing weight, succeeded in designing an iron whose head tends to follow through naturally. As Jones himself expressed it, "the blade seems to flow through the ball."

This redistribution of weight—the heavier blade and lighter hosel—gives better control, too. The center of percussion is two inches lower than it is on hickory-shafted irons, and an inch lower than it is on other steel-shafted irons. This makes the clubhead easier to direct, and gives a more perfect instrument for shot control.

Another factor which contributes to control is the flange sole, which seats itself in back of the ball with the accuracy of a putter. This feature relieves the player of the distracting business of fussing with the lie of the blade, and lets him concentrate on the stroke itself.

In these clubs, Jones also cuts the number of stances right in half, by introducing the brand new idea of matching in pairs as to length and lie! This means that you need master only *one* stance for every *two* clubs. And, every club is matched with every other club in swinging weight—so that one swing and one timing are correct for every club in the set!

"Poems in Wood"

Bobby Jones is recognized as one of the greatest wood players of all time. And his uncanny skill is reflected in the new woods which he designed. One famous expert, when first examining them, said—"They're poems in wood." When perfectly sane golfers get to talking like that about these clubs, they *must* be magnificent!

In addition to the customary woods, Jones contributes a new Senior Set of *Five* Graduated Woods—introducing two completely new woods to take the place of the Numbers 1 and 2 irons. Senior golfers will find, in this Set, a solution of the difficulties they now have with their long iron shots.

Look! It's Calamity Jane!

That interesting looking club on the end is none other than Calamity Jane—an exact duplicate of the famous lady herself. Legend has it that Bobby Jones clings to this great putter because he considers it "lucky." In a way, that's true. Calamity Jane's magnificent balance and deadliness make it a lucky club in any golfer's bag.

Lower prices for all

The new Jones Clubs have the famous Spalding Cushion-neck. The sets are Registered, so that you can always get an exact duplicate of any club. And the prices are the lowest ever asked for Spalding fine clubs.

CUSTOM-BUILT REGISTERED IRONS
Set of 9 $75   Set of 8 $67   Set of 6 $50
(Cushion Shaft Irons, $5 each)

**CUSTOM-BUILT DE LUXE
REGISTERED WOODS**
Set of 4 $48   Set of 3 $36   Pair $24

**CUSTOM-BUILT STANDARD
REGISTERED WOODS**
Set of 4 $40   Set of 3 $30   Pair $20
(Autograph Woods, separately, $8 and $10 each)

Custom-Built De Luxe Senior Graduated Registered Woods, $60 for set of 5. Senior Graduated Matched Woods, $40 for set of 5. Calamity Jane Putter, $6.

Spalding
ROBERT T. JONES, JR.
GOLF CLUBS

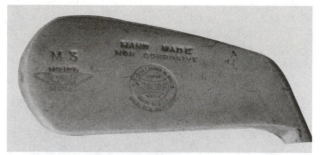

MONEL METAL IRONS

$50   **$65**   **$95**

Circa 1912-1913. "Ball with Wings" and "Baseball" mark.

SEELY PATENT IRONS

$450   **$750**   **$1,750**

Circa 1912-1919. "Forked hosel" with "Gold Medal" marks.

CUSTOM SERIES IRONS

$400   **$650**   **$1,300**

Complete set 1-9 custom irons.

"M" SERIES IRONS

$35   **$45**   **$90**

Circa early 1920s. Irons 1 through 9 with deep line scoring.

"F" SERIES IRONS

$40   **$55**   **$100**

Patented 1-3-1922. #1 iron. "F" numbers marked on sole at toe.

SEMETRIC SERIES IRONS

$35   **$45**   **$90**

Circa late 1920s. Irons 1 through 9.

FIRE BRAND SERIES IRONS

$40   **$50**   **$110**

One year only, 1923. "Arm and Torch," various irons.

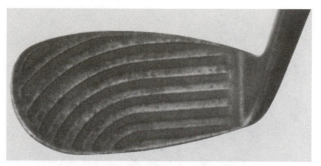

WATERFALL IRONS

$400   **$500**   **$800**

Circa 1920. Single waterfall "F" Series.

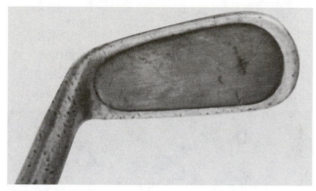

CRAN IRONS

$500   **$950**   **$1,750**

Circa 1897-1915. Wood face insert. "The Spalding", "Crescent," and "Gold Medal" marks.

MAXWELL HOSEL IRONS

$60   **$90**   **$135**

Ten or 12 holes in hosel. Cleek, mid iron, mashie, mashie-niblick, and niblick all with flanged backs.

SPRING FACE IRONS

$300   **$550**   **$1,000**

Circa 1897-1915. "The Spalding," Crescent," and "Gold Medal" marks.

BALL BACK IRONS

$400   **$650**   **$1,000**

Circa 1905. Smooth-face cleek, iron, and lofting iron with large protruding "Ball" back-weighting design.

DOUBLE WATERFALL IRON

$1,650   **$2,500**   **$5,000**

Circa 1920. "F" series.

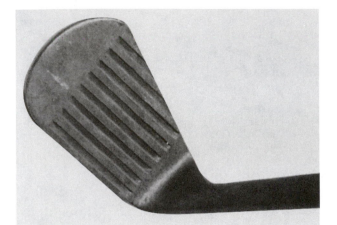

LARD PATENT IRONS

$1,900   **$2,750**   **$4,750**

Circa 1914-1920. Perforated steel shaft. Cleek, mid iron, mashie, mashie-niblick, and niblick.

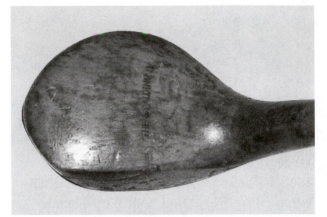

THE SPALDING SERIES WOODS

$190   **$300**   **$650**

Circa 1898-1902. Pear-shaped driver, brassie, and spoon. Heads were usually made from "Dogwood."

THE SPALDING ONE-PIECE WOOD

$950   **$1,600**   **$2,850**

Circa 1898-1902. Driver with leather face insert.

LARD PATENT IRONS

$2,750   **$3,500**   **$5,500**

Circa 1914-1920. Perforated steel shaft. Corrugated deep groove face scoring, any model.

MORRISTOWN SERIES WOODS

$225   **$375**   **$700**

Circa 1902-1905. Spliced-neck, bulger-face brassie with "Morristown" and "Baseball" marks.

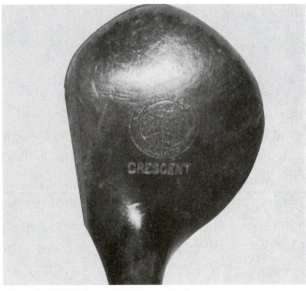

CRESCENT SERIES WOODS

$90   **$125**   **$225**

Circa 1902-1905 Driver, brassie, or spoon with "Baseball" mark.

MORRISTOWN SERIES WOODS

$240   **$390**   **$800**

Circa 1902-1905. Spliced-neck semi-long nose play club or brassie with "Morristown" mark.

HARRY VARDON SERIES WOODS

$160   **$325**   **$700**

Circa 1900-1903. Driver, brassie, or spoon, all with a leather face insert and stamped "Harry Vardon".

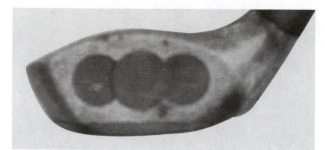

JACOBUS PATENT WOOD

$200	$300	$500

Circa 1910. Three Mahogany dowels arranged in the face. "A G Spalding Bros., Gold Medal" markings.

DUNCAN MODEL WOODS

$80	$100	$175

Circa 1920. Patented one-piece sole and back weight.

FIRE BRAND SERIES WOODS

$90	$125	$200

One year only, 1923. "Arm & Torch" mark.

SKOOTER PATENT WOODS

$125	$190	$325

Patented August 22, 1911. Marked "A G Spalding & Bros." Driver, brassie, or spoon.

ALUMINUM-HEAD WOODS

$135	$250	$550

Circa 1915-1920. Aluminum-head driver and various loft fairway clubs marked "A G Spalding Bros., Makers."

MALTESE CROSS FACE WOODS

$80	$120	$175

Circa 1920s. Red and black Maltese Cross plastic insert.

CROW FACE WOODS

$100	$160	$300

Circa 1920s. Black flying "Crow" in an "Ivorine" insert.

TRIPLE SPLICE PATENT WOODS

$225	$300	$500

Circa 1920. Driver, brassie, and spoon with a "Triple" splice affixing head to shaft.

JUVENILE CLUBS

$30	$40	$65

"A G Spalding Bros., Junior" smooth-face putter, mid iron and mashie.

JUVENILE CLUBS

$65	$90	$150

"A G Spalding Bros., Junior" driver.

SPENCE & GOURLAY
ST. ANDREWS, SCOTLAND

James Spence and George Gourlay went into partnership in 1895 and by 1908 they had built a great reputation and flourishing business. Their business came to an end in 1914 as a result of World War I. Their mark was a "Clover" with "S & G" inside.

OFFSET BLADE PUTTER

$45	$60	$100

Circa 1920-1925. "S & G" inside a shamrock mark.

LONG HOSEL PUTTER

$75	$110	$190

Circa 1920s. "Flag-in-hole." Hosel is 5 1/2 inches.

DOT-PUNCHED-FACE IRONS

$40	$50	$90

Circa 1915. All irons. "S & G" inside a "Clover" mark.

DREADNOUGHT NIBLICK

$65	$100	$175

Circa 1915. Dot-punched face.

ANTI-SHANK IRONS

$100	$160	$275

Circa 1920. All irons. Smith's Patent.

SPENCE, JAMES
ST. ANDREWS, SCOTLAND

After the war, James Spence returned to the business previously operating under Spence & Gourlay. He changed the cleek mark and rebuilt a very successful company. In 1920, he sold out to Robert Forgan & Son. Forgan used the Spence trademark throughout the 1930s, and

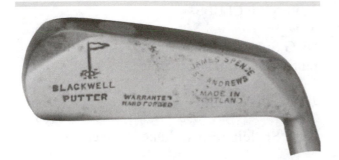

BLACKWELL PUTTER
$55   **$70**   **$110**
Circa 1920s. "Flag-in-Hole" mark on a beveled heel and toe, thick sole offset blade.

BLADE PUTTER
$50   **$65**   **$120**
Circa 1910-20. "Stag" marking.

---

kept the James Spence (St. Andrews) Limited name for a while. He used the "Flag-In-Hole" and monogrammed "JS" marks.

DRIVING IRON
$45   **$65**   **$135**
Circa 1915-1920. Dot-punched face.

SPECIAL APPROACHING CLEEK
$50   **$65**   **$120**
Circa 1915-1920.

MAXWELL HOSEL IRONS
$50   **$70**   **$140**
Circa 1915-1925. All irons. Flanged back, line or dot faces.

LARGE HEAD NIBLICK
$90   **$140**   **$275**
Circa 1915. Dot punched face. Nearly "Giant" size.

SMOOTH-FACE BLADE PUTTER
$50   **$65**   **$120**
Circa 1900-1910. Deep-face, straight, compact blade. "The St Andrew Golf Co., Ltd, Glasgow" stamping.

ST. ANDREW GOLF CO.
DUNFIRMLINE & GLASGOW, SCOTLAND
Began making clubs after 1900. It used the "Running Stag" mark and "Stag." It produced many clubs made from "Hawken's Never Rust," a silvery metal.

STANDARD WRY NECK PUTTER
$50   **$70**   **$135**
Circa 1920. Line-scored offset hosel blade.

HAWKINS NEVER RUST PUTTER
$50   **$80**   **$150**
Circa 1920s. Monel metal flanged-back, offset hosel, line-scored blade.

STANDARD JIGGER
$40   **$55**   **$100**
Circa 1915-1920. Hyphen-scored face.

HAWKINS NEVER RUST IRONS
$50   **$65**   **$120**
Circa 1915-1920. All irons flanged back. "Running Stag" mark.

MAXWELL HOSEL IRONS
$50   **$70**   **$135**
Circa 1915. Flanged back.

CONVEX FACE IRONS
$50   **$70**   **$135**
Circa 1915-1920. "Running Stag" mark. Flanged back.

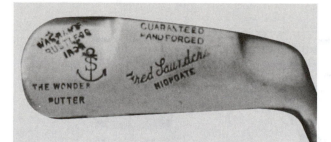

MUSSEL BACK PUTTER

| $50 | $70 | $135 |

Circa 1925. "Anchor & S" mark. Square punched face scoring.

ANTI-SHANK IRONS

| $110 | $170 | $300 |

Circa 1920s. All irons. Fairlie's Patent. "Running Stag" mark.

ST ANDREW SPECIAL WOODS

| $90 | $115 | $190 |

Circa 1915-1920. Driver, brassie, or spoon with large heads.

STADIUM GOLF CO.

LONDON, ENGLAND

The Williamson family owned the Stadium Golf Manufacturing Company, Ltd., and Hugh Williamson was in charge of running the business, helped by manager Jimmie Ross. They produced particularly modern clubs for that time. In 1929, the company folded. They used an "Anchor" with a large "S" mark.

KORECTA PUTTER

| $150 | $250 | $400 |

Circa 1920s. "V" sight groove notched in the "Pagoda" shaped top of the blade. "Anchor and S" mark.

SCUFFLER SEMI PUTTER

| $140 | $190 | $320 |

Circa 1915-1920. "Rivers-Zambra" Approach putter "Reg'd no. 740870" on head.

DOT-PUNCHED-FACE IRONS

| $40 | $55 | $100 |

Circa 1915-1920. All irons with a dot punched face. "Anchor & S" mark.

WHITCOMBE JIGGER

| $40 | $55 | $100 |

Circa 1915-1920. "Anchor" mark at toe.

ANTI-SHANK IRONS

| $110 | $170 | $275 |

Circa 1920s. All irons. "Anchor-S" mark.

STANDARD GOLF CO.

SUNDERLAND, ENGLAND

William Mills broke tradition in the mid-1890s when he made fairway woods and putters from aluminum. "Standard Golf Company, Sunderland, England" was his mark. The company used markings on the soles to indicate model names and the like. Many aluminum woods and putters were

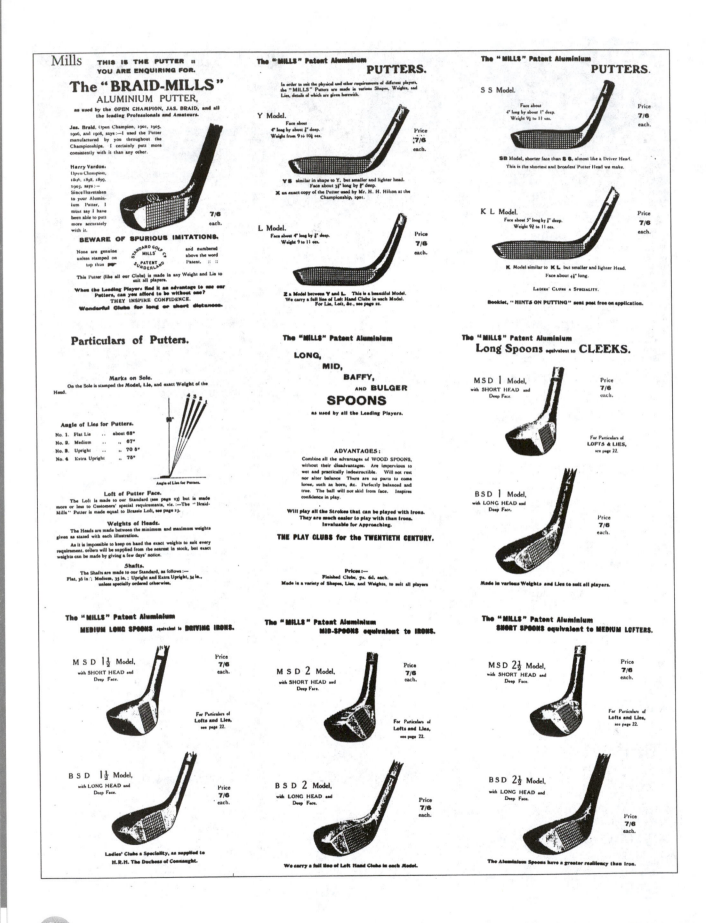

EXAMPLES OF BOTTOM MARKINGS ON PUTTERS

exported to America. The Harry C Lee Co. and BGI were two of the agents that imported vast numbers of "Mills" aluminum clubs.

Peter Georgiady wrote a three-part series on Mills and Standard Golf in the author's monthly publications #88, 89, and 90. Any collector of Mills clubs should include these articles in their library.

Patrick Kennedy produced a reprint of the 1909 Mills Retail Catalogue and this, too, should be required reading.

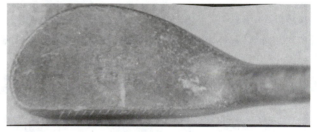

BRAID MILLS MODEL
| $45 | $70 | $140 |
Circa 1905-1915.

NEW RAY MILLS MODEL
| $45 | $70 | $140 |
Circa 1910-1915.

BRAID MILLS 1915 MODEL
| $45 | $70 | $140 |
Circa 1915-1920.

MILLS "SS" MODEL
| $60 | $90 | $150 |
Circa 1915-1920.

NEW MILLS "RNG" MODEL
| $65 | $100 | $175 |
Circa 1910-1915. "T" Bar sight line.

NEW MILLS "RM" MODEL
| $60 | $100 | $175 |
Circa 1910-1915.

NEW MILLS "RBB" MODEL
| $70 | $110 | $190 |
Circa 1910-1915. Thick "sight line" on top.

"MNB" MODEL ALUMINUM HEAD
| $85 | $135 | $220 |
Circa 1910. Offset hosel. "Blade" type aluminum head with 10 to 12 degrees of loft.

BENT NECK "JM" MODEL
| $100 | $175 | $300 |
Circa 1915.

MILLS "YS" MODEL
| $125 | $225 | $400 |
Circa 1905-1915.

NEW MILLS "RSB" MODEL
| $110 | $150 | $275 |
Circa 1910-1915. "Slanted Back" head.

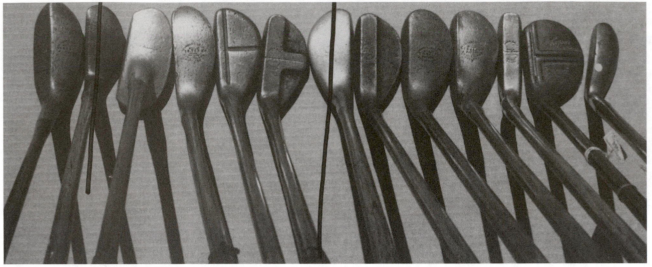

MILLS "L" MODEL

$150 **$250** **$400**

Circa 1900-1910. "L" model indicated long nose.

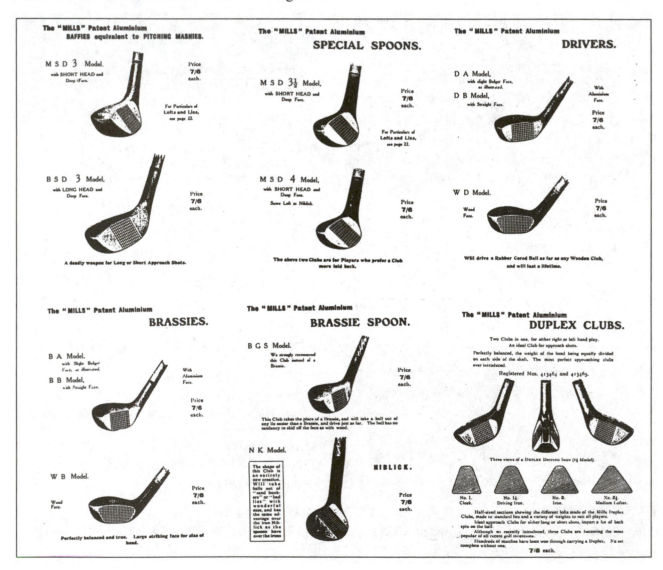

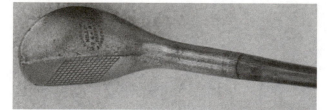

"MSD" ALUMINUM FAIRWAY WOODS
$220   **$350**   **$750**
Circa 1895-1915. Short head. 3 pitching mashie. "BSD" on sole.

MILLS "Y" MODEL
$150   **$250**   **$450**
Circa 1900-1910. Long-nose aluminum putter.

SCHENECTADY-TYPE PUTTER
$160   **$250**   **$425**
Circa 1903-1909. "Sunderland Golf Co" markings.

HILTON "X" MODEL
$160   **$250**   **$450**
Circa 1910-1915. Long-nose head.

MILLS "RSR" MODEL
$150   **$225**   **$350**
Circa 1910-1915. Two hollowed out sight bars on either side of a hollowed out sight line.

MILLS "K" MODEL
$225   **$450**   **$850**
Circa 1900-1910. Very long head.

MILLS "AK" MODEL
$175   **$375**   **$650**
Circa 1910-1915. Rectangular head.

MILLS "RRA" MODEL
$175   **$325**   **$475**
"Circa 1910-1915. Raised right angle aiming sight.

DUPLEX ALUMINUM WOODS
$350   **$600**   **$1,500**
Circa 1900-1915. 1 cleek, 1 1/2 driving iron, 2 iron, and 2 1/2 medium lofter.

MILLS "SB" MODEL
$175   **$275**   **$425**
Circa 1910-1915. Head is nearly "D" shaped.

MILLS "Z" MODEL
$175   **$300**   **$550**
Circa 1900-1910. Long nose head.

"BSD" ALUMINUM FAIRWAY WOODS
$110   **$200**   **$450**
Circa 1895-1915. Long-head clubs. 1 cleek, 1 1/2 driving iron, 2 iron, and 2 1/2 medium lofter. "BSD" on sole.

"MSD" ALUMINUM FAIRWAY WOODS
$110   **$200**   **$450**
Circa 1895-1915. Short-head Clubs. 1 cleek, 1 1/2 driving iron, 2 iron, and 2 1/2 medium lofter. "BSD" on sole.

"CB" SERIES ALUMINUM WOODS
$135   **$225**   **$450**
Circa 1915-1920. All clubs.

MSD ALUMINUM FAIRWAY WOODS
$200   **$325**   **$650**
Circa 1895-1915. Short head. 3 1/2. BSD on sole.

ALUMINUM DRIVERS
$225   **$350**   **$650**
Circa 1900-1915. "D A" bulger face or "D B" straight face.

ALUMINUM BRASSIES
$220   **$350**   **$650**
Circa 1900-1915. "B A" bulger face or "B B" straight face.

BSD ALUMINUM FAIRWAY WOODS
$225   **$375**   **$750**
Circa 1895-1915. Long head. 3 pitching
mashie. "BSD" on sole.

MSD NIBLICK WOOD
$500   **$800**   **$1,600**
Circa 1895-1915. Short head. 4 or "NK."
"BSD" on sole.

STEWART, TOM
ST. ANDREWS, SCOTLAND

By Ralph Livingston

One of the most recognizable maker's
marks is the "Clay Pipe"-shaped cleek mark of
Thomas Stewart Jr. of St. Andrews, Scotland.
The "Pipe of Peace" cleek mark is stamped
into the back of the club head, centered along
the sole. From 1893 to 1904, Stewart used the
pipe and also a "Serpent" (indicated a club for
ladies) cleek mark. In July 1904, his registration mark was approved and from thereafter,
the stamping "T.S.St. A. REG. TRADE-
MARK" was added beneath the "Pipe" mark.

Stewart quickly gained a reputation for
making clubs of the highest quality. Many of
his clients were the top professionals and amateurs of that time. Today, he is best known for
the clubs he made for Bobby Jones, Francis
Ouimet, Harry Vardon, and countless others.

When Stewart would personally supervise
the making of a club, he would stamp a "Dot"
into the toe on the back of the club.
Approximately one in 50 clubs has Stewart's
personal inspection mark. There are other
inspection marks and these are attributed to
his best associate clubmakers.

One of the most logical aspects of his
business was that he sold only club heads.
Most of his production was sold to professionals and retailers who would have their staff do
the assembly. For a small fee, the club heads
were personalized with the professional's
name and golf course or the retailer's advertisement. Consequently, many "Pipe" marked
irons have names other than "Stewart"
stamped on their backs.

R T J PUTTER
$120   **$200**   **$500**
Circa 1930. "Pipe" mark.

PATENTED "V" BACK PUTTER
$250   **$400**   **$700**
Circa 1920. "V" groove hollow back design.

ORD PUTTER
$50   **$65**   **$120**
Circa 1920. Line-scored blade. "Pipe" mark.

PUTTING CLEEK
$50   **$65**   **$125**
Circa 1920. Line-scored faced. "Pipe" mark.

SMOOTH FACE PUTTING CLEEK
$50   **$65**   **$125**
Circa 1910. Marked "Slazenger Special New
York." "Pipe" mark.

GEM PUTTER
$60   **$90**   **$160**
Circa 1915-1920. Rounded back. "Pipe" mark.

NEW ZEALAND CLUBS
$75   **$125**   **$250**
Circa 1910. "Hood & Clements,
Christchurch." Bent neck, smooth-face blade
putter. "Pipe" mark.

BRASS PUTTER
$100   **$175**   **$300**
Circa 1900. No registration marks under
"Pipe" mark.

Excerpts From Tom Stewart's 1930 Catalog

LIST OF GOLF IRON HEADS.

PUTTERS OR PUTT. CLEEKS.

1. Putters or Putt. Cleeks, Ordinary.	
1. Do.	Round Back.
1. Do.	Diamond Back.
1. Do.	Deep Face.
1. Do.	' Accurate.'
1. Do.	„ Round Back.
1. Do.	„ Diamond Back.
1. Do.	Park Pattern.
1. Do.	Special—Blade bent at neck.
1. Do.	Sherlock Pattern.
1. Do.	F. G. Tait Pattern.
1. Do.	Rowland Jones Pattern.
1. Do.	Gun Metal.
2. Do.	Fairlie Pattern.
3. Do.	Logan Pattern.
3. Do.	Celtic Pattern.
1. Do.	R. T. J. Pattern.

3. Putters—Gem or ' 100.'	
3. Do.	Gem ' Accurate ' Bend.
4. Do.	Ballingall.
4. Do.	Smith—Hollow Back.
4. Do.	' Stewart ' Patent.
4. Do.	Kinnell.
Do.	Humphry.
6. Do.	' A.B.' Pattern, as used by Harry Vardon.
3. Do.	Auchterlonie.
6. Do.	' D.S.' Pattern.
Do.	Aluminium.
4. Do.	Maxwell Pattern.
2. Do.	Citizen.

CLEEKS.

Cleeks—Ordinary, Driving and Approaching.	
1. Do.	Ordinary, Long Head.

Sets of Iron Heads made similar to those used by the late Mr. F. G. Tait.

LIST OF GOLF IRON HEADS—Continued.

1. Cleeks—Ordinary, Short Head.	
1. Do.	Bevel Heel.
1. Do.	„ and Toe.
1. Do.	Diamond Back.
1. Do.	Round Back.
1. Do.	Mussel Back.
1. Do.	Bulger Back.
1. Do.	Round Sole.
Do.	Concentrated (Various).
1. Do.	The ' Nipper.''
1. Do.	Sammy.
2. Do.	Fairlie Pattern.
3. Do.	Braid or ' Auchterlonie ' Pattern.
3. Do.	Logan Pattern.
3. Do.	Celtic Pattern.
4. Do.	Smith Pattern.
5. Do.	Smith Pattern—Hollow Back.
4. Do.	Carruthers Pattern.
4. Do.	Ballingall Pattern.
4. Do.	Maxwell Pattern.

IRONS.

Irons—assorted.	
1. Do.	Mid.
1. Do.	Ordinary.
1. Do.	No. 1.
1. Do.	No. 2.
1. Do.	No. 3.
1. Do.	No. 4.
1. Do.	Bevel Heel.
1. Do.	„ and Toe.
1. Do.	Diamond Back.
1. Do.	Round Back.
1. Do.	Mussel Back.
1. Do.	Bulger Back.
1. Do.	Round Sole.
Do.	Concentrated (Various).
2. Do.	Fairlie Pattern.
3. Do.	Logan Pattern.
3. Do.	Celtic Pattern.
4. Do.	Smith Pattern.

Sets of Iron Heads made similar to those used by the late Tom Morris.

LIST OF GOLF IRON HEADS—Continued.

5. Irons—Smith Pattern—Hollow Back.
4. Do. Ballingall Pattern.
3. Do. Auchterlonie Pattern.
4. Do. Maxwell Pattern.

MASHIES.

Mashies—Assorted.
1. Do. Deep Face.
1. Do. Vardon Pattern.
1. Do. Ordinary Pattern—Narrow Face.
1. Do. Herd Pattern.
1. Do. Kirkaldy Pattern.
1. Do. Jamie Anderson Pattern.
1. Do. Bevel Heel.
1. Do. „ and Toe.
1. Do. Diamond Back.
1. Do. Round Back.
1. Do. Mussel Back.
1. Do. Bulgar Back.
1. Do. Round Sole.

Mashies—Concentrated (Various).
1. Do. Extra Deep Face.
1. Do. Lofting.
2. Do. Fairlie Pattern.
3. Do. Logan Pattern.
3. Do. Celtic Pattern.
4. Do. Smith Pattern.
5. Do. Smith Pattern—Hollow Back.
4. Do. Ballingall Pattern.
3. Do. Auchterlonie Pattern.
4. Do. Maxwell Pattern.

JIGGERS.

Jiggers (Assorted).
1. Do. Ordinary.
1. Do. Round Back.
1. Do. Diamond Back.
1. Do. Hilton Pattern (in four different lofts, Nos. 1, 2, 3 and 4.
Do. Concentrated (Various).

Driving Irons made similar to that as used by the late Jack Kirkcaldy.

LIST OF GOLF IRON HEADS—Continued.

2. Jiggers—Fairlie Pattern.
3. Do. Auchterlonie Pattern (or ' Braid ').
3. Do. Logan Pattern.
3. Do. Celtic Pattern.
4. Do. Smith Pattern.
4. Do. Maxwell Pattern.

NIBLICKS.

Niblicks (Assorted).
1. Do. Ordinary.
1. Do. Deep Face.
1. Do. Extra Large Heads.
1. Do. Diamond Back.
1. Do. Round Back.
2. Do. Fairlie Pattern.
3. Do. Logan Pattern.
3. Do. Celtic Pattern.
4. Do. Smith Pattern.
5. Do. Smith Pattern—Hollow Back.
4. Do. Maxwell Pattern.

MASHIE NIBLICKS, etc.
1. Mashie Niblick—Deep Face.
1. Do. ' Benny Pattern.'
3. Do. ' Young Benny ' Pattern.
1. Do. Round Top and Straight Sole.
1. Do. Egg Shape.
2. Do. Fairlie Pattern—Deep Face.
3. Do. Logan Pattern.
3. Do. Celtic Pattern.
4. Do. Smith Pattern
5. Do. Smith Pattern—Hollow Back.
4. Do. Maxwell Pattern.
1. Mashie Cleeks.
1. Do. Irons—Deep Face.
1. Do. „ Bevel Heel.
1. Driving Mashie.
1. Do. Irons.
1. Push-Shot Irons.
1. Lofting Irons, etc., etc.
1. Spade Mashies.

Any pattern of head made to order.
Sets of Iron Heads made as used by Mr. Robert T. Jones.

STEWART'S PATENT PUTTER.

The chief feature of this club is in its broad sole, combined with a heavy top edge, which keeps the ball from 'jumping' when struck.

This pattern of putter is used by many professionals, also many prominent amateurs, including Mr. E. A. Lassen, Ex-Amateur Champion.

"SHERLOCK PUTTER."

This putter is a copy of Jas. Sherlock's own club (Pipe Brand).   'Sherlock' *Autograph* Putters can only be obtained direct from Mr. James Sherlock, Golf Club, Hunstanton.

"A. B." PUTTER.

The 'A. B.' Putter as *used* by Harry Vardon, Open Champion, is after the model of Gem Putter, having a heavy sole and a narrow face.

THE BALLINGALL PUTTER.

This pattern of putter, with a flange sole and invented by Mr. Ballingall, is the favourite style of putter in Ireland, and is used by Mr. Lionel Munn, Irish Amateur Champion, and most of the leading professionals of " Erin."

AUCHTERLONIE APP. CLEEK.

This Approaching Cleek, frequently called the 'Braid App. Cleek,' is the same as made for and played with by James Braid. (The Ex-Open Champion's club is ' *Pipe* ' *Brand*.) This club, which has a centre-balanced blade, is greatly praised by the Ex-Champion (see ' Braid's Book on Golf '), and has now a great hold on the market, both at home and abroad.

Nos. 1, 2, 3 and 4 Irons.

The professional kit does not seem to be complete now-a-days without this set of Irons, which range in loft from a driving Iron to that of a Lofting Iron.

This set of heads is used and played with (all ' Pipe ' Brand) by Arnaud Massy, Alex. Herd, etc.

"VARDON" MASHIE.

The Vardon pattern of Mashie ('Pipe' Brand) is the most 'sought after' pitching club of the day, and is specially made to the direction of the Open Champion.

"SMITH HEADS."

A pattern of club which has received considerable attention of late is that known as the " Smith " pattern.

T. STEWART MAKER IRONS

| $65 | $100 | $160 |

Circa 1910. Smooth-face cleek. "Pipe" mark.

BRASS PUTTER

| $135 | $225 | $400 |

Circa 1895. "Serpent" mark.

TWEENIE IRON

| $80 | $110 | $200 |

Circa 1920s. Rounded sole line scored club. Similar to a "Bobbie" iron. "Pipe" mark.

LARGE HEAD NIBLICK

| $135 | $200 | $400 |

Circa 1900. Smooth face without registration marks under the "Pipe" mark.

DIAMOND BACK IRONS

| $50 | $60 | $100 |

Circa 1910-1920. Dot-punched face. "Pipe" mark.

JIGGERS

| $50 | $70 | $120 |

Circa 1920. With broad flat sole, line scored. "Pipe" mark.

HARRY VARDON IRONS

| $60 | $95 | $150 |

Circa 1920. "Pipe" mark.

BOBBIE IRON

| $70 | $100 | $170 |

Circa 1920. Broad, rounded sole. Line-scored face. "Pipe" mark.

SAMMY IRON

| $75 | $100 | $170 |

Circa 1915. Dot-punched face. "Pipe" mark.

T. STEWART MAKER IRONS

| $80 | $135 | $250 |

Circa 1895-1905. No "registration" stamp below the "Pipe" mark.

SERPENT MARK IRONS

| $110 | $160 | $300 |

Circa 1898-1902. Clubs marked "Slazenger Special New York" smooth face.

T. STEWART MAKER IRONS

| $50 | $60 | $100 |

Circa 1915-25. Dot punched face. All irons.

T. STEWART MAKER IRONS

| $50 | $60 | $100 |

Circa 1920-30. Lined face. All irons.

CONCAVE FACE LOFTER

| $75 | $125 | $250 |

Circa 1900. No registration marks under the "Pipe" mark.

CLUBS FOR CAIRO, EGYPT

| $65 | $125 | $200 |

Circa 1915. All irons. "Pipe" mark.

TOM MORRIS IRONS

| $90 | $140 | $250 |

Circa 1920s. Line scored face. "Pipe" mark.

"R T J" IRONS

| $90 | $140 | $250 |

Circa 1930. Line scored face.

"F O, R T J" IRONS

| $110 | $175 | $300 |

Circa 1930. (Francis Ouimet, Robert T Jones) initials at toe. "Pipe" mark.

TOM MORRIS IRONS

| $100 | $175 | $300 |

Circa 1910s. Dot-punched face. "Pipe" mark.

PIPE MARK AT TOE

| $125 | $200 | $350 |

Circa 1898. Smooth-face general purpose iron.

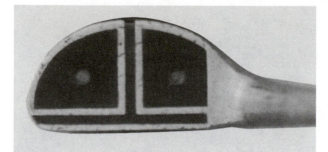

ADJUSTABLE WEIGHT PUTTER

$500	$800	$1,350

Aluminum head with removable head plates. Weights to adjust head weight and coil spring to stop rattle are inside.

TOM MORRIS IRONS

$125	$250	$500

Circa 1905-1915. Smooth face. "Pipe" mark.

ANTI-SHANK IRONS

$125	$225	$350

Circa 1915-1920. Smith's Model. Dot-punched face. "Pipe" mark.

TOM MORRIS IRONS

$200	$375	$750

Circa Pre-1905. Smooth face. No registration marks below "Pipe" mark.

TOM MORRIS IRONS

$175	$350	$700

Circa pre-1898. Smooth face. "Serpent" mark.

RUT NIBLICK

$225	$425	$800

Circa 1895. Medium-size round head. Smooth face. "Pipe" or "Serpent" mark.

THISTLE PUTTER COMPANY
NEW YORK CITY
Famous for the McDougal Patented Putters with aluminum heads, one with adjustable weights.

MCDOUGAL PATENT PUTTER

$150	$225	$375

Aluminum head "T" Square model

CENTER SHAFTED PUTTER

$140	$200	$350

Similar to the patented aluminum head Schenectady putter. The back of the putter is stamped "Jerry Travers, 1 Laurel St, Hartford, Conn."

THORNTON & COMPANY
EDINBURGH, SCOTLAND
Made clubs from about 1895 through the mid-1910s in Edinburgh, and had retail stores in Glasgow and other Scottish cities. Its stamp was a Lion and Shield.

SMOOTH FACE BLADE PUTTER

$55	$70	$110

Name in small block letters.

BENT NECK PUTTER

$55	$65	$100

Line or hyphen face.

GIANT NIBLICK

$950	$1,350	$1,950

3 7/8" X 4 5/8" oversized oval head.

SPLICED NECK WOODS

$150	$225	$375

Thornton & Co, Edinburgh in block or script letters.

TRAVERS, JEROME (JERRY)
HARTFORD, CT.
Travers used a Schenectady Putter to win five U.S. Amateur Championships and also won the U.S. Open as an amateur in 1915 (he did not defend his title in 1916). He produced an aluminum head Schenectady-style putter with his name and address stamped on the back.

ALEX TAYLOR SOCKET WOODS
$75 $95 $150
Stamped with "Alex Taylor" in script. Many were two tone colored heads.

ADJUSTABLE IRON
$850 $1,500 $2,750
Circa 1900-1905. "Urquhart" across face.

TAYLOR, ALEX
New York City
His shop was in New York City during the 1910s and 1920s. Made inexpensive clubs for sale through his shop.

URQUHART, ROBERT
Robert Urquhart first patented an adjustable iron in 1892. His marks were a "U" in a circle and "Urquhart" in large letters on the face of the iron.

VICKER'S LIMITED
SHEFFIELD, ENGLAND
Vicker's Limited operated from 1924 to 1932.

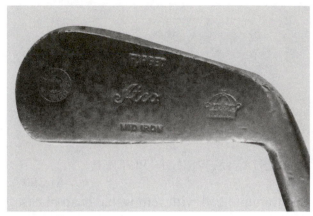

ATCO IRONS
$35 $45 $80
Circa 1920 with line scored face.

IMMACULATE RUSTLESS PUTTER
$50 $60 $100
Circa 1925-1930. Double "K" mark.

It made stainless steel heads sold under the name "Immaculate." Its market also included North America. It used a double "K" on either side of a "V" as its cleek mark.

RUSTLESS IRONS
$50 $60 $100
Circa late 1920s. All irons. "Double K" mark.

VULCAN GOLF CO.
PORTSMOUTH, OHIO
Began making clubs during the mid 1920s. Used "Vulcan" in a monogram as its mark. Made the "Burma" 7-inch-long pencil-thin hosel putter. "Septum" and "Pirate" were other markings.

10   GOLFERS MAGAZINE

Look at These Clubs!

Cut-away illustration of VULCAN V-11 Driver. Note tapered shoulder of the six ivory pins, which hold the black fibre face securely in place. Steel pins through the head absolutely lock the ivory inserts in place. These exclusive features prevent loosening of pins and face due to weather conditions or hard use.

The SEPTEM No. 5 Mashie, shown here, is one of eight perfectly balanced Iron Clubs, including the No. 1 Driving Iron, No. 2 Mid-Iron, No. 3 Mashie Iron, No. 4 Jigger, No. 5 Mashie, No. 6 Mashie Niblick, No. 7 Niblick and No. 8 Putter. VULCAN "Pirate" Irons (popularly priced) are also numbered from 1 to 8.

These are the VULCAN V-11's—Driver, Brassie and Spoon (see cross-section above). A wonderful model finished in Ebony, with broad natural stripe. Shafts of finest steel or selected first-grade hickory—15° bell top of best leather.

IT'S time you got your hands on one of these new VULCANS, gave it a heft and a swing— realized the dawn of a new day in golf cooperation.

Here is *Confidence!* on the end of a shaft of live hickory or steel; confidence that you and these clubs are made for each other—confidence that they are tuned, faced, balanced and shaped to hit a ball how and where you want it to go.

Those who made VULCAN Golf Clubs possible, men who have given many years and famous talents to fine club production, call this "Character." The instant you test a VULCAN club you will recognize it, will sense the confidence it instills.

And just that closer feeling between hands and club marks the difference between yesterday's finest and VULCAN.

VULCAN Character is the product of a group whose special talents have long been given to fine golf equipment, whose leader has supervised production of five million of America's best known golf clubs. This ripe experience, refreshed with new opportunity, has outdone itself.

VULCAN GOLF COMPANY
PORTSMOUTH, OHIO, U.S.A.

VULCAN
Clubs of Character for Every Golfer

NOTE: Ask your Club Professional or your favorite dealer to show you a set of VULCAN Clubs. If he has not yet been supplied ask him to write to us immediately or, better yet, send us his name and address, as well as your own.

© 1927 V. L. Co.

LONG HOSEL PUTTER

| $90 | $150 | $220 |

Circa 1926-1930. 6 1/2 inch long hosel. "Burma 8 Putter" on back.

PIRATE SERIES IRONS

| $35 | $45 | $80 |

Circa 1930. All irons.

LONG HOSEL PUTTER

| $90 | $150 | $220 |

Circa 1926-1930. 6 1/2 inch long hosel. "Septum Putter" on back.

SEPTUM SERIES IRONS

| $35 | $45 | $80 |

Circa 1927. All irons.
OLD ADVERTISEMENT-VULCAN

DRIVING IRON

| $50 | $60 | $100 |

Circa 1930. Stainless steel.

SEPTUM SERIES WOODS

| $75 | $85 | $140 |

Circa 1927. Driver, brassie, or spoon.

WALTER HAGEN & L.A. YOUNG CO.

By Pete Georgiady

If the truth were told, Walter Hagen never made a golf club in his life, though there are thousands that bear his name. His career as a professional and champion was radically different from any of his peers, and Hagen's style of living and playing left an indelible mark on the game of golf.

Born in upstate New York in 1892, he first drew the notice of the golfing world as a dapper young U.S. Open champion at Midlothian in 1914, fast on the heels of Ouimet's sensational victory a year earlier. He was, at that time, the professional to the Country Club of Rochester, N.Y.

Following his win in 1914, Hagen went on a blitz through the next 13 years where he won every major championship at least once. He was twice the U.S. Open and twice the British Open champion, was a five-time American PGA champion (including four straight), he won both the Eastern and Western opens, the North and South opens, the French Open, and a grand number of state championships.

But Hagen did more than win; he won with a style and flamboyance that golf had never witnessed before. He was not the typical pro, making clubs and giving lessons. Hagen passed time with royalty and the most celebrated people in society. He wore the finest clothes and drove the most luxurious autos. He lived on his terms and his terms were that he was allowed in the clubhouse where the professional was formerly forbidden. His high style caused consternation in the ranks, but in the end it helped upgrade the lot of the club pro, whose existence was generally less than honorable.

The never-bashful Hagen was the original endorsement magnet and lent his image to many products. He was said to have carried 25 clubs in his bag at one time just to cover his endorsements. In the early 1920s, Hagen's primary golf club affiliation was with Burke, which manufactured the monel metal Walter Hagen autograph series. Walter also imported clubs for sale in his shop, with Cochrane's of Edinburgh supplying many of the irons bearing Hagen's famous signature.

In the mid-1920s, Hagen was enticed to leave New York, while he was at the Westchester-Biltmore, and move to Red Run Country Club in Royal Oak outside Detroit. The auto business was making Detroit a city on the rise and this prosperity created some new opportunities for Walter.

Prior to this time, Hagen's involvement in the golf club business was minimal. He sold clubs through his shop at the various clubs that employed him, but actually had little part in the clubmaking end, instead employing good workers. He was one of the new breed of pros who sold the clubs of others, spending more time on the course playing competitively.

Hagen's reputation was based on an association with the best of everything. In 1925, he decided to market his own brand of clubs, striking a partnership with his friend, Detroit industrialist Leonard A. Young, owner of a wire and steel company. From 1926 onward, Walter Hagen brand clubs were made exclusively by the L.A. Young Co. Naturally, Hagen played his own brand and, to illustrate the change pervading the club business, he played a mixed set. His deluxe model N2 woods were available only with steel shafts while his Walter Hagen De Luxe registered iron sets came with hickory shafts. The complete set of three woods and nine irons, including putter, cost $115. The most expensive bag in his line was $100. Hagen's top-of-the-line goods were not for the economy-minded person.

But there were clubs for those at the lower end. The same iron sets were also sold in forged steel, in a non-registered series. Then came the Autograph brand, followed by the Triangle brand, and finally WH clubs, with all three brands available in woods and irons. For the beginner, there were Getaway brand irons at $27.50 for the 11 club set.

In premium woods, the Walter Hagen De Luxe models were also fitted with steel shafts, but the Autograph models came with the choice of wood or steel. By 1930, additional mid-grade models included Arrow, Champion, and Star-Line clubs.

The Hagen line contained two unique clubs. Capitalizing on the quality theme, the company produced a very limited number of sterling silver headed blade putters, which could be engraved for use as trophies and awards. Made by Lambert Brothers in New York, they are rare today.

The club most associated with the firm is the notorious Hagen concave sand iron, designed and patented by Edwin McClain. It was the first production club with a "flange" on its sole for the use in sand bunkers. It was also concave, which caused it to be banned from use in 1930. However, flat-faced clubs with the same flange followed and have been indispensable ever since. The next model sand iron, the "Iron Man," was also produced with a hickory shaft for a short time before being transitioned to steel.

Another popular club was the aluminum headed putter called "The Haig." Many had the flat-ended paddle grip and today a few can be found with hickory shafts, though the vast majority was produced with steel.

GETAWAY SERIES PUTTER

$40	$50	$90

Circa late 1920s.

HAGEN AUTOGRAPH PUTTER

$40	$50	$90

Circa late 1920s. Chromed blade.

THE HAIG ALUMINUM PUTTER

$135	$180	$275

Circa 1930-1935. Paddle grip.

STERLING SILVER PUTTER

$700	$900	$1,500

Circa 1930. "Sterling" marked on hosel.

LUCKY LEN PUTTER
$250   **$350**   **$450**
Circa 1930-1935. Wooden-head mallet.

HAGEN AUTOGRAPH IRONS
$35   **$45**   **$80**
Circa late 1920s. All irons.

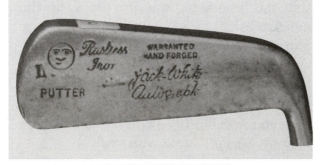

AUTOGRAPH RUSTLESS PUTTER
$60   **$70**   **$110**
Circa 1925-1930. "Sun" mark.

GETAWAY SERIES IRONS
$35   **$45**   **$80**
Circa late 1920s. All irons.

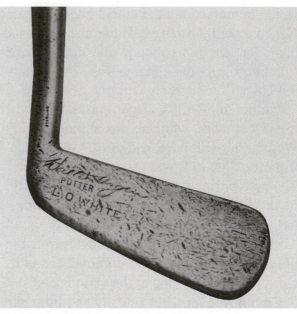

HAGEN AUTOGRAPH WOODS
$75   **$90**   **$160**
Circa late 1920s. Driver, brassie, or spoon.

CONCAVE SAND WEDGE
$300   **$500**   **$850**
Circa 1930. Smooth concave face. Large flange.

IRON MAN SAND WEDGE
$125   **$200**   **$375**
Circa 1930. Large flange. Dot face.

GETAWAY SERIES WOODS
$75   **$90**   **$160**
Circa late 1920s. Driver, brassie, or spoon.

WHITE, JACK
SUNNINGDALE, ENGLAND
Began making clubs in the early 1890s and continued through the late 1920s. Most of his clubs are marked Sunningdale with the "Sun" mark. Famous for making clubs for Bobby Jones.

SMOOTH-FACE IRONS
$200   **$350**   **$1,000**
Circa 1880-1890. General purpose iron or lofter. "R White, Maker, St Andrews" on back.

MUSSEL BACK IRONS
$50   **$65**   **$100**
Circa 1920s. "Sun" mark.

DOT PUNCHED FACE IRONS
$50   **$60**   **$100**
Circa 1915-1920. "Sun" mark.

SUNNINGDALE WOODS
$90   **$135**   **$220**
Circa 1920. Driver, brassie, or spoon.

SPLICED-NECK WOODS
$175   **$300**   **$500**
Circa 1900-19100. Driver, brassie, or spoon.

WHITE, ROBERT
ST. ANDREWS, SCOTLAND
Began making clubs in the late 1870s. Marked his clubs with "R. White, Maker, St. Andrews" in an oval configuration. Clubs with full Robert White markings are scarce and command a premium.

BRASS-HEAD PUTTERS
$200   **$350**   **$800**
Circa 1880-1890. Straight brass blade. "R White, St Andrews, Maker" mark.

SMOOTH-FACE CLEEK
$225   **$400**   **$1,000**
Circa 1880-1890. Cleek. "R White, Maker, St Andrews" on back.

Illustrated by Sharri Lou Casey

MacLeod got so mad at his putter
In his anger he started to stutter.
To those few who were near
It was something to hear.
Such language I never would utter.
By Edwin De Bell

RUT IRON
$900   **$1,800**   **$4,000**
Circa 1880-1890. Small rounded head. "R White, Maker, St Andrews" on back.

WILLIAMS, J H & CO.
BROOKLYN, NY
Began forging clubs prior to 1900 in Brooklyn, NY. Made iron heads for putters and irons, marking them with a tiny "Diamond" and a "W" inside. The mark is found stamped into the hosel. "J H Williams Co, Brooklyn" in block letters was also used. It made fine-quality club heads.

SMOOTH FACE BLADE
$60   **$90**   **$140**
Circa 1895-1900. "Diamond in W" mark on hosel.

OK SPECIAL IRONS.
$60 $80 $140
Circa 1900. All irons. Smooth face.

ONE PIECE WOOD
$1,000 $1,650 $2,750
Circa 1900. Smooth face round head.

PARK STYLE PUTTER
$125 $175 $300
Circa 1900. Severely bent neck blade. "W" in "Diamond" mark.

WILSON, R B (Buff)
ST. ANDREWS, SCOTLAND
Began making clubs in the late 1890s. Marked his clubs with "R B, Wilson, Maker, St. Andrews" in an oval configuration. He used

SMOOTH-FACE IRONS
$200 $350 $850
Circa 1889-1890. All irons. "R. Wilson, Maker, St Andrews" mark.

the "OK" mark to signify irons exported or made in America.

SMOOTH-FACE BLADE PUTTER
$60 $80 $140
Circa 1900. "R B Wilson" in block letters.

GOOSE-NECK PUTTER
$60 $80 $150
Circa 1900. "R B Wilson OK Special" mark.

SMOOTH-FACE IRONS
$60 $90 $190
Circa 1900. All irons. Smooth face.

RUT NIBLICK
$190 $350 $650
Circa 1900. Smooth face round head.

WILSON, ROBERT,
ST. ANDREWS, SCOTLAND
Began forging clubs about 1870 in St. Andrews and continued until about 1905. His marks were "R. Wilson, St. Andrews" and a bent "horseshoe" nail.

PUTTING CLEEK
$250 $400 $1,150
Circa 1889-1890. "R. Wilson, Maker, St Andrews" mark.

SMOOTH-FACE CLEEK IRONS
$250 $400 $1,000
Circa 1889-1890. "R. Wilson, Maker, St Andrews" mark.

WILSON, THOMAS E.
CHICAGO, IL

By Pete Georgiady

Ever since the first national championship unofficially pitted golfers from Chicago against the Boston/New York establishment, the Windy City was a hotbed for early golf in the United States. Its highly-developed industrial manufacturing base quickly adapted and the area became the home of several major golf manufacturing companies.

The Wilson Company, like so many of its contemporaries, entered the golf market as an adjunct to its primary products. In 1913, the group that would soon become Wilson was named the Ashland Manufacturing Company. Located on Chicago's Ashland Avenue, it was a subsidiary of the meat packing firm of Schwartzchild and Sulzberger. Ashland was an outlet for goods delivered from meat by-products, namely intestines and entrails, which they used to produce gut strings for banjoes, violins, tennis rackets, and also surgical sutures. Looking to expand its fortunes, the company also began trading in tennis rackets, hunting and camping equipment, bicycles, phonographs, and automobile tires.

Within a year, Ashland was in receivership and a New York-based bank assumed control. The bank chose a successful meat packing executive named Thomas E. Wilson to head its new investment because of his demonstrated managerial ability. In 1914, the name was changed to the Thomas E. Wilson Co., and the firm moved from its Ashland Avenue location to Chicago's south side. There was great irony in the hiring of Thomas Wilson because the owners of the company had already decided to name the firm the Wilson Company in an effort to draw upon the successes of the very popular President Woodrow Wilson. Still trading in diverse commodities, the rejuvenated Wilson Co. began manufacturing its own products in 1916.

Thomas Wilson was experienced with company acquisitions and charted a similar course for his new firm. Driven to make the company the best in the sporting goods field, he purchased an Ohio company already making leather balls, baseball gloves, and harness gear, and moved it to Chicago. Next, the Indestructo Caddy Bag Manufacturing Co. was purchased and Wilson quickly entered the golf business in a big way.

In 1925, the young company underwent its first name change when it merged with Western Sporting Goods Manufacturing Co., also of Chicago and the newly merged company used the name Wilson-Western Sporting Goods Co. Finally, in 1931, the name changed to the familiar Wilson Sporting Goods.

Earliest Wilson golf clubs are actually marked with the Ashland Manufacturing Company's "A.M. Co." monogram in a circle. Most of these heads were obtained from MacGregor and were additionally stamped with retail or professional's names. The first clubs actually bearing the Wilson name were from the Plus Success series, with the model name in very small block letters, dating from about 1916 or 1917. Slightly later were irons from the same series where the lettering is contained inside a large W. These irons all date from 1917-1918, although Plus Success clubs were available in several other variations continuing into the 1920s.

In the early 1920s, Wilson introduced its Aim Rite symbol, which would appear on many clubs through the decade. In one of these similar designs, it was commonly placed on the face of the club at the sweet spot. Alternately, a mark of concentric circles was found at the sweet spot. Both of these marks were registered as trademarks and they also served to help golfers align the club face with the ball, useful since the vast majority of Aim Rite clubs were sold through stores to economy-minded customers. But the golf market in the 1920s was booming just as the stock market was, and lower-end merchandise was selling very well to the new golfers learning the sport.

The all-time best selling Wilson series was the Wilsonian model of mid-priced clubs. Available throughout the 1920s, it was the mainstay of the company's club selection. All Wilsonian models were available in ladies weights and junior and juvenile sizes. Many of the early Wilsonian irons, as well as other models, were also stamped "Hammer Forged" with the mark of the ball peen hammer, the sign of a better quality product.

Wilson continued low-priced domination throughout the post-war era with many sets of clubs with names like Carnoustie, Cup Defender, Dixie, Lincoln Park, Linkhurst, Pinehurst, Skokie, Streak, and Taplow. Because of their economical nature, most were configured with two woods, four irons (2, 5, 7, 9) and putter. In trying to complete a full set, collectors are often frustrated by searching for the in-between numbers which were never produced. In the late 1920s, brightly colored leather grips became fashionable and several lines were sold with bright red, blue, or green leather.

One of the more uncommon Wilson clubs produced was the Baxpin model deep-groove mashie, which was also stamped for and sold

to another Chicago manufacturer, Burr-key. Early deep-groove clubs can also be found with the old Ashland Manufacturing Co., markings, too. Another unique product is the Walker Cup set, which featured rainbow pattern grooves on the faces of the irons. Introduced in the mid-1920s, the use of that name on a set of clubs is an indication of how important amateur competitions were during those times.

As the company became solidly established as a maker and seller of golf supplies, it also ventured into the country club market for higher grade equipment. Its Red Ribbon and Blue Ribbon sets were positioned for pro shop sales and were used by many tour golfers. Also in the prestige club category was Wilson's Harry Vardon "72" set with its readily identifiable green grips. Two collectible Wilson putter models from this period are the Amby-dex two-way putter and the Kelly Klub. In the 1940s, Wilson would begin its advisory staff program whose roots were established some 15 years earlier with endorsements from young Gene Sarazen, Johnny Farrell, and the mature Ted Ray, who won the 1920 U.S. Open at age 43. All three golfers lent their signatures to Wilson's first autograph lines of clubs.

CUP DEFENDER PUTTER

| $35 | $45 | $80 |

Circa late 1920s.

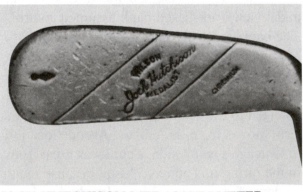

JOCK HUTCHISON MEDALIST PUTTER

| $35 | $45 | $90 |

Circa 1925-1930. Offset blade.

WILSONIAN PUTTER

| $35 | $45 | $80 |

Circa late 1920s.

RED RIBBON PUTTER

| $35 | $45 | $80 |

Circa late 1920s.

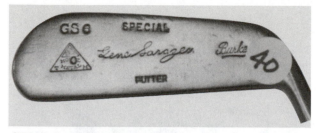

GENE SARAZEN PUTTER

| $110 | $160 | $260 |

Circa 1925-1930. "Pencil" neck 7-inch long hosel.

WALKER CUP PUTTER

| $35 | $45 | $80 |

Circa 1925-1930. Offset blade with a five-inch hosel.

PINEHURST PUTTER

| $35 | $50 | $90 |

Circa 1925-1930. Dot punched face.

TED RAY SEVENTY-TWO PUTTER

| $35 | $50 | $80 |

Circa late 1920s.

SUCCESS PUTTER #2-1/2

| $35 | $50 | $90 |

Circa 1920s. Bent neck line scored blade. All original.

HARRY VARDON PUTTER

| $35 | $45 | $90 |

Circa 1926-1930.

FAIRVIEW PUTTER

| $40 | $50 | $100 |

Circa 1910-1915. Smooth face blade.

TRIUMPH PUTTER

| $45 | $60 | $110 |

Circa 1925-1930. Flanged back.

WILSONIAN BRASS PUTTER

| $60 | $80 | $140 |

Circa 1925-1930. Ball face scoring.

WALKER CUP RAINBOW PUTTER

| $110 | $160 | $275 |

Circa late 1920s. Rainbow face.

PINEHURST IRONS

| $40 | $50 | $80 |

Circa 1925-1930. All irons.

SCHENECTADY PUTTER

| $135 | $200 | $350 |

Circa 1915-1920.

JOHNNY FARRELL IRONS

| $35 | $45 | $80 |

Circa 1930. "Matched Models D1002."

CREST IRONS

| $35 | $40 | $80 |

Circa 1930. All irons.

BOB MACDONALD IRONS

| $35 | $40 | $80 |

Circa late 1920s. All irons.

SUCCESS IRONS

| $35 | $40 | $80 |

Circa 1920s. All irons.

WALKER CUP IRONS

| $35 | $40 | $80 |

Circa late 1920s. All irons.

CUP DEFENDER IRONS

| $35 | $40 | $80 |

Circa 1930. All irons.

JOCK HUTCHISON IRONS

| $35 | $45 | $80 |

Circa 1930. All irons.

WILSONIAN IRONS

| $35 | $40 | $80 |

Circa 1920s. All irons.

TED RAY SEVENTY-TWO IRONS

| $35 | $45 | $80 |

Circa 1930. All irons.

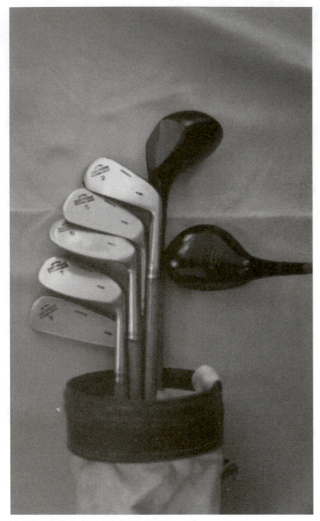

RED RIBBON IRON SET

$300	**$450**	**$850**

Circa 1930. Mid iron, mashie, mashie-niblick, niblick, and putter with 2 woods.

HARRY VARDON IRONS

$40	**$50**	**$80**

Circa 1930. All irons.

FAIRVIEW IRONS

$45	**$65**	**$100**

Circa 1910-1915. All smooth face irons.

DEEP GROOVE IRONS

$90	**$130**	**$225**

Circa 1915-1922. All irons. Corrugated deep grooves.

WALKER CUP RAINBOW IRONS

$100	**$150**	**$250**

Circa 1930. All irons. Rainbow face design.

DEEP GROOVE IRONS

$100	**$140**	**$240**

Circa 1915-1922. All irons. Slot grooves.

RED RIBBON IRONS

$35	**$40**	**$80**

Circa 1930. All irons.

SUCCESS WOODS

$75	**$90**	**$150**

Circa 1920s. Driver, brassie, or spoon.

WILSONIAN WOODS

$75	**$90**	**$150**

Circa 1920s. Driver, brassie, or spoon.

RED RIBBON WOODS

$75	**$90**	**$150**

Circa late 1920s. Driver, brassie, or spoon.

PINEHURST WOODS

$80	**$100**	**$175**

Circa 1925. Driver, brassie, or spoon.

SEVENTY-TWO SERIES WOODS

$85	**$110**	**$175**

Circa late 1920s. Harry Vardon or Ted Ray. Driver, brassie, or spoon.

GENE SARAZEN WOODS

$85	**$110**	**$175**

Circa 1925-1930. Driver, brassie, or spoon.

SMOOTH-FACE IRONS
$225   **$375**   **$900**
Circa 1880-90. General purpose or lofting iron with "W Wilson, Maker, St Andrews" stamping.

JUVENILE CLUBS
$30   **$40**   **$65**
"Gene Sarazen 11-13" on a circa 1925-1930 line scored mashie. Appears all original.

WILSON, WILLIE
ST. ANDREWS, SCOTLAND
Willie Wilson began forging clubs about 1870 in St. Andrews. He marked his clubs "W Wilson, St Andrews" and used the oval "St. Andrews Cross" mark during the 1890s.

BRASS-BLADE PUTTER
$250   **$425**   **$900**
Circa 1880-1890. "W Wilson St Andrews, Maker" mark.

SMOOTH-FACE CLEEK.
$250   **$450**   **$1,000**
Circa 1880-90. "W Wilson, Maker, St Andrews" stamping.

RUT IRON
$900   **$1,650**   **$3,500**
Circa 1880-90. "W Wilson, Maker, St Andrews" stamping.

WINTON, W & CO., LT'D
MONTROSE, SCOTLAND
The Winton family began forging irons about 1890 in Montrose, Scotland. They later added outlets in London and the club heads are

DODO PUTTER
$125   **$190**   **$350**
Circa 1925. Flanged back "Dodo, Little-Johnnie" putter. "Reg'd No. 353972."

---

marked as such. They used a "Diamond" cleek mark. They also made Bobby Jones' first "Calamity Jane" putters.

TAPLOW PUTTER
$40   **$55**   **$90**
Circa 1920s. "Diamond" mark.

PICCADILLY BLADE PUTTER
$40   **$55**   **$90**
Circa 1925. "Diamond" mark.

LINE SCORED FACE PUTTER
$40   **$55**   **$90**
Circa 1920-1925. Long blade putter. "Diamond" mark.

DOT FACE RUSTLESS PUTTER
$40   **$55**   **$100**
Circa 1925-1930. Offset blade. "Diamond" mark.

THE SPIELIN PUTTER
$50   **$65**   **$120**
Circa 1925. Step down hosel. "Diamond" mark.

TWO LEVEL BACK PUTTER
$60   **$100**   **$225**
Circa 1915-1920. "Diamond" mark.

FINESSE PUTTER
$160   **$250**   **$400**
Circa 1920. Shallow dot face blade. Oval hosel and shaft.

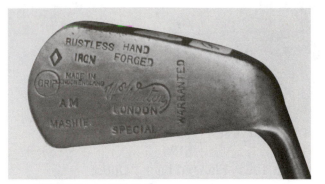

SMOOTH FACE IRONS

$50 **$70** **$135**

Circa 1900. All irons. "Winton, London" mark.

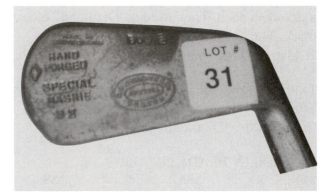

BOGIE SERIES IRONS

$140 **$220** **$375**

Circa 1920. Cavity back. "Bogie" stamped in the cavity.

THE MASCOT PUTTER

$175 **$275** **$450**

Circa 1920. Oval hosel and shaft. Large flange and rounded top line coming to a pointed toe.

JIGGER

$50 **$60** **$100**

Circa 1920. "Diamond" mark on toe.

HARRY VARDON SERIES IRONS

$50 **$60** **$100**

Circa 1920s. All irons. Line scored face. "Diamond" mark.

WIN-ON NIBLICK

$45 **$55** **$90**

Circa 1925-1930. Flanged back.

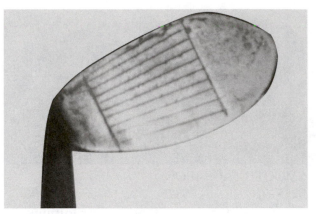

POINTED TOE CANNON PATENT

$125 **$200** **$350**

Circa early 1910s. "Ted Ray's Own." "Diamond" mark.

GIANT NIBLICK

$900 **$1,450** **$2,600**

Circa 1920. Large head. "Diamond" mark.

HOYLAKE SPECIAL IRONS

$45 **$55** **$100**

Circa 1910-1915. All irons. "Criss-cross" face scoring.

THE CERT SERIES IRONS

$55 **$65** **$110**

Circa 1920s. "Diamond" mark.

ANTI-SHANK IRONS

$125 **$200** **$350**

Circa 1910-1915. All irons. "Diamond" mark. Fairlie's Patent.

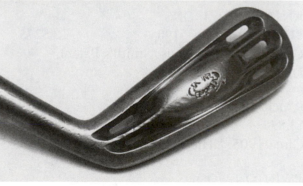

WATER IRONS

$2,750   **$4,800**   **$9,500**

Circa 1905. Horizontal slots perforating head
at heel and toe. Fancy flower face.

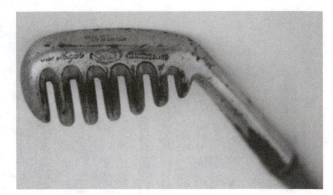

WATER IRONS

$2,750	$4,800	$9,500

Circa 1905. Horizontal slots perforating head at heel and toe. Fancy flower face.

FLANGED BACK IRONS

$55	$65	$110

Circa 1915. Diamond mark at toe.

DREADNOUGHT NIBLICK

$85	$140	$275

Circa 1920. Large head. "Diamond" mark.

ANTI-SHANK IRONS

$110	$190	$275

Circa 1920s. All irons. Smith's Patent. Diamond mark.

RAKE IRONS

$3,850	$5,750	$9,500

Circa 1905. "The Major." Seven pointed tines.

J WINTON WOODS

$80	$100	$170

Circa 1920. Driver, brassie, or spoon.

SPLICED NECK WOODS

$135	$200	$350

Circa 1910-1920. All woods.

SEMI-CIRCLE W & D PUTTERS

$300	$650	$1,500

Circa 1895-1897. Brass or Steel smooth-face blade with "Wright & Ditson, Boston" mark in a semi-circle at the toe. Screw-in shaft.

WRIGHT & DITSON

BOSTON, MA

Wright & Ditson began selling golf clubs at its Boston location about 1895. All clubs were purchased from A. G. Spalding & Brothers. Wright & Ditson added its own markings on the blank backs and wood heads for advertising purposes.

Jim Cooper has written the definitive work on Spalding, which is profusely illustrated. Every Spalding collector should have this reference in his or her library. It is available from the author, or Jim Cooper. There are also Wright & Ditson Retail Catalogue reprints from 1913, 1920, 1925, and 1930 available from the author of this book.

SEMI-CIRCLE W & D PUTTERS

$175	$350	$700

Circa 1895-1897. Brass or steel smooth-face blade with "Wright & Ditson, Boston" mark in a semi-circle at the toe.

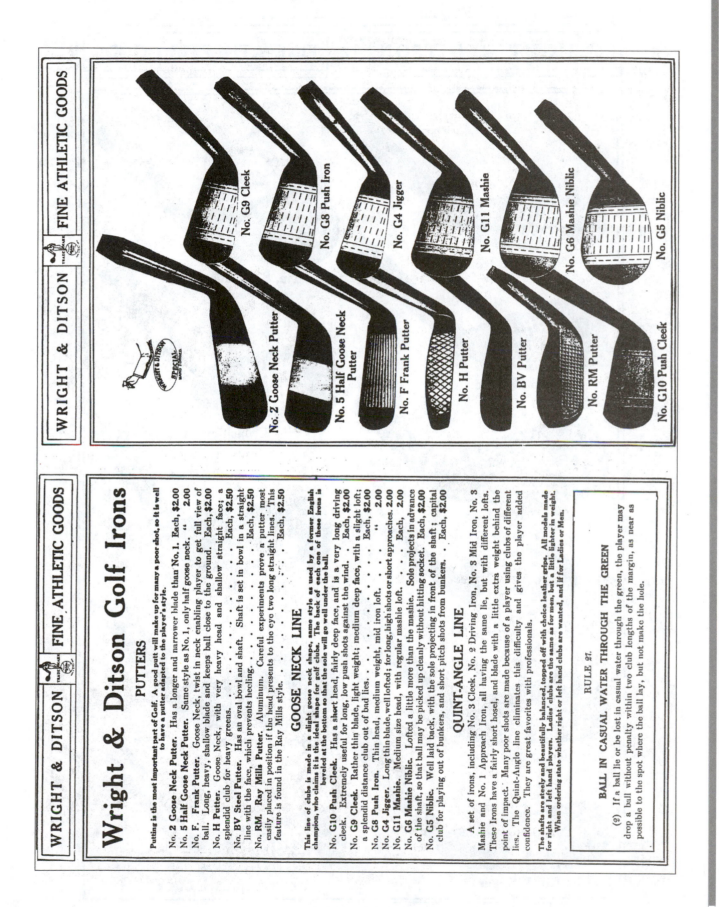

WRIGHT & DITSON   FINE ATHLETIC GOODS

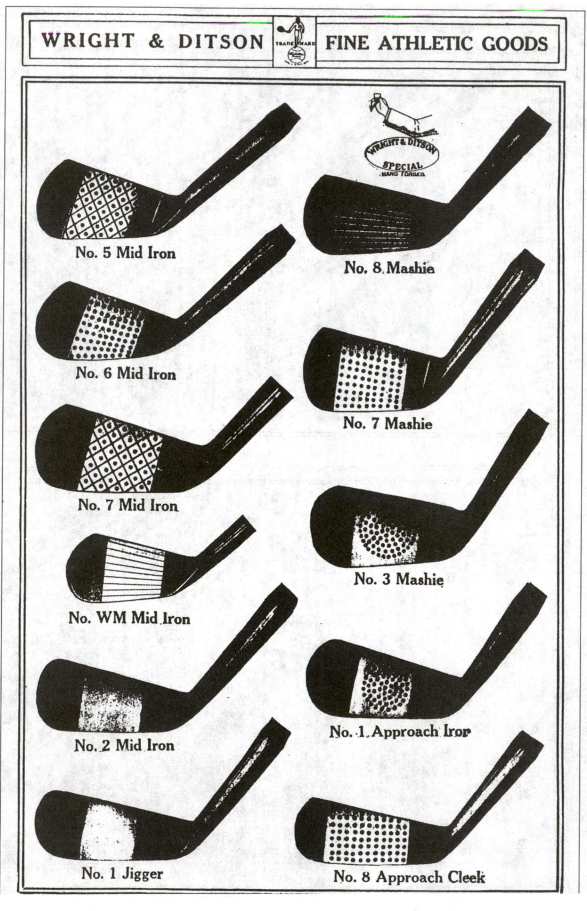

No. 5 Mid Iron

No. 8 Mashie

No. 6 Mid Iron

No. 7 Mashie

No. 7 Mid Iron

No. WM Mid Iron

No. 3 Mashie

No. 2 Mid Iron

No. 1 Approach Iron

No. 1 Jigger

No. 8 Approach Cleek

| WRIGHT & DITSON | FINE ATHLETIC GOODS |

Wright & Ditson Golf Irons

MASHIE NIBLICS

No. 3 Mashie Niblic. A new club with a flat sole, well laid back, with concave face, and will take a ball out of any bad lie; is also a fine club for pitching over bunkers or on to greens that lie up hill, and puts extreme backward spin on ball. Each, $2.00

No. 6 Mashie Niblic. A wide blade, well lofted, making a splendid approach club and fine for cut shots, causing the ball to drop dead. . . . . . Each, $2.00

NIBLICS

No. M Niblic. Is well laid back, with a long, deep face and a very thin sole, so that a ball may be played out of any hazard. The long blade with the thin sole puts a back spin on the ball that is certain to make it drop "dead" with hardly any roll, which makes this club an ideal one for short pitching. . . . . . Each, $2.00

No. 4 Niblic. A very heavy club for digging ball out of sand or other hazards. " 2.00

No. 6 Dreadnought Niblic. Has a very broad and flat face. . . . . " 2.00

PUTTING CLEEKS

No. 8 Putting Cleek. Has long blade; medium weight; the same length as a putter and is upright in lie. The face is slightly laid back in order to put a "drag" on the ball, and is the nicest club to use on rough putting greens. . . . . . Each, $2.00

No. 7 Putting Cleek. Similar to No. 8, but lighter weight and shorter blade. " 2.00

PUTTERS

Putting is the most important part of Golf. A good putt will make up for many a poor shot, so it is well to have a putter adapted to the player's style.

New Model Fownes. Made of wood and beautifully balanced. Splendid for either short or approach putts. . . . . Each, $3.00

No. RL. Wood face and brass back. A very handsome and useful putter. " 3.00

No. BM. Aluminum. Very popular with expert players, and is used for long approach putts. Flat, medium and upright lie. . . . . Each, $2.50

Hammer-Head Aluminum Putters improve your putting. Used and highly endorsed by many prominent players. . . . . Each, $2.50

Straight Face Putter. Regular style, in gun metal and steel; for novice and juvenile. 2.00

No. 1 Goose Neck Putter. Bent slightly in the neck, so that one can get a direct sight on the ball. Tapers gradually from a narrow top to a wide sole without any loft. Ball runs close to the ground. Has a long, shallow face. . . . . . Each, $2.00

The shafts are steely and beautifully balanced, topped off with choice leather grips. All models made for right and left hand players. Ladies' clubs are the same as for men, but a little lighter in weight. When ordering state whether right or left hand clubs are wanted, and if for Ladies or Men.

RULE 27.

(1). Casual water in a Hazard, drop behind the Hazard or in the Hazard under penalty of one stroke.

RULE 6.

A competitor shall not ask for or willingly receive advice except from his caddie.

RULE 30.

When the player's ball lies on the putting green he shall not play until the opponent's ball is at rest.

| WRIGHT & DITSON | FINE ATHLETIC GOODS |

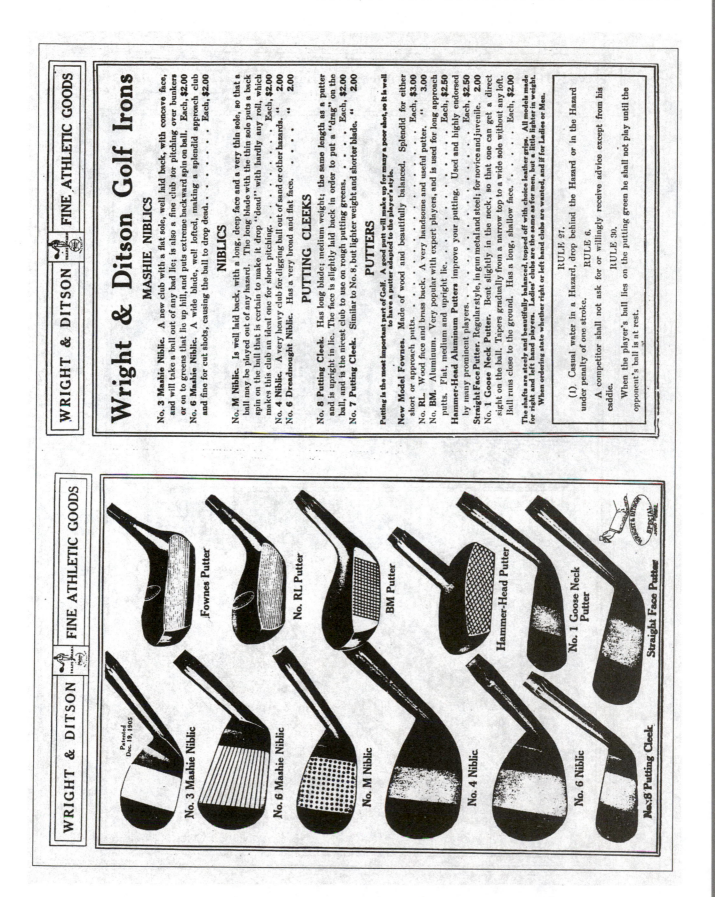

Patented Dec. 19, 1905 — No. 3 Mashie Niblic — Fownes Putter — No. 6 Mashie Niblic — No. RL Putter — No. M Niblic — BM Putter — No. 4 Niblic — Hammer-Head Putter — No. 6 Niblic — No. 1 Goose Neck Putter — No. 8 Putting Cleek — Straight Face Putter

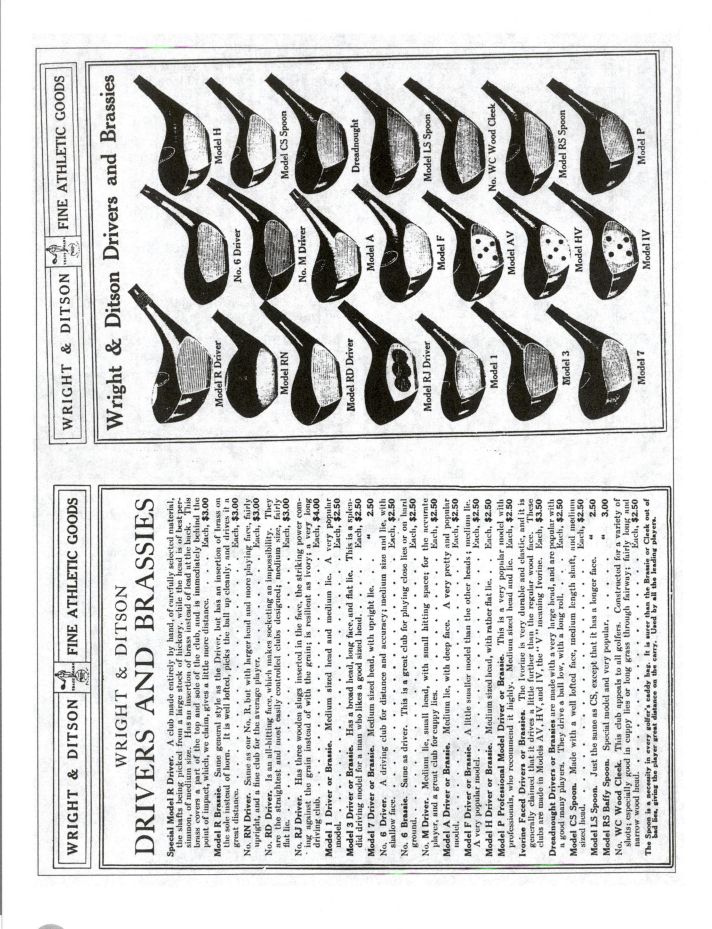

ONE SHOT SERIES PUTTERS
$45 $55 $110
Circa 1915. Offset blade.

ST. ANDREWS SERIES PUTTERS
$40 $50 $100
Circa 1910. Square punches on face.

WRIGHT & DITSON, MAKERS, ST. ANDREWS
$60 $80 $160
Circa 1898-1903. All irons.

WRIGHT & DITSON
$60 $80 $160
Circa 1898-1903. All irons.

WRIGHT & DITSON SELECTED PUTTERS
$90 $125 $250
Circa 1898-1903. Severely bent neck in the "Park" style.

ONE SHOT SERIES PUTTERS
$60 $90 $160
Circa 1915. Smooth-face brass blade.

ONE SHOT SERIES PUTTERS
$70 $110 $220
Circa 1915. Flanged back with "Maxwell" holes drilled into the hosel.

"F" SERIES PUTTER
$45 $65 $100
Circa 1922-1925. Deep scoring lines on bottom of face; top is smooth.

A H FINDLAY PUTTERS
$50 $65 $130
Circa 1900-1905. Smooth face, straight steel blade.

A H FINDLAY PUTTERS
$60 $80 $150
Circa 1900-1905. Twisted neck gem-type wide-sole putter.

A H FINDLAY PUTTERS
$65 $85 $150
Circa 1900-1905. Smooth face straight Brass blade.

BEE-LINE SERIES PUTTERS
$35 $45 $80
Circa 1920s. Offset hosel and a line-scored blade.

KRO-FLITE SERIES PUTTERS
$35 $45 $80
Circa 1926-30 Sweet Spot "R F Putter" with long hosel and offset blade. Patented Sept. 13, 1927.

VICTOR SERIES PUTTER
$35 $45 $80
Circa 1920s. Blade putter.

A H FINDLAY IRONS

$50	$70	$140

Circa 1900-1905. Smooth-face iron or lofting iron.

BEE-LINE SERIES IRONS

$35	$40	$70

Circa 1920s. All irons.

RAINBOW SERIES PUTTERS

$35	$45	$80

Circa 1920s. Dot-punched face. "Rainbow" mark.

ALUMINUM HEAD PUTTERS

$85	$125	$225

Circa 1915-1920. "B M Wright & Ditson Special."

WRIGHT & DITSON SELECTED IRONS

$50	$70	$140

Circa 1898-1903. All irons.

A H FINDLAY IRONS

$60	$80	$160

Circa 1900-1905. Smooth-face cleek.

ONE SHOT SERIES IRONS

$40	$60	$100

Circa 1910-15. All smooth-face irons.

ONE SHOT SERIES IRONS

$110	$140	$250

Circa 1920. Corrugated deep groove "Dedstop Jigger".

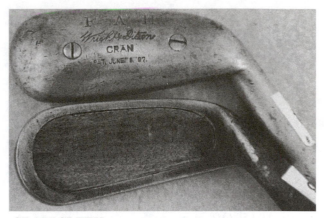

CRAN CLEEK

$500	$1,000	$2,250

Circa 1897-1915. Wood face insert.

ST. ANDREWS SERIES IRONS

$35	$40	$70

Circa 1915-1925. All irons.

"F" SERIES IRONS

$40	$50	$90

Circa 1922-1925. F-2 through F-7 or F-9 with deep scoring lines on bottom of face, top is smooth.

ONE SHOT SERIES IRONS

$40	$50	$90

Circa 1915. All marked face irons.

"F" SERIES IRONS

$40	$50	$90

Circa 1922-1925. F-1 with deep scoring lines on bottom of face; top is smooth.

ONE SHOT SERIES IRONS

$40	$50	$90

Circa 1920. "#8" Sky-iron or Jigger.

"F" SERIES "SKY-IRON"

$50	$70	$125

Circa 1922-1925. Deep scoring lines on bottom of face, top is smooth.

ONE SHOT SERIES IRONS
$90 $125 $200
Circa 1915-1922. Corrugated or slot-type deep groove mashie, mashie-niblick, or niblick.

KRO-FLITE SERIES IRONS
$35 $40 $70
Circa 1926-1930. Sweet spot. 1 through 8 and 19.

VICTOR SERIES IRONS
$35 $40 $70
Circa 1920s.

RAINBOW SERIES IRONS
$35 $45 $75
Circa 1920s. Dot-scored face.

WATERFALL IRONS
$350 $500 $900
Circa 1920. "Bee-Line" markings.

DOUBLE WATERFALL IRONS
$1,600 $2,400 $4,500
Circa 1920. "Bee-Line" markings.

SPLICED-NECK WOODS
$135 $225 $500
Circa 1898-1903. "Wright & Ditson" in script. Driver, brassie, or spoon. Some have leather face inserts.

SPLICED-NECK WOODS
$220 $325 $800
Circa 1898-1903. Pear-shaped, persimmon head, bulger-face driver, or brassie. Some have leather face insert.

A H FINDLAY WOODS
$85 $110 $200
Circa 1900-1905. Driver, brassie, or spoon. Many with leather face inserts.

A H FINDLAY WOODS
$110 $135 $275
Circa 1900. Bulger driver or brassie with a leather face insert. Very thick, oval shaped socket hosel.

VICTOR SPECIAL SOCKET WOODS
$90 $120 $220
Circa 1900-1910.

WRIGHT & DITSON WOODS
$75 $85 $150
Circa 1910-1920 Driver, brassie, or spoon.

BEE-LINE SERIES WOODS
$75 $85 $150
Circa 1920s Driver, brassie, or spoon.

ST. ANDREWS SERIES WOODS
$75 $85 $150
Circa 1920s. Driver, brassie, or spoon.

ST. ANDREWS SERIES WOODS
$80 $110 $200
Circa 1920s. Small head wooden cleek or Bull Dog head.

VICTOR SERIES WOODS
$75 $85 $150
Circa 1920s Driver, brassie, or spoon.

ALUMINUM HEAD WOODS
$110 $150 $300
Circa 1910-1920. Various lofts.

JUVENILE CLUBS
$30 $40 $75
Circa 1920. "Y" Youth series putter or irons.

Gripping:

Cut the grip on a bias and attach to top of shaft with tack.

Wrap the grip so each wind fits snug. You should be stretching the grip for a tight fit. If you prefer a thicker grip, put the grip over cloth wraps (underlisting) then apply grip. Tack at a point where you want to end the grip and cut grip below the tack.

Cosmetic whipping:

Form an "L" with the whipping and cover the "L" with four to 10 wraps. Make a "loop" from a piece of the whipping and place over the windings. Cover the loop with three to four turns, cut the whipping and place the end thru the loop. Pull the loop through and cut off the excess whipping. If your club does not have an end cap, you should also whip about 1/2 inch down from the end.

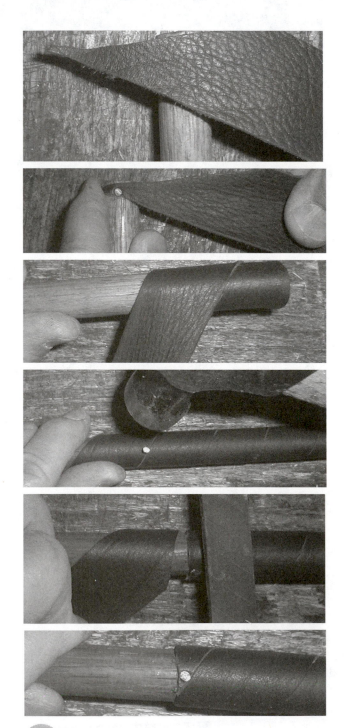

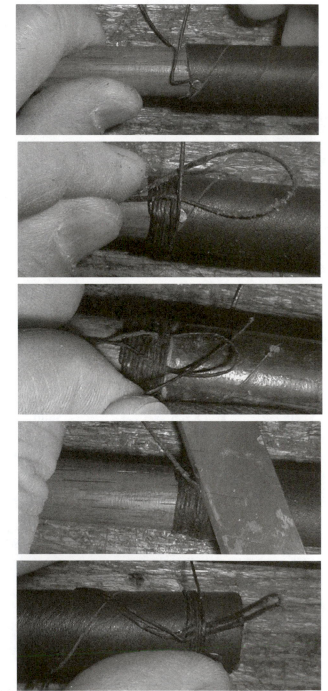

Chapter 5

Golf Balls

Golfers through the ages have played with balls made from many different materials: wood, feathers stuffed into a leather cover, gutta-percha, wound rubber centers with celluloid covers, balls with "honey" centers, solid balls made of "space age" plastics, graphite windings, Cadwell Geer, syrlin, balata, and zinthane covers.

The ball most people associate with pre-1850 golf is the "feather" ball. A skilled worker took three pieces of leather, two round and one rectangular strip, and sewed the three together with heavy waxed thread. Before the last few stitches were completed, it was turned inside out to hide the seams. A quantity of boiled feathers, enough to fill a top hat, were stuffed through the tiny unsewn opening and the closing stitches finished the ball. Many ball makers soaked the leather in "alum" and when the cover dried, it shrunk. At the same time, the drying feathers inside expanded, making a surprisingly hard, very playable golf ball. *The Encyclopedia of Golf Collectibles* by Olman and *The Curious History of the Golf Ball* by Martin provide lengthy descriptions of how the feather ball was made.

A skilled worker could only make three or four good balls in a day and, as a result, the balls were rather expensive. It is thought that a feather ball in the early 19th century (expressing value in 2000's dollars) cost the golfer $50 or more! Only royalty and the very wealthy could afford these expensive balls.

In the 1840s, experiments making golf balls from gutta-percha transformed the ancient game that had been played for 400 years with hardly a change. Gutta-percha, dried sap of the Malaysian sapodilla tree, was used during that time the same way we use Styrofoam peanuts to pack fragile items. The gutta-percha was heated in boiling water and rolled into a sphere by hand, then left to "cure" for a few weeks before being painted. In a day's work, a skilled worker could make

An assortment of individually wrapped and boxed golf balls is a collector's dream.

This gutty ball was made by Allan Robertson, circa 1853.

A smooth gutty mold has a clamping device, circa 1850.

A hand-hammered gutta-percha ball dates to 1855.

10 times as many "gutties" as he could featheries. The price of the gutties was about one-fifth the price of the feather ball, with remade balls even less. Many who previously could not afford to play began to use this new inexpensive ball.

The transition from the feather ball to the gutta-percha ball was not as rapid as most golf writers and auctioneers make it out to be. Robert Forgan recalled: "… (in 1856) gutta-percha balls were just getting established, and as they were much cheaper than the feather ball, golf soon began to spread …" Featheries were most likely still played by many traditional Scotsmen well into the 1860s.

Gutta balls that had been scuffed and nicked during play were found to fly straighter and longer than the new smooth balls. Some players gave new balls to their caddies to "knock them around" before play began. Somewhere along the line, an enterprising ball maker used the "claw" of his hammer to nick the ball's surface. Patterns were cut into the ball using a chisel, until another enterprising maker decided a metal mold with raised markings could mold the gutta-percha into a uniform ready-made "scored" ball.

Golf was propelled into the modern game we know today by the Haskell Patent of April 11, 1899. Working for B.F. Goodrich of Akron, Ohio, Coburn Haskell and Bertram Works developed a process, in 1898, of winding thin rubber strips around a central core and covered these windings with a cover of gutta-percha. Again, everyone did not change from the guttie to the rubber-core balls overnight. In fact, the only player in the 1902 British Open field playing the new Haskell ball was Sandy Herd, the eventual winner. By 1910, though, only the diehards were playing gutties.

As the game grew during the later part of the 19th and early 20th centuries, golfers demanded a better ball, and hundreds of ball makers began molding balls with a variety of

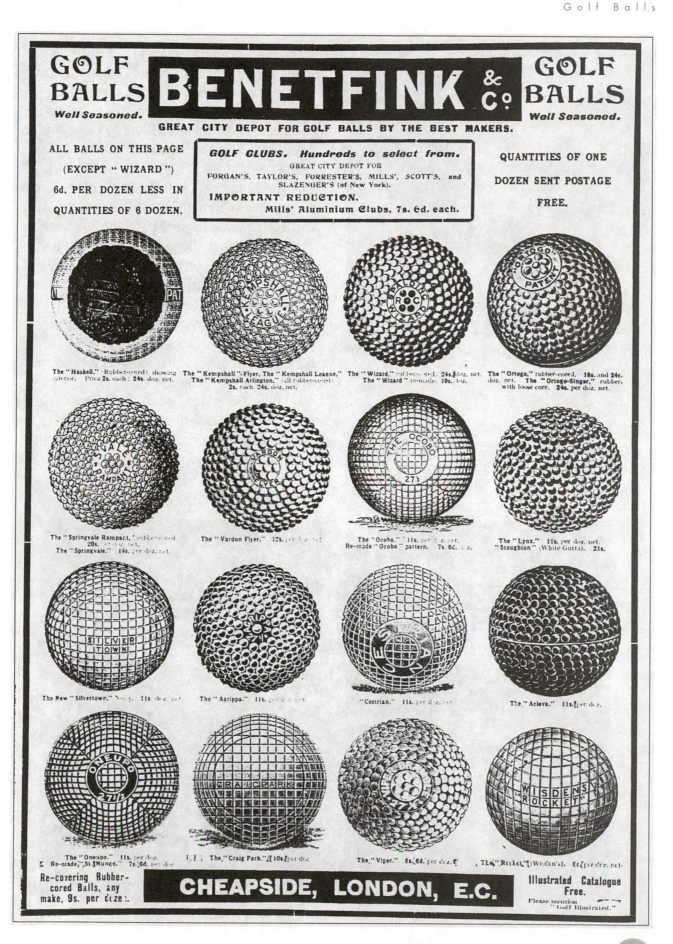

Smooth and dimpled golf ball molds are made of brass and iron.

cover patterns. Covers had circles, dots, stars, swirls, crescents, squares in circles, triangles, hexagons, octagons, dimples, brambles, and were cut with lines. The "Pneumatic" ball was filled with air and there were some balls that emitted smoke or an odor to aid in finding it in the rough. There were also balls made to float on the water.

Literally thousands of patterns and combinations of patterns were used by the manufacturers to single out their ball from all others available.

During the period from 1895 to 1940, most balls came in a wrapper with a paper seal that carried the advertisement and the ball's name. Many companies thought wrapping the ball justified the high prices for golf balls. We must understand that during the Great Depression balls were selling for 50 cents to $1 each. Balls were truly expensive when considering the price of steak, potatoes and milk. Even in the bountiful "Roaring '20s," $1 was a large sum to pay for a golf ball.

There are several good references on golf balls worth looking into, including *The Curious History of the Golf Ball,* 1968, by Martin; *The Encyclopedia of Golf Collectibles,* 1985, by Olman and *Antique Golf Ball Reference Guide,* 1993, by Kelly.

Collecting golf ball boxes can be as challenging as collecting balls.

D&M GOLF BALLS

The D&M **SKULL**   75c

No. 16. The D&M "Skull" is a golf ball that is popular among golfers from the tournament player down to the beginner. It has the "click" and long "carry" that pleases the hard-hitting low-handicap player. It is absolutely true in flight and roll, and has a cover equal to any ball on the market for taking punishment from misplayed shots. Supplied in the new standard size and weight. Multi-dot markings in four colors.
No. 16. Skull, mesh only....................$.75

The D&M **BLUE FOX**   75c

No. 12. This ball represents a splendid combination of distance and durability. It has a speedy get-away, flies far and true and has a protective covering that will stand the gaff of hard usage. Marked in four colors and available in dimple markings only. New standard size and weight.
No. 12. Dimple only, price.................$.75

The D&M **OWL**   50c

The outstanding feature of this ball is service. It will stand up and give complete satisfaction for general play. It is responsive to all shots, has good carry, and has a particularly tough but elastic cover that will not cut easily. The "Owl" is a wonderfully fine ball for the price. Available in new size and weight to conform to new requirements adopted by U. S. G. A.
No. 14M. Mesh. Price.....................$.50
No. 14D. Dimple. Price.................... .50

The D&M **CRICKET**   3 for $1.00

No. 18. For a "three for a dollar" golf ball the D&M Cricket has much to offer in distance and accuracy in flight and roll. It has plenty of stamina to withstand the abuse it may get from a beginner's irons. An ideal ball for golf driving ranges, miniature golf courses and regular golf play. New standard size and weight. Price, each $.35. Three for $1.00.

PRACTO GOLF BALLS

These balls are very light and soft. Ideal for outdoor or indoor practice. They have a strongly knit cover that will stand up under many hard shots from wood and iron clubs.
No. P1. Practice Balls. Price...............$.25

TURNER PRACTICE GOLF BALLS

The Turner practice balls are of thin hollow rubber. A flanged base is provided for teeing the ball up for practice shots. They are very soft, light and durable.
No. PT5. Turner Practice Balls. Price.......$.25

PRICES
Golf Balls

GENERAL PRICING:
The following pricing is by major type only. Prices are for the common balls of that type or cover pattern.

FEATHER BALL		
$2,400	$4,200	$8,500

SMOOTH GUTTA-PERCHA		
$1,200	$2,400	$6,000

HAND HAMMERED GUTTA-PERCHA		
$1,200	$2,200	$5,000

LINE CUT GUTTA-PERCHA		
$190	$350	$850

BRAMBLE GUTTA-PERCHA		
$175	$350	$800

BRAMBLE GUTTA-PERCHA COVER WITH RUBBER CORE		
$140	$350	$950

BRAMBLE RUBBER OR CELLULOID COVER		
$125	$250	$750

SQUARE MESH COVER		
$40	$75	$225

Prices are for grades G-5, G-7, and G9.

NO MAKER'S NAME
FEATHER BALL

$4,400	$5,750	$12,000

Circa 1800. Large size.

GOURLAY, JOHN
MUSSELBURGH
FEATHER BALL

$5,750	$8,750	$13,500

Circa 1840-1860. "J Gourlay" and size number.

NO MAKER'S NAME
FEATHER BALL

$2,400	$4,200	$8,000

Circa 1840-1860. Average size.

FEATHER BALLS

MORRIS, TOM, ST. ANDREWS
FEATHER BALL

$8,000	$15,000	$30,000

Circa 1840-1860. "T Morris" and size number.

ROBERTSON, ALLAN
FEATHER BALL

$5,750	$10,500	$17,500

Circa 1840-1850. "Allan" and size number.

LINE CUT GUTTA-PERCHA
$190 $350 $800
Circa 1895-1905.

NO MAKER'S NAME
SMOOTH GUTTA-PERCHA
$1,200 $2,400 $6,000
Circa 1850-1860. White, brown, or black usually
with a "test" mark.

HAND HAMMERED
GUTTA-PERCHA
$1,200 $2,200 $5,000
Circa 1850-1880. Hand marked with a chisel.

UNKNOWN MAKER (FORGAN STYLE)
RED HAND HAMMERED WINTER BALL
$1,250 $3,750 $10,000

MACHINE CUT GUTTA-PERCHA
$225 $500 $1,800
Circa 1880-1895. Pattern with wavy lines from
line cutting machine.

UNKNOWN MAKERS

LINE CUT GUTTA-PERCHA
$800 $1,200 $2,500
Circa 1895. "Allaway" in rectangular panel.

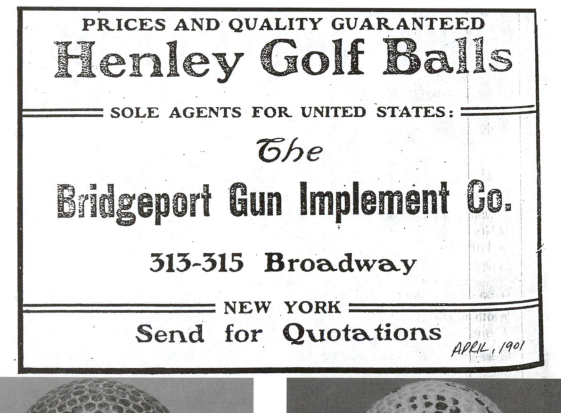

PRICES AND QUALITY GUARANTEED

Henley Golf Balls

SOLE AGENTS FOR UNITED STATES:

The

Bridgeport Gun Implement Co.

313-315 Broadway

NEW YORK

Send for Quotations

APRIL, 1901

BRAMBLE GUTTA-PERCHA
$400   **$900**   **$2,500**
Circa 1895-1905. "Maltese Cross," could have been sold by or made by F. H. Ayres, London

AUCHTERLONIE
ST. ANDREWS
BRAMBLE GUTTA-PERCHA
$800   **$1,200**   **$2,500**
Circa 1895-1905. "Auchterlonie" at pole. (Notice the backwards "N" in the name.) Also collectible as a signature ball.

GUTTA-PERCHA BALLS

REMADE, NO NAME
BRAMBLE GUTTA-PERCHA
$175   **$350**   **$800**
Circa 1895-1905. No name, or maker's name not identifiable.

BRAMBLE GUTTA-PERCHA
$400   **$800**   **$2,000**
Circa 1895-1905. "The Finch."

VARIOUS MAKERS
LINE CUT GUTTA-PERCHA
$175   **$375**   **$900**
Circa 1895-1905. Maker's name marked on ball.

227

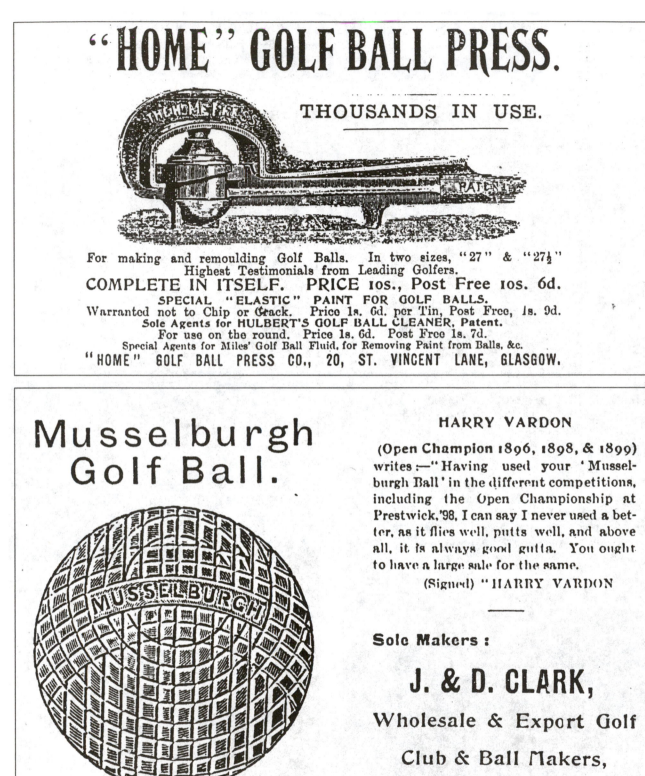

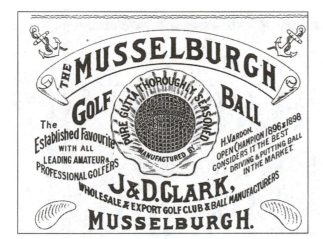

CLARK, J. & D.
MUSSELBURGH
LINE CUT GUTTA-PERCHA
$500   **$1,000**   **$2,750**
Circa 1900. "Musselburgh" across the equator.

COUNTY CHEMICAL CO.
CHEMICO DE LUXE
$800   **$1,500**   **$3,200**
Circa 1900. "Horseshoe" type markings with "Dots." "Chemico De Luxe" at poles. Very scarce.

DUNN, WILLIE
NEW YORK
LINE CUT GUTTA-PERCHA
$500   **$1,000**   **$2,800**
Circa 1895. "Dunn's Record Ball 27."

STARS AND STRIPES GUTTA
$6,000   **$12,000**   **$32,000**
Circa 1897. "Willie Dunn's Stars and Stripes" and "Patented July 27, 1897, No 27441" at the poles. Extremely rare.

HALLEY, J. B.
LONDON
LINE CUT GUTTA-PERCHA
$400   **$800**   **$1,500**
Circa 1895. "The Ocobo 27 1/2."

BRAMBLE GUTTA-PERCHA
$190   **$350**   **$800**
Circa 1895-1905. Maker's name marked on ball.

FORGAN, ROBERT
ST. ANDREWS
HAMMERED GUTTA-PERCHA
$1,200   **$3,000**   **$7,500**
Circa 1855-1880. Stamped "R Forgan" usually with size number.

GUTTA-PERCHA CO.
LONDON
EUREKA LINE CUT GUTTA
$350   **$800**   **$2,500**
Circa late 1890s. Widely spaced lines. "The Eureka 27 1/2" at poles.

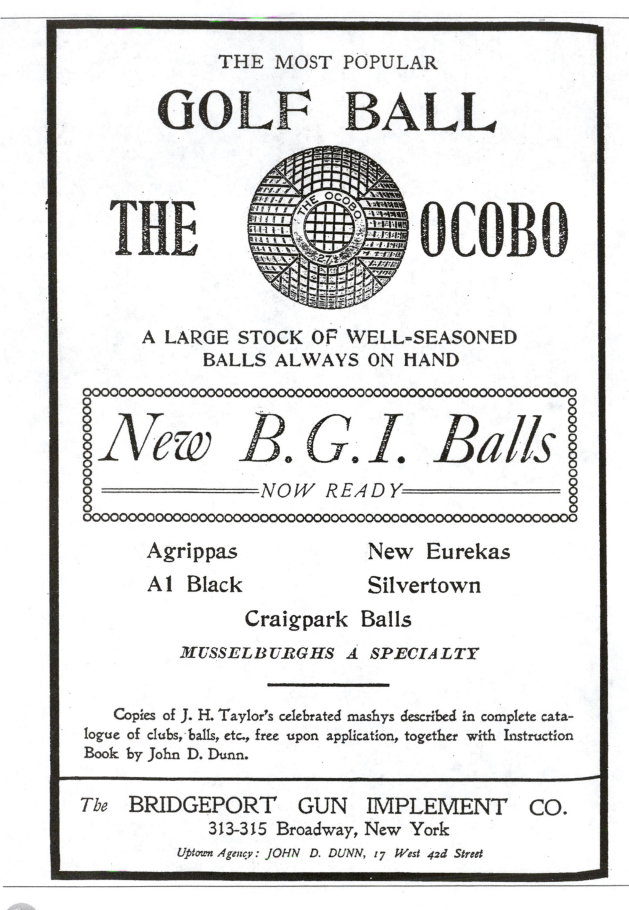

HENLEY'S
LONDON
LINE CUT GUTTA-PERCHA
$400 $800 $2,500
Circa 1895. "Henley" in a rectangular panel.

MORRIS, TOM
ST. ANDREWS
BRAMBLE GUTTA-PERCHA
$1,200 $3,000 $6,000
Circa 1895-1905. "The Tom Morris 27 1/2." Also collectible as a signature ball.

PARK, WILLIE
MUSSELBURGH
LINE CUT GUTTA-PERCHA
$1,500 $3,500 $6,000
Circa 1890s. "Park" in rectangular panel. Also collectible as a signature ball.

PARK ROYAL
HEXAGONAL FACES
$7,000 $15,000 $32,000
Circa 1896. Supposedly designed to minimize speed on downhill putts. Rare!

SILVERTOWN
LINE CUT GUTTA-PERCHA
$225 $500 $1,500
Circa 1890-1905.

HENLEY'S
LONDON
WHY NOT BRAMBLE
$100 $220 $650
Circa 1915-1925 with "Why Not" at both poles.

HUTCHISON MAIN
GLASGOW
SPRINGVALE GUTTA
$200 $450 $1,250
Circa 1900. Line cut.
SPRINGVALE SERIES BRAMBLE
$200 $400 $1,000
Circa 1900. "SVale" Hawk, Falcon, Eagle, Kite, and others.

SPALDING
BRAMBLE GUTTA-PERCHA, VARDON
FLYER
$550 $1,250 $3,000
Circa 1900. "Vardon Flyer" at both poles. Also
collectible as a signature ball.

WHIT & BARNES
THE DIAMOND GUTTA
$1,000 $2,000 $3,500
Circa 1895-1900. "Diamond W & B Co" at equator.
"Diamond" pattern line cut gutta-percha. Very rare.

DIMPLE BALLS

UNKNOWN MAKER
THE RESILIENT
$800 $1,750 $4,000
Circa 1910. "The Resilient" at the poles. Ringed
"Diamonds" pattern. Very scarce.

THE FALCON
$800 $1,250 $2,500
Circa 1910. "The Falcon 27" at poles. Similar
design to the "Diamond Chick."

CAPON HEATON
$600 $1,200 $2,500
Circa 1910. "Capon Heaton" at poles. Five pointed stars inside a large dimple. Very scarce.

FAROID
$1,750 $4,200 $8,800
Circa 1920. "Faroid, This End Up" at poles.
Ringed pattern. Very scarce.

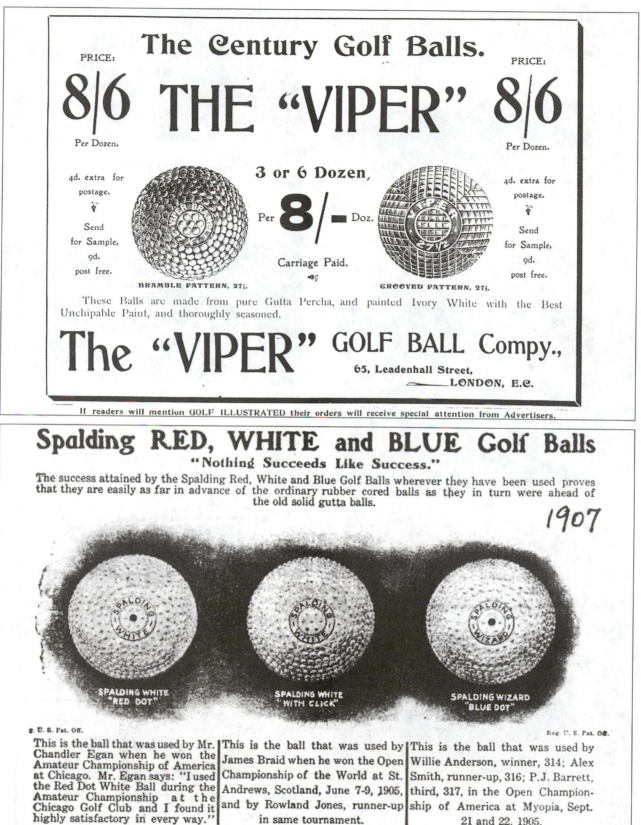

The Century Golf Balls.

PRICE:

8|6

Per Dozen.

4d. extra for postage.

Send for Sample, 9d. post free.

THE "VIPER"

3 or 6 Dozen,

Per **8|-** Doz.

Carriage Paid.

PRICE:

8|6

Per Dozen.

4d. extra for postage.

Send for Sample, 9d. post free.

BRAMBLE PATTERN. 27½.

GROOVED PATTERN. 27½.

These Balls are made from pure Gutta Percha, and painted Ivory White with the Best Unchipable Paint, and thoroughly seasoned.

The "VIPER" GOLF BALL Compy.,

65, Leadenhall Street,
LONDON, E.C.

If readers will mention GOLF ILLUSTRATED their orders will receive special attention from Advertisers.

Spalding RED, WHITE and BLUE Golf Balls

"Nothing Succeeds Like Success."

The success attained by the Spalding Red, White and Blue Golf Balls wherever they have been used proves that they are easily as far in advance of the ordinary rubber cored balls as they in turn were ahead of the old solid gutta balls.

1907

SPALDING WHITE "RED DOT"

SPALDING WHITE "WITH CLICK"

SPALDING WIZARD "BLUE DOT"

g. U. S. Pat. Off.

Reg. U. S. Pat. Off.

This is the ball that was used by Mr. Chandler Egan when he won the Amateur Championship of America at Chicago. Mr. Egan says: "I used the Red Dot White Ball during the Amateur Championship at the Chicago Golf Club and I found it highly satisfactory in every way."

This is the ball that was used by James Braid when he won the Open Championship of the World at St. Andrews, Scotland, June 7-9, 1905, and by Rowland Jones, runner-up in same tournament.

This is the ball that was used by Willie Anderson, winner, 314; Alex Smith, runner-up, 316; P.J. Barrett, third, 317, in the Open Championship of America at Myopia, Sept. 21 and 22, 1905.

CAPPER & CAPPER
CHICAGO
BLACK BUG DIMPLE
$100   **$250**   **$750**
Circa 1920. No name, just a black bug at the pole.

COCHRANE'S LTD.
EDINBURGH
STAR CHALLENGER
$350   **$750**   **$1,500**
Circa 1905-1910. "The Challenger" surrounding a "Star" on the poles. Joined stars circle the ball.

THE GAMAGE
LONDON
GAMAGE'S ARIEL
$300   **$650**   **$1,400**
Circa 1920. "Gamage's Ariel" at poles. Large widely spaced dimples.

HENRY, ALEX
HENRY'S RIFLED BALL
$6,000   **$15,000**   **$32,000**
Circa 1903. "Henry's Rifled Ball" at poles. Cover is a swirl pattern similar to a rifle barrel.

HENLEY'S
LONDON
HENLEY
$3,500   **$6,500**   **$12,000**
Circa 1920s. "Henley" at equator. Triple line pattern that resembles the British "Union Jack" flag. Very scarce.

HENRY C. LYTTON
CHICAGO
BLUE BIRD DIMPLE
$40   **$90**   **$250**
Circa 1920s. No name, just a flying bird on pole.

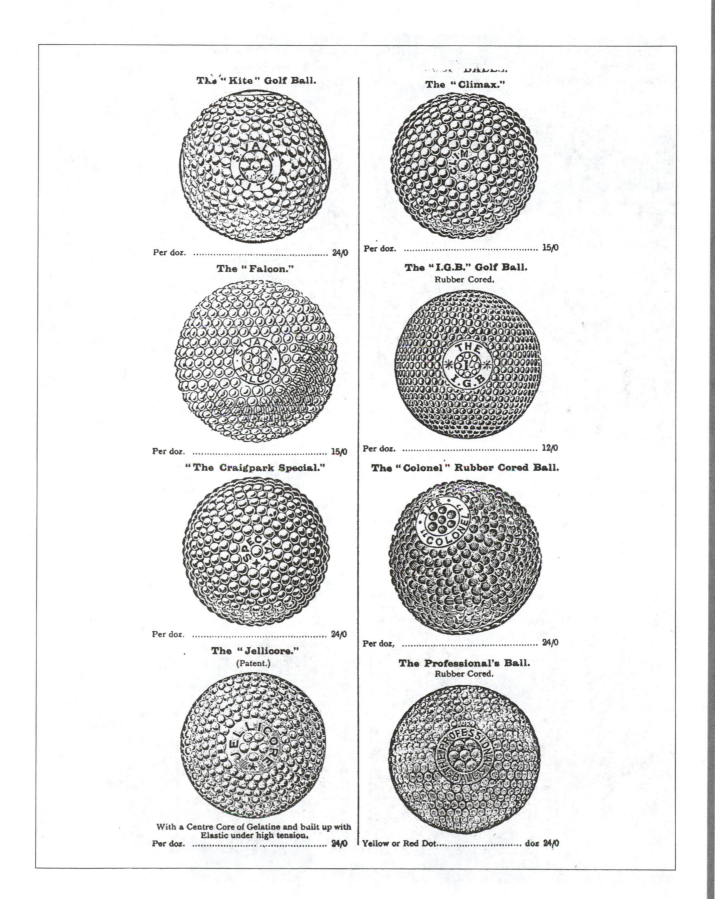

The "Kite" Golf Ball.

Per doz. 24/0

The "Climax."

Per doz. 15/0

The "Falcon."

Per doz. 15/0

The "I.G.B." Golf Ball.
Rubber Cored.

Per doz. 12/0

"The Craigpark Special."

Per doz. 24/0

The "Colonel" Rubber Cored Ball.

Per doz, ... 24/0

The "Jellicore."
(Patent.)

With a Centre Core of Gelatine and built up with
Elastic under high tension.
Per doz. 24/0

The Professional's Ball.
Rubber Cored.

Yellow or Red Dot.......................... doz 24/0

NORTH BRITISH
EDINBURGH
DIAMOND CHICK
$1,500   **$2,500**   **$5,000**
Circa 1910-1915. "Diamond Chick" at poles. A very odd pattern. Very scarce.

SUPER CHICK DIMPLE
 $150   **$350**   **$750**
Circa 1920. "Super Chick 31" at poles. Large dimples. Very scarce.

REACH, A. J.
PHILADELPHIA
REACH EAGLE DIMPLE
$40   **$80**   **$190**
Circa 1920s. "Reach Eagle" at poles. Balls in boxes or wrappers are worth double.

REACH, WRIGHT & DITSON
DIMPLE BALLS
$15   **$40**   **$100**
Circa 1930. Many names. Balls in boxes or wrappers are worth double.
Fig. 1 and 2.

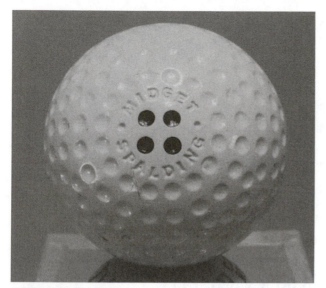

SPALDING, USA
DIMPLE COVER
$40 $100 $300
Circa 1908-1925. Many markings including
Midget Dimple, 40, 50, 60, Dot, Baby Dimple,
Domino, Glory Dimple, Honor, and others.

DIMPLE COVER
$15 $30 $75
Circa 1920-1940. "P G A."

ST. MUNGO, NEWARK, NJ
DIMPLE BALLS CIRCA 1920s
Non-Floaters: Colonel 29, Colonel 30 & Colonel
31
$20 $45 $150

ST. MUNGO, NEWARK, NJ
DIMPLE BALLS CIRCA 1920'S
Floater: Colonel 27
$25 $60 $200

ST. MUNGO, NEWARK & GLASGOW
HEAVY COLONEL
$450 $850 $2,000
Circa 1915. "Heavy Colonel" at poles. Large
widely spaced dimples.

STOW-WOODWARD
BURBANK
$800 $1,200 $2,500
Circa 1930s. "Burbank" crossed vertically and
horizontally at poles. An unusual swirl cover pattern. Very scarce.

MESH BALLS

UNKNOWN MAKER
CUDAHY'S PURITAN MESH
$40 $80 $250
Circa 1920s and 1930s. "Cudahys Puritan" at
poles. Standard square mesh pattern.

UNKNOWN AMERICAN MAKER
ODD PATTERN
$40 $125 $750

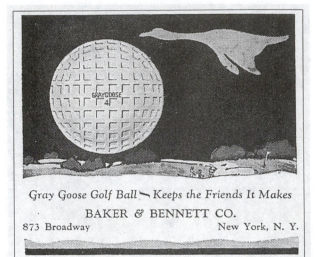

ASSOCIATED GOLFERS
DARBY FLYER MESH
$50 $100 $250
Circa 1920s. "Darby Flyer" at poles. Standard square mesh pattern.

UNKNOWN BRITISH MAKER
GUTTA-PERCHA DIMPLE COVER THE LION
$100 $250 $800
C-1905-1910 with "The Lion" surrounding a "star" at poles.
ST. REGIS MESH
$40 $80 $250
Circa 1930s. Standard square mesh pattern. There is a steel mold for this ball currently on the market. It sold for **$700 in 1995.**

AVON
AVON DELUXE MESH
$50 $100 $300
Circa 1920s. "Avon DeLuxe" at poles. Standard square mesh pattern.

BURKE MFG. CO.
NEWARK, OH
BURKE 50-50 MESH
$50 $100 $300
Circa 1920s. "Burke 50-50" at poles. Standard square mesh pattern.

COCHRANE'S LTD.
EDINBURGH
REX MESH
$40 $80 $250
Circa 1920s and 1930s. Standard square mesh pattern.

DRAPER-MAYNARD
PORTSMOUTH, NH
OWL MESH, D & M SKULL & D & CRICKET
$50 $100 $300
Circa 1930. Standard square mesh pattern.

BAKER & BENNETT
NEW YORK
GRAY GOOSE MESH
$50 $100 $300
Circa 1920s. Standard square mesh pattern. They came in an individual box. A G-7 box will double the value.

DRAPER-MAYNARD
PORTSMOUTH, NH
Circa 1930 DIMPLE
$35 $55 $150
Standard dimple pattern "D & M Blue Fox."

DUNLOP
DUNLOP ENGLAND MESH
$45 $80 $225
Circa 1920s. "Dunlop" and "England" at poles. Pattern similar to the "Super Harlequin" pictured here.

GOLF DEVEL
DUNLOP, ENGLAND
VARIOUS DIMPLE PATTERN BALLS
$20 $40 $100
Circa 1920 "Dunlop Vac 29, and #31.
BROMFORD MESH
$40 $80 $200
Circa 1930s. Standard square mesh pattern.
TEE-MEE MESH
$40 $80 $250
Circa 1930s. Standard square mesh pattern.

GOODRICH, B. F.
WHIZ MESH
$40 $80 $225
Circa 1920s. Standard square mesh pattern.
WHIPPET MESH
$40 $80 $225
Circa 1920s. Standard square mesh pattern.

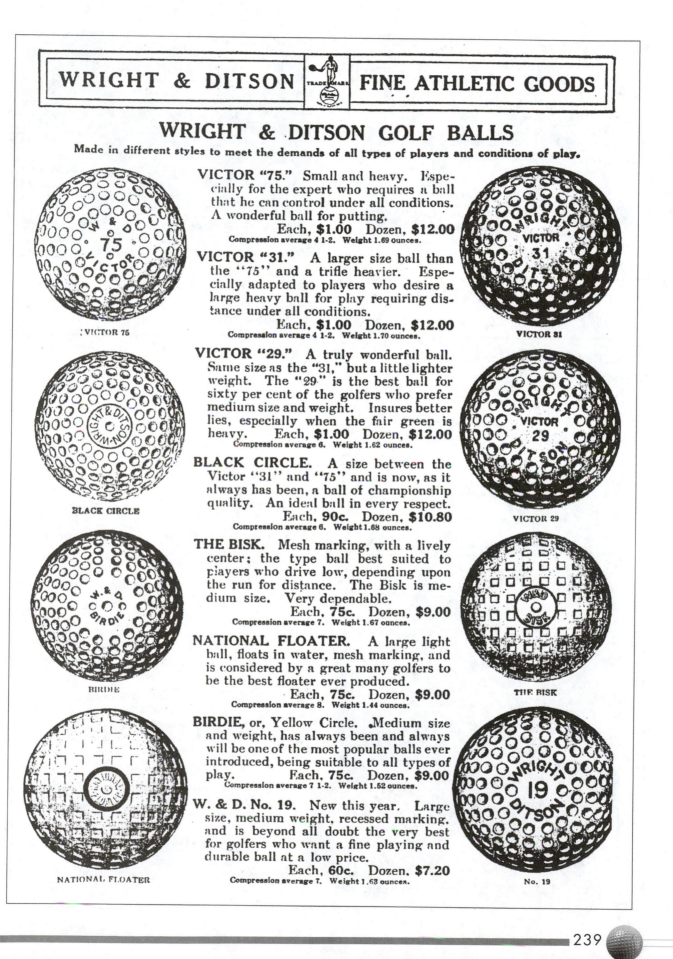

WRIGHT & DITSON | FINE ATHLETIC GOODS

WRIGHT & DITSON GOLF BALLS
Made in different styles to meet the demands of all types of players and conditions of play.

VICTOR "75." Small and heavy. Especially for the expert who requires a ball that he can control under all conditions. A wonderful ball for putting.
Each, $1.00   Dozen, $12.00
Compression average 4 1-2.   Weight 1.69 ounces.

VICTOR "31." A larger size ball than the "75" and a trifle heavier. Especially adapted to players who desire a large heavy ball for play requiring distance under all conditions.
Each, $1.00   Dozen, $12.00
Compression average 4 1-2.   Weight 1.70 ounces.

VICTOR "29." A truly wonderful ball. Same size as the "31," but a little lighter weight. The "29" is the best ball for sixty per cent of the golfers who prefer medium size and weight. Insures better lies, especially when the fair green is heavy.   **Each, $1.00   Dozen, $12.00**
Compression average 6.   Weight 1.62 ounces.

BLACK CIRCLE. A size between the Victor "31" and "75" and is now, as it always has been, a ball of championship quality. An ideal ball in every respect.
Each, 90c.   Dozen, $10.80
Compression average 6.   Weight 1.68 ounces.

THE BISK. Mesh marking, with a lively center; the type ball best suited to players who drive low, depending upon the run for distance. The Bisk is medium size.   Very dependable.
Each, 75c.   Dozen, $9.00
Compression average 7.   Weight 1.67 ounces.

NATIONAL FLOATER. A large light ball, floats in water, mesh marking, and is considered by a great many golfers to be the best floater ever produced.
Each, 75c.   Dozen, $9.00
Compression average 8.   Weight 1.44 ounces.

BIRDIE, or, Yellow Circle. Medium size and weight, has always been and always will be one of the most popular balls ever introduced, being suitable to all types of play.   **Each, 75c.   Dozen, $9.00**
Compression average 7 1-2.   Weight 1.52 ounces.

W. & D. No. 19. New this year. Large size, medium weight, recessed marking, and is beyond all doubt the very best for golfers who want a fine playing and durable ball at a low price.
Each, 60c.   Dozen, $7.20
Compression average 7.   Weight 1.68 ounces.

VICTOR 75

BLACK CIRCLE

BIRDIE

NATIONAL FLOATER

VICTOR 31

VICTOR 29

THE BISK

No. 19

X L CHALLENGER

$250	$700	$1,250

Circa 1917. "X L Challenger" on equator. New basket pattern for 1917.

DUNLOP GOLD CUP MESH

$40	$80	$250

Circa 1920s. "Dunlop" and "Gold Cup" at poles. Standard square mesh pattern.

MACGREGOR
DAYTON, OH
JACK RABBIT MESH

$50	$100	$300

Circa 1920s. "Jack Rabbit" at poles. Standard square mesh pattern.

NORTH BRITISH
EDINBURGH
NORTH BRITISH MESH

$40	$80	$250

Circa 1920s-1930s. "North British" at poles. Standard square mesh pattern.

REACH, A. J.
PHILADELPHIA
REACH PARAMOUNT MESH
$50   **$100**   **$225**
Circa 1920s. "Paramount" at poles. Standard square mesh pattern.

REACH, WRIGHT & DITSON
MESH BALLS
$40   **$80**   **$225**
Circa 1930. Many names.

SCOTTISH INDIA RUBBER CO.
GLASGOW
MAXIM MESH
$40   **$80**   **$250**
Circa 1920s. "Maxim" at poles. Standard square mesh pattern.

U.S. RUBBER CO.
NEW YORK
U.S. ROYAL MESH
$35   **$70**   **$160**
Circa 1930s. Standard square mesh pattern.
FAIRWAY MESH
$35   **$70**   **$160**
Circa 1930s. "Fairway" on poles. Standard square mesh pattern.

WALGREEN'S
CERTIFIED MESH
$35   **$70**   **$160**
Circa 1930s. Standard square mesh pattern.

WANNAMAKER
NEW YORK
FLASH MESH
$40   **$80**   **$225**
Circa 1920s. Several varieties marked "Flash." Blue, Yellow, Red, Long and others. Standard square mesh pattern.

WANNAMAKER
NEW YORK
RADIO BALL
$35   **$60**   **$200**
"Radio" twice printed on each pole. Standard '20s dimple pattern.

WORTHINGTON
OHIO
DIAMOND SERIES MESH
$50   **$100**   **$300**
Circa 1920s. Diamond King, Jack, Four, Chip and others. Standard square mesh pattern.

D&M GOLF BALLS

The D&M **SKULL**   75c
No. 16. The D&M "Skull" is a golf ball that is popular among golfers from the tournament player down to the beginner. It has the "click" and long "carry" that pleases the hard-hitting low-handicap player. It is absolutely true in flight and roll, and has a cover equal to any ball on the market for taking punishment from misplayed shots. Supplied in the new standard size and weight. Multi-dot markings in four colors.
No. 16. Skull, mesh only.....................$.75

The D&M **BLUE FOX**   75c
No. 12. This ball represents a splendid combination of distance and durability. It has a speedy get-away, flies far and true and has a protective covering that will stand the gaff of hard usage. Marked in four colors and available in dimple markings only. New standard size and weight.
No. 12. Dimple only, price.................$.75

The D&M **OWL**   50c
The outstanding feature of this ball is service. It will stand up and give complete satisfaction for general play. It is responsive to all shots, has good carry, and has a particularly tough but elastic cover that will not cut easily. The "Owl" is a wonderfully fine ball for the price. Available in new size and weight to conform to new requirements adopted by U.S.G.A.
No. 14M. Mesh. Price......................$.50
No. 14D. Dimple. Price...................   .50

The D&M **CRICKET**   3 for $1.00
No. 18. For a "three for a dollar" golf ball the D&M Cricket has much to offer in distance and accuracy in flight and roll. It has plenty of stamina to withstand the abuse it may get from a beginner's irons. An ideal ball for golf driving ranges, miniature golf courses and regular golf play. New standard size and weight. Price, each **$.35**. Three for **$1.00**.

PRACTO GOLF BALLS
These balls are very light and soft. Ideal for outdoor or indoor practice. They have a strongly knit cover that will stand up under many hard shots from wood and iron clubs.
No. P1. Practice Balls. Price................$.25

TURNER PRACTICE GOLF BALLS
The Turner practice balls are of thin hollow rubber. A flanged base is provided for teeing the ball up for practice shots. They are very soft, light and durable.
No. PT5. Turner Practice Balls. Price........$.25

****

Golf ball values are based on scarcity, condition, and demand over the past five years. A large quantity of mesh pattern and bramble pattern balls have been recovered from lakes in England and Scotland. Balls with water damage are commonly called "pond" balls and are worth between 25 percent and 50 percent of the full value, depending upon the extent of the water damage. Always consult an expert before purchasing "pond" balls for full catalogue value.

****

REACH PARAMOUNT

TRIANGLE
$75   **$175**   **$500**
Circa 1920s. "Reach Paramount" at poles. Triangle pattern.

SILVERTOWN

LYNX MESH
$40   **$80**   **$250**
Circa 1930s. "Lynx" at poles. Standard square

RUBBER CORE

WRIGHT & DITSON

BOSTON, MASS.
WRIGHT & DITSON "VICTOR" DIMPLE
$35   **$65**   **$225**
Circa 1920s standard dimple pattern.

VARIOUS MAKERS

BRAMBLE, RUBBER CORE
$175   **$350**   **$950**
Circa 1900. Gutta-percha cover.
BRAMBLE, RUBBER CORE
$140   **$350**   **$950**
Circa 1905-1920. Celluloid or rubber cover.

SPALDING BALLS, USA

MESH COVER
$40   **$80**   **$225**
Circa 1920-1935. "PGA" made in both British and American sizes. Square markings.

MESH COVER
$40   **$80**   **$225**
Circa 1920-1935. "Spalding" and "Kro-Flite" at poles. Square markings.

UNKNOWN MAKERS

BRAMBLE, RUBBER CORE
$250   **$450**   **$1,000**
Circa 1905-1915. "The Resilient" at poles.

A. J. REACH, WRIGHT & DITSON, INCORPORATED

GOLF BALLS

THE REACH EAGLE

The essential qualities for which the Reach Eagle is noted are distance, control and durability. Eagle balls can be depended on for the full measure of distance in accordance with the power put into the stroke. No halting or lagging but straight and sure in flight or roll. When hit true, an Eagle ball flies true. On the green the accuracy of response inspires confidence in putting. The tough, lasting covers, stand terrific punishment yet remain in good playing shape for a remarkable length of time. Mesh marked. Also furnished with the new Multidot marking—twelve colored dots painted on the regular Eagle ball. . . . . *Dozen $9.00 Each 75c.*

THE WRIGHT & DITSON BLACK CIRCLE

Mesh marked. Exceptionally true in action, remarkable for distance and durable to an extreme degree. Great carry from all shots. These balls are particularly suited to all general forms of play—the average golfer's ball. Dependable in every respect. Size and weight conform with standard requirements.
Dozen $6.00 Each 50c.

THE REACH PARAMOUNT

Mesh marked. A high grade golf ball, suitable for the discriminating golfer. The quality of this ball has made it one of the most popular on the market. Careful, accurate construction is responsible for playing features which fully meet the expectations of players who prefer to use a ball at this price.
Dozen $6.00 Each 50c.

All the above balls can be supplied in either the 1930 size of 1.62 inches, weight 1.62 ounces or the 1931 size of 1.68 inches, weight 1.55 ounces.

THE WRIGHT & DITSON NATIONAL FLOATER

Mesh marked. Due to its light weight construction, this ball is long in driving quality. Excellent for soft turf conditions. Especially good for ladies' use, for light hitters and beginners. As the name implies, this ball floats in water. The use of this type of ball for water holes reduces mental hazard. Standard floater size and weight. . . *Dozen $6.00 Each 50c.*

A. J. REACH, WRIGHT & DITSON, INCORPORATED

GOLF BALLS

THE WRIGHT & DITSON RECORD

Made for durability and distance. This ball is guaranteed not to cut or nick in actual play. Tests have proven it to be one of the longest distance balls ever made. We have produced in this ball a wonderful degree of durability without sacrificing its distance qualities. *Record* golf balls fully live up to the players' expectations in every kind of shot. Absolute dependability in the continuous uniformity of the Record ball will inspire confidence which improves the player's ability. Mesh marking. Also furnished with the new Multidot marking. Each ball is painted with twelve colored dots. This new marking gives the player greater visibility, easier to identify and easier to hit accurately. . . . *Dozen $9.00 Each .75*

THE WRIGHT & DITSON BULLET
Dimple Marked

Approved Dimple marking. Made for distance. Special type of marking, and very high-powered. Golfers are surprised at the great distance to be obtained with it. Flies especially well into the wind and holds direction better than any ball we know of. In addition to its wonderful flight, it is very accurate in approaching and putting. Its durability is very satisfactory—more so than is usually found in a high-powered ball. These balls are also furnished with the new Multidot marking. *Dozen $9.00 Each 75c.*

THE WRIGHT & DITSON BULLET
Mesh Marked

We furnish the Bullet with a mesh marking. Also with the new Multidot marking; Specify kind, otherwise our regular Dimple Bullet will be furnished on mail orders. *Dozen $9.00 Each 75c.*

All the above golf balls can be supplied in either the 1930 size of 1.62 inches, weight 1.62 ounces or in the 1931 size of 1.68 inches, weight 1.55 ounces. Multidot golf balls are supplied in the following colors: Red, Blue, Green and Maroon.

ST. MUNGO, NEWARK & GLASGOW
MESH COVER
$45   **$90**   **$250**
Circa 1920-1935. "Arch Colonel" and "1.55,"
"1.62," or "1.68" at poles. Square markings.

NOBBY MESH
$250   **$550**   **$1,250**
Circa 1930s. Truck tire pattern.

COLONEL MESH
$50   **$100**   **$250**
Circa 1915-1920. Many names including "F S,"
"29," "31," "27," "Click" and others. Balls in
boxes or wrappers are worth double.

WILSON, THOMAS E.
CHICAGO
WILSON MESH
$50   **$100**   **$250**
Circa 1920s and 1930s. Many including Crest,
"W," Top Notch, Success, Pinehurst and Hol-Hi.
Standard square mesh pattern.

The D&M "OWL" GOLF BALL

50c

The outstanding feature of this ball is service. It will stand up and give complete satisfaction for general play. It is responsive to all shots, has good carry, and has a particularly tough but elastic cover that will not cut easily. The "Owl" is a wonderfully fine ball for the price. Available in new size and weight to conform to new requirements to be adopted by U.S.G.A. January 1, 1931 (1.68 in. 1.55 oz.) or in present standard size 1.62 in. and weight 1.62 oz.

Unless the new size and weight are specified, the present standard size ball (1.62 in. 1.62 oz.) will be furnished on all orders.

No. 14M. Mesh. Price.....$0.50　　　　**No. 14D. Dimple. Price....$0.50**

The D&M "BLUE FOX" GOLF BALL

75c

This ball represents a splendid combination of distance and durability. It has a speedy get-away, flies far and true and has a protective covering that will stand the gaff of hard usage. Marked in four colors and available in either mesh or dimple markings. Available in present standard size only (1.62 in. 1.62 oz.).

No. 12M. Mesh. Price.....$0.85　　　　**No. 12D. Dimple. Price....$0.85**

PRACTO GOLF BALLS

These balls are very light and soft. Ideal for outdoor or indoor practice. They have a strongly knit cover that will stand up under many hard shots from wood and iron clubs.
No. P1. Practice Balls. Price.............$0.25

TURNER PRACTICE GOLF BALLS

The Turner practice balls are of thin hollow rubber. A flanged base is provided for teeing the ball up for practice shots. They are very soft, light and durable.
No. PT5. Turner Practice Balls. Price $0.25

[29]

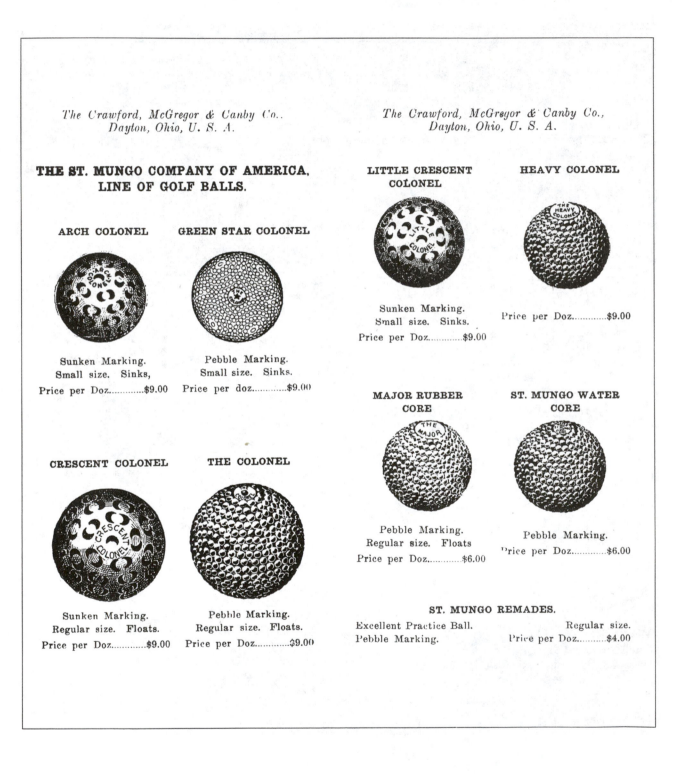

The Crawford, McGregor & Canby Co.,
Dayton, Ohio, U. S. A.

The Crawford, McGregor & Canby Co.,
Dayton, Ohio, U. S. A.

THE ST. MUNGO COMPANY OF AMERICA, LINE OF GOLF BALLS.

ARCH COLONEL

Sunken Marking.
Small size. Sinks,
Price per Doz............$9.00

GREEN STAR COLONEL

Pebble Marking.
Small size. Sinks.
Price per doz............$9.00

CRESCENT COLONEL

Sunken Marking.
Regular size. Floats.
Price per Doz............$9.00

THE COLONEL

Pebble Marking.
Regular size. Floats.
Price per Doz............$9.00

LITTLE CRESCENT COLONEL

Sunken Marking.
Small size. Sinks.
Price per Doz............$9.00

HEAVY COLONEL

Price per Doz............$9.00

MAJOR RUBBER CORE

Pebble Marking.
Regular size. Floats
Price per Doz............$6.00

ST. MUNGO WATER CORE

Pebble Marking.
Price per Doz............$6.00

ST. MUNGO REMADES.

Excellent Practice Ball.
Pebble Marking.

Regular size.
Price per Doz..........$4.00

BRAMBLE, RUBBER CORE

$1,250	$2,500	$6,500

Circa 1900-1905. "The Bruce Cored Center" with a "Spider" and "Web." Gutta-percha cover.

HARRINGTON SPECIAL

$100	$250	$550

Circa 1920s. "Harrington Special" at poles. Squares and rectangles in an odd design.

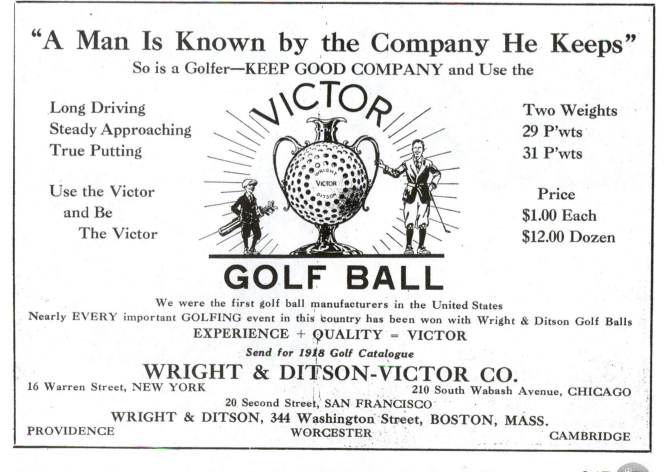

COUNTY CHEMICAL CO.
CHEMICO TRIUMPH
$75   **$175**   **$450**
Circa 1920. "Chemico Triumph" surrounding a
"Cross" at the poles. Small concentric squares
form the pattern.

CRAIG PARK
GLASGOW
WHITE FLYER
$500   **$1,200**   **$2,250**
Circa 1915. "White Flyer" at poles. Circles with a
"Cross" inside. Very scarce!

DUNLOP
BIRMINGHAM, ENGLAND
WARWICK
$45   **$125**   **$350**
Circa 1925-1935. Alternating rows of square and
dimple markings. Beware, many "Pond" examples.

GOODRICH, B. F.
AKRON, OH
BRAMBLE, RUBBER CORE
$750   **$1,250**   **$2,250**
Circa 1899-1905. "Haskell" and "Pat. Apr. 1,
1899" at poles. Gutta-percha cover.

BRAMBLE, RUBBER CORE
$325   **$550**   **$1,250**
Circa 1899-1905. "Haskell" and "Pat. Apr. 1,
1899" at poles. Celluloid cover.

LINE CUT RUBBER CORE
$1,500   **$3,800**   **$6,500**
Circa 1902. "Haskell" and "Pat. Apr. 1, 1899" in
rectangular panels. Gutta-percha cover. Photos of
front and back below.

BRAMBLE, RUBBER CORE
$400   **$900**   **$1,800**
Circa 1910. "Haskell Royal" with a celluloid cover.

BRAMBLE, RUBBER CORE
$600   **$1,000**   **$2,200**
Circa 1905. "The Pneumatic" at poles. These were rubber cored with a center of compressed air.

THE METEOR
$250   **$500**   **$1,350**
Circa 1920. "The Meteor" at poles. Concentric triangles.

GOODYEAR "A"
$75   **$200**   **$500**
Circa 1920. "Goodyear A" at poles. Odd pattern of squares.

GOODYEAR RUBBER CO.
OHIO
BRAMBLE, RUBBER CORE
$300   **$600**   **$1,500**
Circa 1905. "The Pneumatic" at equator. These were rubber cored with a center of compressed air.

HARLEQUIN
SUPER HARLEQUIN
$150   **$350**   **$850**
Circa 1920s. "Super Harlequin" crossed at poles. Unusual arrangement of squares.

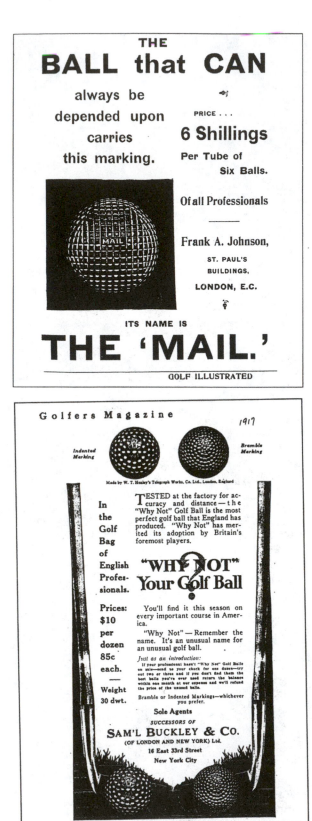

IMPROVED GOLF BALLS
LONDON
BRAMBLE, RUBBER CORE

$250	$500	$1,000

Circa 1902-1905. "I R" at poles. These were recovered "Haskell or other cored balls." Gutta-percha cover.

HUTCHISON
SPRINGVALE FALCON BRAMBLE

$100	$175	$650

C-1920 CAME IN COLORFUL WRAPPER.

THE MERSEY BRAMBLE
ENGLAND

$75	$175	$650

C-1915-25

KEMPSHALL
NEW JERSEY
RUBBER CORED BRAMBLES

$175	$375	$900

Circa 1905-1920. Many, including: "Chick," "Flyer," Arlington," "League" and others.
DATED BRAMBLE

$190	$400	$1,350

Circa 1905-1908. Large numerals on one pole, patent date on other pole.

HENLEY'S
LONDON
WHY NOT BRAMBLE

$175	$350	$900

Circa 1915. "Why Not" at both poles.

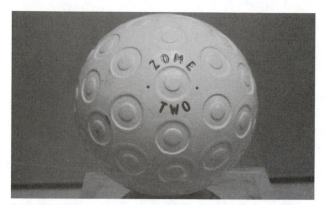

MARTINS
BURMINGHAM
ZOME ONE or TWO
$300   **$650**   **$1,750**
Circa 1900-1910. "Zome Two" at poles. Large circles with a raised center.

UNKNOWN MAKER
ECLIPSE GUTTA-PERCHA
$300   **$800**   **$2,500**
C-1905-1910

NORTH BRITISH
EDINBURGH
CLINCHER CROSS
$200   **$450**   **$950**
Circa 1915. "Clincher Cross" and size number at poles. Ball is lined into four sections. Triangles and rectangles make up the pattern.

SILVERTOWN
BRAMBLE, RUBBER CORE
$190   **$350**   **$900**
Circa 1905-1915. "Silver King" at poles.

DIAMOND COVER
$75   **$150**   **$400**
Circa 1920-1930. Entire cover with diamonds. "Spalding" at poles.

ST. MUNGO, NEWARK & GLASGOW
PATENT COLONEL RED WINTER COVER
$190   **$400**   **$1,200**
Circa 1915-25.

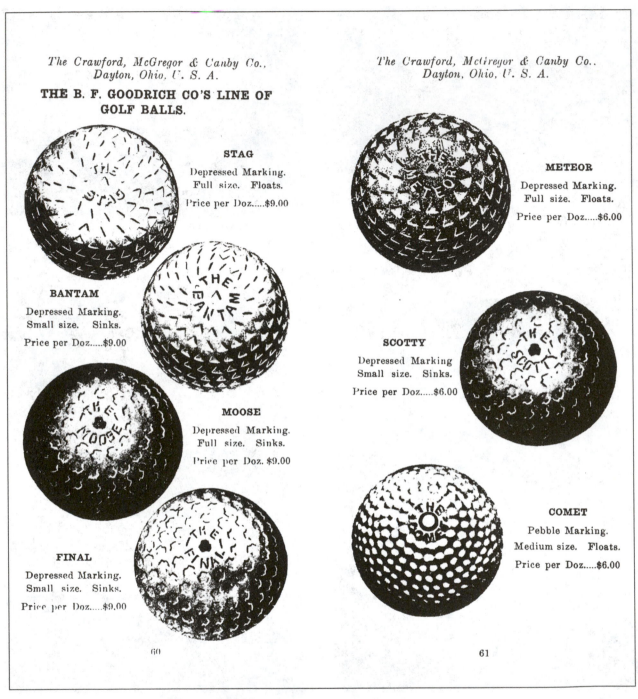

The Crawford, McGregor & Canby Co.,
Dayton, Ohio, U. S. A.

THE B. F. GOODRICH CO'S LINE OF GOLF BALLS.

STAG
Depressed Marking.
Full size. Floats.
Price per Doz.....$9.00

BANTAM
Depressed Marking.
Small size. Sinks.
Price per Doz.....$9.00

MOOSE
Depressed Marking.
Full size. Sinks.
Price per Doz. $9.00

FINAL
Depressed Marking.
Small size. Sinks.
Price per Doz.....$9.00

60

The Crawford, McGregor & Canby Co.,
Dayton, Ohio, U. S. A.

METEOR
Depressed Marking.
Full size. Floats.
Price per Doz.....$6.00

SCOTTY
Depressed Marking
Small size. Sinks.
Price per Doz.....$6.00

COMET
Pebble Marking.
Medium size. Floats.
Price per Doz.....$6.00

61

From the McGregor catalogue of 1913

ST. MUNGO, NEWARK & GLASGOW
CRESCENT COLONEL
$175 $350 $800
Circa 1920s. "Crescent Colonel" surrounds a
"Crescent." Pattern is opposing crescents.

WILSON, THOMAS E.
CHICAGO
WILSON BRAMBLE
$600 $1,200 $2,500
Circa 1920. "Wilson" at poles. Pattern is large flat
brambles.

U.S. RUBBER CO.
NEW YORK
U. S. TIGER
$250 $750 $1,800
Circa 1920. "U S Tiger" at poles. Large circles.
Was made in white and yellow cover colors.

SPALDING
USA
RUBBER CORED BRAMBLES
$150 $300 $800
Circa 1906-1920. Many, including: "White,"
"Wizard," "Dot," "Blue Circle," "Spalding
Bramble," "Spalding Bob," and others.

SPALDING
USA
SPALDING DIMPLE
$40 $90 $450
Circa 1905-1912

ST. MUNGO, NEWARK & GLASGOW
"DONE IT" CRESCENT MARKINGS
$900 $2,500 $6,500
Circa 1920s.

U.S. RUBBER CO.
TIGER MESH
$50 $100 $250
Circa 1930s.

WILSON, THOMAS E.
CHICAGO
CREST MESH
$30 $65 $190
Circa 1930s.

**UNKNOWN MAKER
(POSSIBLY WORTHINGTON)**
WINFIELD MESH
$35 $70 $190
Circa 1930s.Full Sleeve (as photo) brings 25 per-
cent more per ball.

UNKNOWN MAKER
ACE MESH
$35 $70 $190
Circa 1930s. Came in clear cello wrapper.

UNKNOWN MAKER
PIONEER MESH
$35 $70 $190
Circa 1930s. Came in clear cello wrapper.

REACH EAGLE DIMPLE PATTERN MINT
NEW IN BOX
$175

Circa 1925

WORTHINGTON
OHIO
THE WONDER BALL
$300   **$750**   **$2,000**
Circa 1920s.

UNKNOWN MAKER (ENGLAND)
ENGLAND MESH
$35   **$70**   **$190**
Circa 1930s.

WORTHINGTON
OHIO
WHITE FLAT BRAMBLE
$600   **$1,250**   **$2,500**
Circa 1910-1915. "White Worthington" at poles.
Large flat brambles. Very scarce.

WRIGHT & DITSON
BOSTON, MA
CIRCLE SERIES,
RUBBER CORE BRAMBLE
$150   **$300**   **$800**
Circa 1906-1915. "Wright & Ditson" and patent
dates inside colored circles.
Blue, Green, Orange Floater, Black and others.

SILVER KING
ENGLAND
MESH PATTERN MINT NEW IN BOX
        $250

WRAPPED AND BOXED BALLS

Golf ball manufacturers began wrapping
balls about 1895. Dunlop, Slazenger, Penfold,
Spalding, Wilson and several other companies
continued through the 1980s. The first wrappers were made of paper with an advertising
seal; later wrappings were of colored cellophane.

REACH, A.J., CO.
PHILADELPHIA
REACH EAGLE MESH PATTERN MINT NEW
IN BOX
        $250

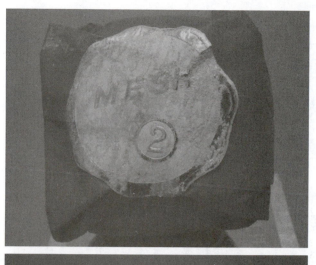

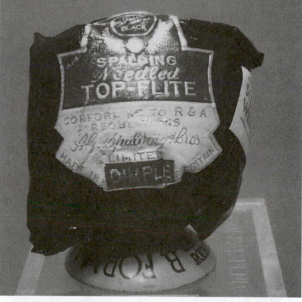

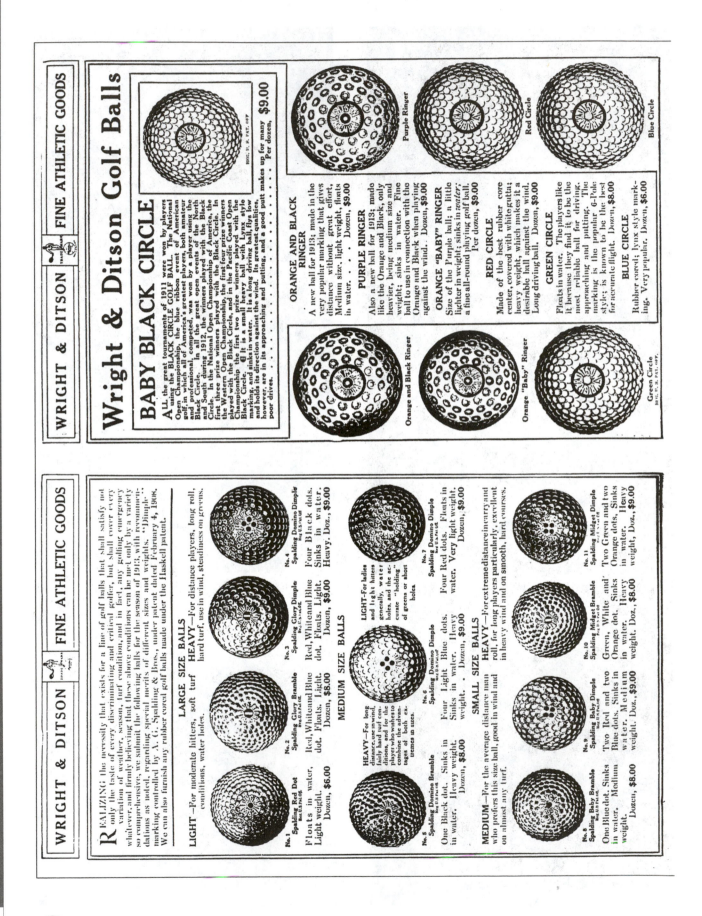

DIMPLE PATTERN MINT NEW IN BOX
$175
Circa 1930s

WANNAMAKER
NEW YORK
CIRCA 1924 DIMPLE BALLS

$20	$40	$100

Circa 1925. Dimple patterns. Many names, including "Red Flash," "Radio Crown," "Xray," "Taplow," and others.

BALL BOXES AND CONTAINERS
All prices given are for empty boxes and containers.

UNKNOWN MAKER
RE-MOULDED DOZEN BOX

$50	$90	$175

Circa 1920s. Dozen box, dimple or mesh.

VARIOUS MAKERS
INDIVIDUAL DIMPLE BALL BOXES

$5	$20	$50

Circa 1940s-1960s. Individual boxes for dimple balls.
INDIVIDUAL DIMPLE BALL BOXES

$15	$35	$75

Circa 1920s-1930s. Individual boxes for dimple pattern balls from the period pre-1935.
INDIVIDUAL MESH BALL BOXES

$20	$45	$90

Circa 1920s-1930s. Individual boxes for mesh pattern balls from the period pre-1935.

DUNLOP
DUNLOP 65 BALL TUBE

$10	$25	$60

Circa late 1930s-1950s. Three-ball screw-top tube sleeve.

DUNLOP 65 BALL BOXES

$20	$50	$100

Circa late 1930s-1950s. Boxes for dimpled Dunlop 65 marked "Recessed."
DUNLOP BALL BOXES

$40	$75	$125

Circa 1920s-1930s. Boxes for mesh or dimple pattern balls.
DUNLOP BALL BOXES

$75	$125	$250

Circa 1905-1920. Boxes for bramble pattern balls.
DUNLOP METAL DISPLAY BOX

$300	$500	$1,000

Circa 1920s. Metal box for displaying two dozen balls on countertop.

NORTH BRITISH
GLASGOW
NORTH BRITISH SLEEVE BOX

$40	$75	$150

Circa 1920s. Cardboard sleeve box for three balls, mesh or dimple.

SILVERTOWN
SILVERKING DIMPLE DOZEN BOX

$75	$150	$300

Circa 1930. Balls encircling the globe, dozen box.

ST. MUNGO
GLASGOW
ONEUPO DOZEN BOX

$100	$225	$500

Circa 1900. Box for gutta-percha balls.

ST. MUNGO
NEW JERSEY
ARCH COLONEL MESH DOZEN BOX

$75	$150	$350

Circa 1920s. Colorful box picturing "The Colonel."

SILVERTOWN GUTTA
DOZEN BOX
$100   **$225**   **$450**
Circa 1900. Slip case type dozen box.
FLEETWING MESH PATTERN GOLF BALLS
MADE IN USA
$35   **$70**   **$175**
Circa 1930s

U. S. RUBBER
NEW YORK
US 444 SLEEVE BOX
$30   **$60**   **$150**
Circa 1930s. Cardboard sleeve box for three balls,
mesh or dimple.

WORTHINGTON
OHIO
WORTHINGTON
DOZEN BOXES
$35   **$60**   **$100**
Circa 1930s and 1940s. Dozen boxes for mesh or
dimple.

WORTHINGTON
DOZEN BOXES
$50   **$90**   **$150**
Circa 1920s. Dozen boxes for mesh or dimple.

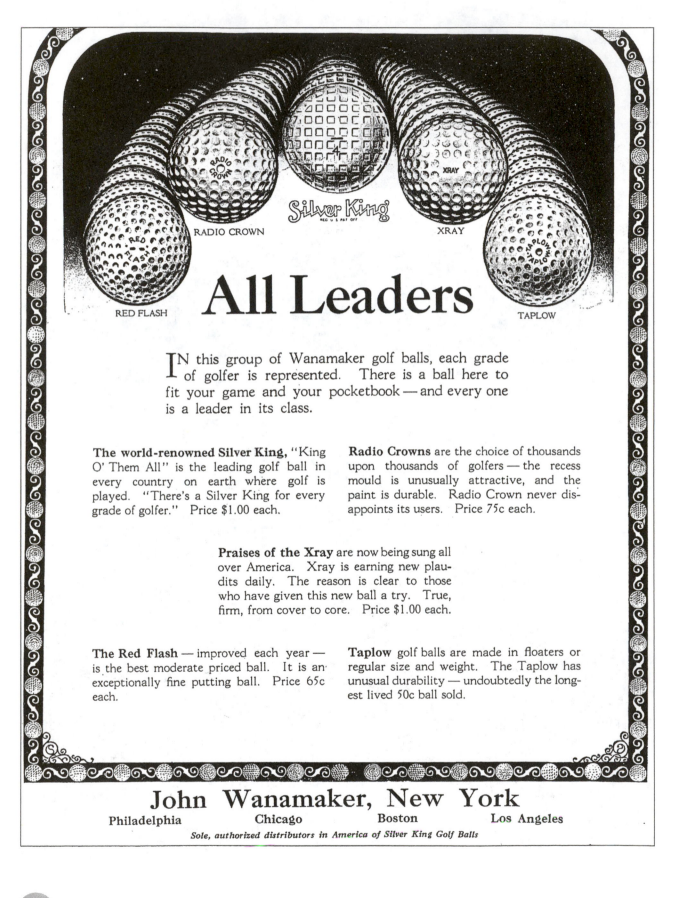

RADIO CROWN

Silver King
REG U S PAT OFF

XRAY

RED FLASH

TAPLOW

All Leaders

IN this group of Wanamaker golf balls, each grade of golfer is represented. There is a ball here to fit your game and your pocketbook — and every one is a leader in its class.

The world-renowned Silver King, "King O' Them All" is the leading golf ball in every country on earth where golf is played. "There's a Silver King for every grade of golfer." Price $1.00 each.

Radio Crowns are the choice of thousands upon thousands of golfers — the recess mould is unusually attractive, and the paint is durable. Radio Crown never disappoints its users. Price 75c each.

Praises of the Xray are now being sung all over America. Xray is earning new plaudits daily. The reason is clear to those who have given this new ball a try. True, firm, from cover to core. Price $1.00 each.

The Red Flash — improved each year — is the best moderate priced ball. It is an exceptionally fine putting ball. Price 65c each.

Taplow golf balls are made in floaters or regular size and weight. The Taplow has unusual durability — undoubtedly the longest lived 50c ball sold.

John Wanamaker, New York

Philadelphia   Chicago   Boston   Los Angeles

Sole, authorized distributors in America of Silver King Golf Balls

Chapter 6

Signature Balls

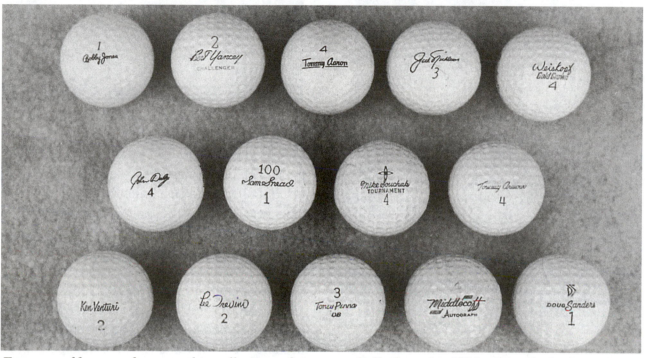

Famous golf names decorate this collection of signature balls from the 1950s through the late 1970s.

One of the most asked questions by would-be ball collectors is, "What is a signature ball?" Signature balls are imprinted, at the time of manufacturing, with a professional's name. Golf balls signed by a professional, president or celebrity (usually with a "Sharpie" felt tip pen) are NOT SIGNATURE balls. They are autographed balls and are classified as autographed items.

The first signature golf balls were feather balls. Willie Park, about 1890, made gutta-percha balls and simply marked them "Park." Harry Vardon was the first professional golfer to receive monetary compensation for the use of his name when, at the turn of the century, A.G. Spalding & Brothers made the "Vardon Flyer" gutta-percha ball.

Over the years, literally thousands of different named balls and varieties bearing those names (about 140 different varieties of the MacGregor-made balls marked with Jack Nicklaus' name have been classified) have been collected singly, in sleeves, or in original half dozen and dozen boxes.

Paul Biocini has authored the *Signature Golf Ball Collector's Guide*, 1995, and has been gracious enough to write the introduction to this chapter:

It all started in Scotland when the names Morris, Gourlay, Allan (Robertson), etc., were imprinted on the feather balls they had made. Forgan, Park, Auchterlonie, and others were the best ball makers during the gutta-percha period, 1860-1900, and they, too, imprinted their names on balls.

But why were the names put on the ball? Quality, recognition, favorite professional, posterity, or just a way to promote sales; whatever the reason, it was here to stay.

Originally, many of the early American golf professionals were golf pros from Scotland and England. This was the case with John Dunn of New York, who when remolding used and damaged gutties, imprinted his name on the ball, thus creating the first signature ball made in the U.S., circa 1898.

A.G. Spalding & Bros. introduced the Vardon Flyer with Bramble markings in 1900, which became the first manufactured signature ball. During 1905-1915, there were hundreds of newly formed golf ball manufacturing companies producing a variety of exotic balls, but only the J. H. Taylor Company's "JH" Bramble Ball (1915) and later the "JH" Mesh Ball (1925) were stamped with a professional's name.

Starting in the late 1920s, Worthington, Wilson, and other companies produced both mesh and dimple design balls imprinted with the names of the stars who played them. As a result, collectors today ardently search for balls bearing the names of Walter Hagen, Gene Sarazen, Jock Hutchison, Johnny Farrell, Tommy Armour, and others. This was the first attempt by ball companies to create the "Professional Staff" concept.

Wilson was also the first company to sign a lady professional in 1933 and "Helen Hicks" became the first woman's name to appear on a manufactured ball. "Babe" Didrickson was the second when the Goldsmith Co. made a ball bearing her name in 1935. Wilson, in 1937, also made a "Didrickson" ball but, to my knowledge, no collector has reported having found one.

Around 1936, the larger golf companies started the "Sold in Pro Shop Only" line of more expensive "Professional" quality balls. This helped promote the sale of the lesser expensive signature balls sold only in retail, sporting goods, and department stores.

During the period from the late 1930s through the 1960s, local golf pros like Wiffy Cox, George Buzzini, Andy Silva, and others began having specially made balls with their name imprinted as an advertising ploy (much like the logo balls imprinted with St. Andrews or Pebble Beach), which sold as an inexpensive over-the-counter ball. Approximately

5,000 pros did so, and today more than 2,000 different names have been reported by various collectors.

Signature ball collecting is a relatively new specialty in golf collecting. The new or experienced collector can still find many treasures through local flea markets, garage sales, friends, old golf bags, professional tournaments, collectibles dealers, or trading with other collectors.

Which signature balls to collect should be determined by where your interest lies. There are many who want to "collect them all" and have hundreds or even thousands of balls in their possession. Others may want to collect only winners of the Masters, or only winners of major tournaments. Presidential, ladies, or celebrity balls are other collectible venues. One individual collects only signature balls of the pros he has seen play in person.

The field is limited only by your imagination, physical storage or display space, and your pocket book.

When placing a value on a signature ball, keep in mind the overall preservation, how much it has deteriorated from mint new, and the name clarity. If the signature name is scuffed or partially unreadable on a nearly new ball, the ball is technically uncollectible, unless it is very rare or the only example available.

The G-5, G-7, G-9 pricing values will represent the following conditions:

G-5

An average ball, with a good clear name, may have iron marks (no cuts), some paint loss, or may be slightly out of round.

G-7

An above average condition ball showing only the slightest evidence of play. The name and all markings are bold.

G-9

Mint new as made. No evidence of play.

COLLECTING SIGNATURE BALL BOXES

(Gary Hilgers has been a long-time collector of signature balls and signature ball boxes. He has graciously submitted a brief overview on collecting ball boxes.)

The manufacture of signature balls reached its peak in the 1960s. During this time, the large golf ball companies such as Wilson, Spalding, and MacGregor led the way in finding those pros who were willing to have their name stamped on a ball and marketed "to the world." While ball performance was (and is) critical to ball sales, the ball companies realized that marketing played an equal key role. Golfers who bought these balls either wanted to emulate the play of a particular golfer or they simply liked the way the ball box looked on the store shelf. Today, the golf ball box collector graces his or her walls with colorful graphics of these golf ball boxes, and the result is a step back in time to get an idea of what people saw on the golfing shelves of that era.

As one might imagine, it is getting more and more difficult to locate balls and boxes. The best sources are antique golf dealers, private collectors, collectibles shows, auctions, and garage sales.

Golf ball boxes of the big name pros such as Palmer, Nicklaus, Snead, Nelson, Sarazen, Hagen, and Hogan are a must for the beginning collector. Discovering a scarce full-dozen box of signature balls stamped with pros' names such as Ted Makalena, Tony Lema, Patty Berg, Babe Zaharias, Porky Oliver, or Wiffy Cox, would be a very enjoyable find!

One subtle fact of signature ball collecting that goes unnoticed is the collector is forced to learn more of the history of the game. With every new ball box (or ball) one acquires, one can't help wanting to find out a little history of the pro himself.

Most signature golf ball collectors seek those boxes that ideally meet four criteria:
1. Have a picture of the golf pro
2. Have the facsimile signature of the pro
3. Have the balls in their original packaging
4. Is of at least a G-5 condition

In recent years, the trend for ball manufacturers has steered away from these pro-specific balls. While the Jack Nicklaus "Golden Bear" ball has been the top seller of all signature balls, over the past 15 years, very few have found their way to store shelves. Balls endorsed by John Daly, Greg Norman, Ben Hogan, and some Tommy Armour balls are a few that can currently be found on store shelves. This trend indicates that golf ball boxes will maintain their value and niche appeal as the supply becomes more and more limited.

Signature Balls—Pricing

TOMMY ARMOUR—MESH
WORTHINGTON BALL CO.
$120 $250 $550
Circa 1931. "Tommy Armour" in black letters. "Great Lakes" monogram "GL" at poles.

TOMMY AARON
MADE IN JAPAN
$10 $15 $25
Circa 1960-1965. Several varieties marked "Japan."
SPALDING, USA
$10 $15 $25
Circa 1965. "Unicore."

TOMMY ARMOUR
WORTHINGTON BALL CO.
$30 $60 $120
Circa 1935. Small or large "Tommy Armour" in black letters. Four red and black dots at poles.

TOMMY ARMOUR—DIMPLE
WORTHINGTON BALL CO.
$25 $45 $100
Circa 1937. "Tommy Armour" 50 or 60 with name in red block letters.

TOMMY ARMOUR
WORTHINGTON BALL CO.
$10 $15 $30
Circa 1958. "Silver Scot."

LAURIE AUCHTERLONIE
DUNLOP
$40 $60 $120
Circa 1957. Block letters on Dunlop 65 ball.

SEVE BALLESTEROS
SLAZENGER, UK
$15 $25 $35
Circa 1980. Name in script.

TOMMY BOLT
KROYDON
$10 $15 $25
Circa 1955-1965.

JULIUS BOROS
WILSON, THOMAS E., CHICAGO
$20 $35 $60
Circa 1958. "100," "Zenith," and others.

LAURA BAUGH
WILSON, THOMAS E., CHICAGO
$10 $15 $20
Circa 1960s-1980s. Most all varieties found.

GEORGE BAYER
MACGREGOR
$25 $35 $50
Circa 1958-1962. All varieties.

PEGGY KIRK BELL
SPALDING, USA
$25 $35 $50
Circa 1965. Spalding Pinehurst.

PATTY BERG
WILSON, THOMAS E., CHICAGO
$45 $65 $100
Circa 1955-1960. Four balls about the same value: "Autograph," "Trophy," "Classic," or the "Patrician."

JACK BURKE
MACGREGOR
$10 **$20** **$45**
Circa late 1950s. Many varieties all about the
same value.

BILLY CASPER
WILSON, THOMAS E., CHICAGO
$10 **$15** **$20**
Circa 1960s-1980s. Most all varieties found.

BILLY BURKE
WORTHINGTON BALL CO.
$30 **$45** **$75**
Circa late 1930s. Three balls about the same value.
"50," "Victory," and "75."

BILLY CASPER
WILSON, THOMAS E., CHICAGO
$25 **$35** **$50**
Circa 1958. "Wilson Tournament" or "Super
Power" with number at bottom.

WIFFY COX—MESH
WORTHINGTON BALL CO.
$125 **$275** **$700**
Circa 1930. Square mesh pattern.

BOBBY CRUICKSHANK
MACGREGOR
$50 **$80** **$175**
Circa 1936. Two dots, red and black.

HARRY COOPER—MESH
WORTHINGTON BALL CO.
$120 **$250** **$700**
Circa 1931. "Harry Cooper" in black letters.
"Star" at poles.

WIFFY COX
WRIGHT & DITSON, BOSTON, MA
$60 **$90** **$150**
Circa 1936. "Wright & Ditson" with four green
dots.

BABE DIDRIKSON
GOLDSMITH CO., NEW YORK
$450 **$700** **$1,250**
Circa 1936. Wilson 75.

BOBBY CRUICKSHANK
WORTHINGTON BALL CO.
$45 **$70** **$140**
Circa 1938. Worthington cured cover.

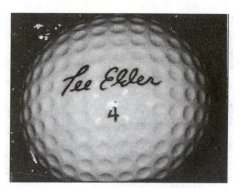

LEE ELDER
FAULTLESS
$10 $15 $20
Circa 1962-1966.

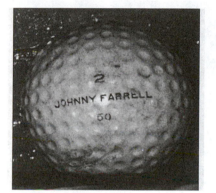

JOHNNY FARRELL
WILSON, THOMAS E., CHICAGO
$45 $70 $125
Circa 1936. "50."

JIMMY DEMARET
MACGREGOR
$25 $35 $60
Circa 1958. All varieties.

BABE DIDRIKSON
GOLDSMITH CO., NEW YORK
$250 $400 $800
Circa 1936. Wilson 35 and 50.

JOHNNY FARRELL
WILSON, THOMAS E., CHICAGO
$125 $250 $700
Circa 1930. Any mesh cover ball.

JACK FLECK
SPALDING, USA
$70 $100 $150
Circa 1956.

RALPH GULDAHL
WILSON, THOMAS E., CHICAGO
$75 $100 $175
Circa 1935. Radio Active 75.

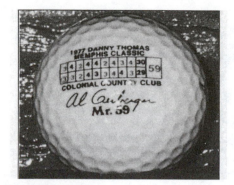

AL GEIBERGER
SPALDING, USA
$50 $75 $125
Circa 1977. "Mr. 59" with score card.

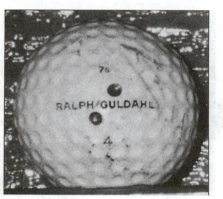

RALPH GULDAHL
WILSON, THOMAS E., CHICAGO
$35 $50 $90
Circa 1936-1939. All varieties.

WALTER HAGEN
HAGEN GOLF CO.
$140 $275 $700
Circa 1930. Any mesh pattern.
HAGEN GOLF CO.
$50 $75 $125
Circa 1935. "Bingo," "Playboy," "Vulcord,"
"Honey Bee," "It's A Honey," or "288 For
Tournament Play."
HAGEN GOLF CO.
$60 $90 $150
Circa 1935. "Hagen PGA" with Honey Bee.

BEN HOGAN
HOGAN
| $5 | $10 | $15 |
Circa 1970-1990. Most all varieties.

KY LAFFOON
WRIGHT & DITSON, BOSTON, MA
| $40 | $85 | $200 |
Circa 1938. Two orange dots above and below name.

HAGEN GOLF CO.
| $20 | $35 | $50 |
Circa 1950-1965. "Sir Walter," "Speed-Flo,"
"Trophy Plus," or "International."
HAGEN GOLF CO.
| $10 | $15 | $25 |
Circa 1955-1965. "The Haig," "The Haig 80-90-100," or "TCW 80-90-100."

HELEN HICKS
WILSON, THOMAS E., CHICAGO
| $50 | $75 | $125 |
Circa late 1930s. All varieties.

JIMMY HINES
WORTHINGTON BALL CO.
| $40 | $75 | $150 |
Circa 1938. Dimple ball. "Victory" and "Jimmy Hines."

BEN HOGAN
MACGREGOR
| $35 | $50 | $90 |
Circa 1950. "Crown."
HOGAN
| $20 | $35 | $50 |
Circa 1955-1960. "River Run," "Hogan Construction," or red "Star."

JOCK HUTCHINSON
WORTHINGTON BALL CO.
| $120 | $250 | $700 |
Circa 1930. Square mesh pattern.

TONY LEMA
KROYDON, NEWARK, NJ
| $25 | $45 | $80 |
Circa 1963. With champagne glass.

LLOYD MANGRUM
WILSON, THOMAS E., CHICAGO
| $25 | $50 | $120 |
Circa 1950. Name in block letters.

JOE KIRKWOOD
WORTHINGTON BALL CO.
| $30 | $40 | $65 |
Circa 1940. All varieties.

TONY LEMA
KROYDON, NEWARK, NJ
| $15 | $25 | $40 |
Circa 1960.

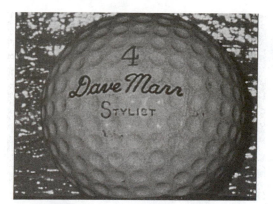

DAVE MARR
WILSON, THOMAS E., CHICAGO
$10 $20 $30
Circa late 1960s. "Stylist" under name. Also "Pinehurst," "Medalist," and "100," all about the same value.

CARY MIDDLECOFF
WILSON, THOMAS E., CHICAGO
$10 $15 $25
Circa 1960. Autograph 100.

NANCY LOPEZ
RAM GOLF CO.
$15 $25 $40
Circa 1970-1972. All varieties.

TED MAKALENA
UNKNOWN MAKER
$60 $100 $150
Circa 1960.

JOHNNY MILLER
WILSON, THOMAS E., CHICAGO
$10 $15 $25
Circa 1969-1980. All varieties.

BYRON NELSON
MACGREGOR
$30 $60 $120
Circa 1935-1938. All varieties.
NORTHWESTERN
$25 $35 $50
Circa 1962-1968. Steel center.

BYRON NELSON
NORTHWESTERN
$15 $25 $45
Circa 1962-1968. All varieties.

JACK NICKLAUS
MACGREGOR
$10 $15 $35
Circa 1964. Three red crowns above name.

PORKY OLIVER
WILSON
$35 $85 $150
Circa 1958. "Autograph" below name.

ARNOLD PALMER
WILSON, THOMAS E., CHICAGO
$25 $40 $75
Circa 1960. "Personal," "Autograph," "Victory,"
"S T C," "100," and "Steel Center."

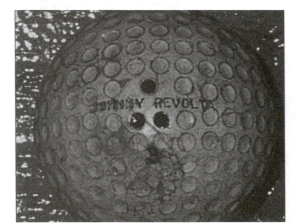

JOHNNY REVOLTA
WILSON, THOMAS E., CHICAGO
$25 $45 $80
Circa 1936-1945. All varieties.

JACK NICKLAUS
MACGREGOR
$15 $30 $60
Circa 1963. Gold-colored Golden Bear.
MACGREGOR
$15 $25 $40
Circa 1962-1968. "Champion," "Century,"
"Supreme," "Ambassador," "Embassy,"
"Diplomat," and "VIP 100."
MACGREGOR
$10 $15 $20
Circa 1970s. Most all varieties.

ARNOLD PALMER
SEARS, ROEBUCK
$15 $20 $35
Circa 1963. Steel center.
PRO GROUP
$15 $20 $35
Circa 1965. Steel center.
PRO GROUP
$10 $15 $25
Circa 1977. Surlyn cover.

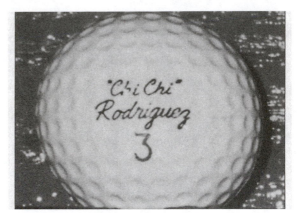

CHI-CHI RODRIGUEZ
WILSON, THOMAS E., CHICAGO
$12 $18 $35
Circa 1962. "Chi-Chi" signature.

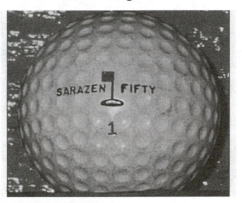

SARAZEN FIFTY
WILSON, THOMAS E., CHICAGO
$25 $40 $90
Circa 1950. Dimple with "Sarazen" and a "Flag-
in Hole" then "Fifty."

JOHNNY REVOLTA
NORTHWESTERN
$15 $20 $35
Circa 1963-1964.

GENE SARAZEN
WILSON, THOMAS E., CHICAGO
$125 $250 $700
Circa 1930. All mesh pattern balls.
WILSON, THOMAS E., CHICAGO
$65 $150 $350
Circa 1932-1935. "50," "75," and "Flag." Tough or
vulcanized covers.
WILSON, THOMAS E., CHICAGO
$15 $25 $50
Circa 1940-1952. "Squire."
WILSON, THOMAS E., CHICAGO
$15 $20 $30
Circa 1960. "Strokemaster" and "Autograph."

DENNY SHUTE
WORTHINGTON BALL CO.
$35 $65 $110
Circa 1940. "Medalist."

SAM SNEAD
WILSON, THOMAS E., CHICAGO
$10 $15 $30
Circa 1960s. "100."

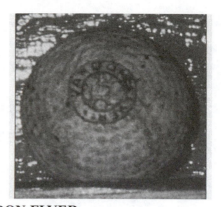

VARDON FLYER
SPALDING, USA
$450 $1,100 $3,000
Circa 1900. Bramble pattern. Gutta-percha.
"Vardon Flyer" at pole.

CRAIG WOOD
DUNLOP, ENGLAND
$50 $90 $150
Circa 1939. "Craig Wood" with "2 6 4" below
name.

DENNY SHUTE
WILSON, THOMAS E., CHICAGO
$40 $60 $90
Circa 1939-1940. "Red 50," "Custom," "Medalist,"
and "Red 75."

SAM SNEAD
WILSON, THOMAS E., CHICAGO
$35 $50 $75
Circa 1938-1939. "White Sulpher" and
"Greenbriar."
WILSON, THOMAS E., CHICAGO
$10 $15 $30
Circa 1950. Blue Ridge.

ALEX TAYLOR—MESH
ALEX TAYLOR CO., NEW YORK
$120 $250 $700

Circa 1930. Two different mesh pattern balls. A
"Taylor Ace" and "Alex Taylor Co" T 30 with a
"T" at the poles.

ALEX TAYLOR—DIMPLE
ALEX TAYLOR CO., NEW YORK
$75 $150 $325
Circa 1930. "Taylor Imp, 31" at the poles.

LOU WORSHAM
MACGREGOR
$20 $30 $50
Circa 1955-1958.

BABE ZAHARIAS
WILSON, THOMAS E., CHICAGO
$125 $175 $600
Circa 1939. Wilson 75.

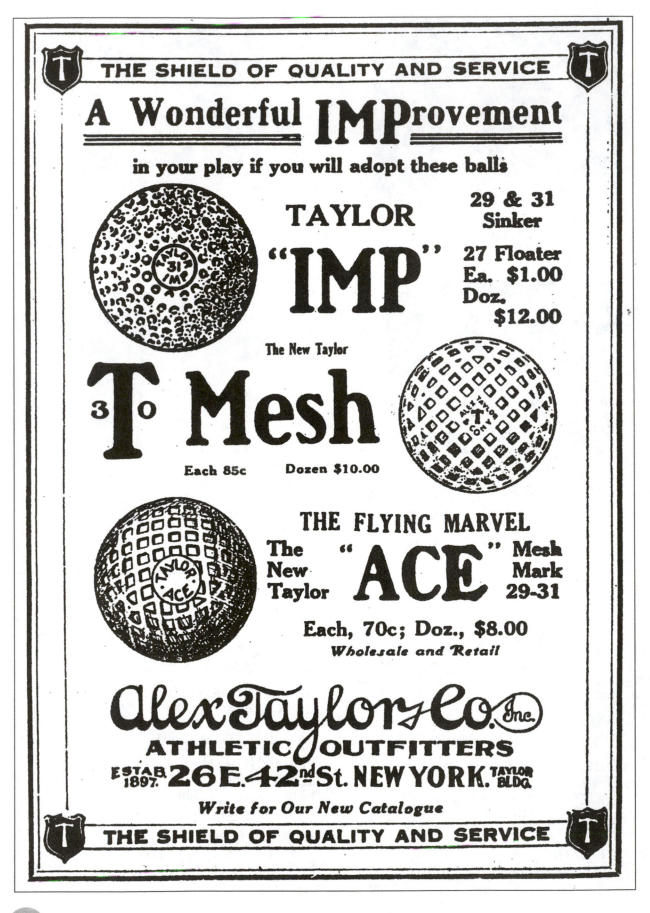

Chapter 7

Collecting Autographs

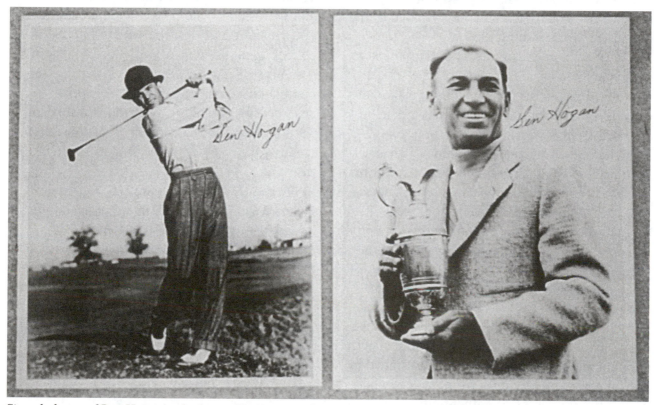

Signed photos of Ben Hogan and other golfing icons make great additions to any collection.

Autographed photographs, gum cards, books, golf balls, letters, and other items are highly sought after by collectors. The first questions collectors pose are about authenticity and guarantees.

There are only two sources from which you can confidently obtain signed items. The first is to get them signed IN PERSON. If you send balls, pictures, cards, etc., by mail to a golf pro, his wife, secretary, or an auto pen may do the signing, not the professional. Jack Nicklaus, Lee Trevino, and several others use an autopen to sign pictures. I've seen many "rubber stamp" Ben Hogan items, especially letters and 3" x 5" cards. Several others have

their secretaries or family members sign items. Your best bet to get in-person signed items is to go to tournaments on practice days. Pros prefer not to sign anything but their official score card on tournament days.

The second, and most convenient, is to purchase your signed items from a reputable dealer or experienced collector who will guarantee the signed items for authenticity for LIFE. This means that anytime during the ownership of the signed item, it may be returned if there is a reasonable doubt the signature is not authentic. When a dealer or collector can give you this lifetime assurance, you can be confident it is an authentic signature.

Many dealers will issue a "Certificate of Authenticity" that is, in fact, a worthless piece of paper unless backed by a LIFE guarantee. California law mandates all autographed items sold in the state or to a California resident for $50 or more must be accompanied by a certificate of authenticity. Many other states may have—or will have—similar laws. Just remember the certificate is only as good as the guarantee of the issuing dealer.

Most auction houses offer no return of any item when purchasing in person at the sale. Make sure you know the signatures you are purchasing are authentic or hire the services of an expert to inspect signed items for you. Experience is great, but the opinion of an expert is almost essential when purchasing at auctions.

Be careful when purchasing autographed golf balls. (These are not to be confused with "signature" balls that are imprinted with a professional's name at the ball factory as a form of advertising.) The dimple pattern and the small size of a ball make it difficult to sign, and many signatures are hard to authenticate. Forgers are acutely aware of this and will take every advantage. Do yourself a favor. Collect only autographed balls you have had signed in person, or again, buy only from dealers who offer a life guarantee of authenticity.

Golfing Autographs: A Brief History

Mark Emerson, a recognized expert and a long-time collector of quality autographed items, has been kind enough to offer his perspective on collecting autographs.

The autograph hobby dates back about 1,000 years, and with the first British Open Championship in 1860, golf began to establish itself as a sport. As a result, autographs of golf's greatest players did not escape interest of collectors.

The first great impresario of the game was Old Tom Morris. Old Tom was the most outstanding player of his day—winner of four British Open titles (1861, 1862, 1864, and 1867)—was a fine clubmaker, golf ball manufacturer, and architect. He also was a visionary, understanding the appeal and collectibility of signed material and, even at the turn of the century, he was signing limited edition prints.

The emergence of "The Great Triumvirate"—Harry Vardon, James Braid, and J.H. Taylor, who between them captured 16 British Open titles—cemented interest in collecting autographs of golf's great stars in the United Kingdom. Signatures were mainly obtained in small leather-covered books designed for collecting autographs. Morris, Vardon, Braid, and Taylor were responsible for creating the spark of collecting golf figures overseas.

In the United States, the U.S. Open Golf Championship began in 1895, but initially it attracted small fields. It wasn't until Francis Ouimet stunned the golf world with his 1913 U.S. Open triumph over Ted Ray and Harry Vardon in that memorable playoff that Americans began to take note of golf heroes. Consequently, autographs of early U.S. Open winners are scarce. The boom in American golf was just around the corner when Gene Sarazen, Bobby Jones, and the flamboyant Walter Hagen began winning numerous major golfing titles between 1914 and 1930.

In the late 1950s, Arnold Palmer's magnetism electrified galleries and television viewers. Crowds at P.G.A. Tour events grew at a faster pace. Today, at nearly any event, players are hounded for signatures on just about anything imaginable.

Why Autographs?

The appeal of autograph collecting generally falls into a few categories. First, collecting signatures in person can be fun and exciting. "In-person" collectors say they enjoy the moment a famous person spends with them, and every once in a while a brief conversation ensues that makes it a life-long memory.

The aspect of collecting older autographed pieces, especially those from deceased individuals, seems to center around the "connection" of an item held by, and then signed by them.

In addition to the fun of autograph collecting, it can also become an investment that might pay off in time. Quality autographs, just like quality collectibles of all kinds, can appreciate in value.

Autographs can also become an outstanding piece of art that can adorn an office, home, or any place. As the collector, you can be the creator of that piece of art that can be fun and satisfying as well.

Whom To Collect

This is a topic every collector should try to come to grips with early on in the process. The best advice in any collecting pursuit is to develop a focus or goal. It is always up to the individual to make this decision, but collecting winners of major championships seems to be the most logical.

Collectible Formats

Once an individual decides whom to collect, it is wise to choose a preferred format for the collection. This is a matter of taste and value. Golf autographs can be on programs, pairing sheets, magazine covers, photos, letters, 3" x 5" cards, golf balls, just to name a few.

In the late 1950s, Arnold Palmer's magnetism electrified galleries and television viewers. Crowds at P.G.A. Tour events grew at a larger pace. Today, at nearly any event, players are hounded for signatures on just about anything imaginable.

Golf Autographs

* Indicates deceased

TOMMY AARON

Photo	$20
Ball	$25

AMY ALCOTT

Photo	$25
Ball	$25

TOMMY ARMOUR

Photo	$1,250
Ball	Unknown
Signature	$375
Typed Letter Signed	$750
Handwritten Letter Signed	$1,250

GEORGE ARCHER

Photo	$20
Ball	$25

PAUL AZINGER

Photo	$20
Ball	$25

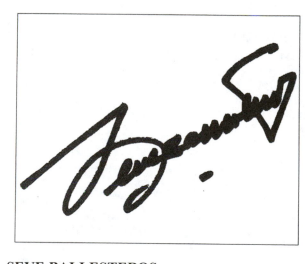

SEVE BALLESTEROS

Photo	$25
Ball	$30

BUTCH BAIRD

Photo	$15
Ball	$20

Photo courtesy of Mounted Memories

MILLER BARBER

Photo	$25
Ball	$25

Photo courtesy of Mounted Memories

ANDY BEAN

Photo	$25
Ball	$25

CHIP BECK

Photo	$20
Ball	$20

PATTY BERG

Photo	$30
Ball	$30

TOMMY BOLT

Photo	$20
Ball	$20
Signature	$5
Typed Letter Signed	$25
Handwritten Letter Signed	$40

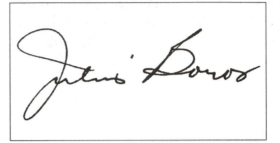

JULIUS BOROS *

Photo	$125
Ball	$225
Signature	$35
Typed Letter Signed	$75
Handwritten Letter Signed	$150

Photo courtesy of Mounted Memories

GAY BREWER *

Photo	$15-$25
Ball	$20-$30

Photo courtesy of Mounted Memories

JACK BURKE
Photo	$20
Ball	$25
Signature	$5
Typed Letter Signed	$25
Handwritten Letter Signed	$50

WALT BURKEMO
Photo	Unknown
Ball	Unknown
Signature	$125
Typed Letter Signed	$250
Handwritten Letter Signed	Unknown

Photo courtesy of Mounted Memories

BILLY CASPER
Photo	$30
Ball	$35

JIM COLBERT
Photo	$15
Ball	$20

GLENNA COLLETT-VARE
Photo	$400
Ball	$450

HARRY COOPER
Photo	$75
Ball	$100
Signature	$15
Typed Letter Signed	$50
Handwritten Letter Signed	$100

HENRY COTTON
Photo	$450
Ball	Unknown
Signature	$150
Typed Letter Signed	$350
Handwritten Letter Signed	$500

FRED COUPLES
Photo	$40
Ball	$40

TOM CREAVY
Photo	Unknown
Ball	Unknown
Signature	$300
Typed Letter Signed	Unknown
Handwritten Letter Signed	Unknown

BEN CRENSHAW
Photo	$30
Ball	$30

FRED DALY
Photo	Unknown
Ball	Unknown
Signature	$100
Typed Letter Signed	$225

JOHN DALY
Photo	$30
Ball	$30

JIMMY DEMARET
Photo	$500
Ball	Unknown
Signature	$175
Typed Letter Signed	$400
Handwritten Letter Signed	$650

LEO DIEGAL

Photo	$350
Ball	Unknown
Signature	$125
Typed Letter Signed	$250
Handwritten Letter Signed	$400

DAVID DUVAL

Photo	$40
Ball	$50

OLIN DUTRA

Photo	$300
Ball	Unknown
Signature	$100
Typed Letter Signed	$225
Handwritten Letter Signed	$350

LEE ELDER

Photo	$15
Ball	$20

Photo courtesy of Mounted Memories

STEVE ELKINGTON

Photo	$15
Ball	$20

ERNIE ELS

Photo	$30
Ball	$30

CHICK EVANS

Photo	$600
Ball	Unknown
Signature	$225
Typed Letter Signed	$425
Handwritten Letter Signed	$650

NICK FALDO

Photo	$30
Ball	$40

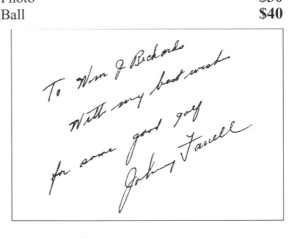

JOHNNY FARRELL

Photo	$250
Ball	Unknown
Signature	$75
Typed Letter Signed	$150
Handwritten Letter Signed	$275

MAXIE FAULKNER

Photo	$50
Ball	$50
Signature	$20
Typed Letter Signed	$50
Handwritten Letter Signed	$100

JIM FERRIER

Photo	**$125**
Ball	Unknown
Signature	**$50**
Typed Letter Signed	**$100**
Handwritten Letter Signed	**$150**

DAN FINSTERWALD

Photo	**$20**
Ball	**$20**
Signature	**$5**
Typed Letter Signed	**$25**
Handwritten Letter Signed	**$50**

JACK FLECK

Photo	**$25**
Ball	**$30**
Signature	**$10**
Typed Letter Signed	**$30**
Handwritten Letter Signed	**$75**

RAY FLOYD

Photo	**$30**
Ball	**$30**

DOUG FORD

Photo	**$20**
Ball	**$20**
Signature	**$5**
Typed Letter Signed	**$25**
Handwritten Letter Signed	**$50**

SERGIO GARCIA

Photo	**$40**
Ball	**$45**

VICTOR GHEZZI

Photo	**$225**
Ball	Unknown
Signature	**$75**
Typed Letter Signed	**$150**
Handwritten Letter Signed	**$250**

HUBERT GREEN

Photo	**$25**
Ball	**$25**

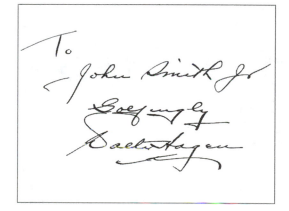

RALPH GULDAHL

Photo	**$1,000**
Ball	Unknown
Signature	**$300**
Typed Letter Signed	**$600**
Handwritten Letter Signed	**$1,000**

WALTER HAGEN

Photo	**$450**
Ball	Unknown
Signature	**$150**
Typed Letter Signed	**$350**
Handwritten Letter Signed	**$500**

CHICK HARBERT

Photo	**$75**
Ball	**$275**
Signature	**$20**
Typed Letter Signed	**$75**
Handwritten Letter Signed	**$100**

CLAUDE HARMON

Photo	**$125**
Ball	**$200**

CHANDLER J. HARPER
Photo	$25
Ball	$35
Signature	$10
Typed Letter Signed	$25
Handwritten Letter Signed	$60

JAY HEBERT
Photo	$15
Ball	$20

LIONEL HEBERT
Photo	$65
Ball	$150
Signature	$30
Typed Letter Signed	$65
Handwritten Letter Signed	$125

BEN HOGAN *
Photo	$200
Ball	$300
Signature	$80
Typed Letter Signed	$175
Handwritten Letter Signed	$400

BOB HOPE *
Photo	$90
Ball	$125

JULIE INKSTER
Photo	$20
Ball	$20

HALE IRWIN
Photo	$20
Ball	$25

LEE JANZEN
Photo	$25
Ball	$25

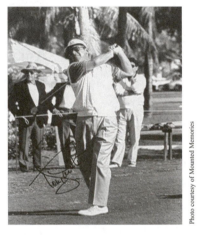

Photo courtesy of Mounted Memories

TONY JACKLIN
Photo	$15
Ball	$20

Photo courtesy of Mounted Memories

DON JANUARY
Photo	$25
Ball	$30

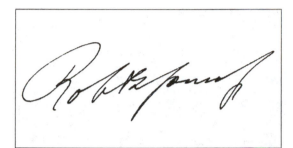

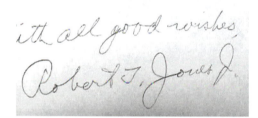

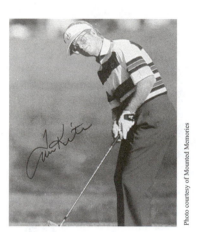

TOM KITE

Photo	**$20**
Ball	**$25**

TED KROLL

Photo	**$30**
Ball	**$100**
Signature	**$15**
Typed Letter Signed	**$30**
Handwritten Letter Signed	**$60**

BOBBY JONES (ROBERT T. JONES JR.) *

Vintage	
Photo	**$7,500**
Ball	Unknown
Signature	**$1,500**
Typed Letter Signed	**$3,500**
Handwritten Letter Signed	**$6,000**
Modern	
Photo	**$2,500**
Ball	Unknown
Signature	**$700**
Typed Letter Signed	**$1,250**

HERMAN KEISER

Photo	**$75**
Ball	**$175**
Signature	**$30**
Typed Letter Signed	**$75**
Handwritten Letter Signed	**$125**

BETSY KING

Photo	**$25**
Ball	**$50**

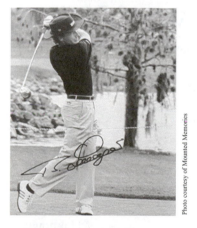

BERNARD LANGER

Photo	**$30**
Ball	**$30**

TOM LEHMAN
Photo	**$25**
Ball	**$25**

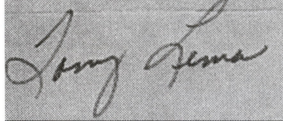

TONY LEMA
Photo	**$750**
Book	**$700**

JUSTIN LEONARD
Photo	**$30**
Ball	**$30**

GENE LITTLER
Photo	**$25**
Ball	**$30**

BOB LOCKE
Photo	**$400**
Ball	Unknown
Signature	**$175**
Typed Letter Signed	**$375**
Handwritten Letter Signed	**$500**

NANCY LOPEZ
Photo	**$25**
Ball	**$35**

DAVIS LOVE III
Photo	**$35**
Ball	**$35**

LLOYD MANGRUM
Photo	**$325**
Ball	Unknown
Signature	**$100**
Typed Letter Signed	**$225**
Handwritten Letter Signed	**$400**

CASEY MARTIN
Photo	**$15**
Ball	**$20**

FRED MCLEOD
Photo	Unknown
Ball	Unknown
Signature	**$200**
Typed Letter Signed	**$400**
Handwritten Letter Signed	Unknown

PHIL MICKELSON
Photo	**$30**
Ball	**$30**

DOC MIDDLECOFF
Photo	**$125**
Ball	**$175**
Signature	**$30**
Typed Letter Signed	**$100**
Handwritten Letter Signed	**$250**

JOHNNY MILLER
Photo	**$20**
Ball	**$25**

Photo courtesy of Mounted Memories

LARRY MIZE
Photo	**$15**
Ball	**$20**

Photo courtesy of Mounted Memories

COLIN MONTGOMERIE
Photo	**$25**
Ball	**$25**

ORVILLE MOODY
Photo	**$15**
Ball	**$20**

Photo courtesy of Mounted Memories

TOM MORRIS*
Photo	**$4,800**

ALEX MORRISON
Photo	Unknown
Ball	Unknown
Signature	**$20**
Typed Letter Signed	**$40**
Handwritten Letter Signed	**$60**

BOB MURPHY
Photo	**$20**
Ball	**$25**

KEL NAGLE
Photo	**$40**
Ball	**$40**
Signature	**$20**
Typed Letter Signed	**$50**
Handwritten Letter Signed	**$100**

BYRON NELSON
Photo	**$25**
Ball	**$40**
Signature	**$10**
Typed Letter Signed	**$40**
Handwritten Letter Signed	**$125**

LARRY NELSON
Photo	**$25**
Ball	**$25**

JACK NICKLAUS
Photo	**$100**
Ball	**$150**

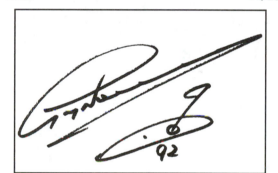

GREG NORMAN
Photo	**$50**
Ball	**$80**

MARK O'MEARA
Photo	**$35**
Ball	**$35**

FRANCIS OUIMET
Photo	**$1,250**
Ball	Unknown
Signature	**$350**
Typed Letter Signed	**$600**
Handwritten Letter Signed	**$1,250**

ALFRED PADGHAM

Photo	Unknown
Ball	Unknown
Signature	**$275**
Typed Letter Signed	Unknown
Handwritten Letter Signed	Unknown

SE RI PAK

Photo	**$35**
Ball	**$35**

ARNOLD PALMER

Photo	**$80**
Ball	**$100**

SAM PARKS

Photo	**$175**
Ball	**$250**
Signature	**$75**
Typed Letter Signed	**$125**
Handwritten Letter Signed	**$250**

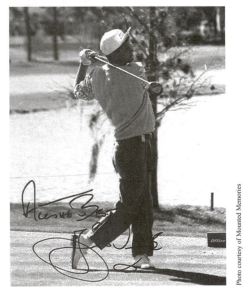

Photo courtesy of Mounted Memories

JESPER PARNEVIK

Photo	**$15**
Ball	**$20**

STEVE PATE

Photo	**$15**
Ball	**$20**

Photo courtesy of Mounted Memories

COREY PAVIN

Photo	**$30**
Ball	**$35**

HENRY PICARD

Photo	**$225**
Ball	**$350**
Signature	**$75**
Typed Letter Signed	**$175**
Handwritten Letter Signed	**$400**

GARY PLAYER

Photo	**$35**
Ball	**$40**

Photo courtesy of Mounted Memories

NICK PRICE

Photo	$30
Ball	$30

BETSY RAWLS

Photo	$40
Ball	$60

JOHNNY REVOLTA

Photo	$150
Ball	Unknown
Signature	$75
Typed Letter Signed	$150
Handwritten Letter Signed	$300

CHI CHI RODRIGUEZ

Photo	$25
Ball	$30

BOBBY ROSBURG

Photo	$20
Ball	$20
Signature	$5
Typed Letter Signed	$25
Handwritten Letter Signed	$50

PAUL RUNYAN

Photo	$75
Ball	$125
Signature	$25
Typed Letter Signed	$60
Handwritten Letter Signed	$100

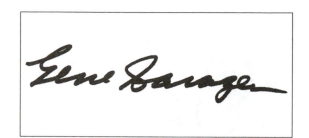

GENE SARAZEN *

Photo	$75
Ball	$125
Signature	$25
Typed Letter Signed	$75
Handwritten Letter Signed	$200

DENNY SHUTE

Photo	$375
Ball	Unknown
Signature	$125
Typed Letter Signed	$250
Handwritten Letter Signed	$400

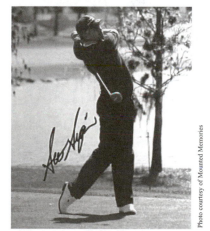

Photo courtesy of Mounted Memories

SCOTT SIMPSON

Photo	$20
Ball	$25

CHARLES SIFFORD

Photo	$25
Ball	$30

Photo courtesy of Mounted Memories

VIJAY SINGH

Photo	**$30**
Ball	**$35**

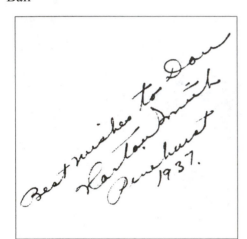

HORTON SMITH

Photo	**$1,000**
Ball	Unknown
Signature	**$400**
Typed Letter Signed	**$700**
Handwritten Letter Signed	**$1,250**

J.C. SNEAD

Photo	**$20**
Ball	**$25**

SAM SNEAD

Photo	**$100**
Ball	**$100**
Signature	**$20**
Typed Letter Signed	**$75**
Handwritten Letter Signed	**$250**

ANNIKA SORENSTAM

Photo	**$50**
Ball	**$60**

CRAIG STADLER

Photo	**$30**
Ball	**$35**

PAYNE STEWART *

Photo	**$75**
Ball	**$125**

FRANK STRANAHAN

Photo	**$50**
Ball	**$50**
Signature	**$25**
Typed Letter Signed	**$75**
Handwritten Letter Signed	**$100**

DAVE STOCKTON

Photo	**$20**
Ball	**$25**

CURTIS STRANGE

Photo	**$30**
Ball	**$35**

HAL SUTTON

Photo	**$25**
Ball	**$30**

PETER THOMSON

Photo	**$40**
Ball	**$45**
Signature	**$15**
Typed Letter Signed	**$40**
Handwritten Letter Signed	**$75**

ROBERT TOSKI

Photo	**$25**
Ball	**$30**
Signature	**$10**
Typed Letter Signed	**$25**
Handwritten Letter Signed	**$50**

JEROME TRAVERS

Photo	Unknown
Ball	Unknown
Signature	**$150**
Typed Letter Signed	**$275**
Handwritten Letter Signed	Unknown

Signature	**$750**
Typed Letter Signed	**$1,250**
Handwritten Letter Signed	**$3,000**

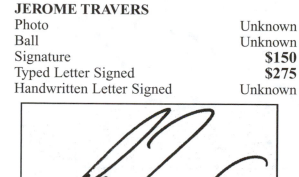

LEE TREVINO

Photo	**$35**
Ball	**$35**

WILLIE TURNESA

Photo	**$75**
Ball	**$150**
Signature	**$25**
Typed Letter Signed	**$75**
Handwritten Letter Signed	**$125**

SAM URZETTA

Photo	**$30**
Ball	**$40**
Signature	**$10**
Typed Letter Signed	**$30**
Handwritten Letter Signed	**$65**

Photo courtesy of Mounted Memories

HARRY VARDON

Photo	**$750**
Ball	Unknown

KEN VENTURI

Photo	**$25**
Ball	**$30**

Photo courtesy of Mounted Memories

LANNY WADKINS

Photo	**$25**
Ball	**$25**

ART WALL

Photo	**$40**
Ball	**$100**
Signature	**$15**
Typed Letter Signed	**$45**
Handwritten Letter Signed	**$75**

HARVIE WARD

Photo	**$35**
Ball	**$35**
Signature	**$15**
Typed Letter Signed	**$40**
Handwritten Letter Signed	**$65**

TOM WATSON

Photo	**$35**
Ball	**$40**

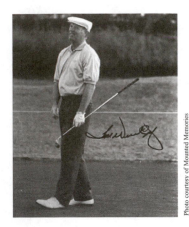

TOM WEISKOPF

Photo	**$20**
Ball	**$25**

JOYCE WETHERED

Photo	**$350**
Ball	**$400**

Photo courtesy of Mounted Memories

LEE WESTWOOD

Photo	**$15**
Ball	**$20**

OSCAR WILLING

Photo	**$200**
Ball	Unknown
Signature	**$75**
Typed Letter Signed	**$100**
Handwritten Letter Signed	**$200**

CRAIG WOOD

Photo	Unknown
Ball	Unknown
Signature	**$600**
Typed Letter Signed	Unknown
Handwritten Letter Signed	Unknown

TIGER WOODS

Photo	**$150-$175**
Framed Photo (UDA)	**$1,400**
Ball	**$450-$500**
Pin Flag (UDA)	**$800**

CHARLIE YATES

Photo	**$100**
Ball	**$125**
Signature	**$50**
Typed Letter Signed	**$100**
Handwritten Letter Signed	**$150**

BABE DIDRIKSON ZAHARIAS *

Photo	**$150-$200**
Ball	Unknown

LARRY ZIEGLER

Photo	**$15**
Ball	**$20**

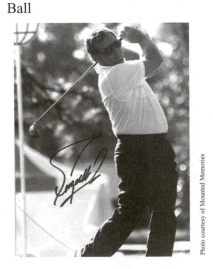

Photo courtesy of Mounted Memories

FUZZY ZOELLER

Photo	**$35**
Ball	**$40**

A painting shows the early days of golf, with a caddy teeing it up for a golfer. Original golf oil paintings are valuable to collectors and to historians of the game.

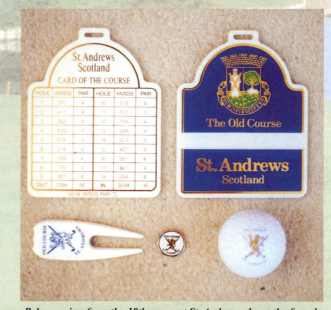

Below, a view from the 18th green at St. Andrews shows the famed Tom Morris Golf Shop, where Old Tom Morris practiced his trade in the mid 1800s. Above, modern souvenirs from St. Andrews will eventually become valuable collectibles.

A rut iron, left, and a giant niblick flank an early golf ball.

Two beautiful clubs made by Robert Forgon of St. Andrew are long nose woods, circa 1880s.

Spliced neck heads are shown before shafting of the golf clubs.

Rut irons are displayed with a rare hand-hammered gutta percha golf ball.

A Hackbarth putter, a golf practice device, and a giant niblick are all sought after collectibles.

There is an interesting variety of face treatments on this group of circa 1920 irons.

Three long nose woods include the top one, circa 1870, middle, from the 1880s, and bottom, from the 1890s.

A rare feather ball and three feather ball-era clubs all date from before 1860.

Some of the amazing variety of putters is shown in these four examples.

Two rare cylindrical putters are displayed.

A group of interesting clubs with back weighting and face inserts are circa 1900.

Putters come in all shapes and sizes, both metals and woods.

293

There are a lot of ways to putt the ball in the hole, as this variety of putters shows.

A group of mallet putters is ready for action on the greens.

If you don't like your putter, make one yourself. This homemade putter is crafted from wood.

This aluminum mallet putter has an unusual deep face and is center shafted.

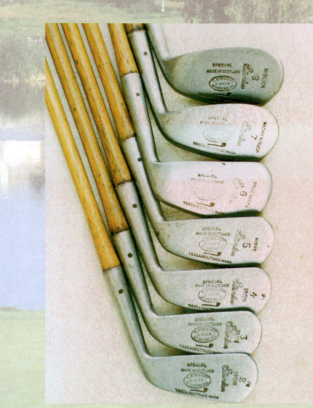

A complete set of Tom Stewart "Pipe" marked irons is circa 1920.

A partial set of Kroydon Ball Face irons is circa 1920s.

A set of Wm. Gilson Akros Model irons, circa 1920, is rare.

Here is a selection of anti-shank irons.

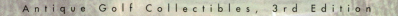

Matched here are a Kroydon Brick Face, top, and a Spalding Waterfall iron.

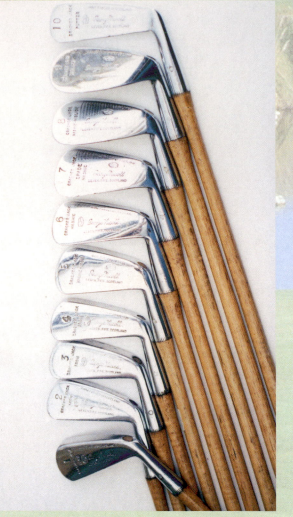

A rare complete set of George Nicoll irons was made in Scotland.

A group of irons shows the interesting variety of face treatments available in early irons.

A pair of Spalding clubs include a Waffle Face, top, and a Waterfall deep groove iron, circa 1916-1918.

Clubs that are a combination of metal and wood were popular in the Roaring Twenties.

Face inserts and aiming aids are features of these woods from the 1920s.

Antique woods with pretty faces look great in displays.

Golf bags from the 1910s and 1920s allowed golfers or their caddies to carry a full set of clubs.

They're effective, but they're illegal. Deep-groove irons from the 1915-1920 period gave golfers an illegal advantage in hitting their shots.

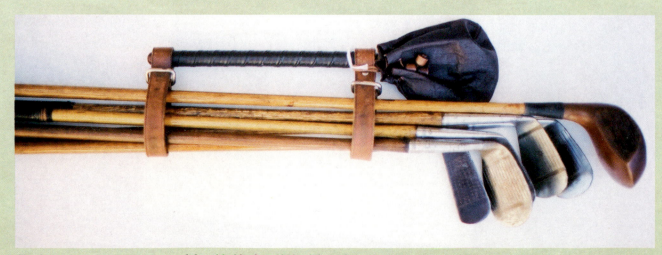

Here's another way to carry a set up clubs, with this circa 1950s club carrier.

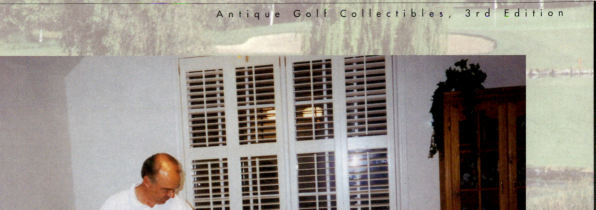

Chuck Furjanic, seated, inspects some antique golf clubs along with collector Chuck McMullin.

"Bobby's" Portable Putting Hole is an interesting practice device, circa 1930.

Another practice device is the Golf Gadjet Driving Range, where "the ball comes back."

A colorful poster for an antique golf equipment auction at Christie's of Glasgow, Scotland, shows a Roaring Twenties golf clubhouse scene.

Bramble cover balls are circa 1905 to 1915.

A group of golf balls from the 1930s are in mint condition.

A great variety of golf ball packaging was available for consumers to choose from in the 1920s and 1930s.

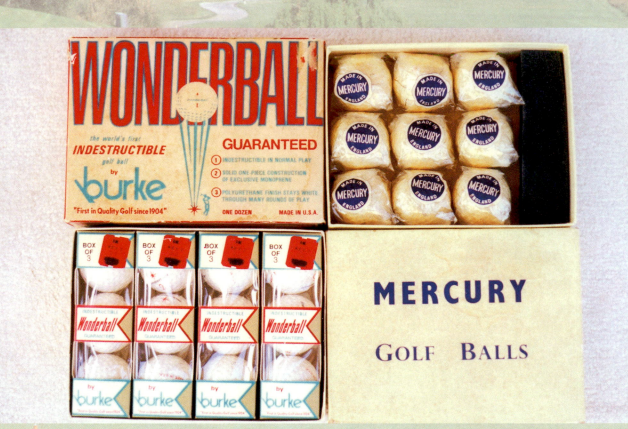

The Wonderball by Burke was advertised as "indestructible," while Mercury golf balls came individually wrapped in a box.

The Kro-Flite Mesh golf ball box and sleeve show the packaging of the 1920s.

Early golf balls show a variety of styles and patterns.

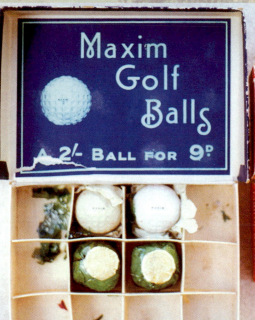

Maxim and Dunlop Warwick golf balls, two popular brands from the 1930s, are displayed in their original boxes.

An assortment of golf balls have odd cover patterns.

An interesting collection of mint-condition golf balls is from the 1920s and 1930s.

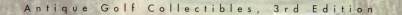

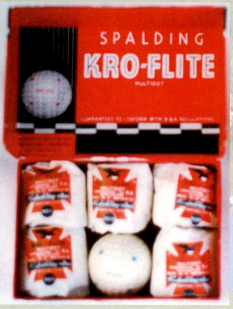

A scarce half dozen mint-condition Spalding Kro-Flite balls are in the original box.

Three golf balls display some interesting patterns.

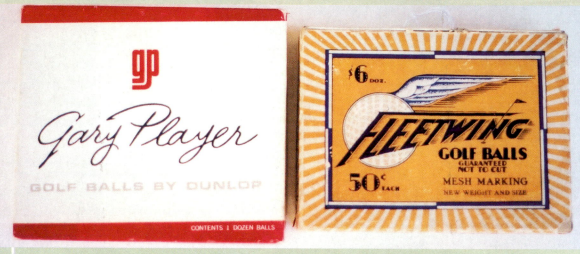

Golf great Gary Player lent his name to Dunlop golf balls, while Fleetwing golf balls cost 50 cents each, or $6 a box, in their day.

Dunlop Gold Cup golf balls from the 1950s are well preserved in their original box.

Many collectors like to display their collections of autographed balls. This one includes Gary Player, Ray Floyd, John Daley, Tom Kite, and other pros.

The antique hickory clubs still get an occasional workout from golf enthusiasts who play in hickory tournaments. The author, right, gets ready to tee off with his foursome in a hickory tournament.

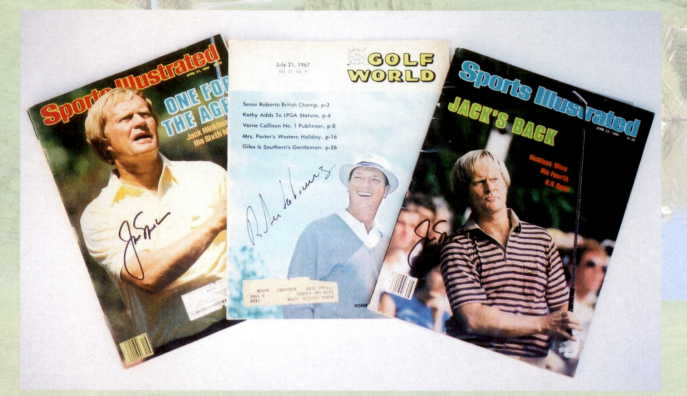

Autographed magazines by top pros, such as Jack Nicklaus, are a popular collectible.

Magazines and programs preserve the printed history of the game of golf.

Programs from the U.S. Open over the years have become a popular collectible.

The Ryder Cup, held every two years, has become a high point in the pro golfing world in recent years and its programs have gained in value.

Tees come in bags, boxes, matchbooks, and envelopes in assorted shapes and sizes.

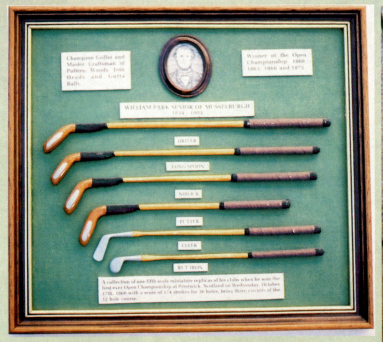

A framed collection of antique golf clubs makes a great wall decoration for a golf collector.

The Novel-Tee, circa 1905, is a booklet of 36 perforated paper golf tees.

Tees in paper bags, dating from the 1950s, were produced by three big names in golf: MacGregor, Walter Hagen, and Wilson.

Tees were packaged in a wide variety of containers in the early years. Also shown are two caddy badges, left center.

Boxes of tees included, from left, the Arrow Tee, Celluloid Tees, and Pryde's Orange Tee, all in colorful boxes.

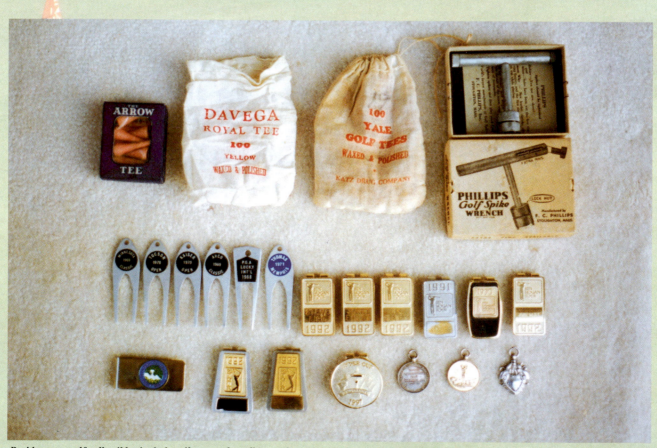

Besides tees, golf collectibles include spike wrenches, divot tools, and several types of golf charms.

The scope of golf collectibles is seemingly endless. This grouping includes a tee, a tee arm, rule books, and a variety of tools.

Ceramic and pewter figurines of golfers make great display pieces for collectors.

Even Santa turns into a golf fanatic on this figurine.

Statuary of golfing figures is collectible as well as decorative.

A real swinging woman golfer is joined by various collectibles, including a teapot, golf shoe spikes, and desk pieces.

More golf collectibles include a comic ceramic figure, golf ball desk sets, and artwork.

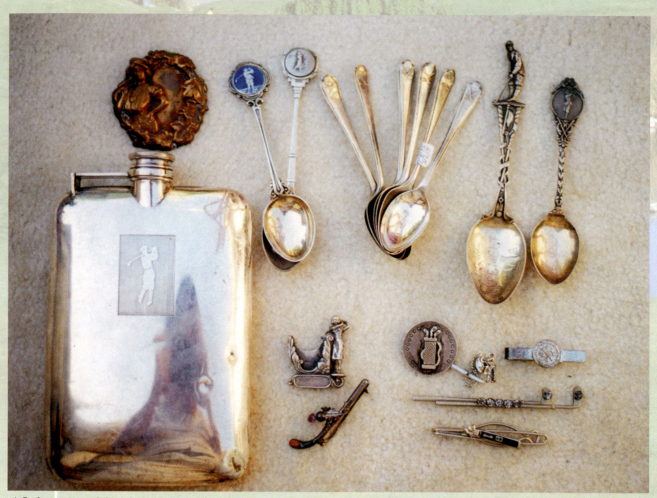

A flask, spoons, and tie tacks are among collectible silver, bronze, and gold golf pieces.

A decorative pipe, spoons, a flask, and other silver and gold pieces are valuable golf collectibles.

One of the more unusual golf items is this English toast rack made in sterling silver, circa 1920.

The Masters in Augusta, Ga., is the site of one of the four Masters tournaments each year and is naturally a focus for collectors of pins, card decks, statuary, and much more.

An autographed Master flag would be prized by any golf collector.

A couple of unusual collectibles are Bobby Jones "Flicker" books and a "Spinoff" golf game, circa 1930s.

A colorful and humorous desk blotter, circa 1900, features an advertisement for Balmosa cream.

Golfers love everything about legend Arnold Palmer and this display pairs his autograph with several photos of his spectacular career.

Auction catalogues are great for acquiring golf collectibles and make excellent reference materials.

Unlike baseball and football, few golf trading card sets have been produced, making these older cards valuable.

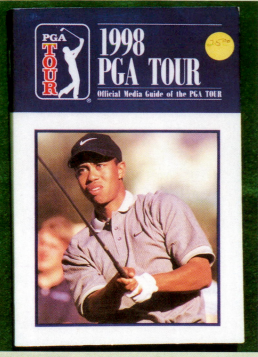

As an emerging pro golf star, Tiger Woods was featured on the cover of the 1998 PGA Tour media guide.

1998 PGA TOUR
Official Media Guide of the PGA TOUR

Golf on TV, Internet, 2E
Four to look for in 2001, 4E
Tour schedules, TV and defending champs, 7E

Bonus Section
Pro golf

Tou act follo

Can Tiger improve on
Quest starts today in

By Harry Blauvelt
USA TODAY

KAPALUA, Hawaii — Against a
leis, luaus and aloha shirts, Tiger
about to start swinging for the
2001.

What better place than Hawa
to find out if he still has a hot
month's hiatus from competiti

He'll tee it up today in The
Champions, on the

The burning question: Can T
millennium magic he weaved
when he won 12 events worldw
three majors, many in runaway

New day: Tiger
Woods starts over

Please see (

PGA TOUR
Another Magical
Mercedes Cha
Thursday 1/11 7:00-10:0
Friday 1/12 7:30-10:3
Saturday 1/13 7:30-10:3
Sunday 1/14 8:00-10:0

Tiger Woods gets lots of media attention. This is USA TODAY's cover of a special pro golf section from Jan. 11, 2001.

Three of the scores of books written about Tiger Woods are among the many collectibles of the young PGA star.

The Grandest

Tiger Woods
THE MAKING OF A CHAMPION

Sports Illustrated
Golf Plus
1997 Masters

SCHOLASTIC BIOGRAPHY
TIGER WOODS
An American Master
by Nicholas Edwards

Tiger Woods has appeared frequently on the cover of Sports Illustrated, including the 1996 Sportsman of the Year issue at left.

A flag autographed by Tiger Woods from The Players Championship in 2001 was authenticated by the PGA Tour and Upper Deck. It brought $1,825 on eBay in 2003.

An autographed pin flag from the 18th green, auctioned by the Tiger Woods Foundation, brought more than $8,600 in on eBay.

Old Tom Morris Golf assembled an impressive group of antique golf collectibles for a recent auction, including clubs, books, a pipe, pottery, and tee-makers.

Chapter 8

Collecting Tees

Tees come in boxes, booklets, match books, bags, packets, and loose.

The "TEE" has played an important role since golf's inception more than 500 years ago. Today we take them so matter-of-factly, we usually don't bother to pick them up after a tee shot.

It may surprise you to know tees were not always made of wood and one could obtain handfuls for free at the pro shop. They were made of aluminum, paper, plastic, steel, wire, zinc, rubber—anything that would raise the ball from the turf. Shapes and forms were stars, triangles, domes, tethers, spinners, molds, and just about anything imaginable and even some unimaginable.

They came individually, in boxes, string bags, paper bags, matchbooks, wheels, tins, and any other marketable containers. Pros stocked numerous varieties in their shops, and the greenskeepers lost their tempers when the new wire tees jammed their mowers. The poor tee was berated, bemused and left on the tee-ing ground, until one day Walter Hagen was paid to use a particular tee, and as a gesture to his fans, left them on the teeing ground after a shot. When the last player in his group hit, and strolled down the fairway, a mad scramble ensued—by who else ... the collector—to pick up the tee Hagen had just used!

An Introduction to Golf Tees
By Lee Crist

Lee Crist has been a collector of tees for many years and has accumulated a vast collection and assortment. He was kind enough to provide the following for your collecting pleasures.

Everyone knows golf tees are those little white trumpet-looking items approximately 1 7/8 inches long. In reality, golf tees have been around for more than one hundred years and, most likely, the first golf tee was a good swift stomp of a golfer's heel. This raised the ground from a common plain to a higher level, giving the player a type of launching pad.

After the heel print attempt came forming a mound of moist dirt (or sand) that would give the ball somewhat of an elevated position, making it easier for contact. Molding each tee by hand constituted a very messy way of accomplishing the feat. Alas, the invention of the sand tee mold came into existence. This approach to forming a consistent tee became popular during the early 1890s. While this form of teeing the ball was not the ultimate, it was definitely a great improvement. Around 1893, more entrepreneurs were at work and individual tees were being developed. Prosper L. Senate of Philadelphia was given credit for inventing and patenting the first portable tee, although I suspect that individuals had made their own …"one-of-a-kind" ... long before this.

As golf became more popular in the United States, so did the quest to find a better way to present the ball for action. The poor golf tee has been the target of abuse ever since and, as of this writing, we have documented 31 variations of sand tee molds.

Collecting golf tees is not a matter of collecting every color in the rainbow or collecting every tee that has a different advertisement. A tee collector, a purist, is a person who has committed his every fiber to finding all the physically different shaped tees that were ever designed, every cloth tee bag ever made, every commercial box manufactured, every advertisement printed and, last but not least, how about patents? Probably none of the collectors started out that way, although it would be very nice to have a few odd looking tees around as a conversation piece.

How to Start a Collection

It is recommended that you communicate with as many of your fellow golfers, friends, golf dealers and antique dealers as you can.

Getting the word out and enlisting the help of others will go a long way. Letting people know that you are "looking" does wonders. It's human nature for people to want to help.

Designing your own business/collector card can also be very helpful and lots of fun. Flea markets and garage sales are a great source for finding tees; never pass up an opportunity to go through the pockets of an old golf bag.

Joining one of the antique golf societies, such as the Golf Collectors Society, is another way of finding fellow collectors who will be more than glad to have someone to correspond with. These people love to buy, sell or trade for something they need in their collection; if you have an opportunity to buy more than one unusual tee—buy it. It's always useful to have extras for trading.

How to Display

Once you start accumulating tees, consideration should be given as to how you are going to sort, display, store, and transport your collection. There are numerous ways to display, as there are many categories of tees: old wooden tees, paper tees, plastic tees, metal tees, pencil tees, surface tees, height tees, novelty tees, tether tees, weighted tees, rubber tees, celluloid tees, swivel tees, and of course, sand mold tees.

Some collections are displayed in jewelry-type trays, others are mounted in styrofoam, some are mounted on plywood with very thin wire, and some use file cabinets, housing the collection in various zip lock bags. The latter is a little cumbersome if you plan to transport and show.

How Extensive is Tee Collecting?

When talking to people about collecting, the one thing you always hear is, "I had no idea that there were so many different tees." There have been more than 1,275 physically different tees catalogued and numbered; much of the credit for this belongs to Art Eden of Florida and Irv Valenta of North Carolina.

As far as "names" of tees, commercial and otherwise, 421 different names have been accounted for.

In the early 1900s, packaging to promote the merchandising of tees became an industry in itself. Tees were packaged in large and small boxes with very ornate designs. Boxes could hold 7, 9, 18, 25, 50, or 100 pieces. There are at least 64 different boxes that have been catalogued.

Another packaging concept was cloth tee bags, similar to a tobacco pouch, which held 50 or 100 tees. Walgreen Drug Co. and Sears Roebuck were two of the early suppliers of the bulk bags; 83 different ones have been catalogued. Paper bags were also used to hold 15 to 25 tees. Most bags were white with the printed advertisement of the golf companies.

Tee packets similar to matchbooks are also collectibles and have been produced since the early 1920s.

Tee advertisements have appeared as early as the 1890s in some sports magazines and are also collectibles.

Pricing

Pricing is a very subjective issue. Many individuals ask what a particular tee is worth. Obviously, the answer is, "Whatever someone is willing to pay."

The following entries and photos are an effort to help you identify some of the tees that you may find, and estimate their approximate value based on condition.

Prices Golf Tees

Prices are for grades G-5, G-7, and G9.

ALL-MY-TEE
VARIOUS
$50 $90 $175
Circa 1920. Red rubber with weighted end.

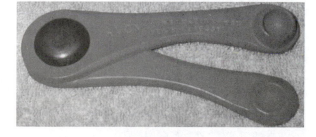

AVON DOUBLE ARM TEE
VARIOUS
$75 $125 $200
Circa 1920s. Made in England of rubber with two tee heights. Approximately five inches long.

BOBBY TEES
VARIOUS
$50 $75 $150
Circa late 1920s. Red wooden goblet-style tees in colorful box. Photo below.

BRASS DOUBLE GOLF TEE STAMP
RANSOME
$600 $1,000 $1,500
Circa 1900. Brass sand tee mold with a deep side for drives and shallow side for irons.

BREAK APART PLASTIC TEES
SPALDING, USA
$70   **$150**   **$250**
Circa 1930s. Twenty red tees that break apart when needed.

CRUICKSHANK STEEL TEES
VARIOUS
$70   **$150**   **$225**
Circa1930. Red wire tees with circular top. Green and red box with Bobby Cruickshank's picture.

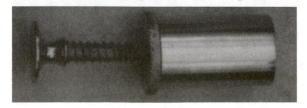

DOUGLAS SAND TEE GUN
VARIOUS
$600   **$900**   **$1,500**
Circa 1910-1920. Cylindrical plunger made of stainless steel. Made in England.

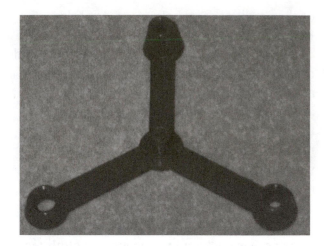

ETERNA TEE
VARIOUS
$40   **$60**   **$100**
Circa 1950s. A three height plastic tee.

\G & S GOLF TEE
VARIOUS
$65   **$100**   **$175**
Circa 1920s. Brass tee with rubber arm that swivels.

GOLD MEDAL GOLF TEE
VARIOUS
$50   **$70**   **$150**
Circa 1930. Twenty wooden tees in box.

K-D SAND TEE MOLD
K-D MFG., LANCASTER, PA

$400	$600	$800

Circa 1920s. Polished aluminum with spring plunger.

INTERNATIONAL GOLF TEE
UNKNOWN MAKER

$100	$200	$400

Circa 1917. Two rubber tees secured by a rubber tether.

JUST PERFECT TEES
VARIOUS

$45	$70	$150

Circa early 1930s. Eighteen wooden tees in pale green box.

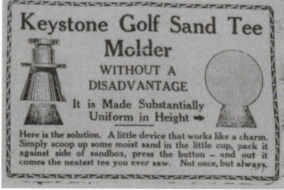

KEYSTONE SAND TEE MOLD
VARIOUS

$300	$400	$500

Circa 1920-1930. Bakelite plastic with spring plunger.

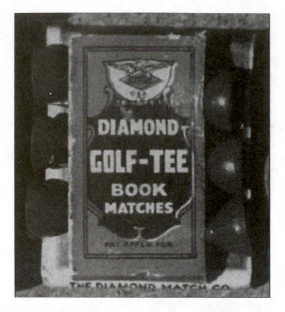

MATCHBOOK TEES
VARIOUS
$15   **$25**   **$50**
Circa 1930s. Matchbook style with three to six tees. Matchbooks from the 1940s and later are worth considerably less.

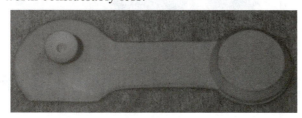

NO-LOOZ-TEE
VARIOUS
$60   **$90**   **$150**
Circa 1950s-1960s. Weighted end. Made of rubber.

NOVEL TEES
VARIOUS
$60   **$100**   **$180**
Circa 1930. Circular Handi-Pack of nine tees.

NOVEL-TEES
SPURGIN MFG., CHICAGO
$50   **$100**   **$200**
Circa late 1920s. A book of eighteen paper tees.

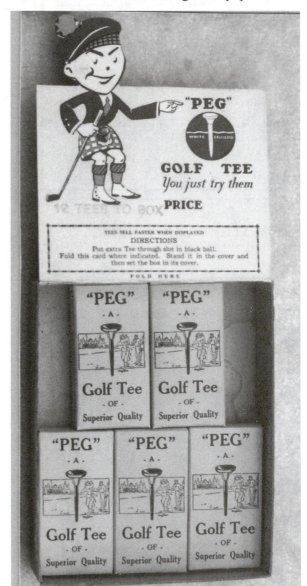

PEG GOLF TEE
VARIOUS
$50   **$80**   **$150**
Circa 1930. Yellow box with twelve tees. (Original display boxes are quite valuable.)

PERFECT GOLF TEE
VARIOUS
$80   **$120**   **$200**
Patented 1927. Molded rubber tee secured in the ground by a nail.

PERFEC TEE
UNKNOWN MAKER
$65   **$120**   **$200**
Circa 1925.

PERMA TEE
VARIOUS
$100   **$150**   **$225**
Circa 1930. Aluminum tee with steel arm that swivels.

PRYDE'S ORANGE TEE
ORANGE MFG. CO.
$60   **$100**   **$175**
Circa late 1920s. Carrot shaped wood tees. Blue and orange box.

THE REDDY TEE
NIEBLO MFG. CO.
$40   **$90**   **$175**
Circa 1930. Wooden tees in green, white and red box.

REX ZINC TEES
THE REX CO., CHICAGO
$70 $120 $200
Circa 1930. Red box. Zinc tees.

RITE PENCIL TEE
WIMO SPECIALTY CO., NY
$10 $20 $35
Circa 1927. Long tee with pencil lead at tip.
Original boxes are scarce. Prices are for single
tees.

ROUND CUPPED DOME METAL TEES
VARIOUS
$40 $60 $100
Circa 1920s. Half-dollar sized "Cupped Dome"-
type tee. Most had advertisements imprinted on
them. Some were made of plastic and are valued
less than the metal dome tees.

RUBBER MANHATTAN TEE
VARIOUS
$75 $130 $200
Circa 1920. Five-inch-long rubber tee with round
weight at one end, tee at other.

SAND TEE MOLD
VARIOUS
$400 $700 $950
Circa 1890-1920. Brass with spring plunger.

THE SCOT-TEE
VARIOUS
$65 $100 $175
Circa late 1920s. Box of eighteen wooden tees.

SELF-ADJUSTING GOLF TEE
MILLAR, GLASGOW
$175 $300 $600
Circa 1900.

TOP NOT TEE
VARIOUS
$50   **$80**   **$175**
Circa late 1920s. Made of both wood and steel.
Orange and white box.

TEES IN BAGS
VARIOUS MAKERS
$30   **$70**   **$120**
Circa 1930s-1940s. Drawstring bags of 50 and 100
wooden tees.

TETHER TEES
VARIOUS
$75   **$100**   **$150**
Circa 1900-1930s. Many varieties with a cord or
"Tether" between weight or colorful thistle and the
tee.

TRIPLE-T GOLF TEE
SIMPLEX MFG.,
CLEVELAND, OH
$10   **$15**   **$25**
Circa 1925. Made for adjusting to three heights.
Original boxes are scarce. Prices are for single tees.

WALGREEN GOLF TEES
WALGREEN STORES
$50   **$75**   **$150**
Circa 1930s. Yellow and black box of yellow-col-
ored wooden tees.

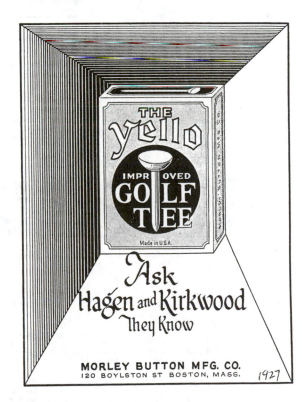

THE "YELLO" TEE
VARIOUS
$60   **$90**   **$160**
Circa 1927. Black-and-yellow box of 18 yellow-
colored wooden tees. Endorsed by Walter Hagen
and Joe Kirkwood.

D&M GOLF TEES

White—
easy to find

Rock Maple—
hard to break

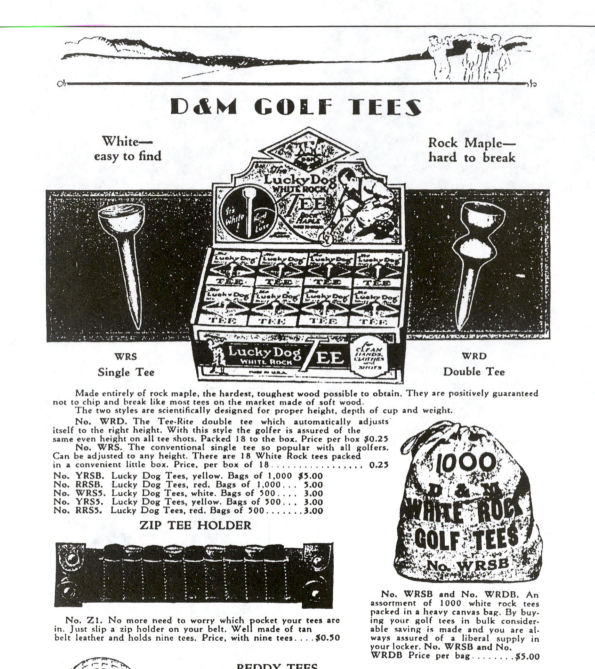

WRS
Single Tee

WRD
Double Tee

Made entirely of rock maple, the hardest, toughest wood possible to obtain. They are positively guaranteed not to chip and break like most tees on the market made of soft wood.

The two styles are scientifically designed for proper height, depth of cup and weight.

No. WRD. The Tee-Rite double tee which automatically adjusts itself to the right height. With this style the golfer is assured of the same even height on all tee shots. Packed 18 to the box. Price per box $0.25

No. WRS. The conventional single tee so popular with all golfers. Can be adjusted to any height. There are 18 White Rock tees packed in a convenient little box. Price, per box of 18 .... 0.25

No. YRSB. Lucky Dog Tees, yellow. Bags of 1,000 $5.00
No. RRSB. Lucky Dog Tees, red. Bags of 1,000 .... 5.00
No. WRS5. Lucky Dog Tees, white. Bags of 500 .... 3.00
No. YRS5. Lucky Dog Tees, yellow. Bags of 500 .... 3.00
No. RRS5. Lucky Dog Tees, red. Bags of 500 ...... 3.00

ZIP TEE HOLDER

No. Z1. No more need to worry which pocket your tees are in. Just slip a zip holder on your belt. Well made of tan belt leather and holds nine tees. Price, with nine tees.... $0.50

No. WRSB and No. WRDB. An assortment of 1000 white rock tees packed in a heavy canvas bag. By buying your golf tees in bulk considerable saving is made and you are always assured of a liberal supply in your locker. No. WRSB and No. WRDB Price per bag........ $5.00

REDDY TEES

No. RT. Turned from one piece of wood and stained a bright red or bright yellow to be easily seen against grass or dirt. This tee enables the golfer to tee his ball at any height he likes best. In ordering specify color desired. Price, per box of 18 .... $0.25

SCOT TEES

No. ST. The Scot Tee is very light and practical. It is conic in shape and well pointed for use on clay as well as grass tees. Bright yellow in color, which makes it easily seen against grass or dirt. Price, per box of 18 .... $0.25

[47]

Chapter 9

Collecting Books On Golf

By Joseph S.F. Murdoch

Joseph S.F. Murdoch, well-known author, book collector and co-founder of the Golf Collectors Society, has kindly written an intro-duction to collecting books.

The collecting of golf artifacts, a hobby that has a history going back several hundred years, has become a major collecting interest in recent years. Among the most popular col-lectible items are books that relate the history of the game, stories of great champions, and, inevitably, books of instruction calculated to improve our skills. Some cynics may proclaim that no one ever learned to play the game from a book, although there are some notable exam-ples of some who did. Walter J. Travis and Larry Nelson are two who come to mind.

Books of every description have been col-lected since the first book appeared about this hobby, which has seized the mind of man throughout the ages. Golf books may not have the lineage of, say, a Gutenburg Bible or the famed poets of England, but for the man who loves the game and likes to read about it, there is a line of books calculated to intrigue him.

One of the many allures of book collecting is that one can select a subject or a subject within a subject, and spend a lifetime pursuing all of the books within this chosen field of interest. Books on golf can be divided and sub-divided into many different categories, each of which may excite the interest of the collector. Books on golf history, the great champions of the game, the building of golf courses, golf humor, golf fiction, golf poetry, golf instruc-tion, or other facets of the game have been written and published over the years, and the collector has the liberty of selecting that sub-ject which is of his greatest interest.

One can, for example, choose books pub-lished in one country or by one writer and form a very nice library of such books. Perhaps a budding young collector may say to himself, "The game has only been played in America for 100 years, so I will collect books on the game which have been published only in America." In restricting himself to this one sphere, he will find great treasures and enough books to fill the shelves, floor to ceil-ing, of a fair-sized room.

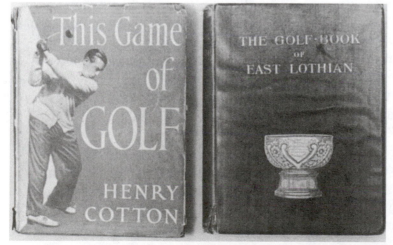

Golf books provide history, enjoyment, and reference materials for collectors.

With the turn of the century, golfers and books proliferated and the books tumbled out of the publishing houses like bogeys from the clubs of a high-handicap hacker. There are books to interest every taste … those who strive for the ultimate par in books of instruction, history of the game, records of the great champions, fiction, poetry, the history of venerable clubs, and, in more recent years, about the sport of golf collecting.

All of these books, now numbering in the thousands, are testimony to man's addiction to the game and a desire to read about it (if fog, sleet, and snow conspire to keep him in the house). Should you be of a persuasion to read and to accumulate a few books on the game you love, you will find great treasures in the library of golf.

Determining Condition and Value of Books

By George Lewis

George Lewis, PGA Master Professional, is one of the largest golf book, ephemera, and collectibles dealers in the world. Established in 1980, George Lewis/Golfiana can be reached at P.O. Box 291, Mamaroneck, NY 10543, or www.golfiana.com.

There have been more than 8,000 golf books published in numerous languages, and it would be almost impossible to list prices for them all. Therefore, to help you determine relative values, the following list of about 100 books includes a few representative titles for each category, such as instruction, history, biography, architecture, essays, reference, etc. Although most of the books listed are still available today, a few of the cornerstone scarce and rare works are also included so that you can get a better feel for the range of pricing.

Prices of books, like so many other collectibles, are determined by condition, edition, scarcity, and desirability. More recent books are not listed, because their value has not yet had a chance to fluctuate significantly from the published price. Also not included are rare works that are out of reach of most collectors, such as *The Goff* by Thomas Mathison, first published in 1743, last auctioned for more than $30,000.

Books that are generally in poor condition (missing pages, broken cover or contents damaged, badly soiled or stained), or library books are not rated. These can be useful for information, but usually are not worth recording as part of your library.

Underlining, margin notes, repair or rebinding all reduce the value of a book. A book that has been beautifully rebound in leather may or may not be worth more than it is with the original binding; most serious collectors would prefer the book in its original state. A leather binding might enhance the value of an inexpensive book, but why spend the money to rebind it? Buy one in very good original condition instead! First printings of first editions command higher prices than later printings.

Lowest price shown is for a first printing in good condition (moderate cover wear, some fading and/or staining, considerable foxing, speckling or browning to pages).

Mid-range price is for a very good copy of a first printing (light signs of age, former owner's neatly inked name, date or brief inscription, perhaps a little foxing or speckling to pages) and if a post-1950 book, in a dust jacket (if it was issued with one).

Highest price is for a first printing that is fine (looks like it is virtually new, with no inscriptions, soil, stain or wear, with dust jacket if issued with one). It is usually quite hard to find pre-1950 books in fine condition, so they may command a significant premium, especially with a dust jacket. Very good or fine condition of the dust jacket may also increase the price, in some instances even doubling the value of the book if the dust jacket is very scarce.

If you want to form a golf library of any significance, it is suggested that you discuss your goals with a reputable and knowledgeable dealer who can advise you and assist you in putting together a more meaningful collection.

Depending upon one's definition of a book, there are two early American prizes to be found, although some would describe them as pamphlets. The first, published in 1893, is *Spalding's Golf,* a thin, paper-covered booklet of 24 pages written by J. Stuart Balfour; the second, a booklet published by the Overman Wheel Company, was written by James Dwight. Each of them is very difficult to find.

The first book, commonly accepted as such, is by James P. Lee and entitled *Golf in America.* Published by Dodd, Mead and Company in Boston, it describes the game, recites a short history of the game in the United States, and is blessed with a number of photographs of early clubhouses. In recent years, it was reprinted in the Rare Book program of the United States Golf Association in an edition of 1,900 copies.

There were only a handful of golf books published in the United States before the turn of the century and one of these, *How To Play Golf,* was the first book of golf instruction published here. It was written by one who was quite qualified to offer advice: H. J. Whigham was a native of England but settled here as a newspaperman in Chicago. Whigham was the winner of our national Amateur Championship in 1896 and 1897. His book was illustrated with the very first action photographs taken of a golfer swinging a club; all previous pictures had been posed.

Considering the scarcity of books published in this country prior to 1900, 1898 saw a veritable flood of books for the relatively few golfers who had taken up the game here. Our annual publication on cricket saw fit to include golf in its summary of activity. This is *The American Cricket Annual & Golf Guide,* edited by Jerome Flannery. It is not easily obtained, but is an interesting record of early golf in this country.

Based on our personal experience, one of the scarcest books in the entire library of golf is *Through The Green & Golfer's Year Book,* edited by Prosper L. Senat and published in Philadelphia. Considering the paucity of information about early golf, this is a gold mine of information and a great prize to be won should it be found.

Two illustrated books are of interest; the first, *The Golfer's Alphabet,* was published by Harper (New York), with delightful illustrations by the early golf illustrator, A. B. Frost; and *An A.B.C. of Golf* by "A Victim" (Blanchard, New York), both of which were, as the titles indicate, a letter of the alphabet given to describe the game of golf.

That same year, the first book of fiction on golf published in this country was published by Harper and written by the same W. G. VanTassel Sutphen who was an early (and verbal) supporter of the game. It is a collection of short stories under the title *The Golficide & Other Tales.*

To complete the list of books published here before 1900, 1899 saw another book of fiction, *Drives and Putts* by Walter Camp and Lilliam Brooks (published by L. C. Page in Boston), and a delightfully illustrated poem by Samuel Peck called *The Golf Girl.* The illustrations were done by Maud Humphrey, a popular children's illustrator of the time and, of some distinction, because she was the mother of Humphrey Bogart, who played golf but won greater fame in the motion pictures.

As the record indicates, although golf had now been played with ever-increasing popularity for some 15 years, the book publishers were slow to find a market for books on the game. On the other side of the Atlantic, many books had already been published and, indeed, there were already collectors of them, but the publishers ignored the American public. There was one exception and, if it is elusive, it remains a target for the collector who may want a complete collection of American-based books. This was *The Art of Golf* by Sir Walter G. Simpson, published in Edinburgh in 1887 and released in an American edition in New York in 1892.

"Buy the BOOK before the collectible" is a statement heard by most beginning collectors.

Prices Golf Books

Prices are for grades G-5, G-7, and G9.

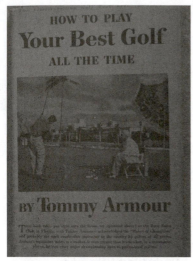

ARMOUR, TOMMY
HOW TO PLAY YOUR BEST
GOLF ALL THE TIME **$8 $25 $50**

CLARK, ROBERT
A ROYAL AND ANCIENT
GAME **$800 $2,500 $3,000**
A library cornerstone. 1875.
Many later editions.

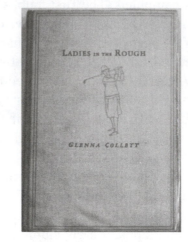

COLLETT, GLENNA
LADIES IN THE ROUGH
$150 $250 $400
Autobiography. 1928.

ALLEN, PETER
FAMOUS FAIRWAYS
$35 $50 $75
Architecture. 1968.

ALLIS, PETER
THROUGH THE LOOKING GLASS
$20 $35 $60
Biography. 1963.
Instruction. 1953. Many later editions.

BAMBERGER, MICHAEL
THE GREEN ROAD HOME
$15 $25 $40
Biography. 1986.

BARNES, JAMES M.
PICTURE ANALYSIS OF GOLF STROKES
$75 $150 $300
Instruction. 1919.

BOOMER, PERCY
ON LEARNING GOLF
$20 $40 $60
Instruction. 1942.

BRIGGS, CLARE
GOLF: THE BOOK OF A THOUSAND
CHUCKLES
$250 $400 $700
Humor. 1916. Originally issued in box.

BROWN, KENNETH
PUTTER PERKINS
$50 $80 $125
Fiction. 1923.

BROWNING, R. H. K.
A HISTORY OF GOLF
$75 $150 $300
History. 1955. An important addition to any
library.

COCHRAN, A. & STOBBS, J.
THE SEARCH FOR THE PERFECT SWING
$10 $30 $60
Instruction. 1968. Reissued.

COMISH, G. & WHITTEN, R.
THE GOLF COURSE
$15 $30 $50
Architecture. 1979.

COUSINS, GEOFFREY
GOLFERS AT LAW
$40 $50 $75
Rules. 1958.

DANTE, J. & ELLIOTT, L.
THE FOUR MAGIC MOVES TO WINNING
GOLF
$15 $25 $45
Instruction. 1962. Reissued.

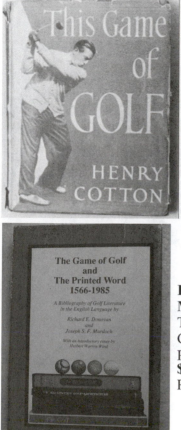

COTTON, HENRY
THIS GAME OF GOLF
$25 $50 $75
Instruction. 1948.

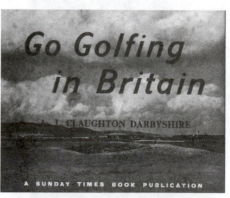

DARBYSHIRE, L. CLAUGHTON
GO GOLFING IN BRITAIN
$35 $50 $67
Architecture. 1961.

DONOVAN & MURDOCK
THE GAME OF GOLF AND THE PRINTED WORD
$40 $80 $100
Reference. 1988.

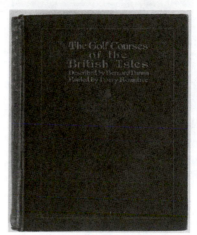

GOLF COURSES OF THE BRITISH ISLES
$600 $1,100 1,750
Architecture. 1910. A library corner-stone.

DARWIN, BERNARD
BRITISH GOLF
| $25 | $50 | $75 |
History. 1946.
GOLF BETWEEN TWO WARS
| $40 | $90 | $120 |
History. 1944.
GREEN MEMORIES
| $250 | $350 | $500 |
Autobiography. 1928. Reissued.

DARWIN, BERNARD, ET AL
HISTORY OF GOLF IN GREAT BRITAIN
| $125 | $225 | $350 |
History. 1952.

DAVIES, PETER
DAVIES' DICTIONARY OF GOLFING TERMS
| $20 | $40 | $50 |
Reference. 1980.

DEMARET, JIMMY
MY PARTNER, BEN HOGAN
| $100 | $150 | $200 |
1954. Books signed by Demaret are worth about a $150 premium.

DOBEREINER, PETER
THE GLORIOUS WORLD OF GOLF
| $20 | $40 | $60 |
History. 1973.

DUNCAN, G. & DARWIN, B.
PRESENT DAY GOLF
| $40 | $90 | $175 |
Anthology. London, 1921.

ELLIOT, LEN & KELLY, P.
WHO'S WHO IN GOLF
| $15 | $25 | $35 |
Reference. 1976.

FLAHERTY, TOM
THE U.S. OPEN 1895-1965
| $12 | $20 | $35 |
History. 1969.

GIBSON, NEVIN
ENCYCLOPEDIA OF GOLF
| $15 | $32 | $40 |
Reference. 1958.

HAMMOND, DARYN
THE GOLF SWING
| $100 | $150 | $200 |
Instructional. 1926.

EVANS, CHICK
CHICK EVANS' GOLF
BOOK
$75 $150 225
Autobiography. 1921.
Also limited edition.

HAGEN, WALTER
THE WALTER HAGEN
STORY
$50 $100 $150
Autobiography. 1956.
Books signed by Hagen
are worth about a $450
premium.

GRAFFIS, HERB
THE PGA
$35 $55 80
History. 1975.

HOGAN, BEN
FIVE LESSONS,
THE MODERN
FUNDAMENTALS
OF GOLF
$10 $30 $40
Instruction. 1957.

HAULTAIN, A.
THE MYSTERY OF GOLF
$125   **$175**   **$250**
Instruction. 1910. Reissued; also 1908 limited
edition.

HENDERSON & STIRK
GOLF IN THE MAKING
$50   **$80**   **$150**
Reference. 1979.

HILL, DAVE
TEED OFF
$20   **$30**   **$40**
1977.

HILTON, HAROLD
ROYAL AND ANCIENT GAME
OF GOLF
$1,000   **$2,000**   **$3,000**
Anthology. 1912.

HOGAN, BEN
POWER GOLF
$15   **$35**   **$60**
Instruction. 1948. Books signed by Hogan are
worth about a $250 premium.

HOUGHTON, GEORGE
CONFESSIONS OF A GOLF ADDICT
$10   **$20**   **$35**
Humor. 1952.

HUNTER, ROBERT
THE LINKS
$400   **$650**   **$1,200**
Architecture. 1926.

HUTCHINSON, HORACE
FIFTY YEARS OF GOLF
$200   **$300**   **$550**
Biography. 1919. Reissued.

JACOBS, JOHN
GOLF
$10   **$15**   **$25**
Instruction. 1963.

JENKINS, DAN
DOGGED VICTIMS OF INEXORABLE FATE
$25   **$40**   **$75**
Humor. 1970.

JONES, ERNEST
SWING THE CLUBHEAD
$40   **$125**   **$200**
Instruction. 1952.

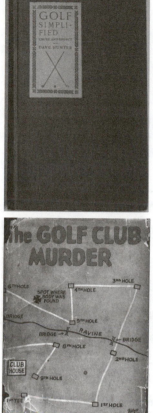

HUNTER, DAVE
GOLF SIMPLIFIED
$10 $20 $35
Instruction. 1921.

HUTCHINSON, HORACE

GOLF, THE BAD-MINTON LIBRARY
$125 $275 $375
Anthology. 1890 and many later issues. Reissued.

JEROME, OWEN FOX
THE GOLF CLUB MURDER
$50 $100 $150
Mystery. 1929.

JONES, ROBERT T., JR.

BOBBY JONES ON GOLF
$35 $60 $90
Instruction. 1966. Reissued.

JONES, ROBERT T., JR.

DOWN THE FAIRWAY
$150 $300 $600
History. 1927. If a book is signed by Jones, the value is determined by whether the signature is vintage or later. Premiums range from $600 to $2,000. The rare Dust Jacket adds a premium of up to $2,000, depending upon condition.

GOLF IS MY GAME
$35 $60 $90
Biography, instructional. 1960. Reissued.

KERR, JOHN

GOLF BOOK OF EAST LOTHIAN
$800 $1,200 $1,500
History. 1896. Reissued.

LOCKE, BOBBY

BOBBY LOCKE ON GOLF
$40 $60 $90
Instruction. 1953.

LONGHURST, HENRY
TALKING ABOUT GOLF
$40 $60 $100
Essay. 1966.

ONLY ON SUNDAYS
$25 $40 $60
Essays. 1964.

MacDONALD, C. B.
SCOTLAND'S GIFT; GOLF
$450 $650 $850
History. 1928. Reprints $35.

MACKENZIE, ALISTER
GOLF ARCHITECTURE
$500 $800 $1,200
Architecture. 1920.

MARTIN, H. B.
FIFTY YEARS OF AMERICAN GOLF
$300 $450 $700
History. First edition, 1936. Limited edition. Reissued.

MARTIN, JOHN STEWART
CURIOUS HISTORY OF THE GOLF BALL
$150 $275 $325
Reference. 1968.

MEHLHORN, BILL
GOLF SECRETS EXPOSED
$30 $45 $70
Instructional. 1984.

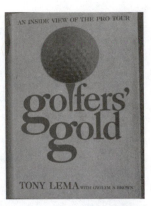

LEMA, TONY
GOLFER'S GOLD
$20 $35 $50
History. 1964.

**McMAHAN,
VALERIE BUMPS**
BUMPSIES: THE
GOLF BALL KIDS
$300 $450 $700
First edition with dust
jacket. Children's book.
1929

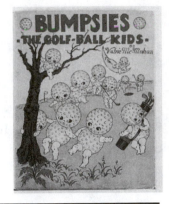

MORRISON, ALEX
NEW WAY TO BETTER GOLF
$20 $30 $45
Instruction. 1940. Many reprints.

BETTER GOLF WITHOUT PRACTICE
$60 $80 $100
Instruction. 1940.

**MORTIMER, CHARLES G. & PIGNON,
FRED**
THE STORY OF THE OPEN GOLF CHAMPI-
ONSHIP 1860-1950
$25 $50 $75
History. 1952.

MURDOCK, JOSEPH S. F.
THE LIBRARY OF GOLF, 1743-1966
$400 $500 $650
Reference. 1968.

NELSON, BYRON
WINNING GOLF
$20 $30 $45
Instruction. 1946. Books signed by Nelson are
worth about a $40 premium.

NICKLAUS, JACK
MY 55 WAYS TO LOWER YOUR GOLF SCORE
$10 $20 $30
Instruction. 1964. Books signed by Nicklaus are
worth about a $75 premium, provided it is not an
"auto pen" signature.

GOLF MY WAY
$10 $20 $30
Instruction. 1974.
THE GREATEST GAME OF ALL; MY LIFE IN
GOLF
$15 $25 $50
Instruction. 1969.

OLMAN, JOHN & MORTON
ENCYCLOPEDIA OF GOLF COLLECTIBLES
$30 $50 $80
Reference. 1985. Also Limited Ed.

PARK, WILLIE
THE GAME OF GOLF
$200 $450 $700
Instruction. 1896.

PARK, WILLIE JR.
THE ART OF PUTTING
$600 $850 $1,200
Leather binding, marbled end papers. 1920.

PLAYER, GARY
GARY PLAYER'S GOLF SECRETS
$10 $15 $25
Instruction. 1962. Books signed by Player are
worth about a $25 premium.

PLIMPTON, GEORGE
THE BOGEY MAN
$10 $15 $25
Essay. 1968.

PRICE, CHARLES
THE AMERICAN GOLFER
$15 $30 $50
Anthology. 1964. Reissued.

REVOLTA, JOHNNY
SHORTCUTS TO BETTER GOLF
$10 $20 $50
Instruction. 1949. Books signed by Revolta are
worth about a $75 premium.

RICE, G. & BRIGGS, C.
THE DUFFER'S HANDBOOK OF GOLF
$75 $125 $175
Humor. 1926. Reissued; also limited edition.

RICHARDSON, RICE & MORRISON, Editors
1938 GOLFERS YEARBOOK
$60 $80 $100
Reference. 1938.

ROTELLA, ROBERT J.
MIND MASTERY FOR WINNING GOLF
$20 $30 $40
Instruction. 1981.

NORWOOD, JOE
JOE NORWOOD'S
GOLF-O-METRICS
$20 $40 $60
Instruction. 1978.

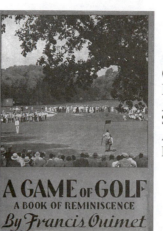

**OUIMET,
FRANCIS**
A GAME OF GOLF
$125 $190 $250
Autobiography. 1932.
Photo of later edition.

PALMER, ARNOLD
MY GAME AND
YOURS
$10 $20 $30
Instruction. 1965.
Books signed by
Palmer are worth about
a $35 premium.

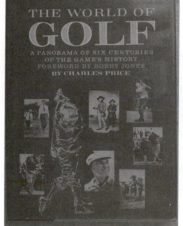

**PRICE,
CHARLES**
THE WORLD OF
GOLF
$25 $40 $60
History. 1962.

SALMOND, J.B.
THE STORY OF THE R. & A.
$50 $85 $140
History. 1956.

SAMPSON, CURT
HOGAN
$10 $12 $15
Biography. 1996.

SARAZEN, GENE
BETTER GOLF AFTER FIFTY
$10 $20 $30
Instruction. 1967. Books signed by Sarazen are
worth about a $100 premium.

THIRTY YEARS OF CHAMPIONSHIP GOLF
$30 $60 $90
Biography. 1950.

SCHAAP, DICK
MASSACRE AT WINGED FOOT
$10 $15 $30
History. 1974.

SHAW, JOSEPH T.
OUT OF THE ROUGH
$25 $60 $80
Fiction. 1934. Many later reprints.

SIMPSON, SIR WALTER G.
THE ART OF GOLF
$650 $850 $1,000
Instruction. 1887, 1891. Reissued.

SMITH, H. & TAYLOR, D.
THE SECRET OF ... HOLING PUTTS!
$12 $25 $40
Instruction. 1961.

SNEAD, SAM
HOW TO PLAY GOLF
$10 $20 $30
Instruction. 1946, 1952.

SOMERS, ROBERT
THE U.S. OPEN
$15 $20 $30
History. 1987. Reissued.

**RICE, G. &
KEELER, O. B.**
MY GAME AND
YOURS THE BOBBY
JONES STORY
$75 $150 $250
Biography. 1953.

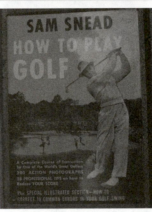

SNEAD, SAM
THE EDUCATION
OF A GOLFER
$15 $30 $50
History. 1962.

STANLEY, LOUIS T.
THIS IS GOLF
$20 $30 $40
Instruction. 1954.

STEEL, DONALD & RYDE & WIND
THE ENCYCLOPEDIA OF GOLF
$60 $100 $125
Reference. 1975.

STEELE, C. K.
THE GOLF COURSE MYSTERY
$60 $100 $200
Fiction. 1919.

SUGGS, LOUISE
GOLF FOR WOMEN
$10 $20 $30
Instruction. 1960. Books signed by Suggs are
worth about a $25 premium.

TAYLOR, DAWSON
THE MASTERS: 3RD SPECIAL EDITION
$90 $125 $150
History. 1981. Handsome leather cover resembles
Masters Jacket. Also plain binding.

**ROBERTS,
CLIFFORD**
THE STORY OF
AUGUSTA
NATIONAL GOLF
CLUB
$60 $90 $110
History. 1976.

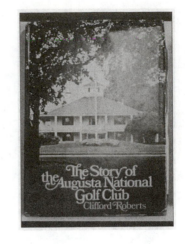

TAYLOR, JOHN HENRY
TAYLOR ON GOLF
$200 $350 $450
Instruction. 1902.

THOMAS, GEORGE C., JR.
GOLF ARCHITECTURE IN AMERICA
$350 $650 $800
1927.

TRAVERS, JEROME D. & CROWELL, J.R.
THE FIFTH ESTATE
$125 $200 $275
Biography. 1926.

TRAVIS, WALTER J.
PRACTICAL GOLF
$150 $250 $350
Instruction. 1901, 1902, 1909 editions.
PHOTO from book

TUFTS, RICHARD S.
THE PRINCIPLES BEHIND THE RULES OF
GOLF
$75 $120 $150
Rules. 1960, 1961. Reissued.

VAILE, P. A.
THE NEW GOLF
$40 $70 $100
Instruction. 1916.

VARDON, HARRY
HOW TO PLAY GOLF
$75 $125 $200
Instruction. First American edition 1912.

WEBLING, W. HASTINGS
LOCKER ROOM BALLADS
$40 $65 $100
Humor. 1925

STANLEY, DAVE
A TREASURY OF
GOLF HUMOR
$15 $30 $45
Humor. 1949.

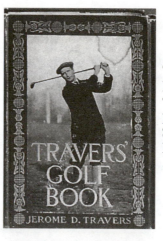

**TRAVERS, JEROME
D.**
TRAVERS' GOLF
BOOK
$35 $60 $75
Instruction. 1913.

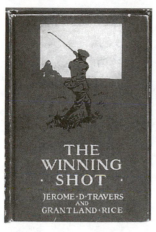

**TRAVERS, JEROME
D. & RICE, GRANT-
LAND**
THE WINNING SHOT
$100 $145 $200
History and reminis-
cences of four-time U.S.
Amateur champion and
U.S. Open champion
Travers. 1915.

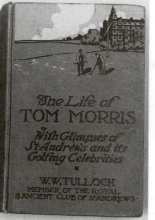

TULLOCH, W. W.
LIFE OF TOM MOR-
RIS
$800 $1,200 $1,500
Biography. 1908.

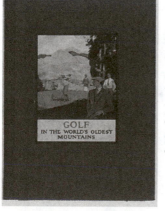

**UZZELL,
THOMAS H.**
GOLF IN THE
WORLD'S OLD-
EST MOUN-
TAINS
$350 $500 $800
Travel. 1926.

VARDON, HARRY
THE COMPLETE
GOLFER
$50 $100 $200
Instruction. 1905.

WHIGHAM, H. G.
HOW TO PLAY GOLF
$200 $300 $400
Instruction. 1897.

WILSON, ENID
GOLF FOR WOMEN
$20 $35 $50
Instructional. 1961.

WIND, HERBERT WARREN
COMPLETE GOLFER
$25 $50 $75
Anthology. 1954. Reissued.

WODEHOUSE, P. G.
GOLF OMNIBUS
$50 $125 $175
Fiction. 1973.

WETHERED, JOYCE & ROGER
THE GAME OF GOLF
$100 $150 $200
Anthology. 1929.

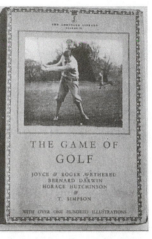

WHITLATCH, MAR-SHALL
GOLF FOR BEGIN-NERS & OTHERS
$30 $60 $100
Instruction. 1910.

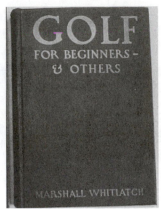

WIND, HERBERT WARRE

THE STORY OF AMERICAN GOLF
$150 $250 $400
History. First edition. 1948. Reissued. Photo is the 1975 Edition.

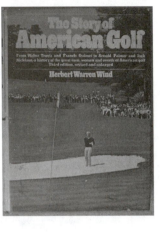

WINGATE, ROLAND
SAVING STROKES
$25 $35 $50
Instructional. Privately printed and scarce. 1934.

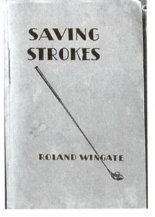

GOLF WITHOUT TEARS
$50   **$125**   **$175**
Fiction. 1924.

WOOD, HARRY B.
GOLF CURIOS AND THE LIKE
$800   **$1,200**   **$2,000**
Reference. 1910.

GOLF CURIOS AND THE LIKE
$40   **$60**   **$80**
Reference. Reprint 1980.

ZAHARIAS, BABE D.
THIS LIFE I'VE LED
$35   **$60**   **$80**
Biography. 1955.

Chapter 10

Collecting Golf Art

A watercolor by Harry Rowntree, "Bembridge Golf Course," is featured in The Golf Courses of the British Isles.

The Pictorial History of Golf: A Suggestion for Collectors

We are indebted to David White (GCS, London) for the article that follows, reprinted from THE CONNOISSEUR, July 1902. It appeared in the Golf Collectors Society Bulletin No. 21, January 1975.

By Martin Hardie

At some moment in every student's career, the question arises whether he shall know a little about everything or everything about some-

thing. So for the collector, there comes the time when he, too, must decide whether he will continue in his pleasant dilettante ways, or devote his research to some special branch of art. Is he to wander at ease in the low-lying meadows, plucking a flower here or there as they please his fancy, or is he to climb the heights in search of edelweiss and the rare blooms? Yet, even when he is drawn to some particular branch of study, be it pictures, or china, or books, or even postage stamps, the possibilities before him are too infinite, and he will feel at once the need of further limitation.

To give an instance from the book world, there is a well-known editor of the present time who devotes his energies to the collection of books of the year 1598.

To suit our present theme, let us suppose that prints are the subject elect for specialization. The study of engravings is endlessly elaborate and complicated, and in making his further limitation the specialist has an unlimited variety of choice. Shall it be a master, a period, or a method? He may give his lifetime to the countless states of Rembrandt, or the 2,000 prints of Hollar. He may choose a period, that of Durer and the Little Masters, or the engravers of the 18th century. He may be attracted by a method-etching or mezzotint, or the color-prints of Japan. As he faces the subject, there are innumerable pleasing vistas of choice.

Now to the collector who is fond of any manner of sport, we would suggest that in tracing its pictorial history he has a new and interesting subject ready at hand. Our present purpose is to show the special attraction offered by the game of golf. And surely every collector ought to be a golfer. Both collecting and playing golf are games in which the individual depends on himself alone. Both have their glorious possibilities, their successes and disappointments, their moments of fortune, their bunkers of despair. It is a serious question for one who plays both games to decide whether he would prefer a hole in one, or to pick up for five schillings in a country village a first proof, say, of the Salisbury Cathedral by Lucas. Let him search his heart and decide whether he would rather be a better golfer or a better collector.

First it may be pointed out that the collection of golf prints may be of the greatest value in settling disputed points in the history of the Royal Game. For the origin of golf, like that of Mr. Yellowplush, is "wropt in mistry" and it is still a moot point whether Scotland or the Low Countries can claim to be the incunabula of the modern game. For its early literary history, the only sources are the Scottish Acts of Parliament and records of Kirk Sessions. "The fut ball and golf be utterly cryit dune" is the stern behest of the Parliament in 1457. So also, a century later in 1593, two golfers were prosecuted by the Town Council of Edinburgh for "play-ing of the Gowff on the Links of Leith every Sabbath at the time of the sermones."

But, while Scotland can produce this documentary evidence, it is to the Low Countries that we go for the pictorial history of the game. Without any doubt, as our illustrations will show, golf was in vogue in Holland in the 16th century, being played on ice as well as on grass. Indeed, early in the 17th century, golf balls were imported to Scotland, for in a letter of 1618, the writer says that "no small quantitie of golf and silver is transported yearlie out of his Hienes' Kingdome of Scotland for bying of golf balls." For pictorial records of the earliest period of the game in the Low Countries, one has to search illuminated manuscripts of the 15th and 16th centuries.

Perhaps the earliest representation of golf, or of a game that must be the primogenitor of golf, is to be found in a manuscript in the Chantilly Collection, and shows figures putting both to a post and to a hole. W.H. Weale, the well-known authority on Flemish painting, has dated this for me as between 1460 and 1470. Another Flemish "Book of Hours" in the British Museum Library, executed at Bruges between 1500 and 1520, shows distinctly that in this period, the golfer putted to a hole. The home green in front of the clubhouse, the red coat of the player, and the steel-faced club are all curiously modern. Hidden away among collections of manuscripts must be many a treasure that would throw light on the early history of the game.

By the 17th century, golf in Holland had become almost entirely a winter game. The Dutch painters of the period seem to have found a peculiar fascination in winter scenes, with their clear, bright atmosphere, and the moving crowds of figures in their various occupations of sledding, skating or golf. As might be expected, many a golfing scene is to be found in the pictures of Van de Velde, Van der Neer, Avercamp, Van Goyen, and others of their school. Several drawings of this period, showing single figures or small groups, give perhaps a better idea of golf at the time.

Two such drawings by Avercamp in the Royal Collection at Dresden, of about the year 1610, are obviously character studies from life, and show us players that, except for their costumes, exhibit a startling modernity. How often have we seen a golfer stand in the pose of this stout Dutchman, pipe in hand, his club held loosely resting on the ground, as he surveys a difficult "lie" and swithers for a moment between this club and that. We wonder who the present owner is of the drawing that fetched 18 schillings at the William Esdaile Sale of 1840, catalogued as "Lot 1178, H. Avercamp: Figures playing at Kolf on the ice—capital"?

For the ordinary collector, however, whose aspirations are limited by the length of his purse, the engravings of the period offer the happiest hunting grounds. Juys, Van Schoel, Jan and Adomen Van de Velse, Van Sichem, and R. de Hooghe are some of the artists whose engraved work contains golfing scenes. A rare etching by Hendrik van Schoel—and the connoisseur will appreciate the fact that neither Bartsch nor Nagler chronicle its existence—shows a reservoir with skaters and golfers, particularly noticeable being a small boy at the top of his swing. Another interesting feature of the picture is the group of curlers in the middle distance on the right. The stones, the kneeling attitude of the player, and the "skip" giving directions with outstretched arm, all show that here we have an early picture of the "roaring game." Several etchings by Jan Van de Velde, from sets representing the 12 months, show figures of golfers playing

Bruntsfield Links Golf Club, painted by Sam Bough, was presented by Captain Alexander Whyte for an 1871 competition won by Andrew Usher.

on ice. Of the late 17th century is an engraving by Romeyn de Hooghe, giving us perhaps the best presentment of a golfer with club in hand that can be found among these Dutch prints.

From France, we have an engraving by J. Aliament of about 1750, after a picture in our National Gallery by Adriaen Van de Velde. It is interesting to note that the plate is reversed, with the result that the player seems to be left-handed. A thrill runs through the golfer when he notices, for the first time in a catalogue of Rembrandt's etchings, the entry "A Kolfer." He is, however, doomed to disappointment, for the Kolf there depicted is the modern Dutch indoor game, only remotely connected with our golf.

In Scotland of the 16th and 17th century, our "rude fore-fathers" had no Van de Velde or Avercamp to chronicle with brush the annals of the game. Records of Kirk Sessions tell of the chastisement of offenders against the Sabbath laws; club minutes relate the winning of casks of wine; but of pictures we have nothing until the end of the 18th century, when there begins a series of excellent portraits of golfers with caddie and clubs. These are interesting to the collector because many have been translated into the beautiful mezzotints for which the period is famous. For the player their value also lies in their historic associations and in the representation they give us of the baffies and spoons and other disused weapons of the game.

One of the best known of these mezzotints is the portrait of William Innes by Val. Green, after L. F. Abbott, dedicated to "the Society of Golfers at Blackheath." Of the original picture, no trace can be found, and it may be presumed that it was destroyed in the fire that burned down the Blackheath Clubhouse at the end of the 18th century. Another beautiful mezzotint is that by J. Jones after the portrait by Raeburn, of James Balfour, an early secretary of the Honourable Company of Edinburgh Golfers. This mezzotint carries the inscription: "Published by Wm. Murray, Bookseller, Parliament Close, Edinburgh, October 1796."

An interesting etching is one of Kay's portraits, dated 1803, showing Alexander M'Keller, a well-known character of the Bruntisfield Links, Edinburgh. The engraving by Wagstaffe of the picture by Charles Lees, R.S.A., "A Grand Match at Golf," 1850, is of great historical interest. It depicts a foursome in which Sir David Baird and Sir Ralph Anstruther are matched against Major Playfair and John Campbell, of Saddell. In the group of onlookers are many distinguished Scotchmen of the day, and in the background are seen the towers and spires of St. Andrews. Many similar engravings of championship meetings have been published of late years, but scarcely of sufficient merit to attract the connoisseur.

The collector of wood engravings of "the sixties" will find two interesting golf illustrations by Doyle of "Punch in London Society" for 1863. In more modern times, capital photogravures have been published by the Fine Arts Society after "The Sabbath Breakers," "The Stymie" and other paintings by J. C. Dollman, R.I., and for those clever prints by Mr. Nicholson and Mr. Cecil Aldin, without which the golf collection will be incomplete.

In the case of most collectors, the length of their purse is an important consideration. "Non cuivis contingit adire Corinthum"—not everyone is fortunate enough to dream of acquiring the "Hundred Guider" print, the "Melancholia", the "Abside" or the "Ladies Waldegrave." But these golf prints can, for the most part, be purchased at a reasonable price, and to the connoisseur who is a golfer as well, his acquisition will add a new interest to his game.

Olman's Guide to Golf Antiques, by John and Mort Olman, 1991, provides the most complete reference on art available to collectors.

Prices Golf Art

Prices are for grades G-5, G-7, and G9.

THE BLACKHEATH GOLFERS
ABBOTT, L.F.
$350   **$500**   **$750**
Circa 1900. A colored engraving of the original from 1790.

THE BLACKHEATH GOLFERS
ABBOTT, L.F.
$1,400   **$1,800**   **$2,200**
A mezzotint. Original 1790. Many later reprints.

THE DRIVE
ADAMS, DOUGLAS
$200   **$300**   **$450**
Circa 1960. Approximately 16 x 24. Colored engraving from the original oil painting circa 1894.

A DIFFICULT BUNKER
ADAMS, DOUGLAS
$200   **$300**   **$450**
Circa 1960. Approximately 16 x 24. Colored engraving from the original oil painting circa 1894.

THE PUTTING GREEN
ADAMS, DOUGLAS
$200   **$300**   **$450**
Circa 1960. Approximately 16 x 24. Colored engraving from the original oil painting circa 1894.

THE PUTT
BROCK, CHARLES EDMOND
$1,200   **$1,800**   **$2,500**
An engraving, circa 1894.

THE DRIVE
BROCK, CHARLES EDMOND
$1,200   **$1,800**   **$2,500**
An engraving, circa 1894.

1ST INTERNATIONAL GOLF MATCH
BROWN, MICHAEL J.
$500   **$750**   **$1,000**
1903. First International Golf Match, England vs. Scotland at Hoylake, 1902. Michael Brown was famous for his "Life Ass'n of Scotland Calendars."

HOYLAKE-PUNCH BOWL HOLE
BROWN, MICHAEL
$250 $375 $500
An original print featuring John Ball, amateur
champion. 1911.

**ROYAL COUNTY DOWN GOLF COURSE,
PLAYING TO THE 11TH HOLE**
BROWN, MICHAEL
$250 $375 $500
Another painting for the "Life Ass'n of Scotland.

DEDICATED TO THE FIELD MARSHALL
CHAMBERLAIN, J.
$250 $350 $500
Engraving. Frost & Reed, publishers, 1955.

WOMAN GOLFER
CHRISTIE, F. EARLE
$155 $200 $250
Print of well-dressed woman with a golf club.

THE RULES OF GOLF
CROMBIE, CHARLES
$150 $225 $300
A humorous series published in 1905 by Perrier.
Many reprints. Prices listed are for reprints.

GOLF PLAYERS
DE HOOCH, PETER
$60 $80 $100
Contemporary prints.

THE SABBATH BREAKERS

DOLLMAN, J.

$175   **$200**   **$300**

Circa 1896 black and white engraving. The original sold for $1,320 in 1992. Prices listed are for circa 1977 lithographs in color.

PUTTING

DOLLMAN, JOHN CHARLES

$1,200   **$1,800**   **$2,500**

An engraving, circa 1900.

FAIRWAY SHOT

DOLLMAN, JOHN CHARLES

$1,200   **$1,800**   **$2,500**

An engraving, circa 1900.

PLAYING OUT OF HEATHER

DOLLMAN, JOHN CHARLES

$1,200   **$1,800**   **$2,500**

An engraving, circa 1900.

REIS GOLF CLUB

DOUGLAS, JAMES

$3,500   **$4,200**   **$6,000**

Watercolor of Wick, Caithness golf course. 1897.

ST. ANDREWS CADDIE

EARLE, L.

$100   **$200**   **$300**

Original, 1908, second printing 1928 and also 1979.

OLD SCOTCH CADDY

EARLE, L.C.

$110   **$150**   **$300**

Circa late 1920s. Approximately 16 x 20. Colored print of the circa 1904 oil painting.

THE TRIUMVIRATE
FLOWER, CLEMENT
$300   **$450**   **$600**
1913 painting, prints 1914 and later.

GARY PLAYER
FORBES, BART
$40   **$60**   **$90**
1980 watercolor reprints.

VARIOUS WATERCOLORS
FROST, A.B.
$20   **$30**   **$50**
Circa 1900 including, "By Sheer Strength,"
"Temper," "Stymied," and others. Prices are for
reprints.

GOLF GIRL
UNKNOWN ARTIST
$175   **$225**   **$300**
Print, c. 1900.

JOHN WHYTE MELVILLE
GRANT, SIR FRANCIS
$300   **$450**   **$600**
Circa 1970. Color print, London, limited edition of
750.

JOHN WHYTE MELVILLE
GRANT, SIR FRANCIS
$75   **$100**   **$150**
Circa 1988 color print of the original.

HISTORY OF GOLF IN AMERICA SERIES
GUSTOVSON, LELAND
$400   **$500**   **$600**
Circa 1960s. Six color prints. "The First
Clubhouse in America, Shinnecock," "The Old
Apple Tree Gang," "Awarding The First USGA
Trophy," "Rober Tyre Jones," "Ouimet Wins The
Open," and "Playoff For Masters Championship,"
Snead and Hogan. Singles are $50-100 each.

NILGERI HILLS, SO. INDIA
HIERIDGE, F.E.
$1,800-$2,000
Signed, framed and matted watercolor.

THE GOLFERS
LEES, CHARLES
$150   **$250**   **$350**
Circa 1920. Hand colored. Approximately 21 X 33. Print of the circa 1849 engraving.

BEN HOGAN
MILOSEVICH, PAUL
$20   **$30**   **$40**
1980s. Prints in sepia.

CRENSHAW WINS 1984 MASTERS
MILOSEVICH, PAUL
$150   **$175**   **$225**
1985. Limited edition of 600.

SLAMMIN' SAMMY
MILOSEVICH, PAUL
$20   **$30**   **$40**
1980s. Prints in sepia.

GORE POINT HUNSTANTON
PARTRIDGE, J.H.
$1,700   **$2,200**   **$2,500**
Watercolor. 1920.

COPE'S TOBACCO
PIPESHANK, GEORGE
$20   **$30**   **$40**
Circa 1900 humorous advertisement print for Cope's Tobacco. Reprints 1970s .

HARD APPROACH AT THE 15TH (TRY AGAIN SIR!)
RAINEY, WILLIAM
$1,500-$2,000
Signed, framed and matted watercolor. C. 1920s.

TOM MORRIS
REID, SIR GEORGE
$4,000   **$6,000**   **$8,000**
A gravure. 1903.

A LITTLE PRACTICE
SADLER, W.D.
$300   **$450**   **$650**
Original print, black and white, 1915. Many reproductions worth less than $50.

A WINTER EVENING
SADLER, W.D.
$300   **$450**   **$650**
Original print, black and white, 1915. Many reproductions worth less than $50.

CARICATURES OF FAMOUS GOLFERS
SIR LESLIE WARD, 'SPY'
$200   **$300**   **$400**
1890s to 1910. Various amateur and professional golfers. Ward used the pseudonym "Spy."

ST. ANDREW'S HELL'S BUNKER
SMART, JOHN
$250,000
Watercolor, 1889.

THE BLACK SHED AT HOYLAKE
SMITH, GARDEN G.
$20,000
A watercolor, 1897.

EVERY PUTT PLEASES SOMEBODY
STARK, F.W.
$800-$1,000
Signed. 1927.

BOBBY JONES
STEVENS, THOMAS E.
$250   **$350**   **$500**
1952. Limited edition prints. Signed prints can bring as much as $3,500.

DUTCH TILES
UNKNOWN MAKER
$200   **$300**   **$500**
Circa 1800.

WALTER HAGEN
VAIL, ARNOLD
$500
1993 original oil. Vail painted famous golf immortals at the request of Chuck Furjanic. Seventeen were done from 1993 until his death in February 1995. Fourteen of his 17 works are pictured in the "Linda Craft Auction" catalogue, May 7, 1995, conducted by Chuck Furjanic, Inc.

JIMMY DEMARET
VAIL, ARNOLD
$500
1993 Original oil. Vail painted famous golf immortals at the request of Chuck Furjanic. Seventeen were done from 1993 until his death in February 1995. Fourteen of his 17 works are pictured in the "Linda Craft Auction" catalogue, May 7, 1995, conducted by Chuck Furjanic, Inc.

A FROST SCENE
van de VELDE, ADRIAEN
$75   **$125**   **$250**
Prints circa 1920s made from originals circa 1600.

MAURITS de HERAUGIERES, AGE 2
van der LINDE, ADRIAEN
$45,000
1595. Oil-on-panel.

WINTER LANDSCAPE
Van Der Neer, Aert
$75   **$125**   **$250**
Prints circa 1920s, made from originals circa
1650.

ST. ANDREWS
WATSON, J.F.
$400   **$500**   **$650**
1977. Limited edition print.

OLD TOM MORRIS
WEAVER, ARTHUR
$200   **$300**   **$400**
Late 1980s.

YOUNG TOM MORRIS
WEAVER, ARTHUR
$200   **$300**   **$400**
Late 1980s.

CARNOUSTIE
WOODS, F.R.
$5,000   **$6,500**   **$7,500**
Oil painting of Carnoustie Golf Links, circa 1920.

GOLF POSTERS

By Will Roberto

MAJOR POSTER ARTISTS	POSTERS
Broders, Roger	Vichy
Deje, L Luc	Hyeres
Villemont, Bernard	Basque & Vichy
Lenzerheide, Peikert	Valbella & Crans Sur Sierra
Francois, George	Evian Les Bains
Thompson, A. R.	L.N.E.R. St Andrews
Johnson, Andrew	L.N.E.R. North Berwick
Purvis, Tom	Cruden Bay
Stevens, Thomas E.	Bobby Jones
Desperthes, Jacques	Eprevue Golf Club
Sobie, Roger	Vichy
Walt Disney Productions	Donald Duck Golfer
Mago, T. Miya	Harone Country Club
Vincent, Renee	Divot & Golf de Sar Labot
Comarond, V	Combloux
Marton	Le Touquet
Courchinox, Edourd	Le Touquet
Gene	Dieppe
Hintermeister, Hy	Danbury Fair (1930 USA)
Scribners Magazine	Early U.S. C 1895 Travel Poster

BRODERS, ROGER
Vichy   **$2,500-$3,500**
Colored lithograph poster laid down on linen. 100 x 62 cm

BRODERS, ROGER
Hyeres   **$2,000-$2,250**
Matted and framed poster, circa 1930s, 38 1/4" x 24 3/4"

COURCHINOUX, EDOUARD
Le Touquet   **$900-$1,400**
Lithograph in colors, 1930 100 x 62 cm

DEJE, L. LUC
Hyeres   **$1,000-$1,500**
Colored lithograph poster, 1933, laid down on Linen. 100 x 62 cm

FRANCOIS, GEORGE
Evian Les Bains   **$1,000-$1,400**
Lithograph in colors, 1935 100 x 62 cm

GENE
Dieppe   **$2,000-$2,250**
Framed poster, circa 1930s, 45 1/4" x 24.4"

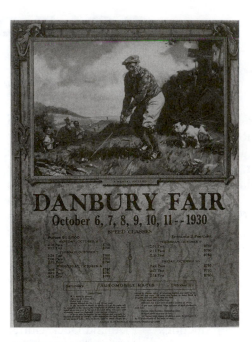

HINTERMEISTER, HY
Danbury (CT) Fair October 1930   **$500-$750**
Framed poster with illustration, 23" x 17 1/2"

JOHNSON, ANDREW
North Berwick L. N. E. R.
$1,200-$2,000
Lithograph in colors, 1935 100 x 62 cm

LENZERHEIDE, PEIKERT
Valbella & Crans Sur Sierra
$800-$1,200
Valbella lithograph poster, 100 x 62 cm

MARTON
Le Touquet
$1,000-$1,400
Lithograph in colors, 1935 100 x 62 cm

MAYER, DICK
Chesterfield Men of America
$200-$300
Matted and framed poster, circa 1950s, 21 3/4" x 20 1/2"

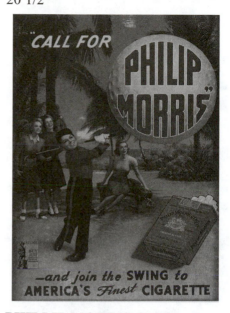

PHILLIP MORRIS & CO.
Cigarette advertisement with U.S. Savings Bond War Defense Logo
$750-$850
Framed poster, 28" x 20 1/4"

PURVIS, TOM
Cruden Bay
$1,200-$2,000
Lithograph in colors, 1935 100 x 62 cm

SATOMI, MUNESUGU
Golf
$500-$750
Lithograph in colors, 1935 100 x 71 cm

SCRIBNER'S
Fiction Number
$400-$500
Framed, circa 1895, 23" x 14 1/4"

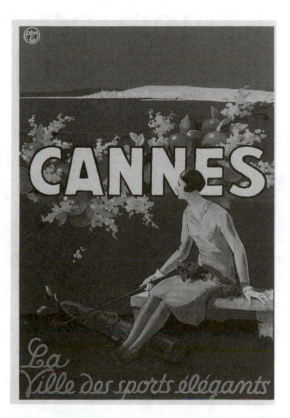

SEM
Cannes La Ville des Sorts elegants
$2,250-$2,500
Framed poster, circa 1930s, 38" x 25 1/2"

WALT DISNEY PRODUCTIONS
Donald Duck
$350-$550
Lithograph in colors, 80 x 60 cm

Chapter 11

Collecting Golf Ceramics and Glass

By Wayne Aaron

Libations were an integral part of golf—especially after the round—and this fancy glassware set the scene.

Wayne Aaron has collected golf ceramics for 25 years and has assembled a very extensive collection. He offers his insight to both the beginner and the advanced collector of golf ceramics.

Golf Ceramics

One of the wonders of collecting golf antiquity is the diversity of fields represented. While clubs, balls, and books dominate the hobby as collecting themes, there is now a heightened level of interest in golf ceramics.

One reason for this growing popularity may be because many are rapidly discovering that while all fields of golf collecting have intrinsic value, ceramics offers additional aesthetic value. Another reason may be the realization that the true social impact of the game can be better understood by studying (and collecting) the artistic artifacts that evolved with the game—such as ceramics, glass, silver, jewelry, art, toys, statuary, medals, and numerous advertising memorabilia items. All of these "aesthetic" categories in their own way help to document, as well as visibly demonstrate, the significant influence golf had on the world around the turn of the century—as it does today.

As one contemplates the joys of collecting golf ceramics, it is wise to recognize at the outset that this endeavor invariably will become a "journey," and as such, never a "destination" that is ultimately reached.

First and foremost, before embarking on this journey it is best to acquire as much knowledge as possible. Only through knowledge can you truly understand what is possible. Also do not be tempted to become a "consumer of quantity" rather than a "collector of quality." A good working definition of quality should not stop at discerning the condition of a potential collectible, it should also encompass historical significance and rarity.

Perhaps the best advice a collector can follow is to always seek out and acquire the very best you can afford. The very scarce items will command a premium price and will appreciate in value at a higher rate than mid to lower end examples. High-end items may even become prohibitively expensive in the future and therefore out of the realm of affordability for many collectors.

It is also helpful to establish clear goals before running head long into the world of golf ceramic collecting. In fact, this is sound advice for any field of golf collecting. In summary, acquire knowledge, define your budget, set your goals, collect only quality, and buy the best when you see it.

While it is academically interesting to possess an encyclopedic level of knowledge covering the history of pottery and porcelain, including supporting terminology techniques, styles, artists, makers, and country of origin, this level of proficiency is not a mandatory prerequisite to become a knowledgeable collector of golf ceramics. While the history of pottery goes back to primitive man, and Chinese porcelain dates to 3000 B.C., ceramics featuring golfers or golfing scenes did not appear until the 17th century when they were used as decoration for Delft tiles. For those who do not subscribe to the "Dutch School" origin of golf, you can jump forward to around 1880 onwards, when golf clubs gave golf ceramics as prizes and golfing sporting subjects found increasing use as embellishments for vases, pictures, tumblers, bowls, steins, plates, and numerous other functional, as well as decorative, items. Focusing on a period running from 1880 to 1940 makes the breadth of knowledge you need to acquire a lot more manageable.

Collectors, dealers, and even auction houses are often confused by terminology. In its simplest form you need to remember the following:

Ceramics is a general term for the study of the art of pottery.

Pottery in its widest sense includes all objects fashioned from clay and then hardened by fire.

Porcelain should only be applied to certain well marked varieties of pottery. It is usually opaque white and is fired at 1,450 degrees Centigrade. Also known as Bone China.

Stoneware is vitrified clay, fired at temperatures of 1,200 to 1,300 degrees Centigrade, which makes it very hard and is tan or gray in color.

Earthenware is not vitrified, retains a porous texture, is fired at no more than 1,200 degrees Centigrade and is usually tan in color.

While some may be driven to become an expert on ceramics and submerge themselves into the world of technique, which encompasses materials, firing, glazes, colors, and metals, it may be best to just understand what is available to collect.

The most definitive discussion to date for golf ceramics can be found in the Olmans' *Guide to Golf Antiques*. Review Chapter 12, pages 153-168. Another excellent reference is *Decorative Golf Collectibles* by Shirley and Jerry Sprung, pages 9-48.

Dates of production by manufacturer, including their marks and country of origin with illustrations of objects, can be found in both of these recommended references.

Where do you start to find collectible golf ceramics? If you are not already a member, by all means join the Golf Collectors Society. Write to P.O. Box 20546, Dayton, OH 45420 for an application form or call (513) 256-2474. After you meet the requirements for membership you will be provided a directory of all members. Each member indicates his or her collecting interests. Look for the letter "C," which denotes ceramics. Start both your education (pursuit of knowledge) and search here. Call 10 or 15 people and you will identify through referrals the serious collectors of golf ceramics. They are the ones to contact because they may have duplicates for sale or trade. They will also get you headed in the right direction to other sources.

I have often been asked why I collect ceramics. It is because I have been stricken by an 18th century imagination. During this period it was a popular belief that porcelain was not just another exotic, but a magical and talismanic substance—the substance of longevity, of potency, of invulnerability—now you know why I collect ceramics.

The following listing is presented as an overview of golf ceramic collecting opportunities and is comprehensive for the majority of desired acquisitions, but is by no means all-inclusive.

An introduction on collecting golf ceramics would not be complete without a brief discussion of what is an acceptable condition (cracks, chips, scratches, repairs, missing parts) before considering an object. The following suggestions are offered:

If the item is truly very rare and you may never see it on the market again, this becomes an issue of price and personal taste. The more the damage, the lower the price. Do not pay a premium for poor quality. Be disciplined enough to walk away, but do not hesitate to purchase if the price is commensurate with condition. A rare item with some damage is a good candidate for a "museum" quality restoration.

Do not be afraid to acquire an item that has undergone a "museum" level repair. The quality will be so high that only the restorer and the individual that paid for the repair will understand the true condition. If the repair is obvious to suggest the restorer was an amateur, walk away from mid to lower end items at any price. You will never be proud of owning junk and you probably will not be able to trade or sell it either.

United States

Ceramic Art Company
(Pre Lenox) Warwick
American Beleek
Weller (Dickensware II)
Enfield Pottery
Rookwood
Buffalo China
Owens (Utopian)
Hanes (Little Arthur)
O'Hara Dial (Waltham Clock Co.)
Viktor Schrechengost
Robinson Clay Products
(Cowan)
Sleepy Eye Indian Mugs
Taylor, Smith & Taylor

England

Doulton Burslem
Doulton Lambeth
Wedgewood
Minton
W.H. Goss
Royal Worcester
Taylor Tunnecliffe
MacIntyre Burslem
Arthur Wood
Willow Art
Grimwades
Royal Doulton (1902 and after)
Kingsware
Series Ware (Charles Crombie) "Pilgrim figures
    & Proverb sayings"
Queensware
Airbrush Brown
Gibson Series
Uncle Toby
H.M. Bateman
The Nineteenth Hole
Morrissian
Bunnykins
Colonel Bogey
Old English
Copeland Spode
Carleton Ware
Arcadian
Bridgewood
Crown Staffordshire
Dartmouth

Shelly
Williamson & Sons
Aonian
A.F.C.
Ambassador
A. Rogers
Burleigh
Cresan
Crown Ducal
Jasperware
Radfords
G & S Ltd.

Germany

Rosenthal
Royal Bonn
Simon Peter Gerz
Hohr-Grenzhausen
Hauber & Reuther
Royal Bayruth
Schwarzburg
Goebel

Villeroy & Boch (Metlach)
Frumper Ware
Schaffer and Vater

Austria

Amphora (Turn-Tepliz, Bohemia, Riessner)

Italy

Richard Ginori

Japan

Noritake
Nippon
Chikaramachi

France

Limoges
Sevres

Spain

Lladro (after 1940)

Netherlands

Dutch Delft Tiles (17th century)

Ireland

Irish Beleek

Collectible Glass

By Jerry Sprung

In the waning days of the Victorian period, through the art nouveau and art deco periods, most items of a personal nature carried some complex design, depicting an event or an item in a representational theme; American Indians for instance, were often depicted on pottery, silver, or bronze.

Ever since golf came to the United States in the late 19th century, it became the subject of many media designers who wished to capitalize on the latest fad. Workers in silver and gold took many of their popular sellers, such as cuff links, tie pins, watch fobs, and match safes for men, and hat pins and compacts for women, and added a golf motif. This was done either by depicting a figure playing golf, or an implement, golf stick, golf ball, or tee.

In addition, silversmiths created trophies with a golfing motif as part of the design. This was done to supply the growing market for tournament prizes. Such makers as Unger Brothers had elaborate catalogs showing a golfer, or a caddy, as the center figure in all of their silver mounted items, from ashtrays to hair brushes to whiskey flasks.

Most bronze golf figures came from Austria. Karl Hagenauer was especially known for his art deco golf figures in the 1920s. Bronze was also used to make decorative humidors and cigarette boxes. Heintz Art Metal Shop and Smith Metal Arts (Silvercrest) of Buffalo, N.Y., were two of the main suppliers of these items.

Most glass golf items were either produced in England or the United States. One of the popular glass designs involved a sterling silver golfer overlay that was attached to the glass bottle, goblet, or pitcher with an adhesive. The same figure is seen in many sizes, adorning glassware made by various manufacturers. Another method was to etch or engrave a golfer or golfing scene directly into the glass. Such companies as Hawkes, Cambridge Glass, and Pairpoint were well-known suppliers of these wares.

Prices Golf Ceramics

Prices are for grades G-5, G-7, and G9.

PORCELAIN HUMIDOR
AONIAN
$1,600   **$1,800**   **$2,000**
ENGLAND
Circa 1900s. Comical golf scene.

WOOD & WOOD BISCUIT BARREL
ARTHUR WOOD & SON
$2,000   **$2,500**   **$3,000**
ENGLAND
Circa 1900. Hand painted porcelain with silver rim, bail, and ornate lid.

EARTHENWARE MATCH BOWL
CARLTONWARE
$150   **$250**   **$375**
ENGLAND
Circa 1920s.

EARTHENWARE HUMIDOR
CARLTONWARE
$450   **$600**   **$900**
ENGLAND
Circa 1920s.

PORCELAIN ASHTRAY
CHIKARAMACHI
$400   **$600**   **$800**
Circa 1930s. Six pieces. Hand painted.

STONEWARE PITCHER
COPELAND SPODE

$600	$800	$1,200

Circa 1900. Golfers in relief, white on blue or green background.

STONEWARE JARDINIERE
COPELAND SPODE

$700	$900	$1,400

Circa 1900. Golfers in relief, white on blue or green background.

STONEWARE EWER
COPELAND SPODE

$700	$850	$1,200

Circa 1900. Golfers in relief, white on blue or green background.

CHINA PITCHER AND CUPS
CRESANT

$1,200	$1,500	$1,800

ENGLAND

Circa 1900s. "Brownie" chocolate pitcher measuring 12 1/2", with matching mugs.

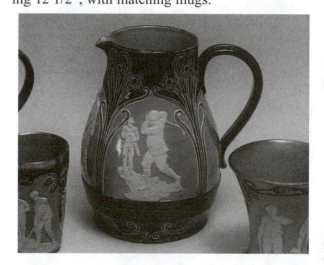

STONEWARE PITCHER
DOULTON

$1,800	$2,200	$2,800

LAMBETH, ENGLAND

Circa early 1900s. Golfers in white relief.

PORCELAIN SPILL VASES
DOULTON

$700	$850	$1,100

LAMBETH, ENGLAND

Circa early 1900s.

TRIVET
DOULTON
$600 $800 $1,000
LAMBETH, ENGLAND
Circa early 1900s. Uncle Toby Series.

CREAMER
DOULTON
$600 $800 $1,000
LAMBETH, ENGLAND
Circa early 1900s. Uncle Toby Series.

HAND PAINTED VASE
DOULTON
$20,000
LAMBETH, ENGLAND
Circa 1885. Burslem.

FLUTE NECK VASE
DOULTON
$20,000
LAMBETH, ENGLAND
Circa 1885. Hand painted, Burslem.

HAND PAINTED HUMIDOR
DOULTON
$12,000
LAMBETH, ENGLAND
Circa 1885. Burslem.

OPEN NECK VASE
DOULTON
$12,000
LAMBETH, ENGLAND
Circa 1885. Hand painted, Burslem.

THE BROWNIES CUP AND SAUCER
GRIMWADES
$400   **$500**   **$600**
STOKE-ON-TRENT
Circa 1910. Porcelain.

ROYAL BONN "DELFT" STEIN
FRANZ ANTON MEHLEM
$15,000
Circa 1890.

THE BROWNIES PITCHER
GRIMWADES
$1,000   **$1,200**   **$1,400**
STOKE-ON-TRENT
Circa 1910. Porcelain.

TOBACCO JARS
HANDLE WARE
$1,000	$1,500	$2,000

MERIDEN
Circa late 1800.

HOTEL DINNERWARE
LIMOGE
$400	$500	$600

PARIS, FRANCE
Circa 1900. Hotel dinnerware "Golf Hotel Le Couquet."

SILVER LID TANKARD
LENOX
$1,800	$2,200	$2,600

LAWRENCEVILLE, NJ
Circa 1905. Lady and gentleman golfers on blue background.

SILVER RIM TANKARD
LENOX
$1,200	$1,500	$1,800

LAWRENCEVILLE, NJ
Circa 1905. Lady and gentleman golfers on green background.

PORCELAIN FIGURINE
LLADRO
$300	$400	$500

VALENCIA, SPAIN
Circa 1950s. Figurine.

PORCELAIN CHINA
NORITAKE
$600 $700 $800
JAPAN
Circa 1930s. Hand painted jar.

PORCELAIN VASE AND ASHTRAY
RICHARD GINORI
$600 $800 $1,000
ITALY
Circa 1920s. Art deco golfers.

PORCELAIN MUG
NORITAKE
$400 $500 $600
JAPAN
Circa 1900s. Hand painted mug marked Nippon.

PORCELAIN BOWL
ROYAL BAYRUTH
$600 $800 $1,000
Circa 1900s. Bowl measuring 10 3/8 inches, signed Brown.

PORCELAIN HUMIDOR
NORITAKE
$400 $500 $600
JAPAN
Circa 1900s. Hand painted humidor marked Nippon.

PORCELAIN BOWL
ROYAL DOULTON
$400 $600 $800
ENGLAND
Circa 1930s. Bunnykins, Royal Doulton.

PORCELAIN PLATE
ROYAL DOULTON
$200   **$300**   **$400**
ENGLAND
Circa 1930s. Bunnykins, Royal Doulton.

PORCELAIN CREAMER
ROYAL DOULTON
$400   **$600**   **$800**
ENGLAND
Circa 1930s. Bunnykins, Royal Doulton.

ROYAL DOULTON, GOLF SERIES WARE
ROYAL DOULTON
$1,500   **$5,000**   **$10,000**
ENGLAND
Circa 1900. Decorated with Charles Crombie figures.

ROYAL DOULTON, GOLF SERIES WARE
ROYAL DOULTON
$200   **$300**   **$400**
Scalloped edge, 9 1/2".

ROYAL DOULTON, GOLF SERIES WARE
ROYAL DOULTON
$200   **$300**   **$400**
Plate, circa 1920, 10".

ROYAL DOULTON, KINGSWARE MUG
ROYAL DOULTON
$200   **$300**   **$400**
Mug, circa 1920s

ROYAL DOULTON WHISKEY BARREL
ROYAL DOULTON
$8,000
ENGLAND
Circa 1900. Whiskey barrel with 19th hole scene at one end and The Club House, St. Andrews, on the other; it has silver spout and bucket.

ROYAL DOULTON, KINGSWARE JUG
ROYAL DOULTON
$500   **$750**   **$1,000**
Jug with stopper, circa 1920, 9".

ROYAL DOULTON, STEIN
ROYAL DOULTON
$100   **$150**   **$250**
Stein with humorous drawing by H.M. Bateman,
5 1/2".

HOTEL DINNERWARE
WARWICK
$300   **$500**   **$600**
WHEELING, W. VA
Circa 1930. Hotel dinnerware depicting Bobby
Jones.

THE NINETEENTH HOLE PLATE
ROYAL DOULTON
$400   **$600**   **$800**
ENGLAND
Circa 1900.

SUGAR BOWL WITH LID
WEDGEWOOD
$650   **$850**   **$1,250**
BURSLEM, ENGLAND
Circa early 1900s. Golfers in white relief.

CREAMER
WEDGEWOOD
$450   **$650**   **$900**
BURSLEM, ENGLAND
Circa early 1900s. Golfers in white relief.

VASE
WELLER
$1,750
ZANESVILLE, OH
Circa 1900. Dickinsware pottery with male golfer scene, 9.4".

VASE
WELLER
$1,200
ZANESVILLE, OH
Circa 1900. Dickinsware pottery with female golfer scene, 8 3/4".

HIGH GLAZE VASE
WELLER
$2,500
ZANESVILLE, OH
Early 1900s. Dickinsware pottery.

VASE
WELLER
$1,750
ZANESVILLE, OH
Circa 1900. Dickinsware pottery with male golfer scene, uncommon brown glaze rim, 9.4".

TEA SET
WILLIAMSONS & SONS
$3,000
ENGLAND
Circa 1900-1910. Porcelain tea set depicting golfers of the period—Vardon, Braid, Taylor, and various caddies.

JUG
GERZ
$1,200 $1,800 $2,250
Jug with golfers in relief, circa 1910, 8".

DECANTER
UNKNOWN MAKER
$250 $350 $550
Circa 1920s. Sterling silver golfer overlaid on blue glass.

DECANTER
UNKNOWN MAKER
$300 $450 $650
Circa 1920s. Sterling silver golfer overlaid on blue glass.

CRYSTAL DECANTER
WATERFORD
$1,500 $2,000 $2,500
Circa 1920. Sterling silver hallmarked neck. Hand painted golfing scene.

COCKTAIL SET
UNKNOWN MAKER
$1,250   **$1,600**   **$2,250**
Circa 1920s. Shaker, six tumblers and six goblets. Sterling silver golfer overlaid on blue glass.

COCKTAIL SET
UNKNOWN MAKER
$550   **$750**   **$1,000**
Circa 1920s. Shaker and six glasses. Sterling silver cap and sterling overlaid golfers.

TANTALUS DECANTER SET
ART DECO CO.
$300   **$500**   **$750**
Circa 1920s. Holder and caps are silver plated. Sterling silver golf scenes overlaid on clear glass.

COCKTAIL SET
UNKNOWN MAKER
$225   **$350**   **$475**
Circa 1920s. Shaker and four glasses. Sterling silver cap and sterling overlaid golfers on frosted yellow glass.

WINE DECANTER
UNKNOWN MAKER
$250 $400 $600
Circa 1920s. Sterling silver golfer overlaid on clear glass.

HAND PAINTED BOTTLE
UNKNOWN MAKER
$200 $275 $375
Circa 1930. 8" high.

AFTER SHAVE BOTTLE
A. R. WINARICK CO.
$100 $125 $175
Circa 1920. 9 1/2" high.

HAND PAINTED GLASS
UNKNOWN MAKER
$50 $75 $100
Circa 1930.

ICE BUCKET
T. G. HAWKES & CO.
$200 $275 $400
Circa 1900. Sterling silver handle. Golf scene engraved on glass.

COCKTAIL SHAKER
T. G. HAWKES & CO.
$450 $600 $850
Circa 1900. Sterling silver lid. Golf scene engraved on glass.

CRYSTAL DECANTERS
T. G. HAWKES & CO.
$1,200 $1,700 $2,000
Circa 1900. Set of two crystal decanters with etched glass golfing scenes, sterling silver caps inoriginal wicker basket carrying case.

WINE BOTTLE
T. G. HAWKES & CO.
$225 $300 $400
Circa 1900. Sterling silver cap. Golf scene engraved on glass.

CLUB SODA BOTTLES
UNKNOWN MAKER
$25 $35 $50
Circa 1920s. Milk glass. Various flavors.

ETCHED GLASSES
HEISSEY
$450   **$650**   **$900**
Circa 1920s. Shot glass with etched golfers.

ETCHED GLASSES
HEISSEY
$450   **$650**   **$850**
Circa 1920s. Tumbler with etched golfers.

COOKIE JAR
HEISSEY
$2,000   **$2,750**   **$3,750**
Circa 1920s. Silver overlay golfers on cut glass.

GLASS SET
CAMBRIDGE
$150   **$200**   **$300**
Circa 1920s. Four pink tumblers and carrying tray
with handle. Acid etched golfing scenes.

LOCKER BOTTLE, ENGRAVED GLASS
T. J. HAWKES & CO.
$275   **$375**   **$650**
Circa 1910. 19th Hole design.

LEADED GLASS BOTTLE
UNKNOWN
$450   **$600**   **$850**
Circa 1910. Painted overlay of two golfers and
ceramic stopper in the shape of a Scot.

CLARET PITCHER
UNKNOWN MAKER
$800   **$1,200**   **$2,000**
Circa 1920. Sterling on glass. 16" tall.

CRYSTAL STEIN-STERLING LID
UNKNOWN MAKER
$1,250   **$1,750**   **$2,250**
Circa 1900. Golfer in relief on lid.

HAND BLOWN PITCHER
UNKNOWN MAKER
$500   **$750**   **$1,000**
Circa 1910. Two inch sterling silver neck band.

CRYSTAL HUMIDOR-STERLING LID
UNKNOWN MAKER
$1,250   **$1,750**   **$2,250**
Circa 1900.

PERFUME BOTTLE
UNKNOWN MAKER
$450   **$600**   **$900**
Circa 1900. Sterling stopper with golfer.

PERFUME BOTTLE
ART DECO
$450   **$600**   **$900**
CZECHOSLOVAKIA
Circa 1930. Cut glass with golfer.

ASHTRAY
H. HOFFMAN
$200   **$300**   **$400**
Circa 1920s. 5" x 3" intaglio cut.

TUMBLER
DE PASSE MFG. CO.
$60   **$90**   **$150**
Circa 1915. Sterling overlay.

ASHTRAY
UNKNOWN MAKER
$40   **$70**   **$100**
Circa 1940s. 2 1/2" x 2 1/2" acid etched glass.

ASHTRAY
UNKNOWN MAKER
$70 $100 $175
Circa 1940s. 4" x 3" acid etched glass.

ASHTRAY
UNKNOWN MAKER
$100 $150 $200
Circa 1940s. Sterling on glass.

CIGARETTE BOX
UNKNOWN MAKER
$200 $300 $400
Circa 1920s. Sterling on glass.

CIGARETTE BOX
UNKNOWN MAKER
$150 $225 $300
Circa 1940s. Sterling on glass.

Chapter 12

Golf Medals and Trophies

Trophies are of many shapes, sizes and metals.

Collecting Medals

By Art Di Prospero

Among my favorite collectibles are medals. There is very little written about them and usually the only sources for obtaining them are the various worldwide auctions. They come in all shapes and sizes, and are made of bronze, brass, copper, pewter, silver, and gold. Most of the silver medals are sterling. The gold medals may vary; the British used mostly 9kt., while Americans used 10kt., 14kt., and .900 fine. Some medals are also silver-plated and 12kt. gold filled.

I have been drawn to medals for several reasons. The initial visual impact is the artwork. Many are in fine detail, both recessed and in relief. The variety of emblems, golfers, clubs, balls, clubhouses, and golfing scenes are sometimes breathtaking.

The pre-1900 British and Scottish medals are not only pieces of art, they tell the history of the game. The names of players, golf course emblems, dates of competition, and other engravings help to identify the better players, where and when they played, and the varied types of competitions of that era.

The early American medals can help "put together" golf in a historical perspective. One of the greatest thrills I can have as a medal collector is to acquire a documented piece from Shinnecock, The National, Merion, Baltusrol, Oakmont, or any of the other great circa 1890-1910 courses. It gives the collector a humbling feeling to know that Willie Anderson, Horace Rawlins, Walter Travis, Walter Hagen, Gene Sarazen, and Bobby Jones competed over these hallowed links.

The feeling is purely spellbinding to hold in my hand a medal won by Walter Hagen, or one of my favorites: the medal presented to Olin Dutra upon winning the 1932 PGA Championship. It contains more than two ounces of gold and has a 1kt. diamond inset. The strike and artwork were absolutely incredible! When holding it, I can almost feel Dutra's euphoria from winning the PGA and being presented with his well-earned medal.

The USGA at Far Hills, N.J., has an awesome display of Bobby Jones medals. Chuck Furjanic's home course, The Four Seasons Resort and Club at Las Colinas, where the

Byron Nelson Tour event is held, has on display all 18 medals won by Nelson during 1945, which include those from his incredible 11 straight wins and the PGA Medal.

When collecting medals, you begin to recognize their historical importance and the part they played in giving the recipients something tangible to remember their "moment of glory." It also gives us a way to identify with the winner's feeling of importance upon being presented with a medal.

Golf Trophies

By Henry Alperin

A trophy or "prize" for the winner of a competition surely must date from the origins of golf. Most notable are the British Open Championship Belt and the British Open Claret Jug, which date from 1860. The original Open Championship Belt was retired by the famous young Tom Morris. The Claret Jug is still being awarded at the end of the championship, with a replica of the original Claret Jug given to the champion. Similar major trophies are awarded for the British and United States amateur titles, and the United States Open Championships. At the Masters, a replica of the original trophy (depicting the Augusta National Clubhouse) is presented to the Masters champion.

Many annual golf events in the United States and abroad have individual characteristic trophies; some are glass and others are silver. Medals are still presented in the amateur championships and to the low amateur at the Masters Championship.

A golf trophy may be any item ranging from the classic silver cup, bowl or plate, to the engraved ribboned medals of gold and silver. Etched and engraved glass trophies are often given at current golf championships, particularly in the United States. Golf trophies have been made using many different materials such as pewter, brass, bronze, plated silver, and ceramics.

Many types of objects have been used for trophies: traditional cups, golf clubs with engraved plaques, mugs, ashtrays, statues, humidors, inkwell sets, decanters, jewelry, cigarette lighters, and mechanical devices such as clocks or watches. All of these items are both collectible and decorative and, while they may cost only a few dollars, they can become a significant investment. There are many collectors within the Golf Collectors Society who specialize in one particular type of trophy; for example, items from a certain era or particular championships. Some individuals may collect only sterling pieces or ceramics, others might collect items pertaining to a certain golfer. Still others may collect a variety of trophies with no particular theme other than the fact it was presented to a winner of a golf tournament. The prices of these items, like other collectibles, relate to the rarity, condition, and demand.

It is always recommended that collectors buy from reputable dealers who will verify the authenticity, particularly of the more expensive items.

There are many specialized texts available that relate to this field of collecting, particularly relating to artifacts of ceramic, silver, and other metals. Previous major auction house catalogs and prior catalogs from golf collectible dealers are also very helpful. The old catalogs, with their prices realized, are good guides for the collector in need of prices of specific trophies.

Where do collectors find trophies? The smaller silver cups and some of the ceramic items can be found in antique shops and flea markets. Sometimes, watches and jewelry, or smoking-related items such as ashtrays and engraved lighters, may also be found at these locations. Many golf collectible dealers carry various trophies, and collectors at golf shows display golf trophies for sale. The large golf auction houses both in the United States and Great Britain often carry many trophies, especially important medals and significant trophy cups. Occasionally an entire collection belonging to a famous golfer may be offered, such as the recent "Bobby Locke" collection, or the large collection of items from the Walter Travis Estate.

The joy of trophy collecting may be in obtaining an item from one's favorite golfer, but many enjoy the history behind the trophy relating to the winning golfer, or the golf society that presented it.

At the United States Golf Association Library, one may research some of the inscriptions as to the particular tournament and the correct date. If the inscription does not contain the name of the golfer winning the trophy, it can be obtained here. Often, the trophy was presented with the date and tournament name, but the winner's name had to be engraved by the recipient.

Sterling silver from Great Britain can be dated as to its manufacturer to see if the date of the presentation and the manufacturer correspond. Sterling silver in the United States is marked with the maker of the company and a sterling mark, but no definite date can be attributed.

Medals and Trophies

By Bob Burkett

MEDALS

From the start of my collecting career in golf, I have always had a special fondness for medals. Unlike clubs, behind each medal there is a story, which can sometimes be found with a little research and imagination. Always, though, these medals represent man's triumph over an opponent, a golf course, and, more importantly, himself.

Medals come in all sizes, shapes, materials, and, of course, values. The value rests on a number of factors, the first being composition. A plain brass medal is usually worth less than one made of 18kt. gold. However, if the brass was won by, say, Horace Hutchison in a British Amateur Championship, and the gold by a local businessman, the values change.

Beauty, as well as content and history, play a part in the value of medals. Some of the best art in the game of golf is depicted on high quality golf medals and most of these have found their way into collections.

Like most collectibles, medals come in vastly different qualities and price ranges. They may vary in price from $40 to $50 for a 1950s base metal item, and up to $50,000 or more for a medal from an important championship such as the British Open or other majors. Each item is individual, and should be judged as such. Obviously, other factors such as age, wear, engraving, and place of origin are to be considered.

The beginning collector should find a focus to his collection. For example, find a specific golf course, a specific time period, famous golfer, or type of medal. Usually your first category choice will be too broad. I started out collecting pre-1930 medals and within a short time it was narrowed to pre-1920 and then, again, to pre-1920 American. It took me 15 years to finally focus on pre-1920 American women's medals.

One last thought: It doesn't matter if you accumulate 10 unrelated medals or 100 related medals, as long as it gives you collecting pleasure. Taking time to research the recipients and places related to your medals may enhance the enjoyment of your collection. On the other hand, you may just want to display them, and that's great too. Remember, the enjoyment of collecting is paramount.

TROPHIES

Trophies come in a wider range of styles and materials than perhaps any other collectible in golf. The oldest known trophy is a silver golf club from the Edinburgh Burgess Golfing Society. Since then, trophies have appeared in every variation the golfer's twisted mind can conceive. China, crystal, gold, silver, wood, leather, pewter, bronze, and only God knows what else have been fashioned into some sort of symbols of achievement—in the addiction we call golf.

As a broad general statement, trophies are more commonly American than British, while medals are more commonly British than American. Having collected both, I will also make the broad general statement that trophies take up an awful lot more space.

Trophies are very visual and come in a wide variety of sizes and shapes. After 15 years of collecting, I have long since given up trying to find an example of each. Unlike medals, trophies can be striking in appearance and somewhat more modest in cost, owing to the materials being more diverse and, in many cases, less expensive.

While some of the early high quality trophies will run easily into thousands, many unusual and decorative trophies from the Art Deco 1920s and 1930s can still be found at a relatively modest price. Find a style, period, and price that fit your taste and budget.

Please avoid the classic beginner mistake of buying any trophy you find at a yard sale, flea market, or antique shop just because it is golf related. There are lots of later (1950s and newer) low quality golf items for sale that have little value now and little hope of appreciation in value.

Having said that, I would also advise that you buy what pleases you. Also, buy the best available. It doesn't matter if you have $50 to spend. Buy the best $50 trophy you can find. If you have $5,000 to spend, the rule is the same. Buy the best $5,000 trophy you can find.

The old saying is still true. The bitterness of poor quality remains long after the sweetness of a cheap price has vanished.

Prices Golf Medals

Prices are for grades G-5, G-7, and G9.

NEW YORK STATE CHAMPIONSHIP MEDAL
$1,750
1921 14K Gold Oval shaped medal. Won by Bobby Cruickshank.

WESTCHESTER COUNTY GOLF CHAMPIONSHIP
$1,000
1926 "Solid Gold" won by Bobby Cruickshank.

NORTH AND SOUTH OPEN CHAMPIONSHIP
$1,750
1943 Pinehurst 14K Gold. Won by Bobby Cruickshank.

BRONZE COIN-SIZE MEDALS
VARIOUS MAKERS
$35   **$50**   **$75**
Circa 1900-1930. Nickel to quarter size with club name and date. Medals with ribbons add 50 percent.

BRONZE COIN-SIZE MEDALS
VARIOUS MAKERS
$60   **$100**   **$150**
Circa 1900-1930. Half-dollar to dollar size with club name and date. Medals with ribbons add 50 percent.

STERLING COIN-SIZE MEDALS
VARIOUS MAKERS
$125   **$175**   **$250**
Circa 1900-1930. Nickel to quarter size with club name and date. Medals with ribbons add 50 percent.

STERLING COIN SIZE MEDALS
VARIOUS MAKERS
$200   **$300**   **$400**
Circa 1900-1930. Half-dollar to dollar size with club name and date. Medals with ribbons add 50 percent.

HOLE-IN-ONE MEDALS
VARIOUS MAKERS
$20   **$35**   **$50**
Circa 1920s through 1960s. Mostly made of bronze. "Royal" is most common.

BRITISH AMATEUR CHAMPIONSHIP
WALKER AND HALL, SHEFFIELD
$15,000   **$18,000**   **$20,000**
Circa 1900. 18kt. gold medal in presentation case. Price is for unmarked or unknown winner. Popular winners command a substantial premium.

1924 BELGIAN OPEN GOLD MEDAL
UNKNOWN MAKER
$7,500
14kt. gold medal. Won by Walter Hagen. Sold at public auction in 1991 for $1,750. Medals won by less popular players are worth substantially less.

STERLING ST. ANDREWS MEDAL
FRICK JEWELERS, NY
$2,000
Circa 1900. Presented to members of the golf team at St. Andrews Golf Club, New York.

BRITISH OPEN MEDAL
UNKNOWN MAKER
$80,000
"Open Golf Championship, 1949" gold medal won by Bobby Locke, in red leather presentation case. Sold at public auction in 1993.

BRITISH OPEN MEDAL
UNKNOWN MAKER
$70,000
"Open Golf Championship, 1950" gold medal won by Bobby Locke, in red leather presentation case. Sold at public auction in 1993.

BRITISH OPEN MEDAL
UNKNOWN MAKER
$125,000
"Golf Champion Trophy, 1885" gilt medal won by Robert Martin, with blue ribbon and in the original box. Sold at public auction in 1996.

BRITISH MEDAL
UNKNOWN MAKER
$350
Gentleman's silver medal inscribed 1893.

U.S. OPEN GOLF MEDAL
UNKNOWN MAKER
$60,000
1955 won by Jack Fleck. Sold at public auction in 1993.

U.S. AMATEUR CHAMPIONSHIP MEDALLION
JOHN FRICK CO., NEW YORK
$2,500
Uninscribed medal c. 1980s, given to tournament dignitary.

TURN OF CENTURY BRONZE MEDAL
UNKNOWN MAKER
$300
Bronze with golfing figure and group scene, circa 1900.

PGA CHAMPIONSHIP MEDAL
UNKNOWN MAKER
$85,000
1921. Won by Walter Hagen. Sold at public auction in 1991 for $8,000.

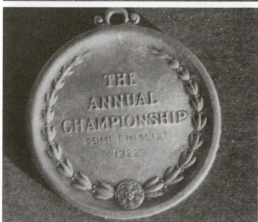

PGA SEMI FINALIST MEDAL
$10,000
1922 Sterling Silver. Won by Bobby Cruickshank.

CANADIAN OPEN GOLD MEDAL
UNKNOWN MAKER
$12,000
1931. Won by Walter Hagen. Sold at public auction in 1991 for $2,000.

2-INCH STERLING RELIEF MEDAL
WM. DUNNINGHAM, ABERDEEN
$2,000
1921 from the Caldonia Golf Club, Carnoustie.

WOMEN'S AMATEUR CONTESTANT MEDAL
VARIOUS MAKERS
$300
Circa 1920-1935. Quarter size and enameled in different colors through the years.

MEN'S AMATEUR CONTESTANT MEDAL
VARIOUS MAKERS
$350
Circa 1920-1935. Quarter size and enameled in different colors through the years.

MEN'S U.S. OPEN CONTESTANT MEDAL
VARIOUS MAKERS
$450
Circa 1920-1935. Quarter size and enameled in different colors through the years.

MEN'S WESTERN OPEN CONTESTANT MEDAL
VARIOUS MAKERS
$150
Circa 1920-1935. Quarter size and enameled in different colors through the years.

GOODNOW CHOICE SCORE TROPHY MEDAL
UNKNOWN MAKER
$100
Sterling silver medal from the Chicago area Bob O'Link Golf Club, inscribed and dated 1919.

VICTORY GOLF MEDAL
VARIOUS MAKERS
$500
A number of medals 2 1/2" in diameter were minted to be gifts to participating golf clubs in a tournament to raise funds for the United War Work Drive. John D. Rockefeller presented the medals.

TURN OF CENTURY BRONZE MEDALS
$1,000-$1,200
Three bronze medals: bronze circular medal awarded to H.W. Beveridge in 1900 at Tooting Bec Golf Club, bronze medal suspended from ribbon from Royal Cromer Golf Club, and bronze 1894 Cheltenham Golf Club medal.

1897 U.S. OPEN GOLD MEDAL
JOHN FRICK, NEW YORK
$125,000
Won by Joseph Lloyd. Sold for $21,000 at public auction in 1990.

Prices Golf Trophies

Prices are for grades G-5, G-7, and G9.

STERLING SILVER LOVING CUP
VARIOUS MAKERS
$125   **$175**   **$275**
Circa 1910-1930. Two-handled sterling loving cup without golfing scene. 5" to 6" tall.

STERLING SILVER CUP
GORHAM
$200   **$375**   **$450**
Circa 1900-1920. Two-handled cup without golfing scene. 5" to 6" tall.

STERLING GOBLET
VARIOUS MAKERS
$100   **$150**   **$250**
Circa 1900-1920. Without golfing scene. 5" to 6" tall.

STERLING SILVER CUP
GORHAM
$600   **$800**   **$1,000**
Circa 1900-1920. Two-handled cup with golfing scene or crossed clubs and ball. 7" to 8" tall.

STERLING SILVER CUP
GORHAM
$300   **$400**   **$500**
Circa 1900-1920. Two-handled cup without golfing scene. 7" to 8" tall.

STERLING GOLFER ON IVORY BASE
UNKNOWN MAKER
$2,000   **$2,500**   **$3,000**
Circa 1910. 6" high including base.

HUMIDOR WITH STERLING LID
VARIOUS MAKERS
$1,000   **$1,500**   **$2,000**
Circa 1900. Glass or crystal with a sterling lid. 6" to 7" tall.

STERLING CHALICE
UNKNOWN MAKER
$5,000
Circa 1850. 7" tall with golfing scene. Pre-1890 trophies are very rare.

STERLING TEA POT
UNKNOWN MAKER
$2,500
Circa 1890-1900. 8" tall with ornate engravings.
Very scarce.

STERLING SILVER LOVING CUP
VARIOUS MAKERS
$1,000   **$1,500**   **$2,000**
Circa 1910-1930. Two-handled sterling loving cup
with golfing scene or crossed clubs and ball. 10"
to 12" tall.

STERLING SILVER LOVING CUP
VARIOUS MAKERS
$375   **$500**   **$750**
Circa 1910-1930. Two-handled sterling loving cup
without golfing scene. 10" to 12" tall.

STERLING LOVING CUP
MADE IN SCOTLAND
J. LAING
$600   **$800**   **$1,000**
Circa 1920s. 6" tall with golfing scene and fine
detail.

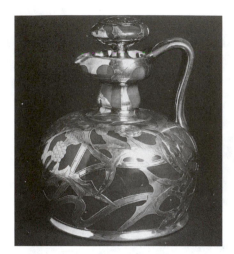

CERAMIC AND STERLING TROPHY
LENOX

$3,000   **$4,000**   **$5,000**

Circa 1900-1910. Opaque green ceramic pitcher with silver overlay. Very scarce.

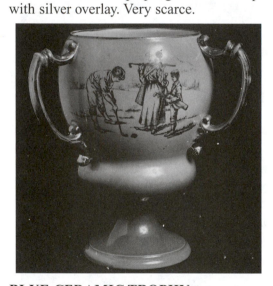

BLUE CERAMIC TROPHY
LENOX

$750   **$1,000**   **$1,250**

Circa 1900-1920. Three-handled trophy with golfing scene. 7" to 9" tall.

STERLING AND BRONZE TROPHY
PAIRPOINT

$800   **$1,000**   **$1,200**

Circa 1900-1920. Three-handled trophy on legs. Sterling on bronze.

BRONZE GOLFER ON BASE
VARIOUS MAKERS

$125   **$200**   **$300**

Circa 1900-1930. Bronze golfer on wood, bakelite or marble base. 5" to 7" tall.

BRONZE GOLFER ON BASE
VARIOUS MAKERS

$250   **$400**   **$600**

Circa 1900-1930. Bronze golfer on wood, bakelite or marble base. 8" to 10" tall.

Chapter 13

Golf Trading Cards

By Mike Daniels

Although sports card collecting has been around for more than 100 years, golf card collecting is still relatively new or unknown to many collectors. Most of us as youngsters collected baseball cards and, even though we played golf, we had never seen a golf trading card. We hope that the next few pages will give you additional information and insight into this wonderful and untapped area of golf collectibles.

The History of Golf Cards

Trade and cigarette cards were the first of the collectible cards. Shop owners and manufacturers handed out trade cards. These cards depicted the manufacturer's products and were printed with the name and address of the shop or shopkeeper. Businesses hoped that if they made these cards attractive, the customer would retain them as an informal business card.

The next step was to produce cards in a series with a particular theme. Flowers, fashion, children, pets, or country scenes were the first series produced.

If you were to review scrap albums from the middle to the late 1800s, you would find evidence of the success of this new marketing strategy both in the United States and Europe. Hence, the card collecting craze began.

About this same time, 1870-1880, a change was taking place in the tobacco habits of people. Cigarettes were taking over from pipes and chewing tobacco. The cigarettes were usually packed in the same fragile packets of their ancestors. This idea of combining a cardboard type of stiffener with the current collecting craze started first in the United

States and soon spread to Australia, Britain, and the rest of the world.

In the period from 1880 to about 1940, sets of cigarette cards were issued in profusion. Thousands of sets were made and the foundation was laid for the continuing card collecting hobby.

Since the majority of smokers prior to 1900 were men, subjects were chosen to appeal to men—military, sports, and women were popular choices.

In the United States, Kinney issued a military series in the late 1880s, Allen & Ginter issued its 50-card great generals set, and Duke did a 45-card famous ships series.

A year or two later, Allen & Ginter offered its first sport series called World Champions, which was a 50-card set. About the same time, Goodwin and Co. issued a 50-card Champions set and Kimball & Co. offered its 50-card Champions of Games and Sport set. Yet, not one of these sets included a golf card.

Around the turn of the century in England, the first golf cards were produced. Felix Berlyn and Cope Bros. and Co. Ltd. produced 25- and 50-card sets of golf scenes and strokes rather than of players. Original complete sets produced by these companies are extremely rare and sell for thousands of dollars. Do not despair, reprints of these and several other early sets were produced during the 1980s and sell for a fraction of the cost of originals.

The earliest American set to depict a golfer or golf scene was the American Tobacco Series of Champion Athletes and prize fighters of 1910—commonly referred to as the Mecca cigarette set. This set had six famous American golfers of the time: Finley Douglas, Alex Smith, Gil Nicholls, George Low, Jack Hobens, and Fred Herreshoff. These are not exactly household names today, but several of these gentlemen had distinguished careers in American golf.

About the same time in England, Odgen's produced its Guinea Gold cigarettes issue of 18 photographic golf cards. This set included Old Tom Morris, Harry Vardon, James Braid, etc., and six scenic cards from an early match played between Vardon and Braid, two of the greatest golfers from this period. By the late 1920s, Churchman felt that there was enough interest in the game and a sufficient number of well-known players to issue its famous golfers 50-card series of photographic cards. Over the next several years, Churchman and other tobacco companies produced many other golf sets.

The success of the cigarette cards became the model for other types of commodities. Cards began to be inserted with newspapers, chocolates, magazines, cereal, tea, and gum packets. Then came a slow and gradual change from a situation where with every stick of gum you were given a few cards, until the time when every pack of cards came with a free stick of gum. Then, finally, why bother putting the gum in the packets at all? We are now in a world of trading cards where series are produced on a commercial basis and sold in packets or as complete sets. Thousands of cards are now produced each year.

Golf cards have gone through a series of cycles over the years, with cards and sets being produced for a few years then going into a form of hibernation, with only a few cards produced annually. Donruss produced two PGA tour sets of 66 cards each in 1981 and 1982. The PGA tour continued to produce sets from 1983 to 1990. These were very similar to the Donruss sets in style and layout. These sets have become quite scarce in their own right since only a few thousand sheets were produced each year and many of these were destroyed. Only a few collectors knew of their existence and managed to save some sets.

The Pro Set company began producing sets for the PGA tour in 1990 and produced sets for three years. The first set consisted of 100 cards, 75 regular PGA tour cards and 25 senior tour cards. These sets were well received by the collecting public and were quite popular by autograph seekers on the American tour.

These sets are no longer being produced, but some new sets have come out of England. Most of these sets are of one theme or small sets of the 1993 or 1995 Ryder Cup Teams.

The huge popularity of Tiger Woods, beginning in the late 1990s, led to the revival of golf card sets in the United States. Upper Deck produced several sets in 2001, 2002, and 2003, including Upper Deck Golf, SP Authentic, and SP Game-Used. They include Woods plus many of the leading golfers such as Sergio Garcia, John Daly, Fred Couples, Justin Leonard, Colin Montgomerie, David Duval, and Phil Mickelson.

The new card sets include such special extras as cards with autographs, and swatches of players' shirts and gloves.

These miniature storybooks tell us much about the history of the game and hopefully some of you will expand your collecting interests into golf cards.

Recommended Reference Books

The following new reference books and price guides have been printed in the last few years. These are excellent checklists, and list all known golf cards in the world through 1994.

A Century of Golf Cards, by Bruce Berdock and Michael Baier, 1993.

The Price Guide to Golf Cards, Part I, Tobacco Cards, by Philip Smedley and Bruce Berdock, 1994.

The Price Guide to Golf Cards, Part II, Non-Tobacco Cards, by Philip Smedley & Bruce Berdock, 1995.

Prices Golf Cards

Prices are for grades G-5, G-7, and G9.

AMERICAN TOBACCO CO.
CHAMPION ATHLETES SERIES
| $30 | $55 | $100 |

Circa 1910. "Mecca" cigarettes. Six cards: A. Smith, F. Douglas, J. Hobens, F. Herreshoff, George Low, and Gil Nicholls.

COLLEGE SERIES
| $20 | $35 | $60 |

Circa 1914. Seven cards.

COLLEGE SILKS
| $25 | $50 | $100 |

Circa 1910. Two sizes of colorful silks. 25 colleges included. Small size 5 1/2" x 3 1/2"; large size 7 3/4" x 5".

BERLYN, FEXIS S.
ENGLAND
BURLINE MIXTURE GOLF CARDS, FULL SET
| $5,500 | $12,000 | $20,000 |

Circa 1910. 25 small-size cards.

BURLINE MIXTURE GOLF CARDS, ONE CARD
| $250 | $450 | $800 |

Circa 1910. 25 small-size cards.

BURLINE MIXTURE GOLF CARDS, ONE CARD
| $400 | $1,000 | $1,500 |

Circa 1910. 25 large-size cards.

BURLINE MIXTURE GOLF CARDS, FULL SET
| $9,500 | $22,000 | $35,000 |

Circa 1910. 25 large-size cards.

CHURCHMAN
CAN YOU BEAT BOGEY AT ST. ANDREWS
| $400 | $700 | $1,000 |

Circa 1934. Complete set of 55 cards.

FAMOUS GOLFERS SMALL SIZE
| $600 | $1,250 | $1,850 |

Circa 1927. Complete set of 50 cards.

FAMOUS GOLFERS LARGE SIZE
| $700 | $1,350 | $2,000 |

Circa 1927. Complete set of 12 cards.

MEN OF THE MOMENT IN SPORTS
| $300 | $500 | $800 |

Circa 1928. Set of 10 golf cards numbering 24 to 33.

PROMINENT GOLFERS SMALL SIZE
| $500 | $1,000 | $1,600 |

Circa 1931. Set of 50 golf cards.

PROMINENT GOLFERS LARGE SIZE
| $550 | $950 | $1,400 |

Circa 1931. Set of 12 golf cards.

SPORTING CELEBRITIES
| $100 | $150 | $250 |

Circa 1931. Set of 7 golf cards, numbering 30 to 36.

DONRUSS
PGA TOUR CARDS

$25	$35	$50

1981. Complete set of 66 cards. All are considered "Rookie" cards.

PGA TOUR CARDS

$30	$40	$60

1982. Complete set of 66 cards.

MEULLER ENTERPRISES, INC.
GOLF'S GREATEST

$25	$30	$60

1992. Complete set of 30 cards.

MILLER PRESS
PRO TOUR CARDS

$90	$150	$300

1983 and 1984. Uncut sheet of 66 cards.

PRO TOUR CARDS

$65	$100	$200

1985, 1986 and 1987. Uncut sheet of 66 cards.

PRO TOUR CARDS

$50	$75	$120

1988. Uncut sheet of 66 cards.

OGDEN'S LIMITED
ENGLAND
OGDEN'S GUINEA GOLD

$25	$50	$100

Circa 1901. Unnumbered cards. The Tom Morris card is worth about double.

LIVERPOOL & LONDON
COPE'S GOLFERS

$1,500	$3,500	$7,000

Circa 1900. 50 numbered cards.

PRO TOUR CARDS

$25	$45	$75

1989 and 1990. Uncut sheet of 66 cards.

B. MORRIS

LONDON

GOLF STROKES by ARTHUR HAVERS

$175	$250	$400

Circa 1925. 25 numbered cards.

PRIMROSE CONFECTIONARY

POPEYE 2ND SERIES

$25	$45	$70

1961. Card #29.

PRO SET, INC.

PGA TOUR INAUGURAL SET

$5	$6	$10

1990. Complete set of 100 cards.

ARNOLD PALMER HOLOGRAM CARD

$50	$55	$60

1991.

BEN HOGAN HOLOGRAM CARD

$80	$90	$100

1992.

NATIONAL EXCHANGE BANK

THE SEVEN AGES OF GOLF

$850	$1,300	$2,250

Circa 1902. Seven card set.

OGDEN'S CHAMPIONS OF 1936
$10   **$22**   **$35**
Pam Barton, A. H. Padgham and H. Thomson.

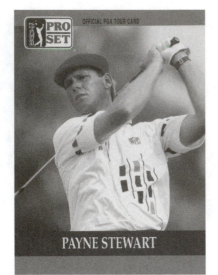

NFL FOOTBALL CARDS
$10   **$20**   **$40**
1990. Payne Stewart special card.

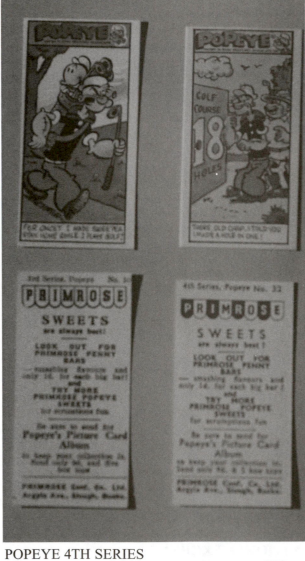

POPEYE 4TH SERIES
$8   **$10**   **$20**
1963. Cards #24 and #32.

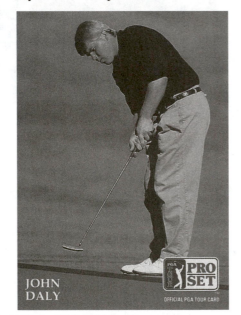

PGA TOUR CARDS
$10   **$15**   **$25**
1991 and 1992. Complete sets of 285 and 300 ards.

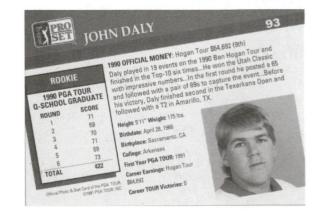

SHERIDAN COLLECTIBLES
THE BOBBY JONES STORY
$5   **$7**   **$12**
1993. Complete set of 12 cards.

FAMOUS COURSES
$250   **$400**   **$650**
Circa 1924. 25 card set.

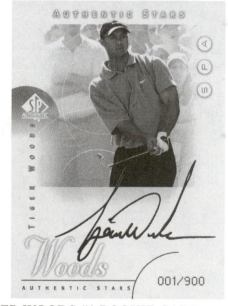

TIGER WOODS #1 ROOKIE CARD
$8   **$12**   **$20**

WILLS
ENGLAND
FAMOUS GOLFERS
$500   **$800**   **$1,300**
Circa 1930. 25 card set.

UPPER DECK
UPPER DECK GOLF
$15   **$25**   **$35**
2001. Complete set of 200 cards.

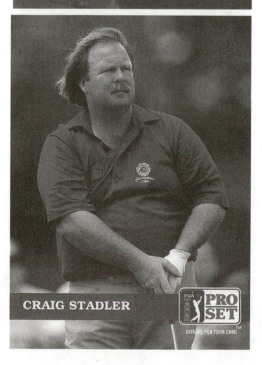

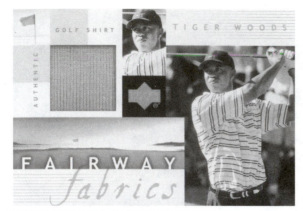

TIGER WOODS FAIRWAY FABRICS
$100   **$150**   **$240**

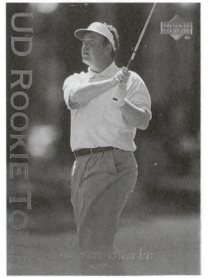

SP AUTHENTIC
$25   **$35**   **$50**
2001. Complete set of 135 cards.
TIGER WOODS AUTOGRAPH CARD
$500   **$750**   **$1,150**
UPPER DECK GOLF
$12   **$20**   **$30**
2002. Complete set of 130 cards.
SP AUTHENTIC
$15   **$25**   **$35**
2002. Complete set of 140 cards.

SP AUTHENTIC GAME-USED
2002. Complete set of 83 cards.
$50   **$65**   **$90**
JACK NICKLAUS SCORECARD SIGNATURES
$125   **$175**   **$225**
UPPER DECK GOLF
$20   **$30**   **$40**
2003. Complete set of 102 cards.

Chapter 14

Silver And Gold Golf Collectibles

An assortment of silver whiskey flasks are decorated with golf themes.

Precious metals were used to make many collectible golf items. Here we will discuss and evaluate those made from gold and silver.

Gold came in various qualities ranging from 9 kt. to 18 kt. and was mainly used for smaller items, such as jewelry in the form of cuff links and tie clasps for men, and brooches, pins, and charms for women.

Silver items were very popular around the turn of the century and were made of sterling or were silver plated. Many of these were for ladies and the home. They included toast racks, knife rests, salt and pepper shakers, coffee and tea servers, various utensils, serving trays, hair brushes, coin purses, and pin cushions. Souvenir spoons were also made for both trophies and the tourist trade at famous course locations like St. Andrews and Troon. For the men there were whiskey flasks, cocktail items, match safes, cigarette cases, watch fobs, inkwells, tie clasps, cuff links, and scoring devices. Some of the prominent manufacturers included: Unger Brothers, Tiffany, Gorham, Wm. Kerr, and Whiting.

Prices Silver and Gold Collectibles

Prices are for grades G-5, G-7, and G9.

BELT BUCKLE - STERLING
UNKNOWN MAKER
$300   **$400**   **$600**
Circa 1900.

CIGARETTE CASE - STERLING
UNKNOWN MAKER
$250
Etched scene of three golfers. Gold wash interior.

BLOTTER
UNGER BROS.
$500   **$750**   **$1,100**
Circa 1905. Golfer on front.

CIGARETTE CASE - STERLING
NAPIER CO.
$200   **$375**   **$575**
Circa 1930. Golfer on front. Knickers in black enamel.

BOOKMARK - STERLING
UNKNOWN MAKER
$225   **$325**   **$450**
Circa 1900-1920. Caddy with bag.

CIGARETTE CASE - STERLING
THE THOMAS CO.
$200   **$375**   **$575**
Circa 1930. Golfer on front.

CIGARETTE CASE - STERLING
NAPIER CO.
$200 **$375** **$575**
Circa 1930. Golfer on front. Place for initials at right front.

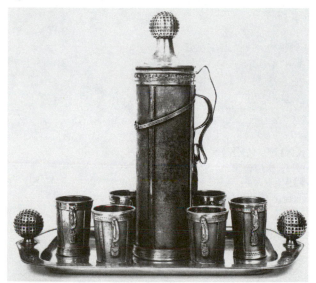

COCKTAIL SHAKER, TRAY AND CUPS
DERBY SILVER CO.
$1,200 **$1,500** **$2,000**
Circa 1920. Silver plated. Mesh ball handled tray, six cups and a 13" tall pitcher.

CIGARETTE BOX – STERLING ON BRONZE
UNKNOWN MAKER
$300
Circa 1912.

CIGARETTE CASE - STERLING
UNKNOWN MAKER
$375 **$575** **$900**
Circa 1900-1920. Golfing scene on cover.

EGGCUP - STERLING
UNKNOWN MAKER
$60 **$100** **$150**
Circa 1920s. Made in England. 3 1/2" tall.

CUPS, SET OF SIX SILVER-PLATED, WITH TRAY
WALLACE
$400
Circa 1900. With knickered golfer logo.

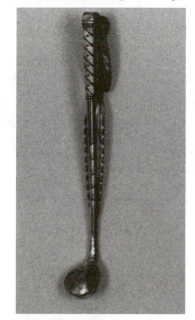

GOLF BAG PIN - STERLING
UNKNOWN MAKER
$75 **$125** **$200**
Circa 1910-1920s. 1 1/2". Bag and clubs.

HAT PIN - STERLING
UNKNOWN MAKER
$60 **$90** **$125**
Circa 1900-1920s. Sterling, wood at top.

GOLD GOLF BALL CUFF LINKS
DUNLOP, NEW YORK
$125 **$175** **$250**
Circa 1920. Nickel-size 10kt. gold mesh golf ball cuff links.

HAT PIN - STERLING
UNKNOWN MAKER
$75 $100 $150
Circa 1900-1920s. Wicker basket at top.

HAT PIN - STERLING
UNKNOWN MAKER
$50 $75 $100
Circa 1900-1920s. Iron head at top.

HAT PIN - STERLING
UNKNOWN MAKER
$60 $90 $125
Circa 1900-1920s. Crossed clubs at top.

INKWELL - SILVER-PLATED
F. BRS. LTD.
$475 $600 $900
Circa 1890. 6 x 11 inches. Two golf ball inkwells,
golfer in center.

LADY'S COIN PURSE - SILVER-PLATED
UNKNOWN MAKER
$200 $300 $450
Circa 1900-1920s. Caddy on front.

KNIFE RESTS
UNKNOWN MAKER
$250 $350 $450
Circa 1900-1920. Silver plated.

LADY'S COIN PURSE - STERLING
UNKNOWN MAKER
$350 $450 $650
Circa 1900-1920s. Lady golfer on front.

MATCH SAFE - STERLING
UNGER, NEWARK, NJ
$400   **$650**   **$850**
Circa 1900-1910. Caddy with bag.

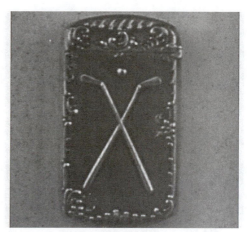

MATCH SAFE - STERLING
UNKNOWN MAKER
$300   **$450**   **$675**
Circa 1900-1910. Ball and crossed clubs.

MATCH SAFE - STERLING
ART NOUVEAU
$400   **$650**   **$850**
Circa 1900-1910. Woman golfer in backswing.

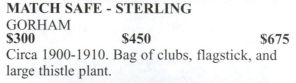

MATCH SAFE - STERLING
GORHAM
$300   **$450**   **$675**
Circa 1900-1910. Bag of clubs, flagstick, and
large thistle plant.

MATCH SAFE - STERLING
UNKNOWN MAKER
$400   **$750**   **$1,000**
Circa 1890. Woman golfer addressing golf ball.

MATCH SAFE - STERLING
La PIERRE MFG. CO.
$300   **$450**   **$675**
Circa 1890. Male golfer in backswing.

MATCH SAFE - STERLING
La PIERRE MFG. CO.
$250   **$375**   **$575**
Circa 1900. Small size with crossed clubs and ball.

NUT TRAY - STERLING
UNKNOWN MAKER
$400   **$500**   **$600**
Circa 1900-1910. 5 1/2" diameter. Golfer in center.

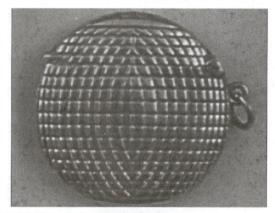

MATCH SAFE - STERLING
H. W. LTD, BIRMINGHAM
$450   **$675**   **$950**
Circa 1900-1910. Golf ball-shaped with line cut
guttie markings.

MATCH SAFE - STERLING
UNKNOWN MAKER
$300   **$450**   **$650**
Circa 1900. Golf clubs and ball.

PIN - STERLING
UNKNOWN MAKER
$100   **$150**   **$225**
Circa 1910-1920s. 3". Bag and clubs.

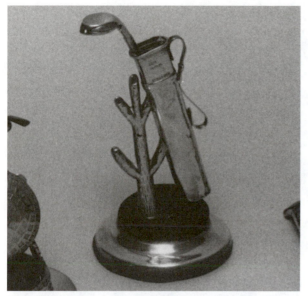

PIN CUSHION-HAT PIN HOLDER - STERLING
UNKNOWN MAKER
$300 $450 $600
Circa 1910-1920. Golf bag pin holder.

SALT DIP
UNKNOWN MAKER
$175 $250 $375
Circa 1900. Silver plate. Gutta ball design with crossed clubs.

PIN CUSHION-WATCH - STERLING
UNKNOWN MAKER
$600 $800 $1,100
Circa 1915-1925. Pin cushion with Swiss watch inside mesh ball cover.

SPOONS - STERLING SILVER
VARIOUS MAKERS
$60 $80 $100
Circa 1900-1930. Golfers on handle.

SPOONS - STERLING SILVER
VARIOUS MAKERS
$60   **$80**   **$100**
Circa 1900-1930. Various handle designs. Larger ornate spoons command double the prices listed.

TABLE SCRAPER
UNKNOWN MAKER
$225   **$325**   **$450**
Circa 1900-1920. Sterling handle, celluloid blade.

TEE INFUSER - STERLING
WATROUS,
WALLINGFORD, CT
$175   **$300**   **$450**
Circa 1910-1915. Shaped like a driver.

TIE CLASP - STERLING
UNKNOWN MAKER
$60   **$90**   **$125**
Circa 1910-1920s. 3". Golf club.

TOAST RACK
DERBY SILVER CO.
$350   **$500**   **$700**
Circa 1900-1910. Four-slice rack.

TOAST RACK
DERBY SILVER CO.
$400   **$550**   **$800**
Circa 1900-1910. Six-slice rack.

VESTA CASE, STERLING
ASPREY & COMPANY.
$1,500
Hallmarked 1906 with enameled golf scene, 1 3/4" diameter.

WHISKEY FLASK - STERLING
KERR & CO., NEWARK, NJ
$500   **$800**   **$1,100**
Circa 1920s. 4" x 8" pint size. Knickered golfers on front.

WHISKEY FLASK - STERLING
UNGER BROTHERS
$650   **$900**   **$1,250**
Circa 1905. Small flask. Caddy with bag.

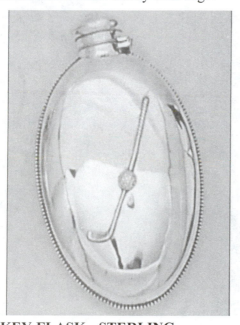

WHISKEY FLASK - STERLING
INTERNATIONAL SILVER CO.
$350   **$500**   **$750**
Circa 1920. Small flask in oval shape. Ball and club on front.

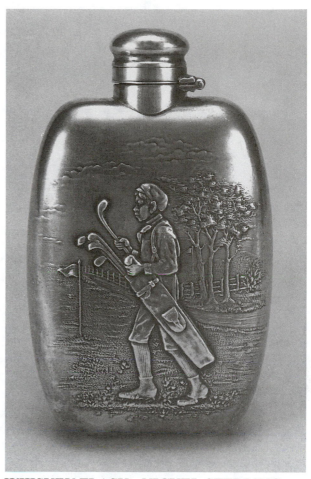

WHISKEY FLASK - NICKEL STERLING
EVANS CO.
$100   **$200**   **$350**
Circa 1920. Golfing scene.

WHISKEY FLASK - STERLING
WATROUS MFG. CO.
$350   **$500**   **$750**
Circa 1920s. Half-pint size. Golfing scene on front.

Several photos were graciously provided by Glentiques, Ltd.

Chapter 15

Miscellaneous Golf Collectibles

During the 1920s and '30s, a variety of golf ball companies made advertising pieces. They are highly collectible today.

Many collectors have wide and varied interests that are not limited to clubs, balls, and books, and extend their search for golf-related collectibles in antique shops, flea markets, and garage sales, as well as fixed price lists, auctions, and dealer offerings.

This chapter will include items such as tournament badges from PGA events, U.S. Opens and the Masters. It also includes watches, scorekeepers, ball washers, drink serving trays, bookends, cigar boxes, games, practice devices, molds, tins, advertising items, golf course equipment, and slot machines.

Prices Miscellaneous Golf Collectibles

Prices are for grades G-5, G-7, and G9.

ACCESSORIES

BALL WASHERS
HALLEY & CO., LONDON
$40   **$60**   **$90**
Circa 1920. Rectangular rubber holder for sponge.

BALL WASHERS
NORTH BRITISH, EDINBURGH
$30   **$45**   **$75**
Circa 1920. Square rubber holder for sponge.

BALL WASHERS
UNKNOWN MAKER
$150   **$225**   **$375**
Circa 1920. Round silver-plated holder for sponge.
Golfing scene on lid.

BALL WASHERS
UNKNOWN MAKER
$125   **$200**   **$300**
Circa 1920. Round brass holder for sponge.

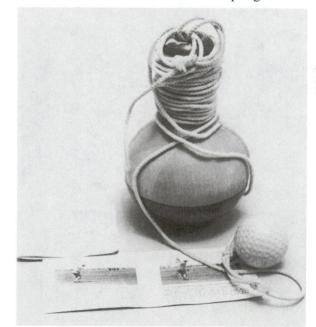

BOTTLE GOLF PRACTICE DEVICE
UNKNOWN MAKER
$150   **$225**   **$350**
Circa 1920s. Bottle-shaped device with mesh ball
at end of long twine tether.

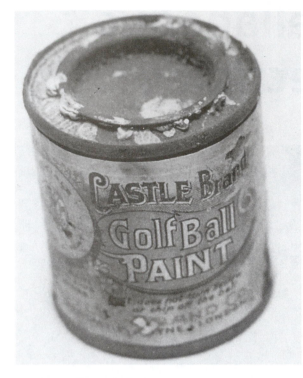

GOLF BALL PAINT
VARIOUS
$150   **$225**   **$375**
Circa 1900-1920.

GOLF SHOE SPIKES
UNKNOWN
$50   **$75**   **$100**
Circa 1920s. "Black Boy" cricket and golf spikes.
Colorful red, green, and white box.

GOLF SHOE SPIKES
UNKNOWN
$50   **$75**   **$100**
Circa 1920s. "Goffix" golfer's cleat that attaches
to street shoes. Add 50 percent for original box.

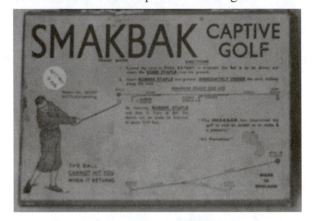

SMAKBAK PRACTICE DEVICE
MADE IN ENGLAND
$75   **$90**   **$125**
Circa 1925. Long metal spike with heavy twine
attached to golf ball. In colorful advertising box.

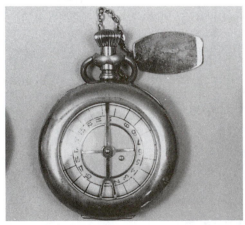

SCORE KEEPER
VARIOUS MAKERS
$150   **$225**   **$450**
Circa 1920s. Pocket watch size.

SCORE KEEPER
VARIOUS
$150   **$225**   **$350**
Circa 1920s. Wristwatch style.

SPOOL OF PITCHED LINEN
VARIOUS
$150   **$225**   **$375**
Circa 1900-1930. For repairing golf clubs. Both British and American makers.

HOGAN BELT WATCH
DUNLOP
$300   **$400**   **$550**
Circa 1950s.

POCKET WATCH
U.S. ROYAL
$100   **$150**   **$250**
Circa 1920s. Open face with mesh ball background.

POCKET WATCH
DUNLOP
$300   **$400**   **$550**
Circa 1920s-1930s. Sterling case in mesh ball pattern.

BADGES

TOURNAMENT MEDIA BADGES
VARIOUS MAKERS
$15   **$20**   **$30**
1960s-1980. 2" to 4", in various shapes: round, rectangular, oval, etc. Made of metal and plastic.

MASTERS PRESS BADGES
VARIOUS MAKERS
$50   **$60**   **$75**
1960s-1970. Rectangular and round. Made of metal.

U.S. OPEN MEDIA BADGES
VARIOUS MAKERS
$20   **$30**   **$50**
1960s-1970s. Press arm bands. Made of felt with elastic band. Various colors.

CADDIE BADGES
VARIOUS MAKERS
$75   **$100**   **$150**
1910-1930. Brass or steel. Golf course name and caddie number. Silver-dollar size.

TOURNAMENT CADDIE BADGES
VARIOUS MAKERS
$20   **$30**   **$45**
1960s-1980. 2" to 4", in various shapes: round, rectangular, oval, etc. Made of metal and plastic.

TOURNAMENT ENTRANCE BADGES
VARIOUS MAKERS
$8   **$12**   **$20**
1960s-1980. 2" to 4" in various shapes: round, rectangular, oval, etc. Made of metal and plastic.

U.S. OPEN BADGES
VARIOUS MAKERS
$15   **$25**   **$45**
1960s-1980. 2" to 4" in various shapes: round, rectangular, oval, etc. Made of metal and plastic.

GAMES

GOLF AROUND THE CLOCK GAME
P.S.P., INC., NEW YORK
$125   **$200**   **$325**
Circa late 1920s. Cast-iron numerals and hole in an advertising tin.

"PLAY GOLF" GOLF GAME
FERDINAND STRAUSS, NY
$125   **$200**   **$350**
Circa 1910. Metal wind-up game.

LAWN GOLF GAME
UNKNOWN MAKER
$250   **$300**   **$350**
Circa 1920s. Four wooden-head clubs, "holes" with discs, one rubber bramble pattern ball, and a wooden storage box.

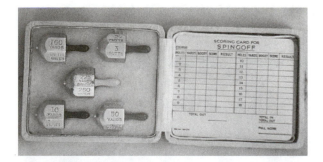

SPINGOFF GOLF GAME
UNKNOWN
$125   **$175**   **$250**
Circa 1920s rainy day golf game.

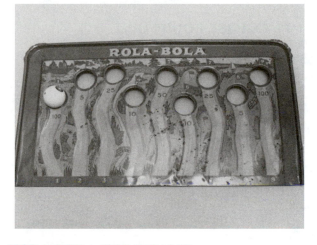

ROLA-BOLA GOLF GAME
VARIOUS
$125   **$200**   **$350**
Circa 1920s. Putting game.

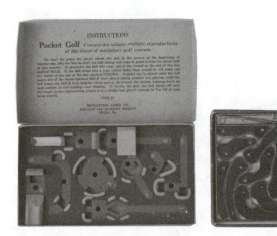

HAND-HELD GOLF GAMES
MINIATURE GAME CO. PHILADELPHIA
$100   **$150**   **$225**
Circa 1940s. Pocket golf and other hand-held
games.

KARGO CARD GOLF GAME
CASTELL BROS., LONDON
$50   **$70**   **$100**
Circa 1920s. Card game.

PAR-IT GOLF GAME
PAR-IT SALES, MILWAUKEE
$25   **$40**   **$65**
Circa 1930s. Card game.

ZWEIFEL CARD GOLF GAME
GROVER C. ZWEIFEL, *TULSA, OK*
$50   **$65**   **$90**
Circa 1930s. Card game.

GOLF BALL SLOT MACHINE
VARIOUS MAKERS
$2,500   **$3,750**   **$5,500**
Circa 1930s-1950s. Jennings and Mills brands.
Countertop model.

GOLF BALL SLOT MACHINE
VARIOUS MAKERS
$2,500   **$3,750**   **$5,500**
Circa 1930s-1950s. Jennings and Mills brands.
Standing model.

GOLF COURSE EQUIPMENT

GOLF COURSE EQUIPMENT
VARIOUS MAKERS
$50   **$75**   **$100**
Circa 1900-1910. Hole or cup liner made of steel.

GOLF COURSE EQUIPMENT
VARIOUS MAKERS
$150   **$250**   **$400**
Circa 1900-1910. Hole cutter.

GOLF COURSE EQUIPMENT
VARIOUS MAKERS
$200   **$300**   **$450**
Circa 1900-1910. Green aerator. The tines were
hollow.

GOLF COURSE EQUIPMENT
VARIOUS MAKERS
$200   **$300**   **$450**
Circa 1900-1910. Sod mover.

GOLF COURSE EQUIPMENT
VARIOUS MAKERS
$100   **$175**   **$275**
Circa 1920-1930. Fringe mower.

GOLF COURSE EQUIPMENT
VARIOUS MAKERS
$100	$175	$275

Circa 1900-1930. Sand tee box. The box pictured was in use at the 11th tee, Baltusrol.

MAGAZINES
GOLFING MAGAZINE
$25	$40	$65

Circa 1930s.

AMERICAN GOLFER
$60	$80	$120

Circa 1905-1916. Edited by Walter Travis.

GOLF ILLUSTRATED
$50	$70	$110

Circa 1920s. Large size.

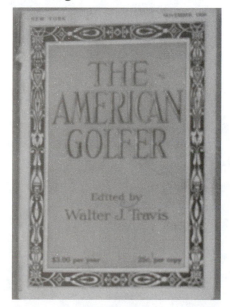

AMERICAN GOLFER
$50	$70	$100

Circa 1920-1930. Large size.

GOLFER'S MAGAZINE
$60	$80	$125

Circa Teens.

TINS & BOXES

COUNTRY CLUB CIGAR TIN
VARIOUS MAKERS
$125	$225	$350

Circa 1920s. Colorful cigar tin.

BISCUIT TIN
ROBERTSON BROS., TORONTO
$200	$300	$450

Circa 1920s. Hand painted. Approximately 10" tall.

HANDKERCHIEF BOXES
UNKNOWN MAKER
$50	$75	$100

Circa 1920s. Hinged wooden boxes with colorful men and lady golfers on lid.

SPICE TIN
VARIOUS MAKERS
$50   **$70**   **$100**
Circa 1920s. Small 1 1/2" x 3 1/2" tins for spices.

TIN BOX
SPALDING, DYSART, FIFE
$150   **$250**   **$350**
Circa 1920s. Large tin box with colorful golfing scenes.

TOMATO CAN
ROYAL BRAND
$50   **$70**   **$100**
Circa 1920s. Lady golfer on label.

COUNTRY CLUB CIGAR BOX
VARIOUS MAKERS
$40   **$70**   **$100**
Circa 1920s. Wooden cigar box.

MISCELLANEOUS

BOOKENDS
UNKNOWN
$100   **$125**   **$150**
Circa 1950s. Heavy granite, 7" tall with crossed clubs and ball.

WHITE METAL BOOKENDS
VARIOUS MAKERS
$100   **$125**   **$150**
Circa 1920s. Golfer in plus fours.

TOMMY GREEN SCHOENHUT GOLFER
SCHOENHUT CO.
$350   **$450**   **$600**
Circa 1920s. 5" wooden golfer at end of control rod.

SISSY LOFTER SCHOENHUT GOLFER
SCHOENHUT CO.
$450   **$600**   **$800**
Circa 1920s. 5" wooden golfer at end of control rod.

ICE CREAM MOLDS
VARIOUS MAKERS
$100   **$150**   **$200**
Circa 1910-1920. Made of pewter. Many shapes including a mesh golf ball mold not pictured.

DUNLOP MAN
DUNLOP
$250   **$400**   **$600**
Circa 1920s. Papier-maché colorful golfing figure with golf bag. Stand marked "We Play Dunlop." pproximately 18 inches tall.

SILVER KING ADVERTISING FIGURE
SILVERTOWN
$300   **$450**   **$650**
Circa 1920s. Papier-mache with mesh ball head.
Approximately 10 inches tall.

PENFOLD OR BROMFORD MAN
PENFOLD
$250   **$400**   **$600**
Circa 1920s. Papier-maché golfing figure with
large "Hogan"-type hat. Stand marked "He Played
a Penfold, or Bromford." Approximately 22 inches
tall.

SCOTTIE DOG ADVERTISING FIGURE
NORTH BRITISH, EDINBURGH
$250   **$375**   **$550**
Circa 1920s. Made in both metal and pottery.
Advertising for the North British Ball.

SILVER KING ADVERTISING FIGURE
SILVERTOWN
$300   **$450**   **$650**
Circa 1920s. Papier-maché with mesh ball head.
Approximately 8 inches tall.

PLASTER ADVERTISING PAPERWEIGHT
UNKNOWN MAKER

$250   **$400**   **$600**

Circa 1920s. Whiskey advertisements made of plaster. Usually with golfer and mesh pattern ball.

METAL SERVING TRAY
VARIOUS MAKERS

$50   **$75**   **$100**

Circa 1930s. Many with beer advertisements.

DESKTOP THERMOMETER
UNKNOWN MAKER

$250   **$325**   **$450**

Circa 1910. 6" with golfer on top. Made of white metal with dark brown patina.

CAST-IRON DOORSTOPS
VARIOUS MAKERS

$175   **$250**   **$400**

Circa 1920s. Colorfully painted.

MASTERS SERIES BADGES

Prices are for grades G-5, G-7, and G9.

1934 Horton Smith			1963 Jack Nicklaus		
$6,000	**$8,000**	**$12,000**	**$400**	**$500**	**$650**
1935 Gene Sarazen			1964 Arnold Palmer		
$4,000	**$5,000**	**$6,500**	**$325**	**$425**	**$525**
1936 Horton Smith			1965 Jack Nicklaus		**$750**
$2,500	**$3,500**	**$5,000**	1966 Jack Nicklaus		**$350**
1937 Byron Nelson			1967 Gay Brewer		**$190**
$2,500	**$3,500**	**$5,000**	1968 Bob Goalby		**$190**
1938 Henry Picard			1969 George Archer		**$175**
$1,200	**$1,800**	**$2,500**	1970 Billy Casper		**$160**
1939 Ralph Guldahl			1971 Charles Coody		**$160**
$700	**$850**	**$1,200**	1972 Jack Nicklaus		**$225**
1940 Jimmy Demaret			1973 Tommy Aaron		**$135**
$750	**$900**	**$1,250**	1974 Gary Player		**$135**
1942 Craig Wood			1975 Jack Nicklaus		**$160**
$650	**$750**	**$1,000**	1976 Raymond Floyd		**$110**
1943-45 Tournament was not held			1977 Tom Watson		**$120**
because of WWII			1978 Gary Player		**$100**
1946 Herman Keiser			1979 Fuzzy Zoeller		**$100**
$450	**$650**	**$850**	1980 Seve Ballesteros		**$90**
1947 Jimmy Demaret			1981 Tom Watson		**$100**
$450	**$650**	**$850**	1982 Craig Stadler		**$75**
1948 Claude Harmon			1983 Seve Ballesteros		**$70**
$400	**$575**	**$700**	1984 Ben Crenshaw		**$85**
1949 Sam Snead			1985 Bernhard Langer		**$65**
$450	**$650**	**$850**	1986 Jack Nicklaus		**$160**
1950 Jimmy Demaret			1987 Lary Mize		**$60**
$400	**$600**	**$700**	1988 Sandy Lyle		**$50**
1951 Ben Hogan			1989 Nick Faldo		**$50**
$500	**$750**	**$1,100**	1990 Nick Faldo		**$40**
1952 Sam Snead			1991 Ian Woosnam		**$40**
$400	**$550**	**$675**	1992 Fred Couples		**$50**
1953 Ben Hogan			1993 Bernhard Langer		**$40**
$475	**$700**	**$1,000**	1994 Jose Maria Olazabal		**$40**
1954 Sam Snead			1995 Ben Crenshaw		**$45**
$375	**$475**	**$650**	1996 Nick Faldo		**$40**
1955 Cary Middlecoff			1997 Tiger Woods		**$100**
$350	**$450**	**$550**	1998 Mark O'Meara		**$40**
1956 Jack Burke, Jr.			1999 Jose Maria Olazabal		**$40**
$325	**$425**	**$525**	2000 Vijay Singh		**$40**
1957 Doug Ford			001 Tiger Woods		**$60**
$325	**$425**	**$525**	2002 Tiger Woods		**$60**
1958 Arnold Palmer					
$500	**$600**	**$750**			
1959 Art Wall					
$300	**$375**	**$475**			
1960 Arnold Palmer					
$400	**$500**	**$650**			
1961 Gary Player					
$325	**$425**	**$525**			
1962 Arnold Palmer					
$400	**$500**	**$650**			

Chapter 16

A Short History Of Golf Bags

By Peter Georgiady

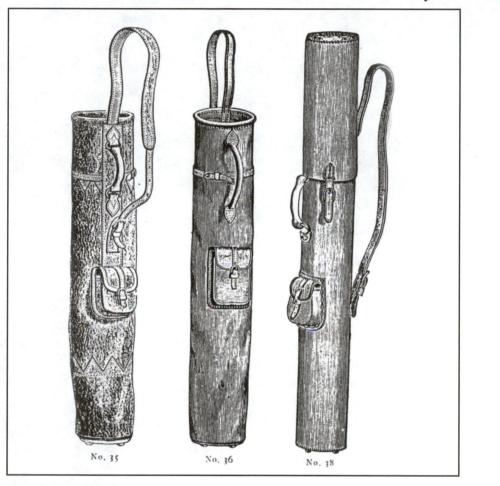

No. 35   No. 36   No. 38

Leather golf bags date to about 1900.

The number of years that golfers have used bags or other carrying devices for their clubs is greatly outnumbered by the years that clubs were simply carried under the arm. That is to say, golf bags are a fairly recent innovation in the history of the sport. There are two separate groups of implements to be examined: bags, or as they were once known, "covers," and carrying devices of another nature.

GOLF BAGS

Going back through centuries of golf, players carried their clubs under their arm without the assistance from any device. It might be said that golfers really never had a need for such devices because it was their caddies that actually did the carrying, however uncomfortable or awkward it might have been.

This match took place at St. Andrews, 1847. Notice the caddies carried the clubs under their arms as bags and other carrying devices were not used until the 1890s.

There was a second reason for the lack of requirement for a carrying valise or bag, and that was the relatively small number of clubs each player carried. Seven clubs was considered a large number, and four or five was often the selected set. Many players carried only three clubs, at a time when a man inventing a shot was more important than having a club that specialized in a particular loft or distance of shot.

Eventually, the bag, or cover, came into use primarily as a device for keeping club handles (grips) dry during the frequent and unpredictable rains that Britain is known for. The first of these covers were simply cloth sacks, long and tubular in shape like a long burlap pillowcase. There were no carrying handles or straps, no ball pockets or towel clips. They covered the handles and most of the wood shafts to keep them dry. Clubs were still just tucked under a player's or caddie's

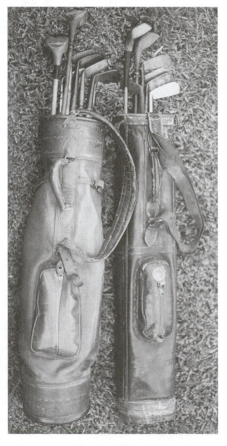

All-leather bags are quite scarce in above average to superb condition.

arm and carried as before. The lone characteristic to separate one bag from another was the use of stenciled initials or a monogram on the fabric.

The first person recorded to have used a bag cover for his clubs is David Stocks of Edinburgh, who allegedly did it to amuse his friends on the links in 1862. Whether or not he is responsible for other golfers adopting this new trend is not known, but they must have seen some merit in it, for Stocks' company later made a good business out of manufacturing golf bags. The popularity of such accouterments rose in the 1880s. Because of the primitive nature of these covers, few, if any, have survived today. They can, however, be seen in period photographs. While the advent of club covers occurred in the 1880s, they were not universally accepted for at least two decades. Period photos show caddies with

unprotected bundles of clubs under their arms as late as 1900.

The natural outgrowth of these early covers was a more advanced cover with new features. Leather was used to cover the base, so the bag could be rested on the ground without the fabric absorbing moisture. Leather was also added to the open end of the bag, with a large circular metal ring allowing the opening to accept the insertion of clubs without difficulty. A handle was applied to the bag for easier carrying and this was ultimately joined by a shoulder strap. These deluxe covers began appearing in the early 1890s. The final parts would come in the form of the ball pocket and stays to keep the bag rigid in its length and prevent it from folding or collapsing. The ball pocket feature eventually grew to accept everything from balls to wardrobes of clothes.

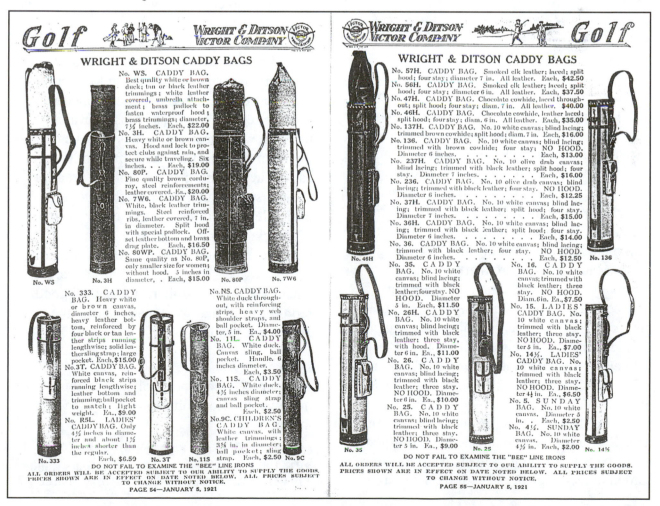

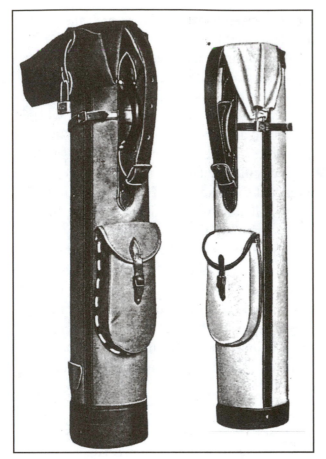

By the mid 1890s, the humble cloth cover had been supplanted by the new golf club bag made of leather. It was rigid with a strong base, had heavy-duty shoulder straps and handles and growing pockets. At a time when the sport was rapidly growing in both America and Great Britain, the large golf manufacturers like Spalding, MacGregor, Burke, Wright & Ditson, B.G.I., and Forgan were offering a complete line of golf requisites, including golf bags. Many of these are marked with their company names, although they were outsourced from saddlers and luggage manufacturers. Firms entering the golf bag manufacturing business came from the ranks of leather tanneries, luggage makers, and golf grip manufacturers, as well as the golf club makers themselves.

By about 1910, the form of the modern bag was fairly well established. Most of these early bags were circular in shape, now often called quiver bags because of their resem-

blance to an archer's arrow-holder, though their size was growing from an opening diameter of three inches to four inches to six inches and larger. Eventually, the amount of leather in the larger bags made them so heavy that canvas sides were joined with leather top, bottom, and straps to make a lighter weight kit.

Virtually all bags were circular until about 1930, when oval bags entered the market. This was in reaction to the number of clubs being carried, often more than 15. A circular bag large enough to accommodate this number of clubs was becoming barrel-sized and cumbersome. Oval or flat-shaped bags were easier to carry while walking four to five miles per round.

Collecting Bags

So far, the collecting of golf bags has been primarily for the display of old clubs. The criteria for aesthetic display include good preservation of the leather, the ability to stand upright, size—usually the smaller the better—and completeness of straps and accessories. Leather has a tendency to begin to rot after 50 years, especially when not conditioned with oil on a regular basis. The most prevalent problem with most old bags is that the carrying strap or its fixtures have broken. If they can stand upright, they can still be used for static display. But a complete bag is more desirable and will be worth more over time.

Wicker bags were popular circa 1900. Original examples are quite scarce and bring prices between $600 and $1,200. Be careful when purchasing, as there are several good reproductions that were made during the 1970s and 1980s.

Desirability

In order of importance, collectors should seek these varieties of golf bags. Values are approximate.

CLOTH SACK OR CLUB COVER
PRE-1900. $500-$1,500
This earliest of all golf bags is very scarce.

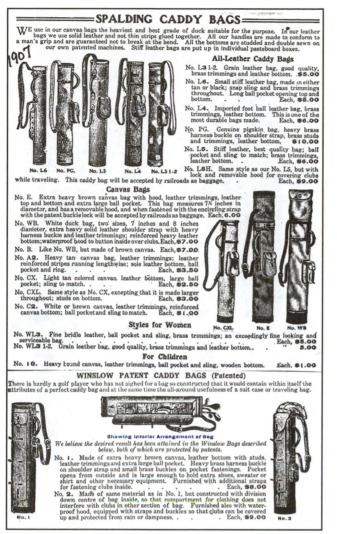

An all-leather "Quiver" bag ranges from 3" to 5" sizes.

Examples extant today show they were usually made of brown sack cloth or canvas, finished at the opening and stenciled with the owner's initials.

EARLY CLOTH BAG

CIRCA 1890-1900.   **$200-$600**

This type of bag was usually fitted with leather around the opening and at the base. They were fitted with one small ball pocket, a cinch strap, a carrying handle, and a shoulder strap that was so lightweight it indicated that this sort of bag only carried six or seven clubs at most. Many early bags were made without stays to keep the barrel rigid, similar to the old cloth club cover.

THE "QUIVER" BAG

CIRCA 1895-1925.

3" BAGS, ALL LEATHER	$300-$800
4" BAGS, ALL LEATHER	$150-$400
4" BAGS, CANVAS TRIMMED WITH LEATHER	$75-$250
5" BAGS, ALL LEATHER	$125-$350
5" BAGS, CANVAS TRIMMED WITH LEATHER	$50-$200

This is the quintessential wood shafted golf club bag stereotypically included in any graphical representation of old golf. Smallest was the 3" bag. Most common was the 4 3/4" diameter bag. Relative age can often be seen in the size and style of pockets, the quality of straps and closure devices, rain/dust hood, metal base reinforcements, the use of side stays, and decorative additions. These bags were popular for many years and it is often difficult to tell the age of the bag from its workmanship alone.

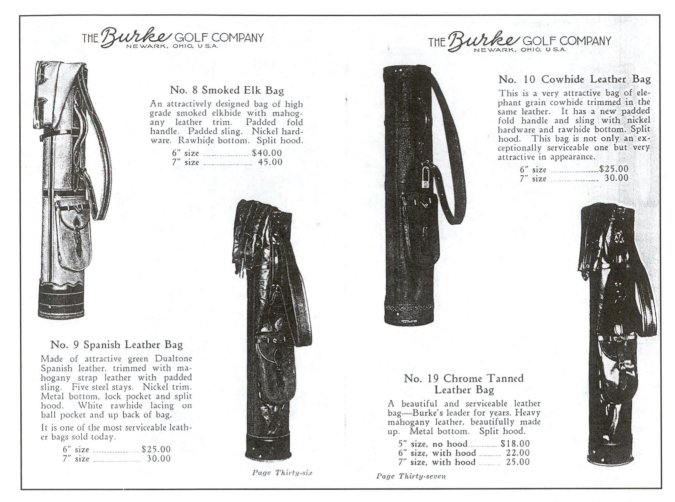

THE Burke GOLF COMPANY
NEWARK, OHIO, U.S.A.

No. 8 Smoked Elk Bag

An attractively designed bag of high grade smoked elkhide with mahogany leather trim. Padded fold handle. Padded sling. Nickel hardware. Rawhide bottom. Split hood.

6" size $40.00
7" size 45.00

No. 9 Spanish Leather Bag

Made of attractive green Dualtone Spanish leather, trimmed with mahogany strap leather with padded sling. Five steel stays. Nickel trim. Metal bottom, lock pocket and split hood. White rawhide lacing on ball pocket and up back of bag.

It is one of the most serviceable leather bags sold today.

6" size $25.00
7" size 30.00

Page Thirty-six

THE Burke GOLF COMPANY
NEWARK, OHIO, U.S.A.

No. 10 Cowhide Leather Bag

This is a very attractive bag of elephant grain cowhide trimmed in the same leather. It has a new padded fold handle and sling with nickel hardware and rawhide bottom. Split hood. This bag is not only an exceptionally serviceable one but very attractive in appearance.

6" size $25.00
7" size 30.00

No. 19 Chrome Tanned Leather Bag

A beautiful and serviceable leather bag—Burke's leader for years. Heavy mahogany leather, beautifully made up. Metal bottom. Split hood.

5" size, no hood $18.00
6" size, with hood 22.00
7" size, with hood 25.00

Page Thirty-seven

LARGE DIAMETER CIRCULAR BAG
CIRCA LATE 1910s AND 1920s ONWARD.

6" BAGS, FULL LEATHER **$100-$300**
6" BAGS, CANVAS TRIMMED WITH LEATHER **$40-$175**
7" BAGS, FULL LEATHER **$90-$250**
7"-8" BAGS, CANVAS TRIMMED WITH LEATHER **$30-$125**

These larger bags reflect the increase in the number of clubs carried. Bags came in 6", 7", and 8" diameter sizes. Other details reflect on the quality of the bag when new. Different grades of leather were used in leather bags. At the upper end were materials like smoked elk hide and stiffer bag leathers. Softer kid leather and suede were good. Canvas or duck were usually at the lower end of the price range, although the tartan plaid canvas was the most expensive of the cloth bags.

The J. Goudie Company of Glasgow (purchased by Leyland, Birmingham Rubber Company in 1920), a factory for golf equipment as early as the 1870s, was another pioneer in the manufacture of golf bags. Goudie was the first company to utilize the "zipp fastener" (zipper) in a golf bag, about 1925, and the oval shaped bag in about 1930.

Good quality bags had features like a wooden reinforcement plate in the bottom, a lock on the ball pocket flap and hood, a blocked or double blocked ball pocket, and decorative leather trimming. Approximate values of these bags—**$50-$150**.

Many whole bags and portions of golf bags were granted patents. Unusual patent bags include bags wider at the base than the top to provide more stability while standing, bags with spikes or supports to give similar stability, and bags with uniquely shaped pockets and club holding accessories.

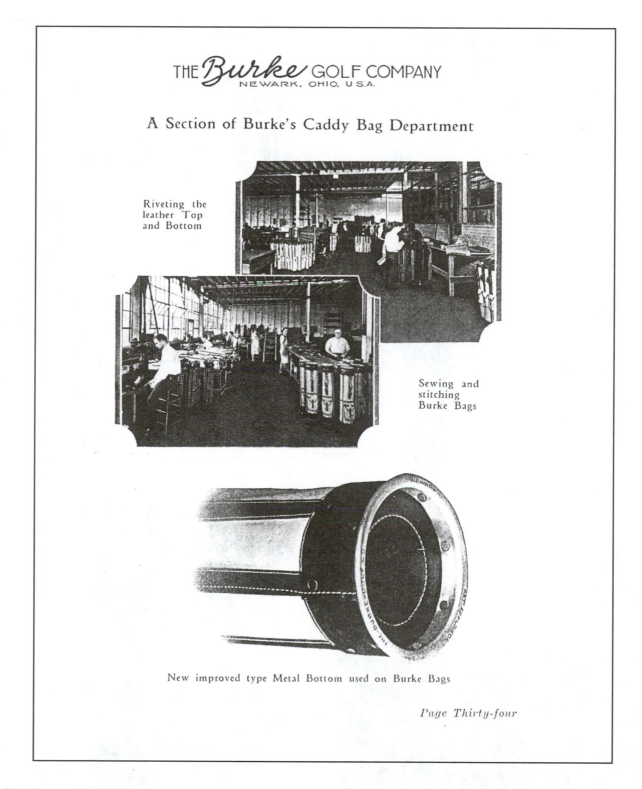

THE *Burke* GOLF COMPANY
NEWARK, OHIO, U.S.A.

A Section of Burke's Caddy Bag Department

Riveting the leather Top and Bottom

Sewing and stitching Burke Bags

New improved type Metal Bottom used on Burke Bags

Page Thirty-four

CLUB CARRIERS

A second group of club-carrying devices includes all items not classified as golf bags. There are dozens of these implements including club caddie stands, club holders, straps, stands, rings, and satchels.

AUTOMATIC CADDIES

In the 1890s and early 1900s, several inventors tried to perfect a golf bag with bipod legs in an effort to dispense with the services of a caddie. Most sought-after of this variety of carrier equipment is Osmond's Patent. It is

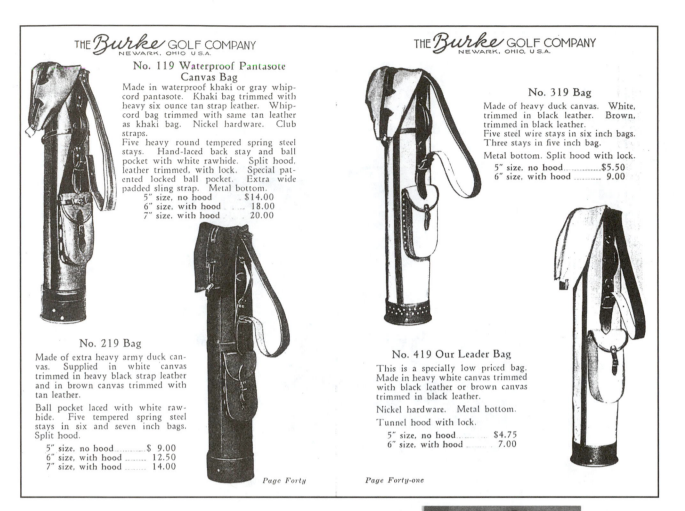

THE *Burke* GOLF COMPANY
NEWARK, OHIO U.S.A.

No. 119 Waterproof Pantasote Canvas Bag

Made in waterproof khaki or gray whipcord pantasote. Khaki bag trimmed with heavy six ounce tan strap canvas. Whipcord bag trimmed with same tan leather as khaki bag. Nickel hardware. Club straps.

Five heavy round tempered spring steel stays. Hand-laced back stay and ball pocket with white rawhide. Split hood. leather trimmed, with lock. Special patented locked ball pocket. Extra wide padded sling strap. Metal bottom.

5" size, no hood		$14.00
6" size, with hood		18.00
7" size, with hood		20.00

No. 219 Bag

Made of extra heavy army duck canvas. Supplied in white canvas trimmed in heavy black strap leather and in brown canvas trimmed with tan leather.

Ball pocket laced with white rawhide. Five tempered spring steel stays in six and seven inch bags. Split hood.

5" size, no hood		$ 9.00
6" size, with hood		12.50
7" size, with hood		14.00

Page Forty

THE *Burke* GOLF COMPANY
NEWARK, OHIO, U.S.A.

No. 319 Bag

Made of heavy duck canvas. White, trimmed in black leather. Brown, trimmed in black leather.

Five steel wire stays in six inch bags. Three stays in five inch bag.

Metal bottom. Split hood with lock.

5" size, no hood		$5.50
6" size, with hood		9.00

No. 419 Our Leader Bag

This is a specially low priced bag. Made in heavy white canvas trimmed with black leather or brown canvas trimmed in black leather.

Nickel hardware. Metal bottom.

Tunnel hood with lock.

5" size, no hood		$4.75
6" size, with hood		7.00

Page Forty-one

the most widely known, but there are another half dozen of similar age and stature that appeal to collectors.

OSMOND'S PATENT	$700-$2,000
OTHERS - SIMILAR	$500-$1,500

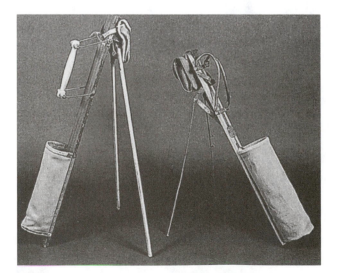

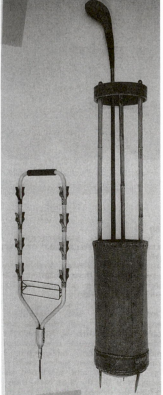

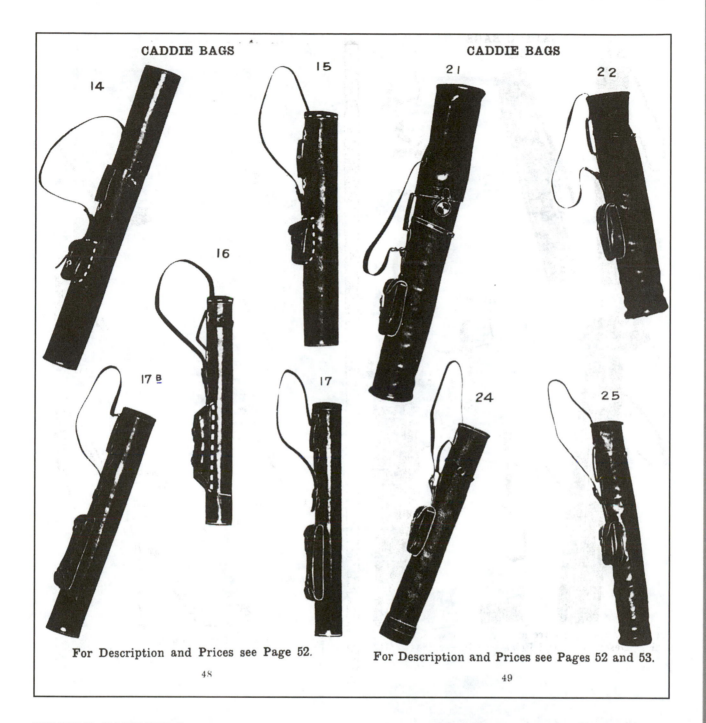

CADDIE BAGS

14 15 16 17 B 17

For Description and Prices see Page 52.

48

CADDIE BAGS

21 22 24 25

For Description and Prices see Pages 52 and 53.

49

SIMPLE CARRIERS

Another variety of carrier was a simple hand grip with brackets for a half dozen clubs. It usually consisted of a handle with clips to hold clubs by their shafts. The hand grip took the form of a leather handle, a strap or wood bar.

CLUB STANDS

Club stands catered to the golfer who never saw the need for a bag and continued to carry clubs under his arm. When making a shot, instead of laying clubs in the fairway grass, a stand kept the grips in the air, avoiding dampness. Several types of spiked stands were sold. The golfer would stick the pointed end in the ground and rest the club handles in a retaining bar or ring. Another such device was a three-legged tripod, which supported clubs much as soldiers stacked muskets.

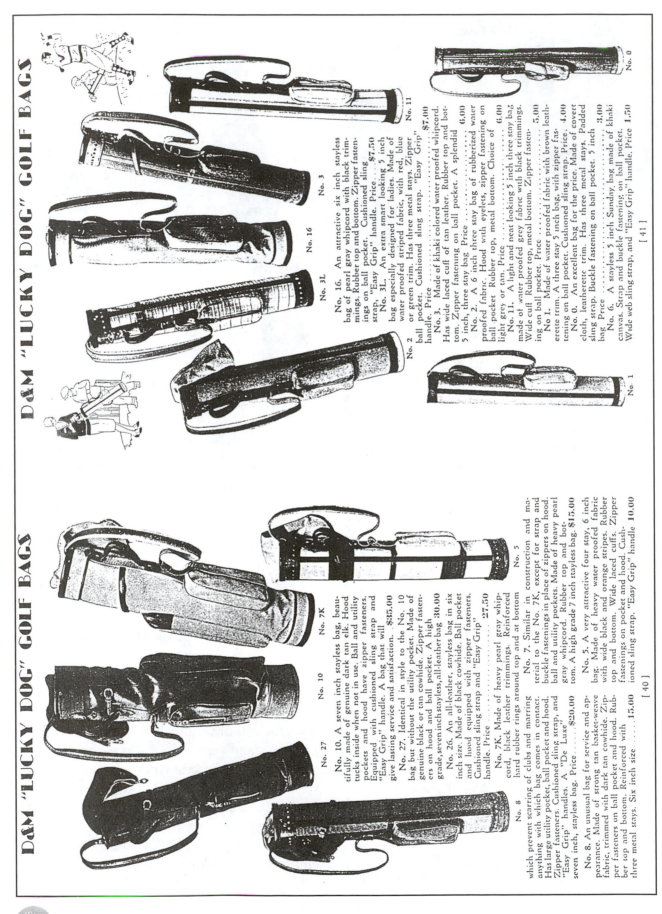

D&M "LUCKY DOG" GOLF BAGS

which prevent scarring of clubs and marring anything with which bag comes in contact. Has large utility pocket, ball pocket and hood. Zipper fasteners. Cushioned sling strap, and "Easy Grip" handles. A "De Luxe" seven inch, stayless bag. Price.....$20.00

No. 8. An unusual bag for service and appearance. Made of strong tan basket-weave fabric, trimmed with dark tan cowhide. Zipper fasteners on ball pocket and hood. Rubber top and bottom. Reinforced with three metal stays. Six inch size.....15.00

No. 10. A seven inch stayless bag, beautifully made of genuine dark tan elk. Hood tucks inside when not in use. Ball and utility pockets and hood have zipper fasteners. Equipped with cushioned sling strap and "Easy Grip" handle. A bag that will give lasting service and satisfaction. $35.00

No. 27. Identical in style to the No. 10 bag but without the utility pocket. Made of genuine black or tan cowhide. Zipper fasteners on hood and ball pocket. A high grade, seven inch stayless, all-leather bag .30.00

No. 26. An all-leather, stayless bag in six inch size. Made of black cowhide. Ball pocket and hood equipped with zipper fasteners. Cushioned sling strap and "Easy Grip" handle. Price 27.50

No. 7K. Made of heavy pearl gray whipcord, black leather trimmings. Reinforced hard rubber rings around top and at bottom

No. 7. Similar in construction and material to the No. 7K, except for strap and buckle fastenings in place of zippers on hood, ball and utility pockets. Made of heavy pearl gray whipcord. Rubber top and bottom. A high grade 7 inch stayless bag. $15.00

No. 5. A very attractive four stay, 6 inch bag. Made of heavy water proofed fabric with wide black and orange stripes. Rubber top and bottom. Wide laced cuffs. Zipper fastenings on pocket and hood. Cushioned sling strap, "Easy Grip" handle 10.00

[40]

D&M "LUCKY DOG" GOLF BAGS

No. 16. An attractive six inch stayless bag of pearl gray whipcord with black trimmings. Rubber top and bottom. Zipper fastenings on ball pocket. Cushioned sling strap, "Easy Grip" handle. Price.....$7.50

No. 3L. An extra smart looking 5 inch bag especially designed for ladies. Made of water proofed striped fabric, with red, blue or green trim. Has three metal stays. Zipper ball pocket. Cushioned sling strap. "Easy Grip" handle. Price $7.00

No. 3. Made of khaki colored water proofed whipcord. Has wide laced cuff of tan leather. Rubber top and bottom. Zipper fastening on ball pocket. A splendid 5 inch, three stay bag Price 6.00

No. 2. A 6 inch three stay bag of rubberized water proofed fabric. Hood with eyelets, zipper fastening on ball pocket Rubber top, metal bottom. Choice of light grey or tan. Price 6.00

No. 11. A light and neat looking 5 inch three stay bag made of water proofed grey fabric with black trimmings. Wide cuff Rubber top, metal bottom. Zipper fastening on ball pocket. Price 5.00

No. 1. Made of water proofed fabric with brown leatherette trim. A three stay 5 inch bag, with zipper fastening on ball pocket. Cushioned sling strap. Price 4.00

No. 0. An excellent bag for the price. Made of covert cloth, leatherette trim. Has three metal stays. Padded sling strap. Buckle fastening on ball pocket. 5 inch bag Price 3.00

No. 6. A stayless 5 inch Sunday, bag made of khaki canvas. Strap and buckle fastening, on ball pocket. Wide web sling strap, and "Easy Grip" handle. Price 1.50

[41]

Chapter 17

How And Where To Purchase Golf Collectibles

There are several antique golf stores: one at the Lodge, Pebble Beach, Calif.; Scottsdale, Ariz.; and Cincinnati, Ohio, as well as others scattered about the U.S. You can make an appointment to visit the author's offices where you can browse through thousands of wood shaft clubs and other collectibles. Jeff Ellis, Leo Kelly, and George Lewis would also welcome you on an appointment basis.

Gatherings of golf associations and societies are where collectors meet to buy, sell, and exhibit their collectibles. The Golf Collector's Society and British Golf Collectors Society have numerous meetings, swap, and trade shows, as well as tournaments where golf with hickory shafted clubs is played.

The BGCS' best attended gathering is during the British Open. "Boot" sales, hickory tournaments, and breaking bread together are the highlights.

The GCS has its national annual meeting in the fall and approximately 500 members gather to play golf with hickories, buy, sell and trade collectibles, attend the annual dinner, and generally have a great time meeting and making friends.

The GCS is divided into 10 regions and, usually, each region has at least one meeting each year. For example, Region 4, (Texas, Oklahoma, New Mexico, Arkansas, and Louisiana) has its annual hickory tournament, show/sale, and dinner in the spring of every year in Irving, Texas. For the convenience of the collectors, Chuck Furjanic, Inc. also holds a major live auction sale that same weekend. About 100 collectors and dealers attend the two events.

ACQUIRING THROUGH AUCTIONS

Auctions are another source to acquire collectibles, but the "Buyer Beware" adage is in force here. You either must be very knowledgeable or have someone knowledgeable represent you at these sales.

* Consigned items should be in the auctioneer's hands at least 60 days ....prior to the sale. Proper cataloguing, photographs, printing, and mailing the catalogues takes time.

* There may be charges to the consignor for unsold lots (listing fees), photography, insurance, and storage.

* Settlement for payment of sold lots is usually between 30 and 45 days after the sale closes. Items must to be paid for and shipped, and items returned may be sent to under bidders. Payments to consignors from a CFI sale average 31 days after the sale.

* Depending upon the arrangements made with the auction company, sales may be credited towards purchase of items in that auction. This is a convenient way for the collector to sell duplicates and acquire items for their collection without the exchange of funds.

KNOW MORE THAN THE ANTIQUE DEALER

One of the most frequently asked questions from beginning collectors who purchased the previous editions of my book was: "Where can these items be purchased?" Most collectors and curious golfers begin with garage sales, flea markets, and antique stores. Unless you are very knowledgeable, you will be disappointed with your purchases. People selling items at garage sales, flea markets, and antique stores usually have very limited knowledge or enough to be dangerous to you, the beginner.

I get e-mail and phone inquiries by the hundreds telling me of items touted as very rare, owned by "Walter Hagen" or "Gene Sarazen" and, especially, Robert T. Jones Jr. clubs with coated steel shafts being offered as hickory shafted clubs.

Make sure the seller has indisputable documentation (provenance or pedigree) to accompany collectibles allegedly to have been the property of a famous golfer. There are many misrepresented Arnold Palmer, Jack Nicklaus, Bobby Jones, Gene Sarazen, etc., items being offered at lofty prices. One of the most common is the "Calamity Jane Putter" that Bobby Jones made so famous. I am offered one of the "Original Six" 10 to 15 times a year! And to my knowledge, Arnold Palmer has never sold or given any of his putters to anyone. Yet, I get calls and inquiries on a regular basis saying his putters are being offered for sale.

Unless you like being taken advantage of, you should first join a golf collector's association or society, buy a good reference book, see the Bibliography, and contact the contributors. Then, when you are armed with more knowledge than the garage sale, flea market, and antique store merchants, you can start having some fun.

ORDERING FROM MAIL ORDER CATALOGUES

The most logical sources would be dealers, like myself, who publish catalogues on a regular basis. Jeff Ellis and I are the only club and ball dealers publishing catalogues on a regular basis. Ellis publishes three or four yearly, while I publish monthly. Leo Kelly, Old Chicago Golf Shop, is on the World Wide Web. George Lewis, Golfiana, publishes two or three extensive book catalogues a year, and there are several dealer/collectors who send lists periodically.

Furjanic, Ellis, and Lewis are among the most respected authorities in the hobby and treat customers with respect, answer their inquiries and offer return privileges on all items. You can order confidently from these dealers as they are committed to the hobby and to the clients they serve.

Chuck Furjanic, Inc., Old Tom Morris, LLC, Christie's, Bonham's, Bob Gowland's International Golf Auctions, Mullock & Madeley, and Pacific Books conduct live auctions on a regular basis. There are several dealers and collectors who conduct mail sales.

The catalogues are very helpful to the bidder, whether a beginner or expert. Estimates, indicating the range between wholesale and retail, are listed for each lot. Good descriptions, items rated using the 10 point grading standards, and numerous photos of the collectibles offered aid the collector to submit bids confidently.

The biggest advantages in buying at auction is attending the live sales and actually being able to view and handle a vast assortment of collectibles, from all areas of the sport, in one place. Rare and seldom offered collectibles are more likely to be offered through major auctions than through dealer listings, Internet or shows. You will also be able to meet and consult with experts and other collectors in attendance. The value of hands-on viewing and inspecting the collectibles, meeting and making new friends with your same interests, and acquiring items at your price, can be one of the most rewarding experiences of your life.

Buying over the Internet can be costly and dangerous to your collecting health. If you must use the Internet, buy from established dealers you know and trust, or who are recommended to you by dealers or collectors you trust. I put the Internet, and Internet auctions, in the same category as garage sales, flea markets, and antique stores. Know more than the seller or do not buy.

SELLING THROUGH AUCTIONS

Auctions are a convenient vehicle for dealers and collectors to sell their collectibles. Established auction houses have extensive mailing lists of clients to whom your collectibles will be exposed, hopefully generating top dollar and fair market value. Most auction houses follow similar guidelines.

Seller's fees range from 5 percent to 20 percent, depending upon the value of the consignment and the value of individual lots.

Selling items personally and depositing funds (conducting business) will require you to file IRS Schedule "C" (Profit or Loss from business). If you make sales to buyers within your own state (and your state has a sales tax law), you must have a license to collect sales tax.

Unless you are prepared to accept the responsibilities of running your own business, (selling through the Internet is just that), it's best to leave auctioning to the experts.

SELLING THROUGH INTERNET AUCTIONS

There are numerous Internet auctions through which you may list and sell your items, many without a fee. Keep in mind, the Internet auction companies only provide the vehicle to offer your collectibles and inform you of the high bidders. You are responsible for collecting the money, being sure the funds are "good" (many bidders want to pay by credit card or with personal checks), physically shipping the items and being prepared for damage to the collectibles while en route. You must also make provisions for returns if your high bidder is not satisfied.

Thanks to Bob Gowland, International Golf Auctions, Chester, England, for contributing information that has been incorporated in this article.

Bob Kuntz, co-founder of the Golf Collectors Society, and Paul Wood inspect clubs.

GOLF COLLECTOR SOCIETIES AND ORGANIZATIONS

No one likes to collect alone. Collectors want to hear from others with their same interest, meet, talk, and show off their prized possessions. One way to meet others is to join an organization or society. Here we will list three that provide a printed bulletin or newsletter for their members.

Welcome to the Golf Collectors Society!

By Tom Kuhl, former Editor of the Bulletin, GCS Newsletter

Any new collector of golf memorabilia (or antiques in general) will eventually come to the point where he or she will seek broader horizons, to branch out, to meet other people who share the same enthusiasm for the game and its various artifacts. Golf collectors have been around for many years, long before the game arrived in America, but they were always scattered hither and yon and never organized. A famous early collector was Harry Wood, an Englishman from Manchester who wrote the masterpiece on collecting, *Golf Curios and the Like*, in 1911, now a valuable item in any golf book collector's library. Other early prominent golf collectors of the 20th century include Alex Findlay, O.M. Leland, Jack Level, and Otto Probst. They, and others like them, shared an intense passion for the memorabilia of the game, but not until 1970 was an official body of golf collectors organized under the title of the Golf Collectors Society.

It began with a small band of 27 collectors in September 1970. On the 25th anniversary of the Golf Collectors Society (GCS) in 1995, there were more than 2,200 members in the United States, with nearly 200 others from all parts of the golfing globe. The largest foreign contingent is from the United Kingdom and Canada, with other members from Japan, Taiwan, Australia, South Africa, continental Europe, and a dozen or so other nations.

From the very start, and on into the present day, the purpose of the GCS is: *To serve as a means of getting golf collectors together...To establish friendships between those who share a love of the game...And to facilitate the exchange of information about collecting and the game.* Founded in 1970 by J. Robert Kuntz of Dayton, Ohio, and Joseph Murdoch of Philadelphia, the GCS remains a not-for-profit fraternal organization.

GCS members collect all golf memorabilia from A to Z. Some specialize in old hickory-shafted clubs, or even earlier valuable long-nose playclubs from the mid-19th century. Others might collect balls, books, ceramics and artwork, medals, old tees and ephemera, early magazines and tournament programs, or maybe just modern era putters only, or a varied combination of all the numerous collecting categories...and a whole lot more!

While some members might specialize in collecting items as small as ball markers or scorecards, there are others who own museum quality collections of the highest caliber. And speaking of museums, the curators of all the world's great golf museums are GCS members as well, including the USGA's Golf House; the R&A Museum at St. Andrews; the James River (Va.) CC Museum, the oldest private golf museum in the United States; the Ralph Miller Library and Museum at City of Industry, Calif., named after one of the GCS founding members; and the new World Golf Hall of Fame, near St. Augustine, Fla. All of these people have a mutual love for the game and its artifacts, equally sharing in the express purpose of the Society to bring people together and to exchange memorabilia and information. The fact that several dozen books exist on golf collecting, authored by GCS members, indicates that information on collecting for new and veteran members alike is a highly sought-after commodity.

One of the single most unifying events toward this stated purpose is the regional trade show and Hickory Hacker. Based on membership population density, the GCS has a Board of Directors covering 10 geographical regions. Several times per year, within each region, a GCS gathering of varying size occurs. Generally speaking, it comprises a one- or two-day show where golf memorabilia is bought, sold, traded or just simply exhibited for educational or entertainment purposes. Members enjoy these events if for nothing more than to meet and share their knowledge, ideas, and experiences concerning the game, its artifacts, and treasures.

But the accumulation of knowledge and golf memorabilia is not always the primary focus for many GCS members at these regional meetings. To get out on the golf course and play with the old "weapons of the game" is a fun occasion that members look forward to. In these Hickory Tournaments—or Hickory Hackers, as some like to affectionately refer to them—participants often outfit themselves in the old plus fours (or knickers as they are called here in the U.S.) and play with the old hickory-shafted clubs from the 1920s or earlier. Like Jones, Sarazen, Vardon, Hagen, and all of the early golfers before them, the GCS Hickory Tournament participants go back in time to the days of golf when wood—not steel or graphite—was the shaft that made the ball go "far and sure."

At these regional trade shows—and especially the GCS Annual Meeting in late September or early October at various locales across the country—expect to find any golf collectible your heart desires. The Annual Meeting is by far the largest show, with more than 200 display tables and 500 to 600 collectors commonly in attendance. Among a number of other locations, the following large and long-running regional golf collecting shows annually take place, and all members and collectors, from anywhere in the world, are always invited.

Dayton, Ohio, in January, "Cabin Fever"

USGA, Far Hills, N.J., in the early spring

The Texas gathering in Irving during March or April

A South Florida event in February, and another at Dunedin, usually in March

The Midwest event in Chicago, at Rolling Meadows, in May

Three or four events throughout the year in the Mid Atlantic region, near Washington, D.C.

The Carolinas gathering, at least twice per year

Western meeting, in Southern California in November or December

Heart of America in June, in either Kansas City, Omaha, or Iowa

Two or three Canadian events in the Toronto area

You won't find anyone pitching golf resorts or golf course real estate, and very little of the overpriced and oversized "new stuff" at these shows. Instead, you will find tables full of the old hickory-shafted clubs, common and rare, or the more valuable and unusual implements of the game. Then there are collectible clubs of the more "modern era" of the game, for example, Tommy Armour woods, Pings, and highly collectible Wilson putters from the 1960s. Back to the good old days, you will discover mesh and gutty balls, and usually some pre-1850 featherie balls; early and modern books offered by a number of collectors, as well as recognized golf book dealers; fine old golf pottery, ceramics, jewelry, and the like; long out-of-print golf magazines, hard-to-find autographs, medals, and much, much more. As our GCS co-founder, Joe Murdoch, has stated time and again when talking about the regional and Annual Meeting trade shows: "If you think you have seen everything there is in golf, you'll be pleasantly surprised to see something new and different at the trade show."

Each GCS member receives our newsletter, The Bulletin, on a quarterly basis. Articles include golf history, featured collections and collectors, golf book reviews, patent information, unusual clubs and artifacts, current golf auction news and results, and coverage of GCS Regional Events. It also has a small classified ad section, where members are offered buy/sell/trade opportunities.

Members also receive an annual Membership Directory issued in the first quarter of the year. Among the address, telephone and e-mail numbers, vital collecting interests of each individual member are identified. The Director of the Golf Collectors Society is Karen Bednarski.

Golf Collectors Society

PO Box 3103
Ponte Vedra Beach, FL 32004-3103
(904) 825-2191

THE GOLF CLUB HISTORICAL SOCIETY OF CANADA

555 Eastern Avenue
Toronto, Ontario, Canada, M4M 1C8
Tel. (416) 465-8844

The Golf Historical Society of Canada was formed in 1988 when four founding members reasoned that there must be other souls who share a love of golf and the game's rich heritage. Today, this collective helps members indulge in their passion for golf history, its artifacts and treasures.

A quarterly bulletin is published covering a wide range of member interests. Trade shows are organized so that members can share their knowledge and build their collec-

tions of golf books, trophies, clubs and memorabilia. Special interest is placed on the preservation of Canadian golf history and traditions. A spring and fall "Hickory Hacker" golf tournament is held and many sets of restored wooden-shafted clubs are once again helping their owners enjoy the "Grand Ould Gayme."

The British Golf Collectors Society

The British Golf Collectors Society exists to promote an interest in the history of golf and the collecting of items connected with that history. The Society journal, Through The Green, is published quarterly and distributed to some 460 members who reside in the U.K. and in 17 overseas countries, including 80 members in the U.S. It contains articles of historical interest and collecting topics.

The Society has three major golfing meetings: President's Day at the Royal Liverpool G.C., Hoylake, in May; The Scottish Hickory Championship, in which wooden-shafted clubs must be used, at Gullane near Muirfield, in May; and The Open Championship meeting at a course (usually one of the Open qualifying courses) in the vicinity of the Open on the Wednesday before it starts. There are also a number of regional meetings and the Society regularly fields a team, in period dress and playing with wooden-shafted clubs, in matches associated with the Centenary celebrations of clubs.

Contact address: The Hon. Secretary, BGCS, PO Box 13704, North Berwick, East Lothian, Scotland EH39 4ZB.

Chapter 18

Collecting Golf Memorabilia
A Collector's Personal View

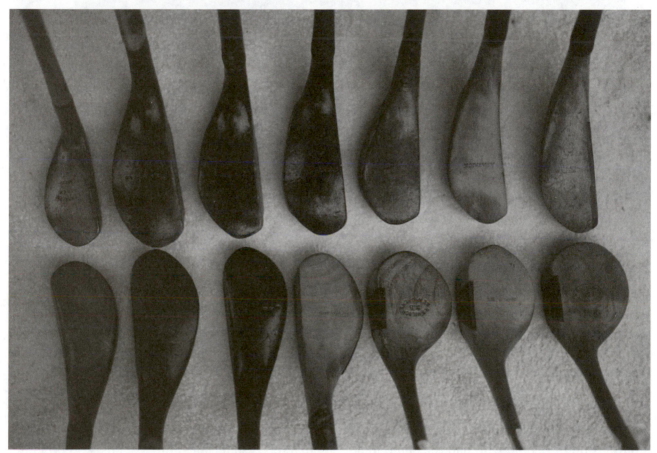

An assortment of wooden head golf clubs dates from 1880 to 1900.

By Johnny Henry

I've known Johnny Henry for nearly 15 years. He can still shoot his age (75) with steel or hickory clubs, has a fine collection of golf artifacts, and has just about the finest collection of golf related memories and friends of anyone I know. A book on collecting golf would not be complete without including his impressions.

People frequently ask me when I started collecting old golf items, and I always reply, "I don't know, but I was collecting for a long time before I knew it." Golf has been a large part of my life since I started playing at age 6 (in 1933) with a set of Spalding juvenile, hickory-shafted clubs. Since then, I have been involved with golf-oriented occupations: Toro turf equipment salesman, golf course irrigation designer, PGA professional, golf archi-

A display cabinet filled with porcelain, glass, and silver golf collectibles shows off a collection.

tect, and greenskeeper. Over the years, the opportunity had arisen to probe for clubs at the various golf courses and I had amassed some 18 to 20 hickory clubs. Then, in 1975, my wife gave me a golf trip to Scotland for an anniversary gift, and that was a serious mistake! While on the trip, I met Ken Smith (GCS #0076); he suggested I join the Golf Collectors Society, which was then just a small group of people who had the same interests as us.

Before Phillips, Christie's, and Sotheby's auction houses began to have golf sales about 1980, it was possible to ferret out collectible clubs from individuals-retired professionals, widows, caddies, "boot sales," as well as thrift shops and pros at old courses in Great Britain. This was the "fun era" of collecting.

While touring the various courses in Scotland and England, I would find pros who would have a few hickories on the wall or back in the club storage area that were for sale. In many cases, they would also give me leads as to where I might find clubs in the area.

Sadly, those days are gone forever. With headlines in the London Times reading "GOLF CLUB MAKES RECORD PRICE AT SOTHEBY'S SALE," the public became reluctant to sell for fear the old clubs in their possession were worth more than this "Colonist" was offering to pay. Other than flea markets, estate sales, thrift shops, and other collectors, probably the best source is purchasing items from dealers. They attend auctions here in the U.S. and in the U.K. to maintain inventories of items we all look for.

My collection, while modest in quantity (240 clubs), is adequate in quality. It consists of 25 long-nose clubs, including a Philp and an 18th century play club made by a bow and spear maker. I also have most of the patent clubs such as the Cran, Seely, spring face, Lard whistler, anti-shank irons, Mills aluminum clubs, along with a giant niblick, tran-

Hand-painted ceramics and china are some of the most sought after golf collectibles.

sitional woods, bulger scares, and deep-grooved irons. There are about 50 putters including: a Calamity Jane, Gassiat, Schenectady, a Kismet with rollers on sole, Ivora Perfection, and various blade and Mills putters.

My collection of balls includes two featheries, 20 gutties, and about 100 wound balls with different markings.

Scattered about in my golf room are various miscellaneous items relating to golf, including pottery by Doulton, O'Hare, Carlton, Wedgwood, Weller, and others. There are also silver and gold medals, silver hat pins, spoons, and glass items by Cambridge and Steuben. My library has about 150 books, none of which are "classic" volumes, but those that I like to read.

This room is an excellent place to relax after a hard day on the links. While sipping a beverage, I can scan the walls, and each club has a story behind it. I can remember where I

was, from whom it was acquired, and the circumstances and haggling that transpired. Collecting memories, making friends, and reminiscing are as important to me as the collection itself. It's amazing how close a bond exists among people with a common interest.

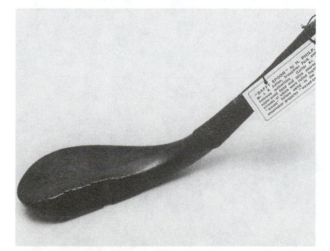

A Baffie Spoon was made by the legendary Hugh Philp in St. Andrews between 1840 and 1855.

A wonderful den display includes a St. Andrews Captain's jacket as the centerpiece.

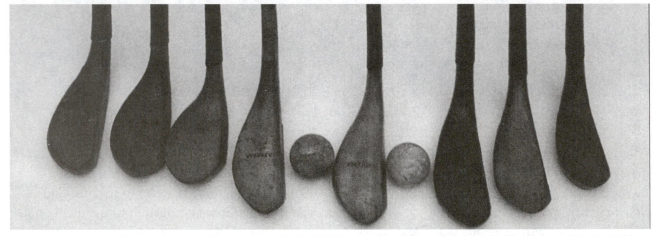

An assortment of long-nose clubs, circa 1840-1890, surround two feather balls, circa 1840-1860.

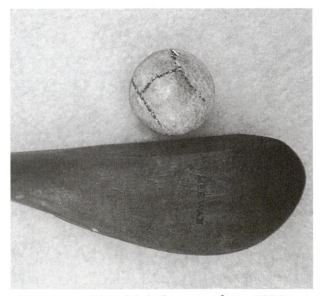

A McEwan Play Club dates to about 1800.

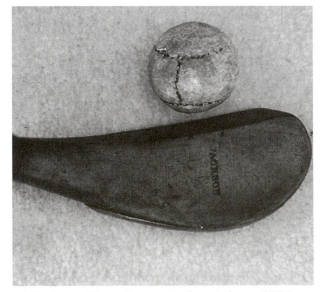

A Jackson Short Spoon is from about 1825.

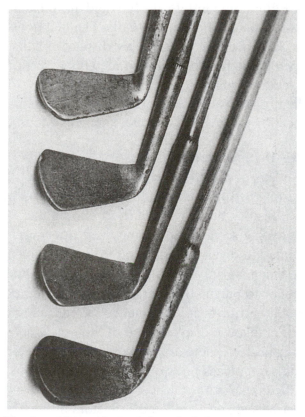

Blacksmith-made iron-head clubs were in use prior to 1875.

Smooth gutta-percha balls date to the 1850s.

Line cut gutta-percha balls were made in 1885-1900.

These are two of the cornerstone books of a collector's library, The Life of Tom Morris, and Golf - A Royal And Ancient Game.

Hand-painted Daulton ceramics are quite scarce.

The sand tee box dates this painting to near 1900.

An early depiction of St. Andrews, from the Road Hole (No. 17), is by Thomas Hodge, 1881.

Collecting Pre-1875 Golf Artifacts

By Will Roberto

Will Roberto, attorney at law, is a long-time collector who specializes in pre-1875 golf collectibles and artifacts. Roberto has kindly outlined this era.

Pre-1875 golf artifacts are very scarce and seldom offered at auction or private sale. The few examples known are in museums, clubhouse displays, and in several advanced collectors' hands. The USGA at Far Hills, N.J., has an outstanding display of long-nose and early hammer-forged iron head clubs. In St. Andrews, Scotland, there is a museum, and in the Royal & Ancient Club House, the Members Room is adorned by many golfing artifacts. Historical courses such as Royal Liverpool, Prestwick, and The Royal Company of Edinburgh Golfers at Muirfield, have extensive displays of clubs and balls. The clubhouse at Gullane has an outstanding display of balls, one of which is the "Map of the Globe" ball. Archie Baird also has a small museum next to the pro shop at Gullane where, by appointment, Dr. Baird will conduct a personal tour.

Pre-1875 Artifacts

This period of collecting covers the era starting in 1457 - a span of nearly 420 years of golf history-but is really a short blip on the collecting scene. Golf during these times was limited to royalty, clergy, and the wealthy businessmen, as only the affluent had the time and money to pursue the sport. Most of the highest quality artifacts are impounded in museums and clubhouse displays, and of those available to collectors, there are many below average or damaged pieces not worth having in a serious collection. As a result, very few quality collectibles are available and collectors diligently seek them when offered privately or at public auction.

The recent auction of the Thistle Club memorabilia pushed ephemera prices to an all time high. Some of the earliest scorecards, notebooks, and letters have since been sold at more than twice the auction prices, as collectors have realized these one-of-a-kind historical items are just as collectible as early clubs, balls, and medals. These are "history" in the hand of those unknown players who kept the game alive when it almost died out in the early 1800s in Scotland.

Golf Clubs

During this era, very few iron-head clubs were marked with manufacturers' identification and they are difficult to date and authenticate. Wooden-head clubs were usually marked with the maker's name, but use, abuse, refinishing, and repair render many unidentifiable, some not worthy of an advanced collection. With these items, accurate provenance or opinions from experts would be the only way a collector could feel comfortable before and after acquisition. There are about 50 major collectors worldwide and a few dealers who concentrate on pre-1875 memorabilia. They could be good sources for identification, dating and authentication. Elsewhere in this book is mention of the Golf Collectors Society and other worldwide organizations that can supply names of experts.

Since the previous edition of this book, current scholarship has advanced the push that the earliest known golf clubs currently in major collections are the spur toe irons, which are light and heavy irons. These clubs date to the 17th century. There are also several wooden clubs, which may be late 17th century but are most certainly of early 18th century vintage. As these clubs have no makers' names or marks, and only limited provenance to assist in dating, the collector golf historian must rely on the crudeness of manufacture, larger size as compared to clubs of a more certain vintage, and written references describing clubs such as these earliest bludgeons, as they are indeed massive tools of the game. They appear to have several generations of design advancement among the few known examples, which only the most expert eye can notice.

Several new theories about wooden clubhead sizes and shapes have been advanced. Foremost among these is that due to the difficulty of travel in the earliest days of the game (50 miles was considered a long trip), many seaside makers of woods and irons never saw what their inland counterparts were producing unless a traveling player was in town for a game or needed a repair. Sometimes the differences were no doubt adopted by the repairer or maker seeing the idea for the first time. The theory as propounded is that inland makers, due to the firmer soils of inland "greens," made wood clubs that had larger, heavier heads characterized by thicker necks and deeper faces. The early coastal clubmakers, such as Philp & McEwan, made smaller, more delicate heads for use on the softer links land such as St. Andrews, Leith links and Musselburgh. Early irons, being "trouble clubs," have not shown such a difference whether made by early inland or seaside makers. They tended to be stout and heavy clubs used to extricate featheries and early gutties from the worst of lies.

The most difficult to obtain are pre-1800 clubs. There are very few authenticated and properly dated pre-1800 clubs in collector hands. Most of these are wooden-headed clubs, as the early players only carried a few irons for use from trouble lies. There are also some pre-1800 iron putters to be found, but not many.

The period from 1800 to 1850 provides the collector more clubs than the pre-1800 period—most likely based on age and preservation rather than numbers originally manufactured. The numbers of golfers did not vary substantially from 1750 to 1845; in fact, during the period from 1820 to 1845 golf nearly died out in Edinburgh. Robert Forgan wrote in a letter to T. H. Bairnsfather, Feb. 3, 1899, "...there was not work for three men making golf clubs in 1856 when I first went to it..." The attrition rate of pre-1800 artifacts was far greater than clubs from the first half of the 19th century. Again, most of the clubs from the 1800-1850 period in collectors' hands are woods, with a few bunker, rut, and putting irons.

Clubs from the period 1850 to 1875 are somewhat more plentiful but cannot be considered common. Some pre-1875 clubs have a maker's name or mark on them that can help date them.

How can a collector date woods and smoothface irons with or without identifying markings? Many wood clubs were marked with the maker's name and sometimes with his mark. Reference books listing known makers can help place a "McEwan," "Philp" or "Jackson" stamped club in a probable time period by size and shape of the stamping and general overall construction of the head and neck.

Many uninformed collectors assume unmarked irons are rare. Most clubs forged in the 1880s and early 1890s were made to look like the old style but were imprinted with the maker's name or mark. Caddies used "Emory" paper to clean rust from the iron heads and, while sanding away the rust, the caddies also sanded away the markings. Rare unmarked irons were usually made by a blacksmith and have a crude hammered appearance, longer hosels, heavier hosel nickings, and usually exhibit forging lines or seams. The hole at the top of the hosel where the shaft is inserted is usually wider in diameter than clubs forged by the post-1885 club maker. Many pre-1875 irons had shafts made of ash, not hickory.

Collectibility of these pre-1875 clubs is determined by quality, provenance, the maker's place relating to the history of the game as a player, maker, or both, and the scarcity of a particular club. A club from 1870 would be far more valuable if the owner could produce a provenance verifying Young Tom Morris used this particular club while winning three British Opens, versus one without provenance probably belonging to a businessman or clergyman.

Balls

As with clubs, pre-1800 balls are scarce. Pre-1860 gutty balls are scarcer than featheries. Named maker balls of both types are even scarcer. Balls with markings on them from this period are among the rarest. There are also a few balls painted for winter play that are highly sought after. While most are red or orange, there have been blue, yellow, and black balls noted.

Early balls continue to be found, with the unusual marked gutties pushing the envelope on auction prices. Marked feather balls by the earliest makers continue to command premium prices and those few of the rarer named featheries rival the gutties.

Early gutty balls were smooth and were hand rolled. The early players realized they flew poorly and marked them by hand using a hammer or knife. (Some gave the smooth spheres to caddies to knock them around before play, rendering them with cuts and marks, thus making their flight more consistent.) Later patterns, such as those made by Forgan, became more common and other makers developed different styles as a form of advertising. Just as club making became more sophisticated, so did ball making.

As golf grew, and with it the demand for balls, heavy iron molds (rare and very collectible) were used to mold and mark the gutta-percha spheres. Various devices to cut patterns in the balls were developed in an attempt to improve the flight of the ball.

Books

Pre-1875 books are very scarce, as few were written. Major titles are Robert Clark, *Golf - A Royal and Ancient Game,* 1875; H.B. Farnie, *A Golfer's Manual,* 1857; Robert Chambers, *A Few Rambling Remarks on Golf,* 1862.

Pre-1875 books have achieved record auction prices in some cases regardless of condition, primarily based on rarity. Easier to come by and equally important are some books published from 1875 to 1910.

Art

Very little pre-1800 art, not already in museums, is available to private collectors and these pieces rarely appear at auctions. There are, however, many fine prints, pieces of sculpture, and paintings being offered from time to time. Also many later generation reproductions of fine quality are available to decorate a collection room.

Several fine pieces of pre-1900 art have sold in the last couple of years. Paintings by J. Michael Brown, Thomas Hodge, Major Hopkins (Shortspoon), and several others have seen record prices achieved.

General

Many important items associated with the game are available. Original letters between players challenging one another are very rare and expensive. Written documents of the game such as rules, scorecards, receipts, club secretary records, and notebooks, occasionally become available.

Clothing, such as the red coats worn by the captains at St. Andrews, leather caps, top hats, tweed waistcoats, and wool plus fours are prized pre-1875 collectibles.

Smoking-pipes with carved golfing scenes, pottery, mugs and beer bottles as well as jewelry, watch fobs, and whiskey flasks are also highly sought after by the historically bound collector.

Clubmaker's tools and maker's die stamps are another avenue as well as feather ball-maker's tools. At an auction in 1989, a complete set of feather ball tools in a wooden case was offered for sale.

Medals

The early clubs and golf societies gave prizes of balls or clubs, a claret of wine, but most often medals. There are numerous medals won by competitors on display at old links such as Muirfield, St. Andrews, Prestwick, and in museums. On occasion, medals are sold through auction and their value determined by the club giving the medal, names of winners thereon, and whether the medal is gold or another metal. Most British-made medals were of 9kt. gold, sterling or bronze.

There have been several good early medals at recent auctions, but they have been few indeed. As expected, those from the earliest clubs have done well.

It is suggested that new collectors contact the many dealers and advanced collectors who can advise and assist in assembling a collection or refining an existing one.

Knowledge in any antique hobby takes years or research and in this hobby it requires

---

SUGGESTIONS FOR A PRE-1875 STARTER COLLECTION

- Long Nose Woods -   T. Morris, Forgan, McEwan, Park
- Blacksmith Irons -   No maker's nameæearly cleeks, lofters, general irons c. 1860 or earlier in any condition are scarce, if not rare.
- Named Irons -   c. 1850-60   by Carrick, Gray
c. 1870s   R. Wilson, W. Wilson, Park, Forgan, Morris, Anderson
Some of the named clubs were made for the seller, often a player or a manufacture of wooden clubs, but are still attractive period pieces.
- Books -   R. Clark Golf A Royal & Ancient Game
John Kirr Golf Book of East Lothian
Alastair Johnston, Chronicle of Golf, 1990
These are cornerstone books for all collectors.
- Art -   Watercolors by Hodge or Hopkins
- Medals -   Any pre-1890 medals from the early clubs
- Balls -   Feather ball, named or unnamed. Smooth gutty, hand hammered gutty, line cut gutty.
- Ceramics -   Pieces that can be dated to pre-1900

many nights of reading old, scarce books (when they can be accessed), or trips to visit private museum collections in the U. S. and abroad.

As thousands of dollars often change hands for sought-after items, subtle variations that shave only a few years off an item's age often mean the difference between a good buy and overpaying. Sometimes these differences are so subtle some of the more sophisticated dealers and collectors miss them due to specialization within the hobby. There are, however, several well-known collectors and dealers with in-depth knowledge willing to help newcomers avoid the heartbreaks. The old doctrine "Caveat Emptor" applies because the well-intentioned adviser could not have been negligent, due to the limited information in the public domain and the difficulty of seeing and handling pieces in museums and private collections because of security concerns.

Even Ex-Presidents Enjoy Golf Collectibles

Former President George Bush visited Montgomery, Ala., on Nov. 8, 1996, and played golf at the Montgomery Country Club. While at the club, President Bush expressed an interest in the golf collectibles on display there. Forrest McConnell, the club's historian, gave the president the grand tour of the collectibles on display in the clubhouse. The president seemed knowledgeable about antique golf artifacts, wooden-shafted golf clubs, and the makers.

On display were several clubs made by Willie Park Sr. and Willie Park Jr. President Bush was keenly aware of the Parks, when and where they made their clubs. He was also keenly aware of their collectible popularity, value, and historical significance in the development of modern-day golf equipment. He was entranced by the long nose putter and rut iron made by Willie Jr. and inspected them closely with the help of McConnell.

The president expressed that he was a student of golf history and has visited many of the old courses in Scotland and England. He is especially fond of the club room at the Royal and Ancient, and the Museum at St. Andrews.

Forrest McConnell is a long-time collector specializing in the history and club making of the Park family. As the historian at Montgomery C.C., Forrest has developed interesting and informative golf displays centering around the Parks. We thank McConnell for sharing the president's visit with our readers.

Former President George H.W. Bush visits with collector Forrest McConnell at the display in the clubhouse at Montgomery (Ala.) Country Club.

Former President Bush inspects a long-nose wood with collector Forrest McConnell.

British Golf Traditions

Prestwick, St. Andrews and..........
Musselburgh: The three course "Rota" for the
British Open from 1872 to 1889

By Keith Foster

Keith Foster is a golf course designer who has two great Texas courses to his credit: The Quarry and Texas Star. He also reconstructed the bunkers and greens at Colonial Country Club, home of the PGA Tour Colonial Invitational Tournament, Ft. Worth, Texas. He is an avid collector and has a particular fascination for pre-1890 left handed long-nose clubs.

All who embrace the wonderful game of golf know that nothing contributes more greatly than the endless variety of courses, shots or conditions. This variety is a very distinct feature of the game. Such variety can be found at golf's hallowed grounds at St. Andrews, Prestwick, and Musselburgh. Most of us are already familiar with St. Andrews, less knowledgeable of Prestwick and have heard little or nothing of Musselburgh. Yet, the three courses were the gold centers of the game within Scotland back in the early, mid, and late 1800s.

St. Andrews, Prestwick, and Musselburgh were golf's big three courses and they formed the Open Rota from 1872 through 1889, while also hosting most of the big matches of the day.

In today's game, it is easy to look at the three courses for what they are not. But rather, to truly appreciate the game and its history, it is far better to look at St. Andrews, Prestwick, and Musselburgh for what they were and still are to the game.

Consider that St. Andrews was once 22 holes, Prestwick was originally 12 holes, while Musselburgh started out as five holes and then pushed out to total nine holes.

The charm of all three courses is the simple truth. There are the holes, play them as you like. That is how the game was intended to be played. Today, we expect courses to fit our games, our talents. This was not the case

with early golf courses, where golfers were to discover and improvise golf shots for a given situation.

Growth Within the Game

While this chapter will look at the three courses more closely, it is helpful to understand how golf courses were maintained then and what helped spread the game within Scotland itself.

Early in the game, the "featherie" was the ball used. Its cost was so high that this alone kept few from enjoying the game, except the well-to-do. But in 1848, the introduction of the gutta-percha ball opened the game to the common man.

The gutta-percha ball also created a rift between Tom Morris and Allan Robertson in St. Andrews. A couple of years later, Tom Morris moved to Prestwick.

As for early golf course maintenance, it should be noted that until the 1860s early golf courses had no real water source. During droughts, the links simply had to weather as best they could. In the 1870s, some courses sunk wells to keep greens moist during extended periods of drought. Around the turn of the century, courses began to introduce primitive watering systems for greens.

The equipment of the day was one's back, a wheelbarrow, shovel, and a spade. Holes were hand cut by a knife to a diameter of 4 1/2", still the standard today. It wasn't until Old Tom put in a lead liner at the soft 7th green at St. Andrews around 1880 that anyone had ever even thought of a cup for the hole in the ground.

The introduction of mechanized equipment to mow turf followed shortly, thereby beginning the quest for improved turf conditions and further grooming of the links.

Musselburgh was a hotbed of golf in the 19th century. Willie Park Jr. and Sr., Douglas McEwan, J.&D. Clark, R. Neilson, Mungo Park and Waggott all had clubmaking businesses there. The Musselburgh links hosted six British Opens from 1874 to 1889.

MUSSELBURGH

Golf in Edinburgh was originally played on Bruntsfield Links or Leith Links. In 1836, overcrowding at Leith Links moved the Honorable Company of Edinburgh Golfers to Musselburgh. Two years later in 1838, the Royal Burgess Society left Bruntfield for the same reason. By 1840, there were four major golfing clubs playing at Musselburgh, making it the golf center of Edinburgh.

With the top four Edinburgh golf clubs now at Musselburgh, Edinburgh, club maker "McEwan" and William Gourlay, the "best ball maker," both set up shops adjacent to the links. Add to this, Musselburgh was the home of Willie Park, the first Open champion in 1860. In its day, Musselburgh had the largest concentration of men skilled in playing, club-making, and ballmaking. This is quite a fact when you consider that Musselburgh was a very tight and compact nine-hole course.

As for the Musselburgh course, it was originally a five-hole course. Mary Queen of Scots was said to have whacked a ball around the links. Musselburgh was the nearest test of golf to a true links course for Edinburgh. Its compact site is rather flat and devoid of cavernous features, yet within each hole, there were sound design principles; namely, that there is a right line and a wrong line to each hole. This design principle still is the hallmark of sound design today.

One interesting feature of the course was the Bankers' holes, which were adjacent to the 5th green. The Bankers' holes consisted of four holes, each 30 yards long. Willie Park, with his incredible short game, once scored a five on the four-hole course.

Musselburgh's demise came from changes within the game and at the hand of Muirfield. In the late 1880s, Musselburgh became so heavily played that the Honorable Company of Edinburgh Golfers had acquired their own property, and in 1892 wanted the Open Championship to be held on their new course, Muirfield.

Musselburgh remains today as a reminder of how simple the game once was and how big the game has become.

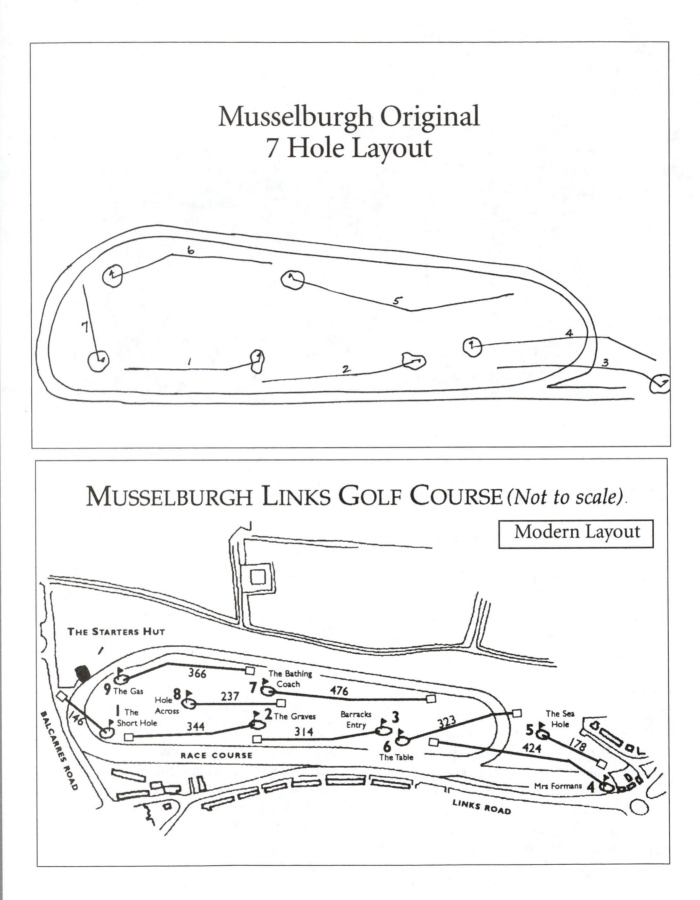

Musselburgh Original
7 Hole Layout

MUSSELBURGH LINKS GOLF COURSE (Not to scale).

Modern Layout

PRESTWICK

With the railway now going through Prestwick around 1840, a primitive links was being started. Tom Morris was persuaded to leave St. Andrews in 1851 and routed a 12-hole course within the links land.

The original 12-hole loop was framed by the railway tracks on its eastern boundary; to the west, the sea. The town was its south boundary and a short stone wall its northern edge. Such great history was made on this rugged ground.

Consider that on such bold terrain there was no machinery, hence nothing could be knocked down or cut into. As such, construction, as we know it, was impossible. The routing of the course at Prestwick worked carefully through and on top of the massive dunes, as in the case of the Alps. Back then, blind shots were regarded as a test of manhood.

Caddies played an important part of pre-1900 golf. Note the clubs were carried under the arms, not in bags. (Allan Robertson is third from left and Old Tom Morris is fifth from left.)

Prestwick's early claim to fame was its promotion of the Open Championship, and from 1860 through 1871, it hosted the first 12 British Open Tournaments. The 12-hole course, although charming, must have been chaotic, due to the number of times holes played across others.

Between 1851 and 1882, Prestwick was and remained a 12-hole course; however, after Tom Morris had returned to St. Andrews, Prestwick followed St. Andrews' lead and became 18 holes. Many of the original greens still remain today, but only the Cardinal (now

Scorecards were prepared for the 1872 British Open Championship.

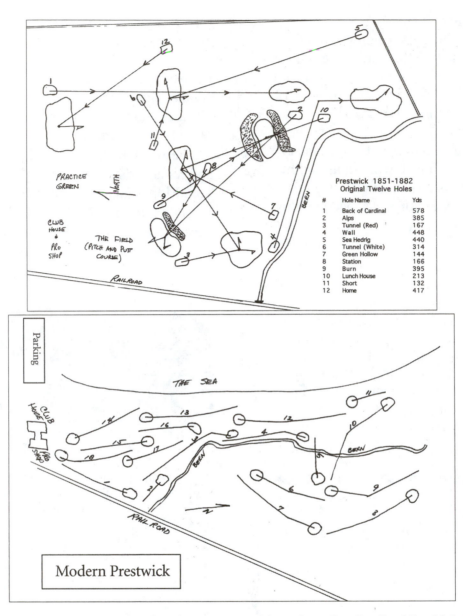

Prestwick 1851-1882
Original Twelve Holes

#	Hole Name	Yds
1	Back of Cardinal	578
2	Alps	385
3	Tunnel (Red)	167
4	Wall	448
5	Sea Hedrig	440
6	Tunnel (White)	314
7	Green Hollow	144
8	Station	166
9	Burn	395
10	Lunch House	213
11	Short	132
12	Home	417

Modern Prestwick

the 3rd) and Sea Hedrig (now the 13th) play as they did originally.

The conversion from 12 to 18 holes was not a smooth one. Prestwick was no stranger to controversy, as some prominent golfers truly loved the rugged and blind shots while others felt the course could be improved by the new routing. Prestwick members still play a tournament on the original 12-hole loop.

Prestwick remains a wonderful golf course where history has been written. Of particular note is, when the re-routing occurred in 1883, many fine holes were created.

The present 1st hole was never part of the original layout, yet I cannot imagine Prestwick

without it. "The Cardinal," which was originally the 4th hole and now the 3rd, remains a testament of the boldness of Prestwick. The 5th hole, "The Himalayas," is of great fame, and was one of the new holes, while the final loop of four holes, which contain holes 15, 16, and 17, are as exciting as any holes in the world. But Prestwick's biggest contribution to golf course architecture might be the 4th. It was the first use of the dogleg, having established the principle of changing direction after the drive.

In 1925, Prestwick's association with the Open was severed, not because of the course, but rather its unsuitability of handling the crowds and its lack of lodging.

ST. ANDREWS

There is never enough that can be said concerning the links at St. Andrews. St. Andrews is after all, the home of the game. Nothing can compare with the town, the shops, the people, and its history. To be at St. Andrews is to be at golf's heavenly gates.

The course at St. Andrews is an acquired taste. At first view, there doesn't seem to be much there. The course is all but fair, yet therein lies its charm. Bobby Jones once com-

A view of the clubhouse at St. Andrews was taken from the Swilken Bridge.

Old Tom Morris is perhaps the most famous of St. Andrews figures.

A match at St. Andrews is shown in an illustration.

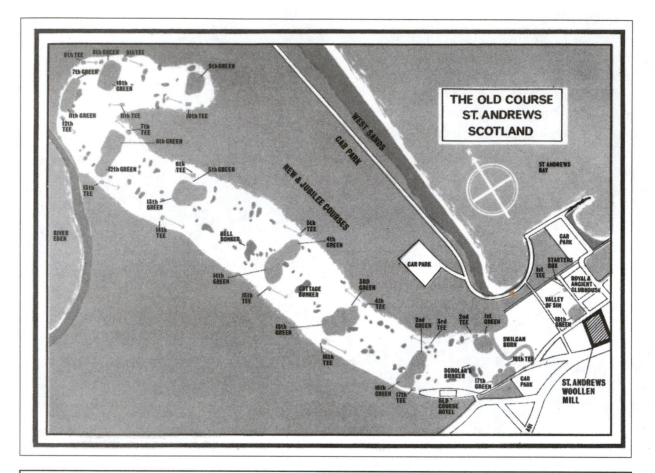

OLD COURSE, ST. ANDREWS

Hole	Name	Distance yds.	Par	Str.	Score
1	Burn	370	4	15	
2	Dyke	411	4	3	
3	Cartgate	352	4	13	
4	Ginger Beer	419	4	9	
5	Hole o' Cross	514	5	1	
6	Heathery	374	4	11	
7	High	359	4	7	
8	Short	166	3	18	
9	End	307	4	5	
	Outward	3272	36		

TOTAL DISTANCE 6566 yds.   Par and S.S.S. 72

Hole	Name	Distance yds.	Par	Str.	Score
10	Bobby Jones	318	4	10	
11	High	172	3	17	
12	Heathery	316	4	6	
13	Hole o' Cross	398	4	12	
14	Long	523	5	2	
15	Cartgate	401	4	8	
16	Corner of the Dyke	351	4	14	
17	Road	461	4	4	
18	Tom Morris	354	4	16	
	Inward	3294	36		

Marked by			Total		
			Handicap		
Date			Nett Score		

LOCAL RULES

1. **OUT OF BOUNDS (Rule 27-1)**
   (a) Beyond any wall or fence bounding the Course
   (b) Beyond the Swilken Burn on the right of the 1st hole and in or beyond the trench marked by stakes on the right at the 2nd hole.
   (c) Beyond the fence behind the 18th green and 1st tee and on or over the white line between sections of this fence
   Note: The trench on the right of the 12th and 13th holes is not out of bounds

2. **WATER HAZARDS (Rule 26)**
   (a) Those parts of the Swilken Burn which are unmarked or are marked with yellow stakes are ordinary water hazards (Rule 26 1a and 1b)
   (b) Those parts of the Swilken Burn to be treated as lateral water hazards are marked with red stakes (Rule 26 1c).

3. **GROUND UNDER REPAIR (Rule 25)**
   Play is prohibited within a GUR demarcated area (Rule 25 1a and 1b applies)

4. **ROADS AND PATHS**
   All roads and paths are integral parts of the Course. The ball must be played as it lies or declared unplayable (Rule 28)

5. **OBSTRUCTIONS (Rule 24)**
   March stones are immovable obstructions (Rule 24-2).

6. **FIXED SPRINKLER HEADS**
   All fixed sprinkler heads are immovable obstructions and relief from interference by them may be obtained under rule 24-2. In addition if such an obstruction on or within the two club-lengths of the putting green of the hole being played intervenes on the line of play between the ball and the hole the player may obtain relief without penalty as follows
   If the ball lies off the putting green but not in a hazard and is within two club lengths of the intervening obstruction it may be lifted, cleaned and dropped at the nearest point to where the ball lay which (a) is not nearer the hole (b) avoids such intervention and (c) is not in a hazard or on a putting green.

7. **STONES IN BUNKERS**
   Stones in bunkers are movable obstructions (Rule 24-1 applies).

ST ANDREWS IS ONLY 75 MINUTES FROM EDINBURGH

Enjoy a lovely visit to this historic wee town! Lots of fun for non-golfers too. As well as the golf see the Historic Buildings, Ancient Castle, Bottle Dungeon, Cathedral and University (founded 1411) – and the beautiful scenery.

Wander Into The Mill And Browse Around !

See lots of interesting displays. Always bargains in Cashmeres, Lambswools, Shetlands, Tweeds, Tartans, Sheepskins, Knitting Wools and lots more.

Lots of good Hotels, Restaurants and Bars nearby!

We pack and post to all countries. Details, brochure and golf tee free!

mented that the more he studied the Old Course, the more he loved it. Time has not changed this fundamental truth.

Long before there was golf, St. Andrews was the pre-reformation capital of Scotland. It is interesting that the routing itself forms a shepherd's crook. The Old Course owes more to the hand of God than that of man and is acknowledged as a masterpiece.

SIR HUGH LYON PLAYFAIR

The concept of the double greens was probably the idea or implementation of Sir Hugh Lyon Playfair, the Provost of St. Andrews from 1842 to 1861. He was also the Captain of the R & A in 1856. Sir Playfair was also credited with carrying out the land reclamation of what are now the 1st and 18th holes.

THE RETURN OF TOM MORRIS

In 1865, Tom Morris returned shortly after the death of Allen Robertson, and was paid £50 a year as "Keeper of the Green," taking entire charge of the course.

Prior to Tom Morris' return, the course at St. Andrews was a narrow and penal golf course. But under his watchful eye and careful study of the course, Old Tom began to enlarge the greens. The purpose was to provide a more comfortable area in which outbound and inbound players could co-exist in safety.

Tom began to learn that the key to links golf was sand. David Honeyman was Old Tom's foreman and Old Tom's words to him would be: "Saund, Honeyman, saund and then mair saund."

Early after Tom Morris' return, he re-grassed several of the greens and claimed ground on the west side of the Swilican Burn, which golfers today play as the 1st green. By the early 1870s, Tom was re-turfing the 1st and 18th fairways, which then led to the re-positioning and enlargement of the 18th green.

With the introduction of the new green west of the Swilican Burn, golfers realized the course could be played clockwise and counter clockwise. For several years, the Old Course routing varied during alternate weeks. The original, preferred routing was and is the way in which we play St. Andrews today.

OF WHINS AND BUNKERS

Within the Old Course, it should be noted that the natural, deep bunkers (those with colorful names) are on the left side of the course. Most of the bunkers on the right of the outward holes are man-made; strategically sited to replace the vast thickets of whin, which once covered the links. Much of the widening of the links was overseen by Old Tom Morris and was completed by the turn of the century.

Old Tom did remove a few bunkers, but one made a triumphant return. That bunker was Sutherland at hole number four. The tale of Sutherland begins with the man.

Sutherland was a flamboyant character, completely and utterly obsessed by golf. Golf was his whole life; anyone who had no knowledge of or no interest in the game was "an ignorant lout." A. G. Sutherland spent his winters on the links at Musselburgh and his summers in St. Andrews.

In August 1869, he walked over the course one day and discovered the bunker had been filled in. He wrote to Major Broothby of the R & A's Green Committee asking if the bunker had been filled in on the authority of the Committee, and at the same time, reminded him that the Committee had no power to remove any bunker from the course. He suggested that the Committee should restore the bunker to its former state or answer for its action in a court of law.

Major Boothby replied he was not aware of any special orders having been given by the Committee for filling up the bunker, but Tom Morris, as Custodian of the Links, had taken the opinion of many golfers who considered that the bunker was unnecessary.

Sutherland was furious. He denied that Tom had the right "to destroy or remodel the links as it pleases him and his clique," and he repeated his conviction that neither the R & A, the Green Committee, nor even the proprietor of the links had the right to change the face of the ground "as nature has placed it."

The lost bunker became the talking point of the day. It was certainly the talking point at a private dinner on Aug. 10, 1869, given by publisher John Blackwood. Sir Alexander Kinlock and Robert Dalzell (both of whom were to become captains of the R & A) were guests at the dinner; and they agreed that the vandalism of the Green Committee was not to be allowed. They made their way to the links where they labored all night, and by morning the bunker was restored. Before they left, they wrote the name "Sutherland" on a piece of paper. Everyone thought it was Sutherland's work, and the bunker is known by the name Sutherland to this day.

THE GAME'S FOUNDATION

Unlike all other golf courses in the world, there is the air of permanence at St. Andrews, and it will forever be linked with the game's origins.

COLLECTIBLES

There are many collectibles available relating to the British Open and the three courses. Actually the list is endless. Here are a few broad suggestions:

Scorecards
Ball Markers
Logo Balls
Programs
Golf clubs made and sold at the courses
Medals & Trophies
Golf Cards (Wills Tobacco)
Post Cards
Photographs
Art
Books

A Word About Collecting

By Rives McBee

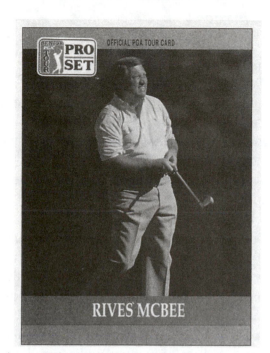

People often ask me, what do you collect and why do you collect? My answer to them is, "I collect almost anything that is related to the game of golf." That includes classic clubs; hickory shafted clubs; clubs with unique shafts, fancy faces and clubheads; golf balls; logo golf balls; golf bags; golf books; golf art; golf autographs; and golf bronzes. I have done exactly what most expert collectors say don't do—that is, get into many areas of different collectibles. Most collectors choose one particular area, such as scorecards, pencils or tees, and stay with just these items. I have chosen to spread out into several areas because I have yet to find the one area that intrigues me the most. I usually can't resist buying something if it is different from what I am looking for originally. An old leather bag may contain a putter or a wood that I want and I buy the whole bag full of clubs.

Why do I collect? It all started in 1966 after my first major tournament appearance, the 1966 United States Open Championship at the Olympic Club in San Francisco. In the second round of the tournament I shot a score of 64, which set the course record and tied the all-time low round for an Open. I went on to finish tied for 13th in the championship, then returned to Midland, Texas, and my job as an assistant golf professional. When I got home, I put the clubs I had used in the Open in the closet, along with a placemat autographed by all of the contestants at the Open. I still have the clubs and the placemat. This started me in the wonderful world of golf collectibles. Adding to my collection has given me many hours of pleasure and meeting fellow collectors around the country has been a fabulous experience.

Collecting can be fun and it can be expensive. Sometimes the pleasure of finding a unique club or ball far outweighs the cost of the item. When a fellow collector asks if he paid too much for a particular find, I usually respond with, "You bought it because you wanted it, so you didn't pay too much." An item is worth what you are willing to pay for it. Most people who sell memorabilia are willing to negotiate and this too can be fun if you know what you are doing.

Now my good friend, Chuck Furjanic, has found a way to help the collector, old and new, by providing this reference and pricing guide. It is filled with illustrations of clubs, golf balls, pottery and ceramics, autographs, golf cards, and many more antique golf collectibles. This book should help all of the new collectors in their search for those "precious finds" at the garage sale or auction, and give them an approximate price for these items. I wish that I would have had this book to help me in my early years of collecting, but I probably would have done what so many of my fellow collectors do. If I like it and can afford it, I buy it!

Golfingly,
Rives McBee
Irving, Texas

A Word About Collectors' Resources

By Pete Georgiady

Twenty years ago there was nothing.

By that, I mean there were no ready resource materials for the collectors of old golf clubs and other golf memorabilia. It didn't much matter because there were almost no collectors. The prospect changed abruptly in 1978 when Englishmen David Stirk and Ian Henderson wrote *Golf in the Making*, an eclectic volume combining colorful bits of golf history with profiles of important club makers and short, but tantalizing, notes on old clubs and other golf items that were rapidly becoming collectible. It is a book that many consider to be the "bible" for golf collectors and deserves a great deal of credit for launching the activities of many of today's collectors.

Without going into great detail, I can say that the shortcomings of one or two of the club-related sections of the Stirk and Henderson book gave me cause to begin my own explorations into the whos, whys, and wherefores of old clubs and club makers. The result of my research is a small group of books devoted to clubs and club makers, the two topics that I have found most self-enlightening. Thus, the pioneering contribution of Stirk and Henderson spawned other collector-writers like me, who will leave teachings for the next generation of golf enthusiasts. After all this time, there is a crying need for even more information about many aspects of the golf collectibles field. Frequently, I am asked if a guide book has been written on this topic or another and, sadly, the answer is usually, "No, not yet." Perhaps golf collectors, most of whom are also golfers, take their game so seriously that it leaves no time for scholarship. Who can blame them?

Voids still remain in the information web, but sooner or later they will be filled. One addition to the collector's library is undoubtedly the volume you are now holding. It has emerged from one among us who has espoused the spirit of old golf with an evangelical fervor. Chuck Furjanic possesses a unique story within the golf collectibles field. A lifelong golfer, coach, and friend of the game, he has made the world of golf collectibles his business. His ability to amass considerable familiarity with clubs, balls, art, and other areas of golf collectibles, as well as knowledge of the persons who were specialists in those areas, has made him a beacon in the field of golf collectibles. This book is a marriage of those two worlds: his daily handling of the game's antiques and his regular contact with collecting novices and experts.

There is no single person who knows everything about all the disciplines of the collectibles we seek, so the natural ideal is a book with an aggregation of information from those highly knowledgeable in the different fields. Chuck has delivered just that. In the years ahead, more books to assist and instruct golf collectors will materialize. Maybe the authors of those future volumes will have been inspired by this price and reference guide, just as we were inspired by another book of 20 years ago.

Pete Georgiady
Greensboro, N.C.

The seeds of Pete's interest in old golf clubs germinated while he was a graduate student at Scotland's Dundee University in the early 1970s. After many years of research and gathering information on old club makers and the clubs they produced, his knowledge has been disseminated in a series of books which include the Compendium of British Club Makers, Collecting Antique Golf Clubs, Views and Reviews: Golf Clubs in the Trade Press, Wood Shafted Golf Club Value Guide, North American Club Makers *and* Cleek Marks and Trade Marks.

A collector of more than 23 years, Pete is a regular contributor on golf topics to golf magazines, the GCS Bulletin, and Chuck Furjanic's monthly catalogue.

About the Author

Charles Michael Furjanic Jr. began playing golf at age 10 during the summer of 1953. Thanks to the parish priest, Father Charles Georgavich, Chuck was gifted his first set of clubs—two woods, four irons, and a putter—all with hickory shafts. In his sophomore year at Swissvale High School in Pittsburgh, Pa., Chuck persuaded a faculty member to sponsor the school's first golf team. Chuck attended Slippery Rock University of Pennsylvania, where he played without compensation. Chuck would, in 1979, establish the "Doc-Chuck" Golf Scholarship Fund in co-sponsorship with coach Dr. Albert "Doc" Schmittlein, providing financial assistance to more than 30 golf students through 1996.

Chuck's lifelong love of golf and collecting led him to turn professional in two areas. Golf came first. He taught lessons at a driving range and played in tournaments, good enough not to embarrass himself, but not good enough to win much more than gasoline money. After nearly four years, he was convinced professional golf was not going to be his lifelong vocation.

Turning to his other love, numismatics, Chuck became one of the nation's leading coin experts and enjoyed working with collectors, building meaningful collections. Chuck was a contributing editor for *A Guide Book of United States Coins* (Red Book) for nearly 15 years, and for the *Handbook of United States Coins* (Blue Book). He authored articles for *CoinWorld, Numismatic News*, and *CoinAge,* gave talks and presentations at local and national organizations, and taught numismatic courses at Allegheny College in Pittsburgh.

In 1986, when packing to move from Pittsburgh to Irving, Texas, Chuck found some old friends in a corner of the garage. The original seven wooden shafted clubs rekindled his interest in golf collectibles and he began in earnest to develop a business around golf, centering attention on the collector.

He published his first retail golf collectibles catalogue for the hobby in February 1989 and launched a new career, not as a professional golfer, but as a golf professional, dealing with collectors and collectibles.

Conducting several successful Mail Bid Sales gave him the expertise to sell the late Linda Craft's golf estate in May 1995 (Linda was an LPGA pro and long-time golf collector). Because of that auction's success, Chuck now conducts spring and fall public sales geared to the collector from both the consignment and sales aspect.

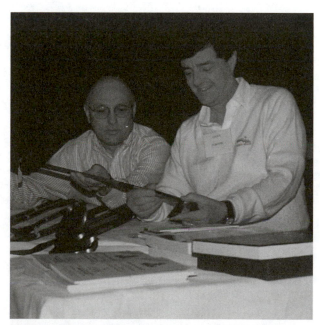

Author Chuck Furjanic, right, and Pete Georgiady inspect a rare golf club at a Golf Collectors Society convention.

Nearly 160 catalogues and this book later, Chuck has found his comfort zone—golf, collectors, and collectibles.

"My philosophy has always been the collector should come first. Customer satisfaction is my most important product, and if the collector is not happy, I'm not happy," he said.

"Yes, we all would like to make mega-thousand dollar sales each time the phone rings, but the collector, who spends his grocery money to buy that $50 ball or $65 hickory shafted club, is the real foundation of the hobby. I take as much time and care filling a $50 order and helping the collector get what he wants, as I do for the $1,000 buyer. I personally try to answer every incoming call because listening to collectors, and helping them find the collectibles or information they seek is very important to me and essential to the hobby."

TO CONTACT THE AUTHOR

E-mail: furjanic@directlink.net or chuckfurjanic@hotmail.com

Web site: http://www.golfforallages.com

Phone: (972) 594-7802   FAX: (972) 257-1785

Mail: Chuck Furjanic, Inc.

P.O. Box 165892

Irving, TX 75016

Bibliography

Berdock, Bruce, and Baier, Michael
A Century of Golf Cards, 1993
Published in Canada

Biocini, Paul
Signature Golf Ball Collector's Guide, 1995
Paul Biocini, Modesto, CA

British Golf Collectors Society
Through The Green

Christie's, Glasgow, Scotland
Auction Catalogues

Cooper, J. M.
Early U. S. Golf Clubs by Spalding & Bros.,
1994
J. M. Cooper, Kannapolis, NC

Donovan, Richard E. and Murdoch, Joseph S. F.
*The Game of Golf and The Printed Word
1566-1985,* 1988
Castalio Press, Endicott, NY

Furjanic, Chuck
Auction Catalogues
Golf Collectibles, Irving, TX

Furjanic, Chuck
Monthly Catalogues 1989 to Present
Golf Collectibles, Irving, TX

Ellis, Jeffery B.
The Clubmaker's Art, 1997
Zephyr Productions Inc.

Georgiady, Peter
Compendium of British Clubmakers, 1994
Airlie Hall Press, Greensboro, NC

Georgiady, Peter

Georgiady, Peter
Wood Shafted Value Guide For 1995
Airlie Hall Press, Greensboro, NC

Georgiady, Peter
Wood Shafted Value Guide For 2000
Airlie Hall Press, Greensboro, NC

Georgiady, Peter
Collecting Antique Golf Clubs, 1996
Airlie Hall Press, Greensboro, NC

Georgiady, Peter and Kelly, Leo M., Jr.
*Quick Reference Guide to Antique Golf Club
Names,* 1993
Old Chicago Golf Shop, Matteson, IL

Gilchrist, Roger E.
Gilchrist's Guide to Golf Collectibles, 1998

Golf Collectors Society
The Bulletin

Hamilton, Charles
Collecting Autographs and Manuscripts, 1993
Modoc Press, Santa Monica, CA

Jackson, Alan F.
*The British Professional Golfers, 1887-1930,
A Register,* 1994
Grant's Books, Worchestershire, England

Kelly, Leo M., Jr.
*Antique Golf Ball Reference &
Price Guide,* 1993
Old Chicago Golf Shop, Richton Park, IL

Kennedy, Patrick
Golf Club Trade Marks, 1984
Thistle Books, S. Burlington, VT

Oliver's

Auction Catalogues
Kennebunk, ME

Olman, John M. and Morton
The Encyclopedia of Golf Collectibles, 1985
Books Americana, Florence, AL

Olman, John and Morton
Olman's Guide to Golf Antiques, 1992
Market Street Press, Cincinnati, OH

Paris, Don
The B.G.I. Company
Self-published 1999

Phillips, Chester England
Auction Catalogues
Smedley, Philip and Berdock, Bruce

*The Price Guide to Golf Cards, Part 1:
Tobacco Cards,* 1994
Published in Canada

Smedley, Philip and Berdock, Bruce
*The Price Guide to Golf Cards,
Part 2: Non-Tobacco Cards,* 1995
Published in Canada

Sotheby's, London, England
Auction Catalogues

Sporting Antiquities Auction Catalogues
Melrose, MA

Sprung, Shirley and Jerry
Decorative Golf Collectibles, 1991
Glentiques, LTD., Coral Springs, FL

Listing of Contributors

Chuck Furjanic
P.O. Box 165892
Irving, TX 75062
(972) 594-7802
(972) 257-1785 FAX
http://www.golfforallages.com
Furjanic@directlink.net

Wayne Aaron
9950 Huntcliff Trace
Atlanta, GA 30350
(770) 993-3611

Hank Alperin
1450 Winter St.
Augusta, GA 30904
(706) 738-7317

Archie Baird
Greyfriars
Aberlady, East Lothian
Scotland EH32 0RB

Paul Biocini
4505 Bluff Creek Drive
Modesto, CA 95355
(209) 527-1162

Bob Burkett
Old Sport Golf
4297 NE Expressway Access Road
Doraville, GA 30340
(404) 493-4344

Jim "Spalding Man" Cooper
1110 Oklahoma St.
Kannapolis, NC 28083
(704) 782-2493

Lee Crist
109 Woodland Terrace
Duncanville, PA 16635
(814) 693-9636

Mike Daniels
Gifts For The Golfer
23 Wilshire Drive
Albany, NY 12205
(518) 869-7103

Art DiProspero
Highlands Golf
P.O. Box 4065
Monroe, CT 06468
(203) 268-2349

Mark Emerson
4040 Poste Lane Rd.
Columbus, OH 43221
(614) 771-7272

Jim Espinola
P.O. Box 54
Dracut, MA 01826
(508) 459-7165

Keith Foster
5615 Old Poag Rd
Edwardsville, IL 62035

Pete Georgiady
Airlie Hall Press
P.O. Box 981
Kernersville, NC 27285
(336) 996-7836
ahp@greensboro.com

Roger Gilchrist
P.O. Box 969
Freeport, FL 32439
(850) 835-1429

Bob Gowland
International Golf Auctions
Chester, England.

Johnny Henry
P.O. Box 776
Ennis, TX 75020
(972) 875-7360

Gary Hilgers
14921 White Oak Drive
Burnsville, MN 55337
(612) 891-1270

Roger Hill
2875 Cascade Springs. Dr. NE
Grand Rapids, MI 49546
(616) 285-6130

Tom & Karen Kuhl
No address available

Bob Kuntz
P.O. Box 300
Dayton, OH 45420
(937) 228-7767

George Lewis, Golfiana
P.O. Box 291
Mamaroneck, NY 10543
(914) 835-5100
www.golfiana.com

Ralph Livingston
831 Freemont NW. Apt #4
Grand Rapids, MI 49504
(616) 451-6020

Forrest Mc Connell
2740 Fernway Drive
Montgomery, AL 36111
(334) 263-6146

Chuck Mc Mullin
Williamsburg, VA

Dick Moore
640 E. Liberty Ave.
Girard, OH 44420
(216) 545-2832

Norm Moreau
12A Mary Gapper Crescent
Richmond Hill, Ontario
Canada L4C 7L9
(905) 737-8629

Joseph Murdoch
Cathedral Village
600 E. Cathedral Road #G307
Philadelphia, PA 19128
(215) 984-8897

Gordon Page
34643 Sunward Loop
Zephyr Hills, FL 33541
(800) 859-9842

Don Paris
98 Sterling Drive
Kensington, CT 06037
(860) 828-5170

Will Roberto
381 Hubbard St
Glastonbery, CT 06063
(888) 653-8666

Jerry Sprung and Glentiques, Ltd
P.O. Box 8807
Coral Springs, FL 33075
(305) 344-9856
2740 Fernway Drive
Montgomery, AL 36111
(334) 263-6146 *